Private Equity: Law and Practice

Private Equity: Law and Practice

Fourth edition

Darryl J Cooke

SWEET & MAXWELL  THOMSON REUTERS

Fourth Edition 2011

Published in 2011 by
Sweet & Maxwell
100 Avenue Road, London NW3 3PF
part of Thomson Reuters (Professional) UK Limited
(Registered in England & Wales, Company No 1679046.
Registered Office and address for service:
Aldgate House, 33 Aldgate High Street, London EC3N 1DL)
Typeset by LBJ Typesetting Ltd of Kingsclere
Printed and bound in Great Britain by CPI Anthony Rowe, Chippenham and Eastbourne
For further information on our products and services, visit
www.sweetandmaxwell.co.uk

No natural forests were destroyed to make this product;
only farmed timber was used and re-planted.

A CIP catalogue record for this book is available from the British Library

ISBN 978-0-414-041660

Thomson Reuters and the Thomson Reuters logo are trademarks of Thomson Reuters. Sweet & Maxwell ® is a registered trademark of Thomson Reuters (Professional) UK Limited.

Crown Copyright material is reproduced with permission of the Controller of HMSO and the Queen's Printer for Scotland. No part of this publication may be reproduced or transmitted in any form or by any means, or stored in any retrieval system of any nature without prior written permission, except for permitted fair dealing under the Copyright, Designs and Patents Act 1988, or in accordance with the terms of a licence issued by the Copyright Licensing Agency in respect of photocopying and/or reprographic reproduction. Application for permission for other use of copyright material including permission to reproduce extracts in other published works shall be made to the publishers. Full acknowledgement of author, publisher and source must be given.

While all reasonable care has been taken to ensure the accuracy of the contents of this book, no responsibility for loss occasioned to any person acting or refraining from action as a result of any statement in it can be accepted by the author or the publishers.

The precedents and commentary contained in this publication are not tailored to any particular factual situation. Precedents in this publication may be used as a guide for preparation of documentation, which may be provided to clients, but distribution to third parties is otherwise prohibited. Precedents are provided "as is" without warranty of any kind, express or implied, including but not limited to fitness for a particular purpose. The publishers and the author do not accept any responsibility for any loss of whatsoever kind including loss of revenue business, anticipated savings or profits, loss of goodwill or data or for any indirect or consequential loss whatsoever to any person using the precedents, or acting or refraining from action as a result of the material in this publication.

© 2011 Thomson Reuters (Professional) UK Limited

To my lovely wife Pam and my two wonderful boys
Ashley and Hayden

Contents

Preface	xi
Contributors	xiii
Private Equity in the United Kingdom—Market Development and Recent Trends	xv
Table of Cases	xxv
Table of Statutes	xxvii
Table of Statutory Instruments	xxix

Chapter 1   Role of Private Equity — 1
1.1   Private equity explained — 1
1.2   Private equity overview — 1
1.3   Rationale for using private equity — 9
1.4   Implications of private equity — 11
1.5   Key points — 14

Chapter 2   Raising Private Equity — 17
2.1   Introduction — 17
2.2   Meeting the investment criterion — 17
2.3   Matching the fund to the proposition — 24
2.4   The fund raising process — 28
2.5   Choosing an investment offer — 38
2.6   Key Points — 39

Chapter 3   Corporate Valuation and Deal Structuring — 41
3.1   Introduction — 41
3.2   Corporate valuation — 41
3.3   Role of the funding instruments — 48
3.4   Structuring a private equity investment — 60
3.5   Key points — 66

Chapter 4   Tax Relief for Equity Investment by Individuals — 69
4.1   Introduction — 69
4.2   Entrepreneurs Relief — 69
4.3   Tax reliefs for equity investment—EIS and VCT overview — 70
4.4   Qualifying companies — 70
4.5   Enterprise Investment Scheme — 72

Contents

4.6	EIS deferral relief	73
4.7	Venture Capital Trusts	74
4.8	Interest relief	75
4.9	Special relief for capital losses against income	77
4.10	Business property relief for inheritance tax purposes	77
4.11	Management shares	78
4.12	Key points	78

Chapter 5 Share Capital — **81**

5.1	Introduction	81
5.2	Maintenance of capital	81
5.3	Shareholders	93
5.4	Types of shares	96
5.5	Sale preference	111
5.6	Key points	111

Chapter 6 Managing the Transaction — **113**

6.1	Introduction	113
6.2	The preparatory phase	113
6.3	The offer phase	114
6.4	Transaction management	115
6.5	International transactions	129
6.6	The completion phase	130
6.7	Pro forma checklist	131
6.8	Key points	136

Chapter 7 Management Due Diligence — **137**

7.1	Introduction	137
7.2	Managing expectations	139
7.3	Problems	140
7.4	Rounded best practice	141
7.5	Deal structures	142
7.6	Covert intelligence operations	142
7.7	Legal and financial searches and checks	142
7.8	Referencing	143
7.9	Outputs of referencing activity	145
7.10	Profiling management teams and structured interviews	145
7.11	Outputs of profiling and interviews	146
7.12	Evaluating the chairman in management due diligence	147
7.13	Conclusion	147

Chapter 8 Due Diligence — **149**

8.1	Introduction	149
8.2	Use of due diligence in private equity transactions	150

Contents

8.3	Types and manner of due diligence	152
8.4	The lawyers' role	153
8.5	Due diligence process	154
8.6	Impact of due diligence on warranty claims: *Infiniteland and Aviss v Artisan*	155
8.7	Accountancy due diligence	156
8.8	Legal due diligence	159
8.9	Specific areas of legal due diligence	165
8.10	Due diligence in public to private transactions	177
8.11	Vendor issues on due diligence	178
8.12	The due diligence report	183
8.13	Post completion audit	184

Chapter 9 Investment Agreement — 185

9.1	Introduction	185
9.2	Conditions	186
9.3	Mechanics of investment	190
9.4	Warranties	191
9.5	Investor controls	217
9.6	Common issues raised by management	226
9.7	Corporate governance controls	230
9.8	Minority protection	236
9.9	Syndication	240
9.10	Exit	241
9.11	Issues arising on buy-outs without private equity	248
9.12	Checklist	252

Chapter 10 Articles of Association — 261

10.1	Introduction	261
10.2	*Russell v Northern Bank Development Corp Ltd*	262
10.3	Minority shareholder protections	267
10.4	Share transfer provisions	269
10.5	Investor director(s)	281
10.6	Ratchets	283
10.7	Miscellaneous	291
10.8	Checklist	292

Chapter 11 Directors and Employees — 297

11.1	Introduction	297
11.2	Duties of directors	298
11.3	Key points	330
11.4	Service agreements	330

Contents

Chapter 12	**Restructuring**	**339**
12.1	The concepts	339
12.2	Restructurings as they occur	344
12.3	Items of particular interest	351
Chapter 13	**Key Issues for Management**	**367**
13.1	Management duties	367
13.2	Business focus	370
13.3	Management of the company	370
13.4	Warranties	371
13.5	Good and bad leaver provisions	373
13.6	The purchase of shares of a departing manager	374
13.7	Ratchets	375
13.8	Service agreements	375
13.9	Heads of terms	376
Appendix 1	*Glossary*	377
Appendix 2	*MBO Model*	405
Appendix 3	*Legal Agreements*	407
Appendix 4	*Manager's Personal Status Questionnaire*	415
Appendix 5	*Common Limitations to Management Warranties*	429
Appendix 6	*BVCA Membership Listing*	433
Appendix 7	*Heads of Terms*	437
Index		445

Preface to Fourth Edition

"If there were nothing wrong in the World, there wouldn't be anything for us to do"
(George Bernard Shaw 1856–1950)

The turmoil in the World's financial markets and the consequences on the World economy could not be expected to leave the world of private equity unaffected. John Kotter, Professor of Leadership at Harvard Business School talks and writes about effective change coming about as a result of the necessity for change, often described as "the burning platform". Companies constantly try to re-engineer themselves into more efficient and successful competitors. This inevitably involves challenging the way everything is done in order to cope with a more challenging market environment coupled with a rebranding to communicate the message that lessons have been learnt and the new better model is now available. Some of these corporate change efforts have been successful. A few fail dismally. Many partially succeed. The challenge to all the players in the private equity arena, investment houses, bankers, lawyers, financial advisors is that change is needed. The burning platform surrounds the industry and now is the time for leaders to come forward in all areas of professional services to deliver a better product, more entrepreneurial, more professional, more efficient and providing greater value.

Effective change begins when the players start to consider the product they deliver. Does it serve the market well? Does it address changing demographics? Does it utilise market experiences? Is it efficient? How is it perceived? Does it respond to changing technologies? Are the processes robust? Does it deliver real value? Is it constantly being challenged? Is it subject to continuous improvement? Transformation programmes require an aggressive challenge of the status quo. The motivation to do that is down to the leading individuals in an organization. Without that motivation, change won't happen. There can be no greater motivation than a threat to a whole industry, which is what the private equity industry has faced these last few years. The challenge now is will it come back stronger, fitter, better equipped, more innovative, leaner, more efficient than ever. Are our private equity houses better able to find the real winners? Are they better able to support them? Have our banks learnt any lessons? Is the process more accountable, more efficient? Are our professional advisors able to deliver a product that provides greater value?

Preface to Fourth Edition

We can only wait and see. No one can doubt the role of private equity in providing foundations for a thriving private sector, but can it grasp the opportunity before it to make it integral to the growth of a wounded economy?

I am grateful to my contributors: James Dow, of Dow Schofield Watts, Paul Quinn of The Quinn Partnership, Colin Ellis Chief Economist at the BVCA, Tony Woolley of Pareto Tax, Martin March and Jo Saunders of Hill Dickinson and Jo Evans of Neil Myerson.

The Law is as at February 1, 2011.

Darryl Cooke
April 2011

Contributors

Darryl Cooke

Darryl Cooke is the founding partner at the corporate boutique law firm, gunnercooke. Prior to that he was head of private equity for EMEA at DLA Piper and head of private equity at Addleshaw Goddard. Darryl is the author of *Management Buy-Outs* and also of *Due Diligence: A Practical Guide*. He is a contributor to a number of other publications and writes a monthly column on *Leadership* drawn from his experience in over 100 buy outs that he has been involved with. He has won numerous awards.

James Dow

James is a founding partner of the corporate finance boutique, Dow Schofield Watts. Prior to its formation he was the corporate finance partner in charge of the North West Region for KPMG Corporate Finance. In total James has spent over 20 years specialising in advising companies, shareholders and funds in the private equity arena. He has particular expertise in deal and debt structuring, recognised as such as the best accountant in the EN Deals of the Year Awards 2001 and as Dealmaker of the Year 2006 in the Insider Deal Awards.

Colin Ellis

Colin is the Chief Economist and Head of Research at the British Private Equity and Venture Capital Association (BVCA), overseeing the strategic direction of the BVCA's Research function. Prior to joining the BVCA, he was European Economist at Daiwa Capital Markets, and a senior economist/manager at the Bank of England. Colin has published a number of research articles and is a Visiting Research Fellow at the University of Birmingham.

Contributors

Paul Quinn

Paul is the founder and Director of The Quinn Partnership and has consistently advised on Deals of the Year for award winning UK private equity investors and is widely regarded as a leading expert on management issues in the UK private equity market. Since establishing The Quinn Partnership in 2005, Paul has asset management teams on deals across a broad raft of sectors and a range of transaction structures with a combined deal value of over £4 billion. As specialists in management due diligence in the UK private equity market, The Quinn Partnership has been voted UK MDD Provider of the Year 2008, 2009 and 2010; in addition they have also been awarded Niche Advisor of the Year 2010.

Private Equity in the United Kingdom—Market Development and Recent Trends

Colin Ellis, Chief Economist and Head of Research,
British Private Equity and Venture Capital Association (BVCA)

Introduction

Since Finance for Industry became a leading financer of management buy-outs in the UK in the 1980s, taking the moniker of Investors in Industry (or 3i) in 1983, the UK private equity and venture capital industries have grown rapidly, becoming an important source of finance both for entrepreneurs and more established businesses. Despite the development of European markets over the past three decades, the UK remains the second-largest hub for private equity in the world, behind the US. During that time the industry has changed dramatically, in terms of its coverage, activities and transparency.

Definitions and types of private equity

Technically, the catch-all term private equity ("PE") refers to the industry as a whole, from the venture capitalist backing entrepreneurs and start-up companies through to the global buy-out houses that buy and sell established multinational companies. However, venture capital ("VC") is often distinguished within private equity as it has some unique characteristics, for instance the fact that VC investments will typically only involve a partial transfer of ownership from entrepreneur to the venture capitalist. At the same time, despite individual VC investments only involving partial ownership changes, entrepreneurs can often end up no longer owning 50 per cent of their business, and hence ceding overall control, given the many rounds of investments that can ensue before a business successfully takes off. In contrast, PE buy-out transactions, which form the bulk of non-VC investments, typically involve outright ownership of a business changing hands at the time of the initial investment.

The differences between VC investments and buy-outs also extend to investment strategies. The traditional VC investment model might involve backing, say, 15 or 20 growing companies or start-ups. In many instances—say for instance seven or eight—the business might fail, and the venture capitalist loses their money. In another six or seven they might make a small loss, or break even. But most of the returns across the portfolio are often generated by the one or two investments that make excellent returns, dragging up the portfolio as a whole. It is precisely because these star performers are hard to identify, and the risk of any individual investment failing is high, that venture capitalists tend to invest in wide portfolios.

In contrast, buy-out investments tend to be more concentrated, and leverage is also more important. The classic buy-out model is not very different from that of a property developer—borrow money against the asset (in this case, the company) to purchase it, do the property up and improve it, and then sell it on for a profit. The role of leverage in buy-out transactions has been widely debated in many different areas, as it does allow PE funds to buy more (or larger) companies than they would otherwise be able to. The resulting leveraged buy-outs ("LBOs") increase the potential return on equity, but at a cost of expanding the overall liabilities of the firm. Other things being equal, higher leverage might be expected to increase the overall risk of the firm as an investment. However, as the recent recession has demonstrated, other things are not equal in the case of PE-led buy-outs: in particular, General Partners ("GPs") at PE firms are more likely to be proactively involved not only in helping to deliver stronger economic performance, but also in taking timely action to assist investee companies and restructure their finances, if necessary, in the event of financial distress.

Private equity buy-outs can take many forms, spawning many different acronyms. The most common of these is the management buy-out ("MBO"), where incumbent management takes control of a business, or sometimes a divested part of the original entity, with private equity backing. Less common—and typically less successful, in terms of economic and financial performance—are management buy-ins ("MBIs"), where the new management come from outside the company. Because of this relative lack of familiarity with the underlying business, compared with incumbent management, MBIs have a higher chance of failure than MBOs. A buy-in/management buy-out ("BIMBO") is a combination of these two forms of buy-out, potentially benefiting both from the new perspective of external management and the expertise of incumbent management.

Apart from MBOs and MBIs, other forms of buy-out have included public to private ("PTP") buy-outs, where listed companies are taken private, and management–employee buy-outs ("MEBOs"), where employees take some of the equity holding. However, the latter in particular are very rare in today's markets. Other relatively rare forms of buy-out include investor-led buy-outs ("IBOs") and leveraged build-ups ("LBUs"). Investor-led buy-outs are acquisitions led by private equity firms, while LBUs are a series of buy-outs with the goal of connecting fragmented industries.

Definitions and types of private equity

Secondary buy-outs ("SBOs") have also increased in importance over recent years. An SBO occurs when one PE house (or fund) wants to exit an investment, and deliver hard returns to investors, but cannot find satisfactory terms via traditional exit routes, namely trade sale or stock market listing ("IPO"). In these circumstances, other PE houses with uncommitted funds may buy the portfolio investment from the first fund, thereby providing liquidity to the market and an exit for the original investors. Provided the second fund can genuinely add value to the underlying portfolio company, it too stands to make a return on its investment.

The importance of adding value to an investee company is common across both VC and buy-out investments. Critics outside the industry sometimes unfairly characterise it as a similar sort of casino investment to some investment banking and hedge fund activities—borrowing money and buying businesses in the hope that the stock market rises, thereby generating a return. In fact, private equity is an active form of management, with a recent study finding that portfolio company managers thought that PE backing added value to their businesses in a number of areas (Table 1). Overall, nine out of ten business managers thought that PE ownership was beneficial for their business. The performance of PE backed businesses through the recent recession, discussed later, tells a similar story of active engagement and long term planning.

Table 1: The impact of PE backing on company performance

Percentage of respondents

	Significant disadvantage	Slight disadvantage	No impact	Slight benefit	Significant benefit
Access to general business expertise	1.0	2.9	20.0	52.2	23.9
Specific sectoral knowledge and experience	2.9	9.8	43.9	34.6	8.8
Detailed operational skills, e.g. improving business processes, financial engineering	3.4	7.3	39.5	41.0	8.8
Contacts and network in the wider business community	0.5	2.9	20.0	51.2	25.4
Engagement with company management on key issues	2.9	4.9	13.2	52.2	26.8

Source: Ellis (2010), "What do business managers think of Venture Capital and Private Equity?", BVCA Research report.

The development of the private equity industry in the UK

After limited activity in earlier decades, the UK private equity market really started to develop in the 1980s, against a backdrop of financial market liberalisation and the shrinking boundary of nationalised industries. Public to private PE backed activity was particularly pronounced in the US, but in the UK there was also a boost to activity from the then-government's privatisation programme. Often this boost was indirect, as newly privatised firms sought to rationalise and focus their activities and sold off non-core divisions. And once UK firms were allowed to provide financial assistance to purchase their own shares in 1981, barriers to entry were reduced. This allowed specialist PE funds to develop in the middle of the decade, frequently with backing from US banks.

Chart 1: Private equity investments as a percentage of GDP

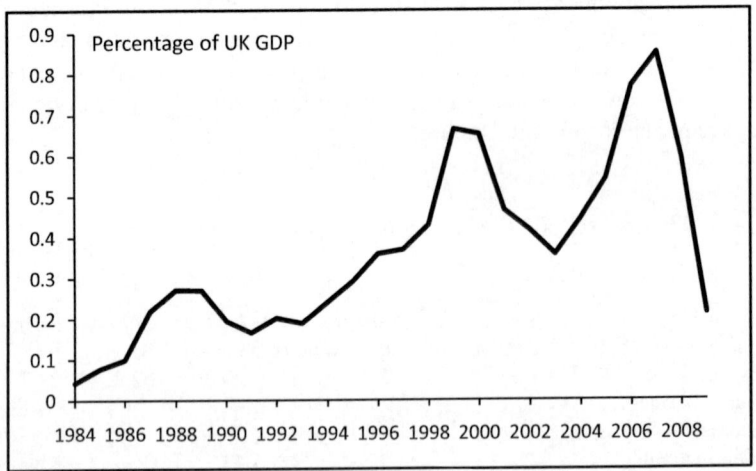

Source: BVCA and ONS

The market has clearly grown in subsequent decades, although overall private equity remains relatively small, compared with the overall size of the economy (Chart 1). Most businesses in the 1980s still relied on bank finance as their lifeblood, something that continues today particularly for small and medium-sized enterprises ("SMEs"). That provided the private equity industry with an opportunity when the early 1990s recession hit, as banks were left as the de facto owners of many businesses that fell insolvent during the downturn. At that time UK banks were not experienced players in the PE arena, so they sold off most of those businesses to PE houses and turnaround funds, which resulted in excellent returns (Chart 2).

Chart 2: Private equity fund performance by vintage year

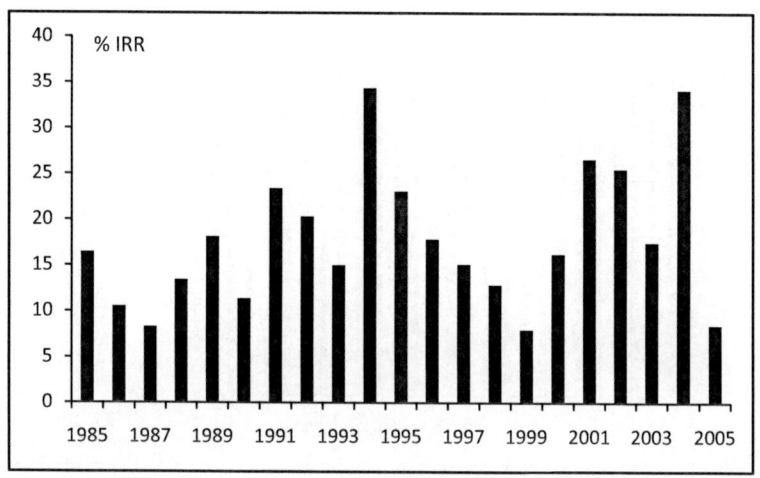

Source: BVCA

These strong returns, and the continued growth and development of the industry, led to a significant increase in PE activity in the late 1990s, leading up to the dot com boom and subsequent bust in the early 2000s. Venture capital firms, in particular, were caught up in the maelstrom wreaked by irrational expectations of unproven future returns, and funds performed poorly.

Following the crash, the UK private equity industry continued its evolution. Firms such as 3i and Apax, which had previously invested at the venture end of the spectrum in the 1990s, started to focus much more on the buy-out landscape, while dominant US players such as Blackstone and KKR also strengthened their European presence. While other European markets also developed rapidly, London's pre-eminence as a financial centre, with high-quality legal and technical expertise, made the UK the obvious location for a European head office. Venture capitalists, meanwhile, started to shy away from somewhat riskier seed and start-up stage funding, and focus on later stage financing instead.

Prior to the 2007 banking crisis and the 2008/9 recession, PE firms enjoyed relatively easy terms on debt, like other borrowers, and took advantage to gear up and purchase some of the largest and best-known brands on the British high street, including Boots, Travelodge and Weetabix. However, with UK-based funds increasingly taking a global perspective, foreign investments rapidly became the bulk of UK funds' new investments by value (Chart 3). The situation is different elsewhere in Europe, where funds focus much more on domestic investments, consistent with London's role as a global financial centre.

Chart 3: UK-led PE investments by location

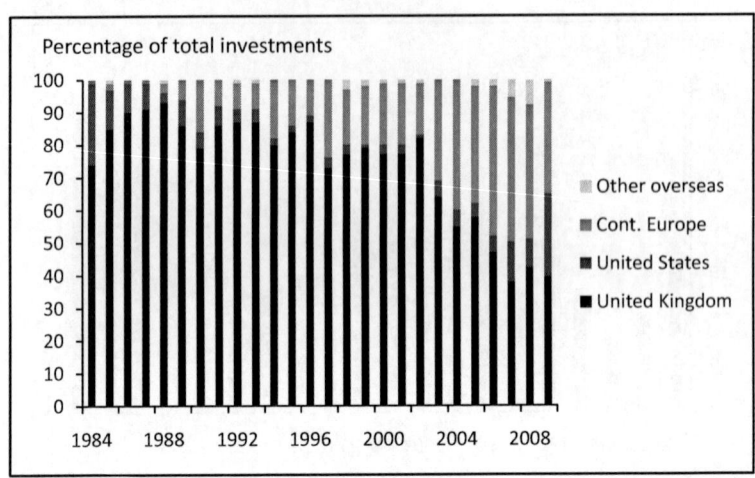

Source: BVCA

When the banking crisis hit in 2007, the financial landscape changed almost overnight. After capital markets dislocated in August 2007, it quickly became clear that banks' balance sheets had grown too large too quickly, while the process of securitisation and trading and re-trading of underlying debts and investments meant that no-one was sure who would be left holding the losses as US house prices fells and mortgagors defaulted on their debts.

At the same time, there were many critics who claimed that private equity would soon suffer the same fate as US mortgage backed securities ("MBSs"). The leveraged nature of PE investments led many commentators to believe that, just as the banks were struggling to reduce the size of their balance sheets, so too the private equity industry would suffer. An infamous 2008 report by the Boston Consulting Group, in particular, confidently claimed that almost half of all PE backed companies would default by 2011, and at least one-fifth of the 100 largest PE firms—and possibly as many as 40 per cent—would go out of business within two to three years.

Chart 4: Financing arrangements for PE buy-outs

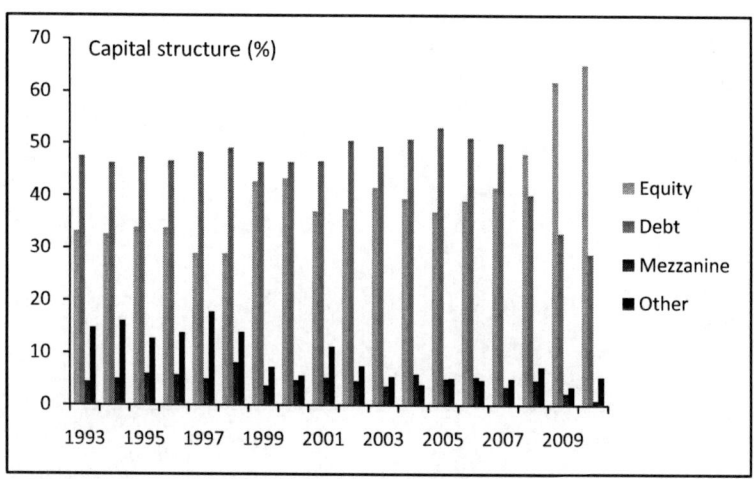

Source: CMBOR

Even without the benefit of hindsight, these claims looked hollow. The deepest recession that the vast majority of the population can remember certainly left its scars on the PE industry, and individual investments and PE houses have failed. But, overall, leverage levels never exploded in the run up to the banking crisis (Chart 4), and the ex post failure rate for portfolio companies and PE houses has been far lower than the industry critics' forecast.

Fundamentally, this outcome can be explained by the private equity's active ownership model. In the period between the start of the banking crisis and the onset of recession, PE houses had already started to focus primarily on managing and nurturing their existing portfolios, rather than new investments and fundraising. At the same time, those funds with high leverage did not just wait for existing agreements to expire, but started to explore new measures and arrangements. Private equity's role as a long term, forward looking, active ownership model stood it in good stead, with recent academic research finding that PE backed buy-outs exhibited a stronger economic performance both before and during the recent recession. Companies that are backed by private equity actually outperformed their peers, and were less likely to fail. For example, PE backed buy-outs had almost 14 per cent higher productivity and 5 per cent higher return on assets ("ROA") during the recession than matched private and listed companies. And insolvencies of PE backed firms have actually been lower than for listed and matched private companies during the recession.

Chart 5: Private equity investments by value and number

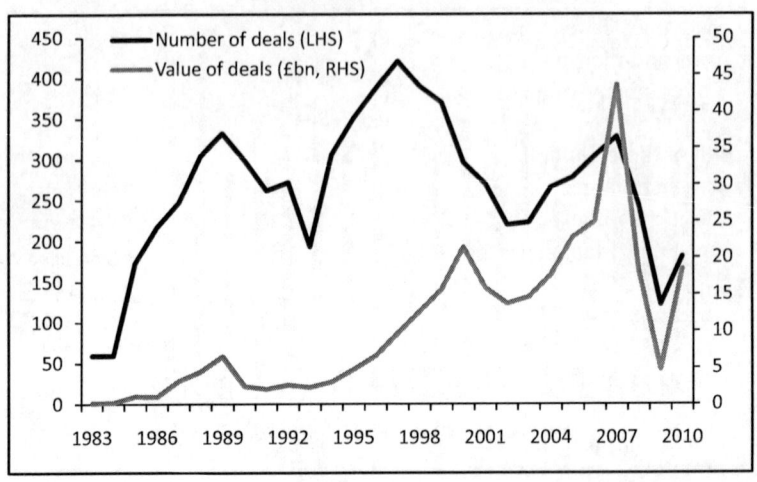

Source: BVCA

This focus on existing portfolios meant that, as the UK economy nosedived, new PE activity in the United Kingdom also fell dramatically (Chart 5). However, with the UK economy now having emerged from recession, albeit more gradually than many hoped, Private equity houses are again looking at new investment opportunities, and activity has partially recovered—over the medium term, it is likely to normalise somewhere between the 2007 peak and 2009 trough. And with the UK Government focusing primarily on deficit reduction over the life of this parliament, the private sector will have to fund the still sluggish recovery. Precisely because of this, the 2011 Budget extended the existing rules regarding the Enterprise Investment Scheme ("EIS") and Venture Capital Trusts ("VCTs"), in an effort to encourage more private sector funding at these early stages of a business' life. With broad support for VC across the political spectrum, and private equity's strong track record of improving businesses, the industry is ideally placed to help back existing and new entrepreneurs, and fund the private sector-led growth that the UK economy so badly needs.

Private equity and transparency

At the same time as it has weathered the recent economic storm, the UK private equity industry has also changed dramatically in terms of its engagement with those outside the industry. Following the Treasury Committee hearings of 2007, the BVCA and larger private equity firms responded swiftly to calls for greater transparency around the industry's activities and investments. The past year saw the publication of the third annual report by the Guidelines Monitoring Group, which was set up to monitor the industry's compliance with the Walker Guidelines for Disclosure and Transparency, introduced in November 2007. These Guidelines called for additional disclosures and communication by private equity firms and their portfolio companies, where the latter are sufficiently large in terms of company value or UK employment.

As a result of these Guidelines, BVCA member firms now provide more information about their larger portfolio investments than many FTSE350 companies. Disclosure is also likely to change once the "Level 2" aspects of the Alternative Investment Fund Managers' Directive ("AIFMD") become clearer over coming months. The AIFMD imposes stricter regulation of alternative funds in the European Union, and the BVCA, like other European associations, has been actively engaged in the development of the directive and will continue to be so. The industry recognises that, with public trust in the financial sector badly damaged following the carnage of the recent recession, it has a public duty to explain what it does and how it is doing it. With that in mind, the Walker Guidelines have evolved and expanded, and the BVCA will respond in a similar manner to European legislative developments. Private equity did not cause or directly contribute to the recent financial crisis, and poses no systemic risk to the financial or banking sectors. But the industry also needs to clearly spell out its role in a market economy, and not just focus on what it doesn't do. And with PE houses set to focus on their core strength of building better businesses in the years ahead, that should benefit consumers, pensioners and workers throughout the United Kingdom and European Union.

Table of Cases

Al Nakib Investments (Jersey) Ltd v Longcroft [1990] 1 W.L.R. 1390; [1990] 3 All E.R. 321; [1990] B.C.C. 517; [1991] B.C.L.C. 7; (1990) 87(42) L.S.G. 37; (1990) 140 N.L.J. 741 Ch D 11–60
Allen v Gold Reefs of West Africa Ltd [1900] 1 Ch. 656 CA 10–09
Alliance Paper Group Plc v Prestwich (No.1) [1996] I.R.L.R. 25 Ch D 11–106
Ammonia Soda Co Ltd v Chamberlain [1918] 1 Ch. 266 CA 5–17
Anthony v Wright (Investments: Auditing) [1995] B.C.C. 768; [1995] 1 B.C.L.C. 236 Ch D 8–08
Aveling Barford Ltd v Perion Ltd (1989) 5 B.C.C. 677; [1989] B.C.L.C. 626; [1989] P.C.C. 370 Ch D 5–09, 5–14, 5–15
Bradford Investments Plc (No.1), Re [1990] B.C.C. 740; [1991] B.C.L.C. 224 Ch D (Companies Ct) 5–56
Bradley v Eagle Star Insurance Co Ltd [1989] A.C. 957; [1989] 2 W.L.R. 568; [1989] 1 All E.R. 961; [1989] 1 Lloyd's Rep. 465; [1989] B.C.L.C. 469; [1989] I.C.R. 301; [1989] Fin. L.R. 253; (1989) 86(17) L.S.G. 38; (1989) 86(3) L.S.G. 43; (1989) 139 N.L.J. 330; (1989) 133 S.J. 359 HL 9–29, 9–30
Bray v Ford [1896] A.C. 44 HL 13–03
Bushell v Faith [1970] A.C. 1099; [1970] 2 W.L.R. 272; [1970] 1 All E.R. 53; (1970) 114 S.J. 54 HL 10–04
Caparo Industries Plc v Dickman [1990] 2 A.C. 605; [1990] 2 W.L.R. 358; [1990] 1 All E.R. 568; [1990] B.C.C. 164; [1990] B.C.L.C. 273; [1990] E.C.C. 313; [1955–95] P.N.L.R. 523; (1990) 87(12) L.S.G. 42; (1990) 140 N.L.J. 248; (1990) 134 S.J. 494 HL 8–08, 11–60
Charterbridge Corp v Lloyds Bank Ltd [1970] Ch. 62; [1969] 3 W.L.R. 122; [1969] 2 All E.R. 1185; [1969] 2 Lloyd's Rep. 24; (1968) 113 S.J. 465 Ch D 5–26
City Equitable Fire Insurance Co Ltd, Re [1925] Ch. 407; [1924] All E.R. Rep. 485 CA 11–01
Credit Suisse Asset Management Ltd v Armstrong [1996] I.C.R. 882; [1996] I.R.L.R. 450; (1996) 93(23) L.S.G. 35; (1996) 140 S.J.L.B. 141 CA (Civ Div) 11–107
Driffield Gas Light Co, Re [1898] 1 Ch. 451 Ch D 5–54
Eurocopy v Teesdale [1992] B.C.L.C. 1067 CA (Civ Div) 9–33, 9–63
Forest of Dean Coal Mining Co, Re (1878–79) L.R. 10 Ch. D. 450 Ch D 13–02
Galoo Ltd v Bright Grahame Murray [1994] 1 W.L.R. 1360; [1995] 1 All E.R. 16; [1994] B.C.C. 319 CA (Civ Div) 8–08
Gambotto v WCP Ltd (1995) 182 C.L.R. 432 10–34
George Newman & Co, Re [1895] 1 Ch. 674 CA 5–18
Halt Garage (1964) Ltd, Re [1982] 3 All E.R. 1016 Ch D 5–09, 5–26
Henry v Great Northern Railway Co (1857) 44 E.R. 858 5–49
Holders Investment Trust, Re [1971] 1 W.L.R. 583; [1971] 2 All E.R. 289; (1970) 115 S.J. 202 Ch D 5–63
Horsley & Weight, Re [1982] Ch. 442; [1982] 3 W.L.R. 431; [1982] 3 All E.R. 1045; (1982) 79 L.S.G. 919 CA (Civ Div) 5–26
Infiniteland Ltd v Artisan Contracting Ltd [2005] EWCA Civ 758; [2006] 1 B.C.L.C. 632 ... 8–11
Ingham v ABC Contract Services Ltd, FC2 93/6609/F CA (Civ Div) 11–106
Kaytech International Plc, Re; sub nom. Secretary of State for Trade and Industry v Kaczer; Potier v Secretary of State for Trade and Industry; Secretary of State for Trade and Industry v Potier; Secretary of State for Trade and Industry v Solly [1999] B.C.C. 390; [1999] 2 B.C.L.C. 351 CA (Civ Div) 12–57

Table of Cases

Kuwait Asia Bank EC v National Mutual Life Nominees Ltd [1991] 1 A.C. 187; [1990] 3
  W.L.R. 297; [1990] 3 All E.R. 404; [1990] 2 Lloyd's Rep. 95; [1990] B.C.C. 567;
  [1990] B.C.L.C. 868 PC (NZ) 11–13
Levison v Farin [1978] 2 All E.R. 1149 QBD 9–55
Malleson v National Insurance & Guarantee Corp [1894] 1 Ch. 200 Ch D 10–02
Morgan Crucible Co Plc v Hill Samuel Bank & Co Ltd; sub nom. Morgan Crucible Co Plc
  v Hill Samuel & Co Ltd [1991] Ch. 295; [1991] 2 W.L.R. 655; [1991] 1 All E.R. 148;
  [1991] B.C.C. 82; [1991] B.C.L.C. 178; (1990) 140 N.L.J. 1605 CA (Civ Div) 11–60
Northern Counties Securities, Ltd v Jackson & Steeple, Ltd [1974] 1 W.L.R. 1133; [1974]
  2 All E.R. 625; (1974) 118 S.J. 498 Ch D 10–05
Office Angels v Rainer-Thomas [1991] I.R.L.R. 214 CA (Civ Div) 11–104
Ooregum Gold Mining Co of India Ltd v Roper; Wallroth v Roper; Ooregum Gold Mining
  Co of India Ltd v Wallroth; Wallroth v Ooregum Gold Mining Co of India Ltd [1892]
  A.C. 125 HL 5–06
Parker v McKenna (1874–75) L.R. 10 Ch. App. 96 Lord Chancellor 11–23
Pavlides v Jensen [1956] Ch. 565; [1956] 3 W.L.R. 224; [1956] 2 All E.R. 518; (1956) 100
  S.J. 452 Ch D 5–39
Post Office v Norwich Union Fire Insurance Society Ltd [1967] 2 Q.B. 363; [1967] 2
  W.L.R. 709; [1967] 1 All E.R. 577; [1967] 1 Lloyd's Rep. 216; (1967) 111 S.J. 71
  CA (Civ Div) 9–29, 9–30
Regal (Hastings) Ltd v Gulliver [1967] 2 A.C. 134; [1942] 1 All E.R. 378 HL 11–22
Ridge Securities Ltd v Inland Revenue Commissioners [1964] 1 W.L.R. 479; [1964] 1 All
  E.R. 275; 44 T.C. 373; (1963) 42 A.T.C. 487; [1963] T.R. 449; (1964) 108 S.J.
  377 Ch D 5–03, 5–09, 5–10, 5–15, 5–26
Roberts & Cooper Ltd, Re [1929] 2 Ch. 383 Ch D 5–51
Rolled Steel Products (Holdings) Ltd v British Steel Corp [1986] Ch. 246; [1985] 2 W.L.R.
  908; [1985] 3 All E.R. 52; (1984) 1 B.C.C. 99158 CA (Civ Div) 5–15
Royal British Bank v Turquand [1843–60] All E.R. Rep. 435; 119 E.R. 886; (1856) 6 El.
  & Bl. 327 Ex Chamber 11–67
Russell v Northern Bank Development Corp Ltd [1992] 1 W.L.R. 588; [1992] 3 All E.R.
  161; [1992] B.C.C. 578; [1992] B.C.L.C. 1016; (1992) 89(27) L.S.G. 33; (1992) 136
  S.J.L.B. 182 HL (NI) 10–03, 10–05, 10–06, 10–07, 10–09
Scottish Insurance Corp Ltd v Wilsons & Clyde Coal Co Ltd; sub nom. Wilsons & Clyde
  Coal Co Ltd, Petitioners; Wilsons & Clyde Coal Co v Scottish Insurance Corp Ltd
  [1949] A.C. 462; [1949] 1 All E.R. 1068; 1949 S.C. (H.L.) 90; 1949 S.L.T. 230; 65
  T.L.R. 354; [1949] L.J.R. 1190; (1949) 93 S.J. 423 HL 5–55
Secretary of State for Trade and Industry v Deverell [2001] Ch. 340; [2000] 2 W.L.R. 907;
  [2000] 2 All E.R. 365; [2000] B.C.C. 1057; [2000] 2 B.C.L.C. 133; (2000) 97(3)
  L.S.G. 35; (2000) 144 S.J.L.B. 49 CA (Civ Div) 12–58
Staples v Eastman Photographic Materials Co [1896] 2 Ch. 303 CA 5–49
TFS Derivatives Ltd v Morgan [2004] EWHC 3181 (QB); [2005] I.R.L.R. 246 11–105
Theatrical Trust Ltd, Re; sub nom. Chapman's Case, Re [1895] 1 Ch. 771 Ch D 5–06
Thomas v Farr Plc [2007] EWCA Civ 118; [2007] I.C.R. 932; [2007] I.R.L.R. 419; (2007)
  151 S.J.L.B. 296 11–105
Trevor v Whitworth (1887) L.R. 12 App. Cas. 409 HL 5–04
Welton v Saffery; sub nom. Railway Time Tables Publishing Co Ex p. Welton, Re [1897]
  A.C. 299 HL 10–04
White v Bristol Aeroplane Co; sub nom. British Aeroplane Co, Re [1953] Ch. 65; [1953]
  2 W.L.R. 144; [1953] 1 All E.R. 40; (1953) 97 S.J. 64 CA 10–09
Will v United Lankat Plantations Co Ltd [1914] A.C. 11 HL 5–53

Table of Statutes

1925	Law of Property Act (15 & 16 Geo.5 c.20)		s.214 .... 12–18, 12–67
	s.91 12–43		(3) 12–79
1927	Landlord and Tenant Act (17 & 18 Geo.5 c.36)		s.238 .... 5–11, 5–25
			ss.238—245 12–66
	s.19(1) 8–42, 8–43		s.314 5–35
1948	Companies Act (11 & 12 Geo.6 c.38) 5–22		s.423 5–25
			Sch.5 5–35
1954	Landlord and Tenant Act (2 & 3 Eliz.2 c.56)		Company Directors Disqualification Act (c.46)
	Pt II 8–41		s.3 11–58
1968	Theft Act (c.60) 13–10		s.11 11–90
	s.15(1) 13–10		Financial Services Act (c.60)
	s.17 11–59	1988	s.47(1) 13–10
	s.19 11–59		Income and Corporation Taxes Act (c.1)
1977	Unfair Contract Terms Act (c.50) 8–29, 9–09		s.707 8–70
			s.776 8–70
1978	Civil Liability (Contribution) Act (c.47) 9–21	2000	Financial Services and Markets Act (c.8) 8–66, 9–26
1979	Capital Gains Tax Act (c.14)		s.397 9–09
	s.88 8–70		Insolvency Act (c.39) 12–83
1985	Companies Act (c.6) ... 9–40, 11–01, 11–15, 11–31, 11–39, 11–44	2002	Enterprise Act (c.40) 12.15, 12–82, 12–84
			Pt 10..................... 12–61
	Pt IV 6–48	2003	Income Tax (Earnings and Pensions) Act (c.1) 10–50
	s.39 5–28		
	ss.99—116 5–07		Pt 7 4–34
	ss.151—153 5–20	2006	Companies Act (c.46) ... 5–03, 5–22, 5–26, 5–31, 5–59, 5–68, 5–69, 9–66, 10–02, 10–34, 11–01, 11–04, 11–09, 11–10, 11–15, 11–27, 11–31, 11–41, 11–48, 11–52, 11–70, 11–76, 11–79, 11–80, 11–87, 11–88, 11–93, 13–04
	s.152(1) 5–19		
	ss.155—188 5–20		
	s.214 12–21		
	ss.263—281 5–11		
	s.311 11–31		
	s.312 11–43		
	s.316(3) 11–43		
	s.317 .... 6–48, 11–27		Pt 17 Ch.5 5–07
	ss.320—322 6–48		Pt 18 Ch.3 5–15
	s.324 6–48		Pt 18 Ch.4 5–15
	s.330 6–48		Pt 18 Ch.5 5–15
	s.425 12–43		Pt 23..................... 5–11
	s.459 9–95		s.26 5–56
	s.744 5–48		s.39 .... 5–27, 11–67
1986	Insolvency Act (c.45) 5–62, 11–01, 11–04, 11–50, 12–83		s.40 11–67
			s.82 11–64
			s.112 .... 5–31, 5–33
	s.76 5–62		s.113 5–32
	s.213 .... 11–49, 12–80		s.162 11–75

Table of Statutes

s.167	11–75	s.425(1)	11–57
s.168	10–04, 11–95	(2)	11–57
ss.170—181	11–09	s.431	11–57
s.171	11–18, 13–04	s.432	11–57
ss.171—177	13–04	ss.434—436	11–57
s.172	11–14—11–16, 13–04	s.455	11–55
s.173	13–04	s.456	11–55
s.174	11–48, 13–04	s.463	11–93
s.175	11–20, 13–04	s.548	5–38
s.176	13–04	s.549	5–68, 11–52
s.177	11–24, 11–26, 11–27, 13–04, 13–06	s.582	5–07
		s.584	5–07
(1)	11–26	s.586	5–07
(2)	11–26	s.610	5–08
(3)	11–26	(2)	5–08
(4)	11–26	s.612	5–49
s.182	11–25, 13–04, 13–06	s.617	10–05
ss.182—187	11–27	s.630	10–33
s.184	13–06	ss.630—634	10–08
s.188	9–100, 11–29	s.633	9–97, 10–06
ss.188—189	11–30, 11–96	s.677(1)	5–19
s.190	11–34, 13–04, 13–06	s.684(4)	5–60
(5)	11–34	s.687	5–59, 5–61
(6)	11–34	ss.713—723	5–61
ss.190—196	11–34	s.735	5–63
s.191	11–34	s.829	5–15
s.192(a)	11–34	(1)	5–15
s.193	11–34	ss.829—853	5–11, 5–17
s.195	5–27	s.830	5–11, 5–50
(4)	5–29	s.831	5–13
s.197	11–36	s.832	5–13
ss.197—214	11–39	s.836	5–14, 5–17, 5–18
s.213	11–41	s.838	5–42
s.214	11–41	s.839	5–42
ss.215—222	11–44	(1)	5–18
s.223(1)	11–36	ss.845—846	5–14
ss.227—230	11–30, 11–96	ss.845—847	5–09
s.237	11–31	s.846	5–14
s.248	11–87	s.847(1)	5–17
s.250	11–04, 12–55	(2)	5–17
s.251	11–04, 12–58	s.851	5–17
ss.252—253	11–34	ss.895—900	5–67
ss.252—256	11–70	s.993	12–80
s.386	11–54	s.994	5–54
s.393	11–54	s.1157	11–72
s.395	9–37	s.1166	5–67
s.396	9–37	s.1177	11–31
s.409	11–79	2007 Finance Act (c.11)	4–04
s.423	11–55		

Table of Statutory Instruments

1985 Companies (Tables A to F)
Regulations (SI 1985/805) ... 11–28
Table A 9–101, 9–103, 10–02,
10–60, 11–07, 11–83
reg.30 5–36
reg.31 5–36
reg.38 5–36
reg.39 10–60
reg.65 .... 10–60, 11–07, 11–85
regs.65—69 10–60
reg.66 11–85
regs 73—77 10–60
reg.83 11–86
reg.88 .... 10–60, 11–82
reg.118 11–71

2001 Financial Services and Markets
Act 2000 (Financial Promotion)
Order (SI 2001/1335)
art.19(5)(d) 10–15
art.49(2)(a)—(c) 10–15

Chapter 1

The Role of Private Equity

James Dow, Dow Schofield Watts LLP

1.1 Private equity explained

Private equity and venture capital describe equity investment in unquoted companies. It is most simply described as "not debt" funding invested in private companies.   **1–01**

It is applicable where the perceived levels of risk, the time horizon associated with the investment or simply the sums required do not suit debt providers or the public equity markets.

These conditions apply to companies in their early stages, or those operating in fast changing environments. It has also become the common mechanism to finance the separation of non-core assets from a parent company, to facilitate management succession in family-owned firms ("management buy-outs") and to delist firms from a stock exchange ("public-to-private transactions").

Private equity providers become co-owners of the companies, sharing risks and returns.

The term "private equity" is the term generally used in the UK to cover the industry as a whole including buy-outs and venture capital. "Venture capital" is a sub-category covering the start-up to expansion stages of investment.

1.2 Private equity overview

1.2.1 Type of private equity firms

There are three main categories of private equity firms: **1–02**

Independents These are the majority of firms which raise their funds from a number of external sources including pension funds, insurance companies, wealthy individuals, and corporate investors. Independent private equity firms usually manage the funds through fixed life limited partnerships. A limited partnership usually has a fixed 10 year life with between 10 to 30 limited institutional investor partners. Within this period the funds invest the money committed and return these funds plus any returns made. This generally requires the investments to be sold before the end of the fund.

The independent acts as a general partner selecting and structuring investments in return for a management fee and usually a share of any upside on achieving capital gains. The upside share is referred to as carried interest.

The independent funds invest 75 per cent to 90 per cent of all UK private equity investment.

1–03 *Captives* These private equity firms obtain their funds from parent organisations which are usually financial institutions. Following the financial crisis, their investment levels have fallen to less than 5 per cent of all funds invested.

Semi-captives Some of the captives also raise funds from external investors. They are known as semi-captives and manage and invest 10 per cent to 15 per cent of all funds invested.

The venture capital trusts ("VCTs") represent a different dimension to the venture capital market. The VCTs are quoted and offer a private investor the prospect of a tax advantage and an opportunity to invest in venture capital. Publicly quoted VCTs also give independently managed private equity firms the ability to raise significant additional capital.

In addition to the type of fund, most venture capital firms can be broken down into two main categories, namely the "generalist" firm and the "specialist" firm.

1–04 *Generalists* Firms which will invest in a wide range of industries and covering all investment categories from start-up businesses to later stage investments.

Specialists Firms which will invest only in certain product categories and/or sector areas of specific interest such as:

- management buy-outs (product specialisation); and
- high-technology propositions (sector specialisation).

1–05 Many of the generalist funds avoid areas which are outside investment criteria or the mandate of the fund. They invariably consist of the following areas:

Product exclusions   Start-ups/early stage investments and/or rescue/turnaround situations.

Sector exclusions   Such as high-technology investments, property investments, gambling or any others set by their investors.

Within the generalist category, most funds have a particular sector or product specialisation, which is derived from past investment experience or the career bias of the fund's investment executives. Conversely, the high-technology funds dedicate their entire focus and resource to the more speculative investment, which often involves dealing with early stage propositions rather than with established companies.

1.2.2 Private equity investments

Private equity investments can typically be subdivided into the following product categories: **1–06**

Management buy-outs/buy-ins

A MBO gives an incumbent management team the opportunity to purchase the company from its present owners. MBOs represent around a half of all private equity funds invested. The average private equity firm equity investment is in the range of £10 million to £20 million. MBOs typically arise in the following situations: **1–07**

- disposal by the parent of a non-core subsidiary;
- succession issue in a family owned company;
- disposal to management as an alternative to a trade sale;
- management buy-back from receivership.

The use of venture capital in MBOs has allowed employees the opportunity to become owner managers and receive a significant equity stake, disproportionate relative to the level of funding invested by the venture capital.

The management buy-in ("MBI") is an extension of the MBO principle in that a manager or group of managers actively search for an acquisition target to buy into. The MBI may be an outright takeover of a company or alternatively the MBI team may join forces with members of the existing management team to form a "BIMBO" (buy-in/management buy-out).   **1–08**

Investment returns have been lower for MBIs, possibly because buy-in candidates are unlikely to have the same level of inside knowledge on the operation of a company than existing management. MBIs represent about ten per cent of private equity funds invested in MBOs.

The most significant recent development has been the rise of the very large MBO, one requiring more than £100 million of private equity investment; this segment represents about one half of all UK private equity investment funding in MBOs.

Rescues

1–09 In a rescue situation, venture capital can have a role to play in re-capitalising a company's balance sheet and provide a contribution to ongoing working capital requirements. Venture capital firms tend to view rescues with extreme caution and do not invest on the proviso that things will change. The management team are held accountable for past mistakes, and without strong mitigating circumstances it is unlikely that the private equity firm will inject new funds. Mitigating circumstances may include:

- a delay in developing a new process or product which creates a financial strain on the company's funding resources;
- production problems brought about by the failure of a key piece of plant or machinery;
- failure of a key customer or key supplier; or more simply an
- overgeared balance sheet.

Rescue or turnaround financing attracts very little private equity investment.

Secondary purchase investments

1–10 This involves a private equity firm purchasing shares in an investee company from another private equity firm, from other shareholders who wish to exit from the company, or refinancing bank debt investments. The number of these investments has increased in recent years and represents five per cent to ten per cent of private equity funds invested.

Purchasing shares from a private equity firm   Despite occasional variations, independent private firms' shares typically raise funds in ten-year limited partnerships. This means the venture funds typically have an investment time horizon of between four and seven years with the need to achieve an exit at the end of this period. Often management of an investee company may wish to develop further the business beyond this timeframe, thereby providing an opportunity for a new private equity investor.

Purchasing shares from existing shareholders In the unquoted company market, it can be difficult for shareholders to exit their position due to the general illiquidity of the shares. The venture capital firms represent liquidity for those shareholders and can also provide additional funding for companies. **1–11**

Shareholders can also realise just a part of their shareholdings. This route can provide owner managers with a certain element of cash and financial independence, without giving up their entire interest in the business. Similarly, private equity firms can be used to fund a settlement of a shareholder dispute, buying-out an exiting shareholder.

Expansion capital

Sometimes known as "development capital" or "growth capital", half of all companies backed are in the expansion capital investments. These are typically existing venture capital investments requiring a fresh injection of private equity to finance growth, refinance debt or to fund acquisitions. The average investment expansion capital is smaller than for management buy-outs, with average financings of around £2 million to £4 million. **1–12**

Early stage investments and start-ups

There is always a strong need for funding in companies at an early stage of their development. Given the associated high risk profile and the historic low investment return most venture capital firms steer well clear of this area, although they still represent around one-third of all companies receiving investment they usually only account for five per cent of funds invested with average equity investments of less than £1 million. Fortunately, there are still some funds which see a real opportunity for significant capital gain by backing such ventures. Early stage and start-up investments represent the difficult end of the market for those seeking funds. In looking at a start-up, it is unlikely that an entrepreneur with merely a good idea will receive significant backing without a demonstrable track record of success in that industry. **1–13**

The start-ups which find most favour tend to be those that have an experienced management team.

To achieve funding for early stage or start-up ventures, proposals must contain some of the following characteristics:

- a well balanced and experienced management team;
- a fully developed product;
- a growing existing market place which is not dominated by a few firms.

1–14 A management team seeking investment in a start-up involving a new product or a new market will find fund raising extremely difficult, irrespective of their track record.

In summary, when reviewing venture capital investments, the MBO and development capital type propositions have generated the highest investment returns for venture capital firms, whilst early stage and rescue propositions have produced the lowest returns.

1.2.3 Recent trends in the industry

Equity gap—£100,000 to £1 million investment range

1–15 Most of the independent private equity firms are principally only seeking investments in excess of £1 million. This is a strong and continuing upward trend as historic investment returns have been better for larger transactions. This has serious implications for the new and emerging businesses in the UK which have a requirement for less than £1 million. On a more positive note, a number of smaller independent funds and government backed regional funds concentrate on the £100,000 to £500,000 sector. However, they are in the minority and generally lack the funding strength to provide significant follow-on investment capability.

There are two major problems with smaller investments: First, investee companies often lack the financial or management resources to withstand adverse changes in trading. Secondly and equally detrimental to the venture capital firms are transaction fees associated with completing an investment below £500,000. On lower end transactions, professional advisors' costs will often account for more than ten per cent of the investment monies raised, these costs divert funds and also erode investment returns.

1–16 Venture capital trusts can fund transactions at the smaller end of the market, but generally they seek equity investment opportunities requiring £2 million or more. VCTs have a duty to make investment returns just as well as mainstream fund management and it is likely that the smaller end of fund raising will continue to be under-serviced.

The equity gap is almost inevitable in any economy, despite continued initiatives to "Bridge the Finance Gap".

Business angels—£100,000 and below

1–17 In recent years a number of networks of high net worth individuals prepared to invest in smaller companies have emerged and these individuals have become known as "business angels". A number of sophisticated "angel networks" have been created across the UK which attempt to match private investors to appropriate opportunities.

The angel formula has a good precedent in the US where many smaller end propositions are now funded through individuals or syndicate groups of private investors. The typical profile of a business angel is someone who has previously generated financial independence in business and wishes to invest in a new venture. It is not uncommon for business angels to monitor their investment in an active way, which often leads to their appointment as a non-executive director. Other angels may wish to be passive investors with the whole aim of realising their investment on the future sale of the company.

Move away from start-ups and early stage

1–18 Many of the independent UK venture capital firms are actively targeting a minimum £2 million investment and ideally only £5 million plus investment propositions. In addition the mainstream primary funds are seeking average equity investment of at least £10 million and there exists a large nucleus of "premier funds" who will only consider investments with a minimum private equity funding requirement of £20 million or higher. Such investment minimums tend to place the focus on expansion capital and MBOs/MBIs. These product groupings are positioned at the lower end of the risk scale, and usually involve dealing with established businesses with proven track records. This trend looks set to continue because large management buy-outs (equity investment over £10 million) have produced the highest long term returns of all private equity investment categories.

The early stage investment or start-up may produce significant up-sides, however the risks of failure are greater. Overall returns for early stage investments are significantly lower than any other private equity categories, thus the investment trend away from these opportunities is likely to continue.

Technology funds

1–19 Until 1998, technology funds undoubtedly suffered from the perception of high-risk and low-return. Then the technology sector became the hottest area of the economy and not surprisingly private equity followed.

UK high-technology companies (communications, software and computer services, biotechnology and medical) receive more private equity than any other industry category: accounting for about one half of the total number of UK companies backed and ten per cent of the total amount invested. The lower

The Role of Private Equity

average value reflecting the fact that over half of the companies backed are early stage investments.

1.2.4 Developments in the MBO marketplace

1–20 Of the total funds raised since 2000, around 70 per cent is expected to be invested in large (over £10 million) or very large (over £100 million) MBO/MBI opportunities.

The MBO/MBI product grouping also usually accounts for around half of UK venture capital investments by value. Given the importance of MBOs to the venture capital industry, it is essential to review the latest trends in the MBO market place.

The very large buy-out funds

1–21 UK private equity fund raising since 2000 has been dominated by the very large buy-out funds and has pushed those private equity firms into the spotlight. Now most public company takeover speculation, no matter what the size, automatically assumes the presence of these financial buyers as well as trade buyers.

Private equity firms could become the main source of fresh capital for companies with more than £100 million if the bias towards bigger companies on the stock market continues.

The bought deal or institutional buy-out ("IBO")

1–22 The development of the large buy-out fund and the increasing size of average investment has led to vendors directly approaching venture capital funds in the sales auction process. Having won the auction, the venture capital firm then assembles the management team, which may include members from outside the target company. This "bought deal" is in stark contrast to the MBOs completed in the 1980s, where the management team obtained the MBO opportunity and then selected their preferred funding provider. The bought deal will continue and reduce the importance of the management team in initiating the MBO process. At the lower end of the buy-out scale, management in conjunction with their advisors are still likely to lead and co-ordinate the MBO process for the foreseeable future.

The BIMBO

1–23 As with all venture capital products, hybrid versions are inevitable and the BIMBO is no exception. The BIMBO is a combination of a buy-in candidate or candidates working with the existing MBO team to effect a MBO. The use of buy-in candidates helps to strengthen an existing management team in an area of weakness. The emergence of the bought deal on larger transactions has also encouraged the BIMBO trend.

Gearing

Gearing represents the amount of debt compared to the amount of equity used to fund transactions. In management buy-outs above £10 million, the ratio of debt to equity is typically in the region of 60:40 to 55:45 with greater amounts of debt being provided to companies with stronger and more predictable cash flows. The focus on cash flow lending has also led to the development of mezzanine funding. Mezzanine funding is debt charging high rates of interest (partially deferred) and with the added bonus of options or warrants to subscribe for equity on preferential terms. Mezzanine finance appears in about 20 per cent of management buy-outs over £10 million. 1–24

1.3 Rationale for using private equity

1.3.1 Limitations of debt funding

In the UK, most companies think of conventional bank lending when it comes to meeting funding requirements. If security cover is good and the funding requirement does not materially affect the level of gearing, many businesses will not require any alternative source of funding. The increasing development of the debtor based finance industry with its invoice discounting and factoring products, means that often a working capital intensive company can continue to meet its funding needs through debt. 1–25

However, banks are in the business of secured lending, and additional unsecured finance must come from private equity. Venture capital firms provide private equity funding in return for a shareholding in the company. The implications of taking venture capital and, in particular, the equity "give-away" factor are discussed in detail at 1.4.

1.3.2 Funding key change

A company's evolution may precipitate the need for venture capital funding. The key changes could include buying-out retiring or dissenting shareholders, funding a management buy-out, to provide new succession or funding organic growth or acquisitions. 1–26

The Role of Private Equity

Organic growth may involve the development of a company's branch network or sales infrastructure, or the building of a new factory and its subsequent equipping with plant and machinery.

1–27 Many companies elect to grow by means of strategic acquisition to obtain an immediate increase, rather than to develop gradually by implementing an organic growth plan. While the acquisition may utilise a considerable amount of management time in consolidating the enlarged operation, the future benefits may be considerable.

Whether growth is organic or by acquisition, private equity may be required if the funding requirements exceed the enlarged company's debt capacity.

1.3.3 Alternatives to private equity firms

Business angels

1–28 Business angels can have a strong role to pay in the smaller funding market place. In the absence of networks of angels, problems can arise, particularly in matching differing private investor requirements.

Agreement on investment deal structures, and taking account of their preferences, can be time consuming. For example, some individuals may wish to invest through offshore trusts whilst others may wish to use some form of tax relief, such as the Enterprise Initiative Scheme. Some investors may want to be active and have a non-executive role within the investee company, which can conflict with the preferences of the existing management team. In terms of exit planning and investment yields, some business angels can have different priorities and it is important to obtain a balanced solution which takes account of most of the individual preferences. Often the best way to achieve consensus amongst business angels is to be prescriptive in setting the investment framework. Under this approach, the business angel has to subscribe on prescribed terms.

The British Business Angels Association ("BBAA") is the UK trade association for promoting angel investing.

Industry partnership

1–29 Industry partnerships or corporate venturing can be a useful way of obtaining funding which would otherwise not be available. In the case of early stage and start-up ventures, the industry partner can often be the most sympathetic investor to a proposition because they are likely to understand the nature of a related industry and can see commercial advantage by backing such a company.

A difficulty of this route may be that a management team may lose both equity control and day-to-day control of the organisation with disagreement most likely in exit planning. In particular, industry partners have firm views on whom the business should and should not be sold to. Conversely, a private equity firm, free of trade interests, backing a management team, will rely on the judgment of management and are focused on maximising exit gains for all shareholders.

Vendor finance

Transactions have been completed entirely using vendor deferred consideration. **1–30** This is where the vendor acts as a deferred lender to the transaction and allows the acquirer to pay the purchase consideration over a period of time. This route lends itself particularly to opportunities which are of little interest to venture funds.

The vendor usually takes the view that unless some form of guarantee or security can be given on the deferred consideration element, the risk factor in not accepting cash consideration may prove to be too great, but the vendor may not have a choice. Where a company is asset rich, security can usually be offered and, in the event of default, equity claw-back provisions can be incorporated into the sale and purchase agreement. It is common to reward the vendor with a commercial rate of interest on the funds deferred and perhaps an additional premium, over and above the acquisition price, is justified to reflect the risk of agreeing to this route.

Vendor finance is also favoured in transactions, requiring speed and the prospect **1–31** of subsequent refinancing of the vendor finance at a later date, post transaction.

Deferred vendor consideration is also used to increase the price paid for the business, meeting the price gap between the vendor's requirements and the abilities of the company to raise external finance. As a "price gap filler", deferred consideration and earn-out arrangements can make a deal happen that would otherwise be considered unfundable.

1.4 Implications of private equity

1.4.1 Equity "give-away" factor

The issue of equity "give-away" in privately owned companies is always an emo- **1–32** tive subject and companies will always seek to meet their funding requirements from sources not requiring an equity share in the business.

Private equity funding is frequently provided as a package which will include ordinary shares with either redeemable preference shares or redeemable loan stock. A prerequisite of most venture capital investments is a requirement to pay dividends on the ordinary shares and a dividend on the preference shares or interest on the loan stock. The ordinary shares owned by the private equity fund will tend to be designated as "A" ordinary shares or preferred ordinary shares or some other variant of that theme in order to differentiate their dividend and minority protection rights from those pertaining to the other ordinary shareholders. The venture fund may insist on a dividend expressed as a percentage of net profits before tax and this is known as the participating dividend. The range of such a participating dividend tends, in the main, to fluctuate initially between five to ten per cent of pre-tax profits, these may also rise rapidly over time to encourage an exit. The redeemable preference shares, or loan stock, are likely to carry a fixed income with a significant premium above commercial bank interest rates.

The redemption of preference shares or loan stock tends to be over a three to six-year period which usually lags, the repayment of bank debt and coincides with the forecast timeframe of the investment. Where cash is a critical issue in the early phase of an investment, it is usually possible to agree reduced or deferred dividend and capital repayments to fit in with the cash flows of the business.

1.4.2 The institutional relationship

1–33 In accepting private equity, the management team will have to abide by a new code of rules as detailed in the share subscription agreement, new articles of association and new service contracts. Whilst most venture capital funds back the judgment and abilities of management, provisions are required which ensure that in the event of default, and/or under-performance of the company, a remedy can be achieved. Furthermore the funds also have safeguards in the articles of association to protect them as minority shareholders.

Venture capital funds generally insist on a service agreement to govern remuneration and service contracts of the directors. This is designed to ensure that directors do not pay themselves more than has been agreed, thereby reducing profits attributable to shareholders as a whole, and will cover matters such as pension and bonus arrangements, and benefits to be provided. The agreements will have provisions to cover arrangements for the management to leave the company as either a "good" or a "bad" leaver. The later usually covering such areas as negligence, incompetence or misappropriation of company funds.

1–34 The articles of association will usually have provisions where if dividends and capital redemptions are in arrears then, during those arrears, the private equity firm can take control (see Ch.9). Similarly, on the theme of control, the shareholders' agreement or investment agreement is likely to contain restrictions relating to the purchase of significant capital assets, the acquisition of any companies, or the

Implications of private equity

ability of management to diversify into other trades without the consent of the venture fund (see Ch.8).

As in all partnerships, the venture capitalist needs to be consulted on significant events and developments within the company. The primary way by which this is done is through the appointment of a non-executive director often the Chairman. The function of a non-executive director is mainly to attend the board meetings of the investee company and to advise management on strategic and business issues. The non-executive director also has a monitoring role and will feed back to the venture capital provider how the company and the investment are developing.

In essence, as a partner in the investee company, the venture capitalist needs to be kept abreast of all material developments which affect the company's performance. While most venture funds are hands-off in approach, regulatory provisions are in place to monitor and control, particularly where events are going badly or in a direction which differs materially from the original business plan.

1.4.3 Pros and cons of private equity

As in most key business decisions, acceptance of venture capital can have important implications on the future of an investee company. It is necessary to summarise objectively the pros and cons of private equity.

1–35

Pros

- In the case of a management buy-out, private equity enables employees to obtain some degree of ownership and control of their company.
- In the case of an existing business, private equity can accelerate the development of the investee company.
- Private equity can strengthen an existing company's balance sheet and cash flow.
- There is the opportunity to obtain second round funding, from the private equity firm.
- A private equity firm as shareholder provides added credibility to the business.

Cons

- The management are bound by the institutional rules and regulations as laid down in the share subscription agreement and articles of association.
- Complete freedom of operation is only possible within the confines of the agreed business plan.

- There is more accountability: a non-executive director and the provision of management information.
- Private equity firms are focused on exits at a time that suits them.

Accepting private equity for a private company is essentially a trade-off between "speed of growth" and "freedom of action and accountability".

1.5 Key points

1.5.1 Private equity overview

1–36
- The emergence of the MBO market in the early 1980s, fuelled by the enterprise culture of the time, led to a rapid growth in the number of private equity firms and levels of investment activity.
- Most of the UK private equity firms are "generalist" in outlook and will consider a wide range of investment opportunities in differing sectors.
- Like any industry, private equity has distinct product groupings which range from early stage investments through to backing well established companies with development capital.
- The venture capital industry continually refines its investment criteria, driven by their returns on investments and the requirements of their investors, which creates trends in deal sizes, industry sectors and deal types.

1.5.2 Rationale for using private equity

1–37
- The debt capacity of a company is limited, beyond this funding can only be provided by venture capital, most of which is provided by the private equity firms.
- Private equity can fund the "key points of change" in a company's life.
- As an alternative to the private equity firms, a company may consider the use of business angels or industry partners to meet its equity funding requirements. In certain circumstances vendor finance; either in whole or in part, may also be a viable option.

1.5.3 Implications of private equity

1–38
- Private equity always involves an element of "equity give-away" which is always emotive despite the overriding commercial logic for increasing the equity base.

Key points

- In accepting a private equity partner the investee company will be bound by a new code of rules, with certain restrictions on management, as laid down in the share subscription agreement and revised articles of association.
- There are pros and cons to private equity, which are probably summarised as a trade-off between "speed of growth" and "freedom of action".

Chapter 2

Raising Private Equity

James Dow, Dow Schofield Watts LLP

2.1 Introduction

Raising private equity can be a time consuming, expensive and unforgiving process for the potential investee company. Like all specialist areas, venture capital has its own set of guidelines and rules, often unwritten, and largely brought about from previous experience of the funds and the managers themselves. The purpose of this chapter is to demystify the fund raising process and identify the key areas and issues involved in raising venture capital. 2–01

2.2 Meeting the investment criterion

Prior to embarking on this process of raising private equity, it is important to determine whether a proposition fits the profile of a typical private equity investment. In judging the investment fit, there are four important criteria on which a private equity firm places emphasis: the management, past performance, future prospects and exit prospects. This section will review each of the key areas in detail. 2–02

2.2.1 Management

Private equity firms are in the business of backing experienced and balanced management teams. It is fair to say that a good management team may perform well in a difficult situation but a poor management team is a catalyst for underperformance and failure. Given that most of the venture funds are "hands-off" in their investment monitoring approach, reliance and trust has to be placed on the "day-to-day" guardians of the investment. 2–03

Venture capitalists are wary in backing the "one-man band" entrepreneur for fear of lack of control, an absence of all round skill base and vulnerability to the well-being and motivation of just one individual. Similarly, a management team with a history of prior failure are unlikely to raise private equity.

There are of course companies where the founding and dominant shareholder has built up a capable and independently minded team. In such circumstances, the venture capitalist will consider investment.

2–04 The ideal management team is an experienced and balanced group of individuals. What does this mean? In looking at the prime age range of a management team, 35 to 50 is the key range. There are of course many exceptions to this age stereo-typing band, however most dynamic management teams comprise individuals in this prime career building age range.

In terms of balance, the ideal MBO team is likely to have a high calibre individual covering each of the major management functions; chief executive, finance, production and sales. Where a weakness exists in a key management discipline, a buy-in candidate can prove to be a useful addition to a management team. The key managers are the chief executive and the finance director. Because of the level of gearing tight financial control is critical to the success of a MBO, and the finance director is a key position.

2–05 In larger transactions, a balanced management team is expected and is the norm. When it comes to smaller transactions, gaps can exist in the coverage of certain management functions where a dedicated role cannot be justified due to the size of the company. Private equity firms understand the need to be flexible when it comes to dealing with smaller investments. However, each key management function needs to be addressed and as the investee company develops, so must the management capability and infrastructure.

2–06 In smaller companies, an alternative to recruiting a full-time member of management to cover a particular function is to appoint a non-executive director with experience in the relevant area. Given that venture funds tend to appoint non-executives, this can sometimes prove to be a useful bridge for the smaller company which cannot justify the full-time resource. A non-executive is no substitute for a full-time member of the team, particularly in the area of the finance function. There is a clear limit as to what an individual can do within a time constraint of one to two days each month.

Professional and balanced management teams are a pre-requisite for the venture capitalist.

Another pre-requisite for a private equity firm, is that the management team must have already invested, or be prepared to personally invest in the company.

2.2.2 Past track record

Arguably the best barometer to predicting future success lies in reviewing the past performance and track record of a business. Past performance is invariably a further indicator of the qualities of the incumbent management team.   2–07

Often the MBO gives management an opportunity to have freedom of thought and action and be owner-managers for the first time. This tends to stimulate motivation to improve on past performance outside the cloak of the parent company. Therefore the MBO can transform an underperforming company's fortunes by having a more committed management paying closer attention to some of the following areas:

- rationalisation of the overhead, both central and divisional, which may lead to a realisation of additional profits and improved performance;
- improvements in product innovation and approach to marketing;
- investment in new capital equipment which was previously denied by the parent company.

The above examples are but a few of the many improvements that can take place, post MBO. To convince a private equity firm of the improvements, the management team will also need to explain why the improvements were not implemented in the past.   2–08

In reviewing ways to improve past performance the venture capitalists will be influenced greatly by the following factors:

Maturity and prospects of the industry   Clearly a company forecasting to trade in line with the industry overall is prima facie more credible than a company anticipating growth ahead of the market.

Changing nature of the technology   An industry which has ever-changing technology is likely to require considerable future investment in research and development, continuing capital expenditure commitments and uncertain prospects.

Production and plant facilities   A business which has underperformed because of poor operational infrastructure has difficulty in raising private equity because of the cost of investment required and the risks that the new investment is not properly managed.   2–09

Competitive marketplace with low barriers to entry   A company which operates in a saturated marketplace, where price-cutting and severe competition are the norm, will cause concern. In the absence of some competitive advantage, the future prospects for the business are unlikely to differ from past performance.

In reviewing rescue or turnaround situations, the venture fund is unlikely to be convinced by a "things will be better tomorrow" scenario. The past has to be explained and quantified and venture capital firms will only consider investing where there have been strong mitigating circumstances.

2–10 Start-ups and early stage investment propositions make up to one-third of the total number of investments made each year, yet account for only five per cent of the total by value. Early stage investments are difficult for private equity firms to invest in since the all important track record cannot be substantiated. In the case of a start-up, often the business plan is the only evidence which a venture fund has available to judge the feasibility of a proposal. The past track record and direct industry experience of management is important in forming a view. The management walkout scenario is most likely to find favour with venture funds, where a management team resign from their former employer and recommence trading as a start-up entity. Providing there are no legal implications surrounding a walkout, this can be a safer way to undertake a start-up venture. The risks being lower: the management team, the product or service and the market have not changed and the forecasts are not dependent on change. Start-ups which require significant capital expenditure or new products or markets are more risky and find fund raising more difficult.

2.2.3 Future prospects

2–11 Whilst the past prospects are the barometer, a private equity firm will only benefit as a shareholder from future performance. To attract private equity investment, a company should show progressive growth to enable good investment returns to be generated from dividends and principally on the ultimate realisation of a capital gain. Since the valuation of a company is normally derived from its earnings stream, rising profits are therefore a prerequisite to a capital gain. Similarly from an investee company's perspective, unless significant progress can be made from utilising venture capital, there is little justification in taking the private equity and giving up an equity shareholding.

As a simple rule of thumb, private equity firms seek to make investments that at least will double in value over three years, which, with all other things being equal, requires a doubling of profits equating to a compound annual growth rate in profits of 25 per cent. When debt is added to the financial structure this will give a private equity return of three times their original investment.

Meeting the investment criterion

This simple rule of thumb is illustrated below. 2–12

Pre-tax profits growth profile

	Growth rate	Yr 0 £000	Yr 1 £000	Yr 2 £000	Yr 3 £000	*Suitable for venture capital?*
Company A	5%	500	525	551	579	No
Company B	25%	500	625	781	976	Yes
Company C	50%	500	750	1125	1687	Yes, if believable

In the case of Company A, profit growth and thus capital value growth is unimpressive and is unlikely to attract venture capital support. Company B shows good profit progression and providing a realistic entry price was paid for the initial investment, a good profit would be achieved on an earnings based valuation. Company C would represent an exceptional opportunity for investment but such rapid growth would need to be capable of reasonable substantiation. Impressive growth as projected by Company C is not necessary to achieve the required venture capital rate of return and setting such high compound growth can lead to subsequent lack of credibility problems when the planned profits targets are not achieved.

In reviewing future prospects, venture capitalists are strongly influenced by factors that are verifiable. Such factors at the micro level include: 2–13

- forward order book;
- number of customers and their prospects;
- stability of the customer base;
- patents and trade licence agreements which protect earnings;
- ongoing capital expenditure requirements;
- product range, product lives and longevity of the product range;
- reliance on suppliers and their prospects;
- number of competitors and their prospects.

At the macro level, venture capitalists will be interested in three key areas: the industry prospects, technology changes and barriers to entry.

Industry prospects

A company operating in an industry which is in decline or in a stagnant phase will warrant closer scrutiny to demonstrate profit growth and upside potential. Clearly in those industry sectors, profit growth which is dependent on cost reductions rather than revenue increases is likely to find stronger venture capital interest. 2–14

Arguably there are no such things as good and bad sectors when it comes to venture capital, instead there are good and bad investment opportunities within each industrial sector. However, a fund manager prefers to back growing companies in growing market sectors, where rapid upside can be achieved, perhaps regardless of management capabilities.

Technology changes

2–15 High-technology companies in areas such as information technology and biotechnology represent high return opportunities for venture capitalists. For such emerging technologies the related risk factor is equally high, particularly in the areas of start-ups and early stage investments.

Invariably the time, effort and cost of developing a product then launching onto the marketplace takes longer than budgeted for. Many venture capitalists treat this area as a cash black hole and avoid such companies. By contrast, specialist high-tech funds concentrate on those opportunities. A factor for those venture funds to consider is the longevity of the product; particularly where an industry is prone to frequent change.

Competitive barriers to entry

2–16 Private equity funds are more interested in companies which have barriers to entry as the barriers reinforce the predictability of future earnings. The following are barriers that prevent new competitors from entering the market:

High capital entry costs An industry which requires significant plant and machinery to enter the market acts as a defence mechanism.

Patent/copyright/government approvals/product brands All of these can act as a barrier to entry given the time and cost of their creation.

2–17 *Niche companies and specialisms* Companies which have a known specialisation or specifically operate in a smaller subset of a marketplace can demonstrate an element of competitive advantage.

The private equity fund manager considers all micro and macro variables in determining whether future profit prospects are achievable.

2.2.4 Exit prospects

2–18 Given that most private equity firms raise their funds through ten-year limited life partnerships, the schedule for a typical venture capital investment is to exit in

Meeting the investment criterion

around three to seven years. The captive private equity firms can claim to be longer term, however, all private equity firms are driven by the need to generate capital gain so as to maximise the investment returns. Because of this, investee companies wishing to attract venture capital must have in mind an exit within this timeframe, investment offers from venture capitalists often contain incentives and/or penalties to encourage exit. For example, increasing dividends or reducing equity shareholding mechanisms can be used to force the exit.

The focus on exit prospects is simply financial: exits produce investment returns, proving the performance of the private equity fund managers. Good fund performance will make fresh fund raising easier and the financial rewards to the managers greater.

In assessing the exit prospects the venture capitalist considers the following routes:

Trade sale

The majority of venture capital investments are exited by way of trade sale to a third-party company. Unlike flotation, a trade sale can be quick and a relatively certain route providing the company has demonstrated a good track record, post private equity investment. **2–19**

Share buy-back

While the option can exist for an investee company to buy back their venture partner's shares, there are two main practical difficulties which have restricted these exits: unwillingness by the private equity firms to participate in these arrangements, driven by suspicion and the problem of funding. **2–20**

Private equity suspicion In these arrangements, effectively the other shareholders become buyers and their economic interests are best served by paying as low a price as possible. Consequently, private equity firms are anxious to avoid being misled as to the value of their shares.

There is always the worry for a venture partner that a "back-to-back" deal has been negotiated by management with another prospective purchaser. **2–21**

Fundability issue The issue of funding the consideration has to be overcome, which is likely to involve at least raising additional debt and may also require additional equity funding from a replacement equity provider, venture capital or otherwise.

Secondary purchase

2–22 The sale of an equity shareholding to another private equity firm, a "secondary purchase" is becoming increasingly more common. The new venture capital partner route can work particularly well where the old venture partner is forcing an exit to meet their own investment criteria preferences while the management believe that further growth potential exists giving rise to a logical exit a few years further on. Secondary purchases can be attractive to investee companies where the relationship with the old partner has broken down irretrievably or that the private equity fund does not have sufficient financial "firepower" to commit to further rounds of investment in the development of the investee company.

Flotation of the company

2–23 Until the emergence of the Alternative Investment Market ("AIM"), the prospect of a full flotation was limited to all but a few investee companies. The large, fast growth and high profile company can lend itself to a flotation and many private equity investments have subsequently floated on the stock market.

Flotation represents a logical exit point for the venture capital provider, giving the flexibility of a complete exit or of a gradual exit of publicly quoted stock over a period of time. Flotation is the most unlikely exit scenario for a private equity backed investment.

2.3 Matching the fund to the proposition

2–24 The British Private Equity and Venture Capital Association ("BVCA"), is the industry body for the private equity and venture capital industry in the UK. The BVCA membership comprises over 230 private equity firms with over £30 billion of funds under management.

The following are six main criteria to consider when matching a proposition to one from a population of over 200 funds.

2.3.1 Size of investment

2–25 All the private equity funds can be differentiated by the size of their preferred investments. However, equally, all firms tend to be flexible in considering opportunities, focusing on the size of the potential financial gain as well as the initial investment.

Matching the fund to the proposition

There are UK private equity firms with funds of over £1 billion; for those funds, average equity investments will need to exceed £50 million. 　2–26

There is also a large number of mid-market firms seeking average equity investments of £10 million to £20 million. Even the smaller to mid-market corporate funds will have a target minimum equity investment level of £2 million and an average of £5 million.

Funding requirements below £2 million are increasingly becoming the domain of government supported regional funds, business angels or private investors. At present, a real equity gap exists in terms of the provision of "professional" private equity in the sub £2 million market.

For practical purposes, the private equity firms provide funds in three distinct segments of the market, namely: 　2–27

(1) large buy-out funds, investing in excess of £30 million of equity;

(2) mid-market firms, investing £10 to £20 million of equity;

(3) smaller cap investing £2 to £10 million.

As a rule of thumb, try to match the fund raising with a fund of 15 to 25 times the size of the fund raising.

Transactions outside the ranges can also be syndicated by firms allowing them to lead on larger transactions. Syndication is where more than one private equity firm will be investing in the deal, usually with one private equity firm acting as lead investor and the other investors following.

Business angels are probably the largest source of smaller amounts of private equity.

2.3.2 Stage of investment

Most of the private equity firms do not invest significantly in early stages, start-ups and turn-around investments because the historic investment returns are the lowest by category for the venture capital industry. Because of this adverse past experience, the higher-risk-type investments tend to find fewer venture capital suitors. Invariably early stage and start-up companies also relate to smaller investment propositions, and as such tend to be avoided by the primary funds. 　2–28

Furthermore, the funds have been raised from institutional investors to invest in buy-out opportunities and specifically not to invest in early stage opportunities.

2.3.3 Industry preferences

2–29 Whilst there are no such things as good and bad sectors, most of the private equity firms will have favourite "pet" sectors at any point dependent on their personal experiences, the demands of their investors and market perceptions.

Generally, most venture funds work to achieve a balanced portfolio across differing sectors. This approach tends to insulate funds from a sporadic downturn in a particular sector and fits in with the primary objective of a portfolio, which is to balance risk. Despite the preference for balance private equity funds will make more than one investment in any successful sector.

2–30 The last point has important connotations for would be investees in that it is important to check whether a venture fund has an existing concentration of investments in the potential investee company's sector.

Each fund tends to have sectors of particular interest and individual fund preferences are disclosed on websites. Many of the generalist venture funds avoid property deals, financial services and gambling, the latter often being a requirement of US institutional investors. Many private equity firms will also avoid "people based" business. The risk of "people businesses" being twofold: firstly, the assets literally do walk out the door every day and secondly there are often no barriers to entry for new competitors.

2–31 Most of the generalist funds avoid high-tech propositions which relate to such areas as biotechnology and information technology. The expertise required to understand such propositions is not suited to the generalist fund manager and usually rests in the domain of high-tech specialist funds. Indeed many of the high-tech propositions come under the category of early stage investments and much of the skill in making money in this area lies in exploiting new ideas and innovations, many of which are not at a stage of production, and are little more than a concept. The specialist high-tech funds are the exception to the principal that venture capitalists avoid early stage and start-up investments.

Whilst avoiding early stage investments, it is also true that all funds are attracted to investments in fast-growing sectors—because fast profit growth is the key driver to faster capital growth and capital value growth is the aim for private equity investors.

2.3.4 Geographical preferences

2–32 Several private equity firms have offices across the UK, with some cities better served than others. Most of the private equity firms are based in London but look to invest across the UK.

Most of the regions in the UK will also have their own region specific funds, which focus resource and effort on seeking local investment opportunities, again this focus being driven by investors.

2.3.5 Degree of involvement

In choosing a private equity partner, it is not only important to know whether their house style is "hands-on" or "hands-off" but also how "hands-on" the "hands-off" style is. Almost all UK private equity firms subscribe to the hands-off approach which is to let management teams operate the company with minimum involvement by the venture partner in the day-to-day running of the business. A "hands-on" approach tends to involve a fund taking a more executive director orientated approach, installing their own executive management, or in the smaller secondary funds having a direct involvement. **2–33**

Fortunately, for investee companies, the majority of the private equity funds back the judgment of management teams to run a company. The private equity fund manager's job is to source, execute and realise investments and not to run businesses, and they do not have the resources to be directly involved. For this reason, all private equity funds appoint non-executive directors to represent their interests at company board meetings. The typical profile of a non-executive is an individual who has experienced a successful career to date at senior management level and who now has sufficient spare time to add value to a company, typically one to two working days per month. The non-executive appointment is designed to give a management team an external and independent perspective using a breadth of experience gained over many years in industry and commerce. The non-executive also represents the interests of the venture capital fund in decision making but can be expected to act in the best interests of all the shareholders.

As part of the normal investment monitoring process, the private equity fund will usually appoint one of their executives as a non-executive or as an observer to the company. The executive will usually visit the company a few times each year to remain close to the investment. In addition to occasional visits, most private equity firms require regular management accounts, cash flow forecasts and other financial information. This information is normally produced in agreed formats and to set timetables. **2–34**

When an investment is going well for management and investors alike, an investee company will have minimal involvement from the venture capitalists. But if an investee company starts to miss budgeted performance, then the variations in "hands-off" will become more apparent. Most private equity firms will act to protect their investment; the variation comes in the timing of action and the actions that would be taken. Usually if an investee company falls into arrears on capital or dividend repayments, the articles of association will allow the venture capitalist to take a more active involvement. This is often effected by changes in voting control triggered by the arrears. This is often a concern for management, however, most private equity firms will rely on the judgment of the management team they originally backed, and when the company experiences difficulties venture capitalists are, by and large, very supportive.

2–35 All private equity firms will restrict the management team in such areas as directors' remuneration and benefits, sizeable capital expenditure decisions, and ability to transfer shares or elements of the business outside the investee company or its related subsidiaries. For the management team which is prepared to abide by the spirit of the investment agreement, such measures should not prove to be unnecessarily restrictive and would have been discussed and agreed in detail prior to completion.

2.3.6 Length of investment

2–36 To emphasise 2.2.4 (exit prospects), most private equity firms are motivated to achieve a capital gain from their investments within three to seven years. This effectively means that an investee company, at some stage over the life of an investment, will have to contemplate a disposal of the company or provide an alternative means for the venture capitalist to realise a capital gain. Therefore management shareholders who wish to remain or grow family dynasties are unsuited to venture capital.

In the management buy-out, the management team are usually equally enthusiastic to achieve an exit in order to create personal financial independence. Family-owned businesses with years of tradition and family heritage will have to convince a private equity firm that they can embrace an exit requirement if they wish to raise venture capital.

2.4 The fund raising process

2.4.1 Role of the financial advisor

2–37 The role of the financial advisor is to advise on the types of funds, typically debt and equity, the mix of those fund types and to effect introductions to the best providers of the required funds.

The success of any fund raising is dependent on the quality of the investment opportunity, and is also dependent on the quality of the guidance and advice given by the corporate finance advisor.

The fund raising process

2–38 The advisor will be active in packaging, presenting and representing the client in the fund raising marketplace from inception of a transaction to its ultimate completion. The process will involve advice on valuation, the requirements of the various investors, negotiation with the investors and advice on the overall capital structure. In selecting an advisor the client should focus on the advisor's credentials.

The best corporate finance advice comes from those organisations with an experienced "hands-on" approach. The emphasis on experience is to match funds with opportunities and creating the right blend of funds. Inexperience will lead to fruitless activity and at worst, to failure. A "hands-on" approach is necessary to ensure that information and financial forecasts are tested before exposure to the rigours of due diligence. The role of the financial advisor should also include client representation and support at all meetings and to pro-actively co-ordinate and negotiate with all parties at all stages up to completion.

2.4.2 The role of other advisors

2–39 In concluding a private equity transaction the investee company is also likely to engage a tax advisor and a solicitor. Their roles are outlined below:

The tax advisor

2–40 The tax advisor will help to ensure that all possible tax reliefs are maximised with attention likely to focus on: obtaining tax relief on interest paid, personal capital gains tax planning and advice on the tax relief of the costs incurred in connection with raising private equity.

The solicitor's role

2–41 The solicitor will advise on the warranties and indemnities sought by the private equity investor, the service contracts for managers and the articles of association required by the private equity firm.

Other advisors

2–42 In addition to the advisors appointed by the investee, the private equity firm will also be appointing professional advisors to conduct financial, legal, management and commercial due diligence, and legal and financial advisors to prepare the legal documents required to document and protect their investment. Other parties, such as the bankers will also want their own lawyers to be involved.

2.4.3 The business plan

2–43 The business plan is the first point of contact with the business for the private equity firm. First impressions are crucial. It is recognised that many good investment opportunities may be passed over principally due to quality and content of the original proposal document sent.

It is important to achieve a "clarity" and "brevity" which invariably is contained in "sharp and punchy" documents. The 200 pages of narrative, graphs and pictures is unlikely to find a willing reader prepared to write off half a day for a first read. Similarly, a marketing-type plan which contains plenty of narrative yet contains one page on the financials and the funding requirement, will find little favour.

2–44 The plan must be written in a concise and understandable manner. Because of this, it is sensible to have any document "proof read" and edited by a financial advisor. The advisor should be experienced in preparing documents to the required standard.

The purpose of the plan is to document the business and outline clearly and persuasively the investment opportunity being offered. A business plan should be prepared to a high standard and be verifiable.

Steps to producing a business plan: A guide

2–45 *Step 1: Prepare an evidence file*   Produce an evidence file covering detailed information on the following areas, where appropriate:

- concept and business explained;
- market opportunity and growth prospects;
- explanation of past track record, financial and otherwise;
- product range(s);
- customer profile;
- competitor analysis and barriers to entry;
- sales and marketing strategy;
- sales process from start to end;
- production process from start to end;
- capital expenditure requirements;

The fund raising process

- market data and research information;
- management team CVs;
- organisation chart;
- strengths, weaknesses, opportunities and threats (SWOT);
- statutory accounts for the past five years;
- copy of the memorandum and articles of association;
- copy of any relevant lender facility letters.

Step 2: Prepare a financial forecast assumptions file Produce a financial forecasts assumptions file providing base data to support the assumptions used to construct a detailed financial model. The following major areas, where appropriate, will need to be covered: **2–46**

- sales assumptions by product volumes and unit selling price; in a manufacturing company it is also necessary to relate sales to production capacity and plant utilisation levels;
- the impact of seasonality on the business: on sales and working capital, the impact of holidays and shutdown periods and the number of working days in a month;
- relate cost of sales components (e.g. direct materials) to sales;
- analyse sales by customer and forecast prospects for three years;
- work out required payroll numbers and specific salaries/pay rates to accommodate planned sales;
- quantify and specify overheads by caption, whether direct or indirect;
- review capital expenditure requirements over the next three years;
- analyse stock and work-in-progress levels and relate to sales activity;
- analyse debtor and creditor days, historically by month;
- quantify all lender and hire purchase repayment profiles.

Using the preliminary work carried out in steps one and two, a clear understanding of the business will have been achieved. The next steps are to produce both the financial model and the written document.

Step 3: Detailed financial model A three-year financial model is required which is capable of producing monthly profit and loss accounts, monthly cash flow statements and monthly balance sheets. The monthly financial statements should be supported by integrated workings covering each of the major areas highlighted **2–47** in Step 2. The monthly cash flows will pinpoint peak funding requirements, which will then have to be met by an appropriate funding structure. In reviewing the corresponding monthly balance sheets and the interest cover levels as shown in the monthly profit and loss accounts, the debt capacity level of a company can be calculated, leaving any funding shortfall to be fulfilled by private equity, and/or deferred vendor consideration.

2–48 *Step 4: Prepare the business plan* The business plan should be a succinct and stand-alone document, presenting a cohesive investment case, consistent with the financial model. The business plan should incorporate a summary of the annualised financial forecasts and contain a dedicated section on the funding requirement. The document needs to "stand alone" providing readers with sufficient information to evaluate the opportunity. It is best to avoid the use of superlatives and statements which are not capable of being substantiated and should chart a cohesive story without unnecessary duplication. At most, excluding the financial section, it should consist of 20 to 30 pages. The detailed financial model should be supplied separately. Arguably, if it takes more than 30 pages to convey a concept it may indicate that management are incapable of demonstrating a convincing and succinct argument. Irrespective of this argument, the private equity manager is unlikely to invest the time in assessing a larger business plan.

Example: A suggested contents index

2–49 A business plan should typically contain the following types of section.

Executive summary of proposition

The executive summary should provide an introduction to the opportunity, an outline of the business and the funding requirement.

The summary should also give an indication of future and past profitability and make a comment on the experience of the management team. The summary should be a stand-alone section briefly outlining the complete story.

Nature of business

The business plan should clearly describe the company's products or services in a non-technical fashion and then describe the industry and the position of the business in that industry. This section should include an assessment of the market and the competition, dependency on suppliers or customers, barriers to entry, the pace of change, the prospects for the industry and the business.

The fund raising process

Business detail

This section should provide further depth on the business, concerning the detail that gives a complete picture of the business. It should cover: **2–50**

- products and customers;
- market position and competition;
- management and employees;
- premises and facilities;
- fixed assets, production processes and required capital expenditure;
- intellectual property, trademarks, goodwill and other intangible assets;
- contingent liabilities;
- SWOT analysis.

The business detail section is one that can clearly be supported by pictures and graphs. The key with graphics is to illustrate the text, too many graphics will disrupt the flow of the text.

In the SWOT analysis it is important to be objective on the weakness and threats since a business proposition which is all strengths and opportunities would imply a lack of realism or understanding of the marketplace. **2–51**

Management team

Given that management is a critical element of any investment assessment, a summary paragraph or two on each senior member of the management team should be included. A factual account of experience and past career is required with the full curriculum vitae kept to the appendices. **2–52**

Financial summary

Based on the past audited accounts and the detailed financial model, the business plan should give a summary of the profit and loss accounts and the balance sheets for the past three years and the future three years. **2–53**

In addition a summary cash flow statement summarising the inflow and outflow of funds is also required. The cash flow statements should clearly show the movements in working capital and historic levels of depreciation and capital expenditure.

It is important that all three statements: profit and loss account, balance sheet and cash flow statement should reconcile with one another. If it is important to adjust the past results to exclude exceptional non-recurring items, the adjustments should be clearly explained and documented in supporting schedules.

2–54 The commentary should describe the historic trading performance and the key assumptions used to prepare the financial model. Sensitivity analysis showing the effect of varying important assumptions should be shown in a stand-alone appendix.

Finance required and purpose

The business plan should clearly articulate the finance being requested and the financial model should be capable of pinpointing funding peaks and troughs.

There is no right or wrong way to write a business plan. Whilst the plan is written by management it is being read by fund providers, and their needs are the ones to be satisfied.

2.4.4 Fund raising in the marketplace

Phase 1: Preparatory stage

2–55 The preparatory phase requires the management team to finalise and know their business plan, to prepare for subsequent meetings with funders and to select the funders.

Know the business plan It is important for management to know the plan inside out. Management must take ownership of the document, even when it feels like the corporate finance advisor has written the plan on behalf of the management team. The management team must know the key assumptions which make up the finance model and the basic profile of the key numbers over the forecast period.

2–56 It is damaging to fund raising if members of management make statements which do not tie into the plan. The funder is left with the dilemma of clarifying whether the statement or the plan is correct, or whether both are wrong.

Prepare for the meetings It is important that a management team interacts effectively with each other, with each team member assuming responsibility for their own particular discipline.

2–57 It is useful to undergo a full dress rehearsal of a meeting with a private equity firm. These sessions should enable the management team to perfect their presentation and also provide useful experience of the question and answer sessions used by private equity managers.

In dealing with questions, it is important not to become defensive or give an answer which is not capable of being substantiated and answers are best short, sharp and factual. Shorter responses allow more ground to be covered in the meeting and also keep the interviewer on their toes. Still on the subject of interview technique, expect most of the questions to be asked as open questions requiring a detailed response rather than a simple yes or no type answer. Venture capitalists are also well schooled in the use of silences.

Select the funders   The different characteristics and preferences of the various private equity firms are explained in 2.3. This role of the corporate finance advisors is to guide the management team on the selection of funds to be approached. **2–58**

While many of the private equity firms use relatively similar investment instruments, terms and conditions can and do vary considerably.

Phase 2: The initial market phase

The fund or funds to be approached will normally be contacted initially by the corporate finance advisor. The aim of this contact will be to prime the private equity firm as to the nature and quality of the opportunity. The business plan is normally then forwarded in advance of a meeting. In this initial period it is unlikely that the private equity firm will invest significant time to the proposition other than to consider the plan submitted. **2–59**

The first meeting   At this stage the private equity manager will be keen to expand on the content of the plan and a series of open questions will be asked to test their own and management's understanding of the business and the key issues. In particular, management will be closely scrutinised at the meeting since the success of a proposition ultimately depends on the management team, and therefore on their preparation for the meeting.

The approach of each private equity firm is down to the individual fund managers concerned. However, all the fund managers regard personal chemistry as very important since a great deal of time is spent with a management team in the run up to completion and beyond. A good meeting is often signalled when a fund manager switches from buyer to seller. This is when the fund manager starts to talk in detail about their fund and their firm and why they are best suited for the investment opportunity. **2–60**

It is probable that a fund manager will finish a positive meeting by proposing to sponsor the proposition to the other fund managers of the private equity firm with a view to canvassing support to proceed to the next stage.

2–61 *The internal case review* Each week most private equity firms hold internal meetings to talk about their investment opportunities. The purpose of these meetings is for the various managers to determine how these various opportunities should be pursued or abandoned.

At these meetings all senior managers of the fund are likely to be present. At the end of this case review process, the decision is taken to continue on an agreed basis or to reject the proposition. The internal case review meeting does not normally mean board approval, but instead represents informal support to move the proposition towards formal board approval stage, in due course.

Phase 3: Getting to conditional offer

2–62 Assuming the proposition is of interest, the fund manager will be keen to become fully familiar with the business and its management prior to issuing an outline offer letter. This period of due diligence may include taking references on the management team. Referees will be a combination of direct business acquaintances and past employers. Deals do fail to attract funding because of poor references, as management credibility is of paramount importance. Before completion all the private equity firms will take out full references on the management team, possibility utilising 360° feedback and psychometric testing and analysis often employing management due diligence experts.

Other due diligence work undertaken by the fund prior to completion will include the taking of customer references and possibly commissioning a market report to review the industry sector and the issues which it currently faces. At this stage it is likely that the assumptions contained in the financial model will be scrutinised in some detail, prior to full due diligence being undertaken by investigating accountants.

2–63 This phase is characterised by a great deal of information flow from the management to the private equity fund manager. Essentially it is a due diligence exercise conducted without external cost to the private equity firm. A deal is far from secure at this stage and the only commitment made by the fund is to devote time to further consider the proposition.

At the end of this phase, the venture capitalist will issue a conditional offer letter summarising the terms for any proposed investment, this will be subject to their own further investigations and the management's business plan standing up to third-party due diligence.

2–64 The offer letter will contain an intended funding scheme, the funding instruments proposed and the required dividend or interest yields and equity rights.

The fund raising process

The approach to offer letters varies between private equity firms. In terms of content and internal approvals required, however, they are usually consistent in seeking exclusivity.

Phase 4: Getting to completion

This fourth phase involves working exclusively with a preferred private equity fund, to eliminate their pre-conditions, completing their due diligence and ultimately concluding with their investment. **2–65**

The pre-conditions are likely to include satisfactory management referencing, keyman insurance and market reports.

There will be a condition precedent that all other required sources of finance are in place by completion. In the case of a management buy-out, it is important for management to source all personal funds required for investment at completion. Some of the conditions precedent will relate specifically to the proposition and may for example cover the need to have all registered approvals and patents prior to completion. The conditions precedent are designed to highlight key areas which are required to be satisfied prior to completion.

The due diligence will include legal due diligence to confirm that the business has all the required assets and rights to trade as planned and to confirm that all potential and contingent liabilities have been disclosed and assessed. **2–66**

Similarly, the venture capitalist will require an investigating accountant to review and comment on the historic financial statements of the company and the assumptions used to prepare the financial model.

The review of the financial forecasts is designed to test the reasonableness of the assumptions applied and, where appropriate, compare them to past performance. Validating the integrity of the financial model increases confidence in the funding requirement intimated and the funding instruments applied to meet that peak requirement.

As part of this process, the investigating accountants will carry out a sensitivity analysis on the key variables to determine the effect on funding requirements and the profit forecast of key changes. The sensitivity analysis is designed to identify the pivotal points of change which make the business proposition untenable. **2–67**

In addition, the investigating accountant will focus on other risk areas, as directed by the venture capitalists. These risk areas might include:

- adequacy of stock valuation methods used and the accounting treatment applied to work-in-progress;

- an assessment of historic and future working capital requirements;
- comment on the trends in sales and costs;
- the accounting policies adopted by the company.

The investigating accountant is also likely to be instructed to assess the adequacy of financial systems and controls which the company has in place.

2.5 Choosing an investment offer

2–68 Often, management teams will have to choose between competing offers from private equity firms. The decision usually rests on the economic arguments, but it is important to consider other issues such as deliverability, personal chemistry and access to further funds.

Investment offer terms and conditions   The ordinary equity percentage required by the venture capital fund is usually the most important consideration, since this element is likely to be the most material element of the cost of the private equity. In MBO situations, the subject of equity can become complex with the introduction of performance ratchets, which require a formula to be applied in calculating the final management equity stake.

2–69 The other terms will deal with dividend or interest rates, the repayment profile of the preference shares and/or any loan instruments and the extent to which an exit is encouraged by penalties, in the form of rising dividends, or rewards in the form of increasing management equity stake. The three constituent components of equity percentage, dividend yield and repayment profile, can be assessed with a discounted cash flow model to provide a uniform basis for comparing different offer letters.

Deliverability   It is important to ensure that the private equity firm can complete the deal on the terms intimated and within the required time.

2–70 To avoid any doubt, it is best for management to agree with the venture capitalist a detailed schedule of events from offer letter stage through to completion.

Personal chemistry   The management team should have some personal chemistry with their intended equity partner. A good working relationship between management and the fund provides a stable platform on which to develop the company.

A potential investee company should not be afraid to ask for references on the fund concerned, which usually entails speaking directly to other investee companies of that fund.

In reality, most investee company relationships are good with their venture partner, particularly where an investment is performing well. It is when a company is doing badly that the worst effects of a bad relationship can be most felt which can, in extreme situations, have direct consequences for members of the management team. 2–71

Access to further funds When deciding on an investment partner, it may also be important to assess both their willingness and ability to inject second round funding. When dealing with a smaller fund, it may be difficult for that fund to commit significant additional investment, particularly in a rescue situation.

2.6 Key points

2.6.1 Meeting the investment criterion

- Private equity firms prefer to back a balanced and experienced management team. 2–72
- In assessing investment propositions, fund managers are influenced by the past track record of a business, as a guide to future profitability.
- The private equity firm's assessment of the business future prospects will determine their investment terms.
- The exit timeframe for a typical venture capital investment is around three to seven years maximum, and most pre-investment analysis focuses on the year three prospects.

2.6.2 Matching the fund to the proposition

- Given the historic investment results and the costs associated with making smaller investments, private equity deal sizes continue to rise with the majority of equity investments being at least £2 million. 2–73
- Most private equity firms will not invest in early stage opportunities. Historically, the investment returns have been higher in larger management buy-outs and most private equity firms focus on these opportunities.
- Most of the generalist private equity firms aim for a balanced portfolio across sectors, but have strong preferences for high growth sectors.
- The investment requirements of the private equity funds are driven by their fund providers the majority of which are US based investors.
- The investment management approach of most private equity firms is "hands-off", leaving the day-to-day control of the investee company with the management team.

- Long established and family owned companies may find venture capital to be a "bridge too far", given the need for a fund to achieve a medium term exit.

2.6.3 The fund raising process

2–74
- The role of the financial advisor is to advise on the types of funds, the mix of funds and the best providers of those funds for the investment opportunity.
- There is no "right" business plan—the key is to produce a document that encourages the reader to invest, after carefully balancing all the risks and opportunities.

Chapter 3

Corporate Valuation and Deal Structuring

James Dow, Dow Schofield Watts LLP

3.1 Introduction

The process of deal structuring is very logical, despite the complex nature of the various financial instruments and their interactive relationships with each other. The purpose of this chapter is to identify a framework for deal structuring which can be applied to private equity investment opportunities. **3–01**

3.2 Corporate valuation

Regardless of whether buy-out or development funding is sought, private equity firms are seeking to meet or exceed their required rates of investment return. One of the most critical influences on their return is the entry price valuation of the investee company—put simply they don't want to overpay on investments. This section briefly discusses the valuation techniques most commonly used by them. **3–02**

There are basically two valuation methods used by private equity firms:

(1) discounted cash flow; and
(2) earnings based valuations.

The examples shown will be based on the following Newco base data. **3–03**

Table 1: Newco base data

Years	0	1	2	3	Thereafter
	£m	£m	£m	£m	£m
EBITDA	3.6	4.2	5.3	5.8	6.0
Depreciation	(1.5)	(1.6)	(1.7)	(1.8)	(1.8)
EBIT	2.0	2.6	3.6	4.0	4.2
Tax @ 30%	(0.6)	(0.8)	(1.1)	(1.2)	(1.3)
Earnings	1.5	1.8	2.5	2.8	2.9
Capital expenditure	1.2	1.1	1.2	1.4	1.8
Working capital	(0.5)	(0.3)	(0.4)	(0.4)	(0.4)
Steady state growth					3%

3.2.1 Discounted cash flow ("DCF")

3–04 The discounted cash flow model explicitly or implicitly underpins all private equity firm analysis of value.

This method values a company as the present value of its expected cash flows, discounted back at a rate that reflects both the riskiness of the project and the financing mix used to finance it.

The key components of value are therefore:

- the expected future cash flows;
- the discount rate applied to those future cash flows.

The expected future cash flows

3–05 The forecast figures used in a DCF valuation should be the most likely figures. Whilst the business plan may portray one scenario, this scenario of the future may not be used by the private equity firm, their DCF analysis will be based on their assessment of the future.

Reliable DCF valuation needs a long explicit forecast period followed by a steady state. This steady state has a continuing value, often referred to as the terminal or residual value. Private equity investments are often made in dynamic growing companies which means obtaining this level of reliable information is often not possible. Consequently, the DCF analysis is often restricted to a three to five year time horizon, mirroring the private equity firm's investment horizon.

Corporate valuation

Example 1: Typical DCF valuation

Years	0	1	2	3	Steady State
	£m	£m	£m	£m	£m
Cash flows					
Earnings	1.5	1.8	2.5	2.9	2.9
Depreciation	1.5	1.6	1.7	1.8	1.8
Capital expenditure	(1.2)	(1.1)	(1.2)	(1.4)	(1.8)
Working capital	(0.5)	(0.3)	(0.4)	(0.4)	(0.4)
Free cash flow	1.3	2.0	2.6	2.9	2.5
WACC/discount factor	15%	0.869	0.756	0.658	5.481
Present value		1.7	2.0	1.9	
Terminal value					13.7
Cumulative NPV		1.7	3.7	5.6	19.3
Cumulative %		9	19	29	100

This example shows that a DCF valuation of £19.3 million for Newco, and 71 per cent of the DCF valuation of Newco is attributed to the terminal value of the cash flows beyond year three.

3–06

Because of its significance, the terminal value is often estimated, not through the use of DCF but by earnings based valuation methods. The important assumption then is what earnings multiple should be applied at the end of the explicit forecast period to calculate the terminal value. Private equity firms most commonly assume that the earnings multiple used in this terminal value calculation should be the same as the earnings multiple that exists at the time of their initial investment. Therefore in this example, the terminal value of £13.7 million is more likely to have been determined by a private equity firm, as an EBIT multiple of five to six applied to year four earnings, discounted back at 15 per cent per annum.

The discount rate

For private equity investments, the cost of capital used is the weighted average cost of capital ("WACC").

3–07

The WACC comprises a weighted average of the costs of all sources of capital. An example WACC is given in Example 2.

Example 2: WACC calculation

	Cost	£m	% Funding	Post tax	%WACC
Debt	6%	10.0	56	4.2%	2.35
Equity	30%	8.0	44	30.0%	13.20
Total funds		**18.0**	**100**		**15.55**

3.2.2 Earnings based valuation

3–08 Earnings based valuation techniques are often used by private equity firms for simplicity, on the basis that earnings should reflect cash flows.

The valuation is calculated as the future maintainable profits multiplied by an appropriate price earnings multiple.

Taking each component in turn:

Future Maintainable Profits ("FMPs")

3–09 Future maintainable profits are the likely recurring profits which an investor could expect to be achieved in the ongoing business. Although the valuation is a future based process, analysis of the past is used to provide a useful guide to the company's prospects.

In analysing past profits, adjustments are often required to determine the maintainable trends. Extracting historic maintainable profits involves analysing and adjusting for the following types of issue:

- extraordinary and non-recurring items such as redundancies, excessive write-offs, provisions or litigation;
- profits or losses arising on sales of assets;
- discontinued and acquired operations;
- non-trading income and expenditure, such as royalties;
- non-arm's length trading with related parties;
- private company items relating to personal expenses, pensions, rent, salaries and benefits;
- items not involving cash, such as accounting charges for goodwill or to amortise previously capitalised research and development costs;

Corporate valuation

- depreciation charges; and
- tax charges.

The above items all share the common characteristic of influencing an investor's perception of past maintainable profits. These items can be both positive and negative. **3–10**

The resultant future maintainable profits will also be adjusted to ensure any interest or other financing costs are excluded. The aim of these adjustments is to determine the valuation of the company independent of its financial structure.

It is possible that an uneven and perhaps declining historic profit will be adjusted to an improving maintainable profit trend.

Example 3: Future maintainable profits calculation

Years	–3	–2	–1	Present 0	Future 1
	£m	£m	£m	£m	£m
EBIT (unadjusted)	1.5	1.8	1.2	1.3	
Adjustments	(0.3)	(0.5)	0.3	0.7	
	1.2	1.3	1.5	2.0	2.6
Growth		8%	15%	33%	30%

Most investors will be heavily influenced by the most recent and the next financial period. The next, future, financial period is the most dominant in this process, as after all it is the performance immediately acquired by the private equity investor. In this example current adjusted EBIT of £2 million looks likely to recur in the future. Taking into account the next financial period, the investors may form a view that future maintainable profits will conservatively be £2.4 million. **3–11**

Profit multiples

Multiples are generally applied to current and prospective maintainable earnings to produce an enterprise valuation. **3–12**

The multiples most commonly used are:

- EBIT;
- EBITDA; and
- P/E.

These multiples are selectively used to eliminate variations due to depreciation rates, tax rates and financial structures.

3–13 The multiples used by investors come from two sources: analysis of the valuation of similar quoted companies and analysis of previous transactions.

The analysis of quoted companies will focus on companies operating in the same market or sector as the investee company and ideally be of a similar size. This analysis has the advantage that because the shares are traded there is a ready market price. There are two major disadvantages: firstly, the share trades represent transactions in relatively small proportions of the equity, and thus do not reflect a control premium, and secondly the quoted companies are usually significantly larger, and effectively therefore less risky investments.

The analysis of previous transactions will remove the disadvantages associated with quoted company analysis, however its main disadvantage is usually the absence of sufficient past transactions to provide comparisons.

3–14 EBIT and EBITDA multiples are more commonly used for enterprise valuation calculations, because they are free of distortions created by variations in financing structures and tax rates. P/E multiples can be misleading.

The impact of financing structures on different multiple calculations is best illustrated in an example.

Example 4: Similar quoted company—valuation multiples

	£m		£m
EBIT	16	Market value of shares	56
Interest @ 6%	(6)	Debt	100
EBT	10	Enterprise valuation	156
Taxation @ 30%	(3)		
	7		

Valuation ratios:

P/E	8	(based on share value)
EBIT Multiple	9.75	(based on enterprise value)

These ratios can be applied to the following private Companies A and B. The Companies are identical except that Company B has £40 million of debt.

Corporate valuation

	Company A	Company B
	£m	£m
EBIT	7.0	7.0
Interest @ 6%	—	(2.4)
EBT	7.0	4.6
Taxation @ 30%	(2.1)	(1.4)
Earnings	4.9	3.2
P/E valuation of equity	39.2	25.6
EBIT valuation	68.2	68.2
Less debt	—	(40.0)
Value of equity	68.2	28.2

This example shows: **3–15**

- an ungeared Company A would be undervalued using a P/E multiple comparison with a geared quoted company;
- A and B are making the same earnings, but company B's shares are worth only £13.6 million less than A's using a P/E multiple to value the shares despite having £40 million more debt;
- EBIT multiples remove the impact of differing financial structures in company valuations.

Enterprise valuation

Having derived a suitable profit multiple and future maintainable earnings, **3–16** simple multiplication of the two derives the valuation.

Example 5: Enterprise valuation calculation

Future Maintainable Profits	£2.4 million
EBIT multiple	9.75
Enterprise valuation	£23.4 million

3.2.3 Asset based valuation

Asset based valuations are unusual in private equity transactions, as private equity **3–17** returns are focused on cash returns to the private equity firm and not on the underlying net worth of the assets of the companies they have invested in.

3.2.4 Private equity returns

3–18 The investment philosophy of the private equity firms is to make significant cash profits from their investments. The rewards enjoyed by the private equity firm managers are directly linked to the returns they make on their investments. Investments are structured solely to provide cash profits. In assessing these cash profits the private equity firms are likely to use discounted cash flow analysis.

Example 6: Private equity returns

Private equity cash flows:

Years	0	1	2	3
	£m	£m	£m	£m
Initial investment	(7.00)			
Yield @ 7%	0.49	0.49	0.49	
Capital redemptions	—	—	1.40	5.60
Sale of investment	—	—	—	5.97
Total cash flows	(7.00)	0.49	1.89	12.06
Required return/discount factor	30%	0.769	0.592	0.456
Present value	(7.0)	0.38	1.12	5.50

3–19 In the example above a private equity firm is contemplating a £7 million investment from which they require a 30 per cent rate of return. The private equity firm would invest if the investment sale proceeds in year three could be expected to exceed £5.97 million. The key determinants of these sales proceeds will be their equity stake and the overall value of the company, which in turn is most dependent on earnings and prospects at that point.

3.3 Role of the funding instruments

3–20 In putting together a transaction involving private equity the optimum funding solution involves a mixture of debt and equity. This section reviews the characteristics of each of the major types of funding instruments and various hybrids.

3.3.1 Debt

3–21 Most businesses develop in the first instance by obtaining external finance from their bank. In reviewing debt capacity banks have been primarily interested in

Role of the funding instruments

secured lending. Primary security is taken from the principal assets of the business by way of fixed and floating charges covered by a debenture.

The development of the private equity market has been mirrored with developments in the senior debt market with the banks restructuring themselves to provide specialist acquisition finance debt teams to support the private equity market.

The increasing competition has led to debt lending by the acquisition finance debt teams being determined by the ability of the company to service debt through operating cash flows rather than asset security. The competition has also led to innovative debt instruments particularly for larger transactions: featuring different classes of debt taking different degrees of risk and return. The deterioration of credit conditions from 2008 has substantially reduced the quantum of debt available to structure private equity backed companies. **3–22**

Asset based finance techniques remain in use at all levels of the market when the assets provide better security for the debt providers rather than the operating cash flows. The debt providers for asset based finance and cash flow lending come from distinct groups.

Banking structures for cash flow lending

Senior debt structures for cash flow lending vary substantially at the top and the bottom of the economic cycles. **3–23**

As far as the historic picture is concerned total debt to equity splits are usually of the order of 60 per cent: 40 per cent, with equity levels dipping towards 30 per cent at the top of the economic cycle and towards 50 per cent at the bottom of the economic cycle.

The established norms for senior debt lending against operating cash flows were a seven year term, roughly two times interest cover and the senior debt being three to four times EBIT. The top of the economic cycle generates different layers of debt with longer maturities and repayment profiles to increase overall debt levels. The bottom of the cycle sees a reduction in all the variables: shorter repayment periods, lower levels of gearing and higher margins.

Banking structures for asset based facilities

Asset based finance with confidential invoice discounting at its core, is debt funding secured against the complete range of a company's assets. Some of the key advantages of asset based funding over cash flow senior debt funding are: **3–24**

- flexibility, as the asset based facility fluctuates with turnover;
- it is often cheaper, as non-utilisation fees and early repayment charges are smaller;
- it is continuous, without a repayment profile, whereas senior debt has a repayment profile;
- financial covenants are focused solely on the asset, and tend to be easier to monitor and to operate within;
- it can result in larger amounts of debt capacity.

Under confidential invoice discounting, the company is effectively generating an overdraft facility linked to the value of the debtor book. These facilities have been extremely effective in funding not only the acquisition price but also the ongoing working capital requirements of the business.

Banking covenants

3–25 Having established the optimum level of debt advance, a lender will wish to monitor the performance of the company, principally in the areas of security cover and cash flow generation. Such monitoring is carried out by establishing financial covenants which the company must work within. Where a financial covenant is broken, in theory a bank can call its facilities in, but in practice financial covenants are used as an early warning system so that underperformance can be pinpointed and corrective action taken. Financial covenants are stipulated at the outset and are based around the financial model shown in the business plan. The covenants set should be tight enough to promote "good housekeeping" but tolerant enough to allow some slippage from the plan. Clearly a well prepared financial model pays rewards at this stage in the process.

3–26 Financial covenants are often expressed as financial ratios and will include the following key ratios for cash flow lending.

- Interest cover. Set to ensure the business is capable of servicing the debt through profit generation.
- Operating cash flow to interest cover. Set to ensure the cash flow generation capability of the company will service debt interest and also make repayments of capital.
- The ratio of debt to equity. The gearing ratios are a secondary driver for the cash flow lenders in determining debt capacity but they are used as a "logic check" on deal structures.
- Trading performance ratios. Cash flow lenders are lending against the ability of the company to generate income and cash, consequently some

covenants will be set to highlight when the ability of the company to generate cash weakens.

Asset based financiers have differing objectives, for these lenders financial performance is secondary to the value of the collateral against which the loan is secured, consequently the covenants are focused on the quality of the security. Their covenants are fewer, less onerous, and will cover: **3–27**

- Asset value covenants. Advances will be determined by asset values. For example, borrowings must not exceed 80 per cent of the debtor's ledger under 90 days old.

- Credit note ratio. The ratio of credit notes issued will have to operate within limits to ensure that the quality of the debtor book is maintained.

- Concentration limits. Advances are also restricted by limiting overall amounts of credit given to certain customers, because of concentration, related trading, credit or other recovery risks.

- Gearing ratios. The asset based financiers generally have fewer gearing ratios, which has enabled "debt only" management buy-outs giving management complete ownership of the equity.

As far as historical lending performance is concerned asset based financiers have been prepared to advance 75 per cent to 85 per cent of the "good quality" debtor book. The precise advance is determined by their assessment of the underlying credit worthiness of the individual debtors and the accounting systems. In determining "good quality" the focus is to avoid lending against "disputable" invoices. They heavily discount the value of contracting debtors (any debtor that can be more easily disputed by the customer). Deductions will also be made for rebates and the normal pattern of credit notes. **3–28**

The asset based financiers may also "over advance" against the debtor book if there is also security in the stock. This distinction is significant as they have been unwilling solely to finance stock. Advances against stock are typically between 0 per cent and 25 per cent dependent on its location, recoverability, shelf life and provisioning.

Repayment profiles

The established norm for senior debt lending is seven years, although five years has become common at the bottom of the economic cycle. As a general rule, senior debt lenders prefer to see repayments from year one and a weighted average profile of four years or less. Debt structures with non-amortising debt elements, where it is anticipated that the debt will only be repaid on an exit, are only available at the top **3–29** of the economic cycle or on larger investment opportunities with stronger credit quality.

For the provision of ongoing working capital, the overdraft is the most appropriate instrument. On larger transactions, a revolving credit or working capital facility may take the place of the overdraft to allow facility advances to fluctuate with trading requirements, providing financial monitoring covenants are adhered to.

3–30 Interest rates are normally expressed as LIBOR plus percentage points. Typical interest rates are between 1.5 to 2.5 per cent above LIBOR rate, depending on the inherent strengths in the business and the competitiveness of the banking market. The tightening credit conditions have seen interest rate margins rise to 3.5 to 5 per cent.

The variable nature of LIBOR can create uncertainty for a highly leveraged transaction, and to safeguard against fluctuating interest rates it is possible to introduce "caps" or "swaps" to fix the interest rate for a period of time.

Other asset finance

3–31 Other asset finance can include finance leases to fund fixed assets and commercial mortgages.

Asset finance can have a material role to play in the funding of fixed assets. As a debt instrument, security is by way of specific chattel mortgage which, like a debenture, allows the asset funder a right of recourse in the event of default by the borrower company. Funding transactions involving major capital expenditure on plant and machinery with asset finance can increase debt capacity as the specialist asset finance provider is focused on the asset's alternative use valuation. These valuations, however, are generally prepared on a forced short term sale basis and consequently they can be considerably less than current book values.

Property loans are also used in funding structures, although commercial mortgages are usually only available for 70 per cent of the value of the security, leaving a funding requirement for the additional 30 per cent. The asset based financiers will often include commercial property in an overall lending package, but in these circumstances have not advanced more than 50 per cent of its realisable value.

3.3.2 Mezzanine finance

3–32 Mezzanine finance is a hybrid financial instrument which holds the middle ground between senior debt and equity capital. Mezzanine is a debt instrument which ranks behind the senior debt but ranks ahead of equity. In return for acting in a junior or subordinated capacity to senior debt a premium return is required which is usually represented in the form of an interest rate of three to four per cent above senior debt rates plus an option to acquire at nominal value a few equity percentage points on the sale or flotation of the company. The equity warrants attached are likely to be in the range of two to five per cent of the equity of the company and are often referred to as an "equity kicker".

Therefore, in considering the role of mezzanine, it may be viewed as an expensive form of senior debt whilst remaining a cheap alternative to equity. Typically, a mezzanine provider would require an overall IRR in the range of 15 per cent depending on the risk profile of the investee company, the economic environment and the competitiveness of the debt market. This compares with a typical venture capital IRR requirement of more than 25 per cent.

Mezzanine is prevalent in about 25 per cent of transactions, in excess of £10 million. **3–33** Mezzanine effectively replaces equity but it retains most of the characteristics and protections of debt. Mezzanine repayments usually start only when a significant portion of the senior debt has been repaid.

In significantly smaller transactions, it is unlikely that mezzanine would be considered, resulting in the use of only debt and equity.

A common exit for mezzanine is to be repaid in full on exit: the sale or flotation of the investee company. Earlier repayments are often not possible until the senior debt providers have seen a significant repayment of their borrowings.

Although mezzanine financial covenants will apply, their requirements will **3–34** usually be less demanding than those pertaining to the senior debt providers. The primary covenant is interest cover, with a likely minimum requirement of 1.5 to 2 times cover.

Mezzanine finance usually only features in funding structures including senior debt based on cash flow lending.

The effect of the mezzanine is to reduce the equity requirement in the funding, allowing the private equity investor to reduce their investment and therefore their required share of the ordinary equity to the benefit of the other holders of the ordinary equity.

3.3.3 Equity

Equity instruments in private equity transactions are most simply described as the **3–35** "other funding" ranking behind debt in terms of security and income rights. They represent the provision of risk capital and in return the private equity investor seeks some upside, in the form of a shareholding in the business.

Through a mixture of ordinary shares, preference shares and medium or long term debt, the venture capital provider can structure investments by which the private equity firm receives an overall return commensurate with the risk.

3–36 The private equity firms structure their investments as "expensive debt" to reduce their equity shareholding. The private equity firm will invest predominantly in either preference shares or loan stock, with little value attributed to their investment in the ordinary shares. This is best illustrated in an example.

Example 7: Private equity as "expensive debt"

A private equity firm is considering an investment of £5 million in a private company. The private equity firm believe that in three years' time, the private company could be sold for £25 million and they would like to see an overall cash return of £11 million (IRR of 30 per cent) on their investment.

Structure A: Private equity as pure equity

	£m
Initial investment in ordinary shares	5
Required return	11
Exit valuation	25
Shareholding required (£11m of £25m)	44%

Structure B: Private equity as "expensive debt"

	£m
Initial investment in preferred shares	4.5
Initial investment in ordinary shares	0.5
Total investment	5.0
Sale proceeds	25.0
Redemption of preference shares	(4.5)
Proceeds for ordinary shares	20.5
Required return from ordinary shares	6.5
Shareholding required (£6.5m of £20.5m)	32%

Role of the funding instruments

Under Structure B, because the private equity investors are receiving £4.5 million from redemption of their preference shares they only require an additional £6.5 million from the sale of their ordinary shareholding, a required shareholding of 32 per cent. 3–37

In structuring their investments as "expensive debt" the private equity provider is effectively ensuring that sale proceeds are initially used to repay their investment, before proceeds are shared. The private equity provider takes a lower shareholding in these structures, which increases the rewards of the other shareholders for performance beyond expectations than would be the case of a "pure equity investment".

Consistent with the structuring of their investment as "expensive debt" and given that most venture funds are "hands off" in approach there are also protections to safeguard a venture fund's position where their investment is put at risk. The protections are contained in the articles of association with provisions relating to the rights and obligations attaching to each class of investment. Where income and/or repayments of capital are in arrears there are likely to be protection provisions which, at their most severe, could result in "swamping rights" giving the venture capital fund voting control in an otherwise minority position. 3–38

Ordinary shares

Ordinary shares represent the permanent and voting share capital of the company which ultimately will generate a capital gain on the disposal of the company. Management tend to receive their shares as ordinary shares, while an institution is likely to denote their shares with a prefix letter such as "A" ordinary shares. This difference of classification is usually done to differentiate the rights of the venture fund from management, as defined in the articles of association. An important institutional benefit may involve special dividend rights, since a venture fund is likely to require a dividend over ordinary shares, which can be expressed as a fixed percentage on cost or participative by linking the amount to the pre-tax profits. The need for pre-emptive dividends is designed to service the investment, like interest on debt, until an ultimate capital gain is achieved on exit. 3–39

The dividend rights attaching to the "A" ordinary shares are often different to those of the other shareholders. The dividend rights may include entitlement to a greater percentage of profit and have cumulative rights.

The private equity firm might structure their interest in Preferred Participating Ordinary Shares, or some similar titled shares. The shares will have a participating dividend which might also be used as a lever to force an exit within their preferred investment timeframe. For example, a participating dividend of seven per cent on 3–40 post tax profits might rise to 30 per cent or more at the end of year four. This tactic encourages the other ordinary shareholders of the investee company to plan an exit prior to any dividend uplift coming into force as the dividend is only paid to the Preferred Participating Ordinary Shareholders.

Unlike debt interest, dividends are only payable where the investee company has sufficient distributable reserves to do so. Therefore a loss making company or start-up venture may have no distributable reserves to pay dividends for the first few years of an investment. In such cases a dividend "roll up" or deferment mechanism may have been agreed at the outset and incorporated into the overall institutional return. Usually dividend arrears are cumulative in that past arrears will ultimately have to be paid once sufficient reserves exist.

3–41 These investments are likely to be titled Cumulative Preferred Participating Ordinary Shares ("CPPOs") or something similar, to denote their specific rights and characteristics. To preserve income rights, equity investments are often therefore in the form of loan stock, a debt investment rather than preference shares. As a result interest can be paid irrespective of profits and the creditor rights of the private equity firm are enhanced.

Management ordinary shares

3–42 Excluding development capital investments, management will receive ordinary shares and the extent of their share ownership will largely depend on the anticipated investment returns for the private equity firm and on the size of the transaction. In terms of ordinary share equity, management will acquire a disproportionate proportion relative to their total cash investment compared with the private equity firm's shareholding and their total cash investment. This discrepancy is often referred to as "management's sweet equity". In practice the management subscribe for their ordinary shares at the same price as the private equity firm, the balance of the private equity investment will be in the form of "expensive debt" higher ranking non-voting instruments: loan stock, mezzanine and preference shares. This disproportionate holding of the ordinary shares can also provide management with a disproportionate gain. A ratchet mechanism can also be used to enhance the overall management stake during the life of an investment. Ratchets are discussed in detail in 3.3.4.

Example 8 illustrates the attractiveness of private equity investment for management. By heavily utilising preference shares or loan stock, the venture capital provider is paying £83,000 per voting percentage point compared to £10,000 from management for each percentage of the ordinary share capital.

3–43 In very large MBOs this differential widens, and management's financial injection is to demonstrate commitment and their equity holding bears little resemblance to any formal financial calculation. In smaller MBOs (below £5 million) there is a strong possibility that management will be in voting control.

Example 8: Management stakes in MBOs

MBO of Newco Ltd	£m	
Acquisition price and costs	18.00	
As funded by	£m	Equity Shareholding %
Senior debt	11.00	Nil
Private equity preference shares	6.00	Nil
Management ordinary shares	0.25	25
Private equity ordinary shares	0.75	75
Total funds raised	18.00	100

Management equity price =	Management investment of £250,000 for 25% equivalent to £10,000 for each 1%
Private equity price =	Total private equity investment of £6.75 million for 75% equivalent to £90,000 for each 1%

In all MBOs, very large or small, management will be required to invest a financial amount that will "hurt". As a guide the private equity firms will be seeking each significant manager to personally invest six to twelve months of gross salary, subject to personal circumstances. **3–44**

Very often a senior debt provider will advance management a personal loan to use for the management. This advance by the senior debt provider is a personal loan requiring the usual personal statements of assets and liabilities, it takes time and should be addressed in advance of completion.

Preference shares or loan stock

As demonstrated in Example 7, private equity firms structure the majority of their investment in the form of either preference shares or loan stock. Whilst the distinctions are important, they both effectively represent equity, as irrespective of structures the finance provided is at risk. **3–45**

Preference shares rank ahead of ordinary shares in the event of a winding up, but they rank behind every form of debt provider and unsecured creditor. Loan stock ranks ahead of ordinary shares and preference shares and has the advantage of ranking at least alongside the unsecured creditors.

3–46 Loan stock interest has the added advantage, subject to meeting certain tax legislation requirements, for the investee company of being tax deductible, whereas dividends on preference shares are not. Dependent on its taxable regime and status the private equity firm is usually indifferent to income received as either dividend or interest. Also the payment of a preference share dividend requires distributable profits whereas loan stock interest does not. Because of these differences and the current tax position private equity investors prefer when possible to use loan stock as their preferred investment structure.

3–47 The preference shares or loan stock are typically redeemable and, depending on cash flow generation capability, are usually repaid throughout the life of the private equity investment. Alternatively, where there is a clear exit strategy at the outset, they may be redeemed only on the sale or flotation of the investee company. Such an approach usually applies to the larger investments where cash flow patterns and recognition of income streams are fairly predictable. For the smaller transaction, the private equity firms like to see their exposure reduce quickly, subject to cash flow generation capability. At best, a one to two year capital holiday will be given with the balance payable over a three to four year period. Where a significant element of senior debt exists, covenants may be put into force which prevents redemption of private equity investment until gearing has been significantly reduced.

The senior debt providers prefer not to see returns to equity, whether income or capital, until their overall security position is improved.

3–48 In some circumstances the preference shares or loan stock may be redeemed at a premium. The purpose of any premium is to boost the investment return. Premia can be used to reduce the private equity firm's shareholding. Effectively, the private equity firm sacrifices some of its share in the capital gain for a 100 per cent share of the premia, which comes from the first piece of equity gain. The loan stock or preference shares usually carry fixed income or dividend rights.

In virtually all private equity investments, preference share dividends are cumulative and arrears must be cleared. Unlike a debt instrument, where interest is payable regardless of reserves or not, preference shareholders cannot force payment of a dividend where there are no distributable reserves present. Similar to the participating dividend on ordinary shares, a preference share dividend can be hiked up by a penal amount to encourage disposal of the business and provide a venture fund with an exit within the agreed timeframe.

Where income and/or capital redemption are in arrears, the articles of association or the terms of the loan stock can contain special rights which transform the non-voting investment into voting shares for the period of the arrears.

3.3.4 Performance related ratchets

Performance related ratchets are used to incentivise management beyond their initial agreed equity shareholding. The ratchets offer management an opportunity to increase their equity shareholdings in the investee company at the expense of the private equity provider. **3–49**

Ratchets are not common and would normally only become effective for "beyond planned" performance. They are unpopular with private equity firms as there is potential for conflict between what is for the "overall good" and the "good of the ratchet holders".

In setting a ratchet mechanism the two principal drivers used are profit or exit value.

Profit related ratchet

A profit related ratchet is based around the calculation of future projected net profits. The inherent problems with this mechanism revolve around different methods of calculating net profits. While accounting standards, policies and principles reduce the scope for judgmental accounting, certain items can remain subjective. **3–50**

For example, the level of provisions applied to the profit and loss account may materially affect the profit outcome for the year. Similarly, a change in accounting policies on, say, depreciation or income recognition may have an impact on the final outcome of the ratchet mechanism. Given the subjective nature of accounts presentation private equity firms tend to view profit based ratchets as difficult to police and verify.

In structuring a profit based ratchet, the private equity firm needs to define profits, to consider whether profits should be averaged, whether the ratchet should be sliding or "hit or miss" and whether the ratchet should be "two way", i.e. negative and positive. There is too much scope for profit based ratchets to be divisive and difficult to document and as a result they are rarely used.

Exit value ratchet

An exit value ratchet is calculated by reference to the final exit valuation of the investee company. This method eliminates the uncertainties associated with profit based ratchets and tends to be the preferred ratchet mechanism used by private equity firms. **3–51**

Example 9: Exit value ratchet example

	Outset	Year 3	Exit valuation
Management equity stake	25%	30%	£25m and above
		28%	£23m–25m
		26%	£22m–£23m

Ratchet—Subject to achieving a minimum capitalisation before the end of year three within each of the stand-alone bands.

The use of a ratchet generally complicates a transaction and can cause friction between management and the private equity firms because they establish different, albeit similar objectives.

3.4 Structuring a private equity investment

3.4.1 Discounted cash flows

3–52 All private equity firms assess investment opportunities by reference to the expected cash flows of the investment and the risks associated with those cash flows. To compare investment opportunities private equity firms will calculate the IRR (internal rate of return) of those expected cash flows.

Put simply the IRR gives the average percentage annual return to the investor over a given period. It is used by the private equity firms to demonstrate their skill in investing, to differentiate themselves from other private equity firms in raising their funds for investment.

The expected cash flows for a private equity investor used to calculate the IRR will include:

Initial investment

3–53 The original cash investment made in ordinary shares, preference shares and loan stock.

Dividends and interest payments

3–54 The dividend income from preference shares and loan stock interest is usually fixed; the ordinary share dividend is usually variable, often expressed as a percentage of profits.

Structuring a private equity investment

Capital repayments

The scheduled repayments of loan stock, or preference shares including where appropriate any anticipated redemption premia. Redemption payments are often restricted, particularly on larger transactions until significant amounts of debt and mezzanine have been repaid. **3–55**

Sale proceeds

The most significant cash flow in the IRR calculation is the assumption regarding the amount and timing of any proceeds arising on the sale of their ordinary shares. In making an assumption on this cash flow the private equity firm must make an assessment of the value of the company at exit. **3–56**

Example 10: Private equity returns

The example below is based on an initial investment of £7 million in a company which has been structured as £6.75 million of 7 per cent redeemable preference shares and £250,000 in ordinary shares. The preference shares are redeemable in five annual instalments from the end of year two and the company will be sold at the end of year three. The private equity firm requires an IRR of 30 per cent on its investment.

Private equity cash flows:

Years	0	1	2	3
	£m	£m	£m	£m
Initial investment	(7.00)			
Dividend @ 7%		0.47	0.47	0.47
Capital redemptions			1.35	5.40
Sale of investment				6.34
Total cash flows	(7.00)	0.47	1.82	12.19
Required return/discount factor	30%	0.769	0.592	0.456
Present value	(7.00)	0.36	1.08	5.56

In Example 10, the private equity firm requires sale proceeds of £6.34 million from its £250,000 investment in ordinary shares to achieve their overall IRR of 30 per cent on their total investment. If the private equity firm believed the exit value of the ordinary shares was £25 million, they would require a 25 per cent **3–57** share (£6.34 million of £25 million), but only a 20 per cent stake if their exit value expectations were £32 million.

Example 10 also shows the significance of the assessment of exit valuation as this determines sale proceeds. The two components used to assess the exit value are projected future profits and the profit multiple that can be attributed at the time of exit. Consequently growth in profits is an essential component in growing the exit value; profits growth will also hopefully equate to cash flow generation to reduce debt. To assist consistency in assessing investment opportunities and for prudence, the private equity firm is likely to assume that the exit profile multiple is the same as the entry multiple paid for the initial investment. Clearly, however, any enhancement in the multiple at the point of exit will also increase capital gains.

3–58 The significance of exit valuations on the overall investment returns made by a private equity firm is well understood and is reflected by increasing due diligence on exit prospects. Private equity firms now as a matter of investment practice will formally commission research on the exit prospects of their investments prior to investment. Furthermore, to protect their rights to receive those anticipated exit proceeds, the use of "tag along" and "drag along" clauses is now prevalent in most articles of association. The "drag along" rights are used to compulsorily "drag" other shareholders into selling their shares if the private equity firm deems an offer should be accepted. The "tag along" rights empower the private equity firm to participate in any offer made for the shares held by the other shareholders.

Example 11: The impact on investment returns of changes to exit multiples

Investment details

	Scenario A	Scenario B
	£m	£m
Future maintainable profits, (*Example 3*)	2.4	
Multiple	6	
Valuation	14.4	
Costs	1.2	
Total funds raised	15.6	
Exit details, year 3		
Future maintainable profits, (*Table 1*)	4.2	4.2
Multiple	6	7
Valuation	25.2	29.4

Structuring a private equity investment

Less: Unpaid debt	(3.5)	(3.5)
Preference shares	(6.0)	(6.0)
Attributable to ordinary shareholders	15.7	19.9
Split—Management 25%	3.9	5.0
Private equity 75%	11.8	14.9
	15.7	19.9

3–59 Under Scenario A, the private equity firm has a total return of £17.8 million from a £6.75 million investment, after three years, an IRR of 38 per cent and a cash multiple of 2.63 times.

Under Scenario B, the private equity firm and the other shareholders have benefited not only from profit growth, but also exit multiple growth. In Scenario B, the private equity firm has a total return of £20.9 million from a £6.75 million investment after three years, an IRR of 46 per cent and a cash multiple of 3.10 times.

3–60 There is no exact science to the quantum of the required IRR for the private equity firms. Each investment is considered individually on its own merits and circumstances. As a general rule, however, private equity firms are looking to treble their money. When making investments, the private equity firms will take an investment "portfolio view": one third will disappoint, one third will be average and one third will perform above expectations. Because of this variation in portfolio performance, a private equity firm is usually unwilling to consider an investment with a fixed upside, or a capped return, without a corresponding protected downside.

IRR sensitivities

3–61 As noted in Example 10, the most significant cash flows are the initial investment and the sale proceeds. Consequently, the private equity firms are focused on not "overpaying" on entry and clearly researching and understanding the exit prospects.

The example also shows that the IRR benefit from adjustments to income or redemption of capital are quite modest—the key cash flows are always the cost of investment and the sale proceeds on exit. The two key variables in determining the sale proceeds are the anticipated maintainable profits at the point of exit and the multiple applied to them to value the company.

3–62 In itself, a one per cent equity percentage change does not produce a material swing in the IRR. But overall the equity percentage does have a material effect on returns and all private equity funds would regard it as a primary variable: their perspective is no different to the other shareholders.

Given the significance of future profits in determining value and the private equity firm's investment returns: due diligence will focus on projected profits. The temptation therefore in raising private equity funds is to present optimistic projections for the future. However, in the final analysis the private equity firm will always use their own assessment of maintainable profits for the future.

3–63 The variables considered by private equity firms to assess investment opportunities can be categorised as primary or secondary drivers. The primary drivers for the private equity firm are:

- entry price;
- projected maintainable profits;
- equity percentage held.

The secondary drivers, which are less important, are:

- dividend rates;
- capital repayment profiles.

The exceptions are transactions that allow short term redemptions of substantially all of the investment capital. Their attraction to private equity firms is they enable funds to be returned to their own investors early and therefore increase the profit share earned by the managers of the private equity firms.

3.4.2 Principles of deal structuring

3–64 The previous sections of this chapter have identified and discussed the key principles surrounding each of the financial instruments. The purpose of this section is to bring together the different instruments and provide a framework for deal structuring.

The steps involved in structuring a deal are as follows.

Step 1: Is the acquisition price reasonable?

3–65 A key requirement of all successful private equity investment is not to overpay on entry.

As a guide, recent history suggests:

- investments of less than £10 million have been typically valued in the range of four to six times EBIT; and
- investments above £10 million in the range of six to nine times EBIT.

Structuring a private equity investment

This is only a guide based on past investment experience, each investment opportunity will be considered on its merits.

Step 2: What is the cash flow debt capacity?

It is always in the interests of the ordinary shareholders to raise debt first: it is **3–66** cheaper and interest is tax deductible. The objective should be to maximise the debt in a deal structure, the balance is ensuring that the debt can be serviced in terms of capital and interest repayments without creating unnecessary stress and risk of default for the investee company.

Cash flow debt capacity does fluctuate during the economic cycle, as a guide based on past deal structures:

- the amount of senior debt will usually be a multiple of three to four times EBIT; and
- the senior debt should be in the region of 50 per cent to 60 per cent of the total funds raised.

Step 3: Is the debt capacity greater with asset based finance?

Asset based debt capacity does vary significantly between businesses. **3–67**

As a guide, based on past experience the asset categories should yield the following debt capacities:

- debtors, 75 per cent to 85 per cent of the "good quality" debtor book;
- inventory, up to 25 per cent dependent on recoverability, and a good quality debtor book;
- plant and equipment, 10 per cent to 25 per cent, dependent on its alternative uses; and
- property, 50 per cent to 70 per cent of immediate reasonable value.

Step 4: Will the funding structure support any mezzanine?

Consistent with Steps 2 and 3, this step is to determine whether there is any other **3–68** debt available prior to confirming the equity funding requirement. As a guide based on past experience:

- mezzanine is really only prevalent in funding transactions in excess of £10 million;

- mezzanine represents between 10 per cent and 15 per cent of the total financing and is usually in the range of 0.75 to 1.25 times EBIT; and
- mezzanine is normally only prevalent in structures with senior debt based on cash flow lending.

Step 5: What is the total equity funding required?

3–69 This is usually the final piece being the total funding requirement less the available debt.

Based on past experience equity typically represents 40 per cent to 50 per cent of the total funding.

Step 6: Does the investment generate the required returns for equity?

3–70 Having determined the equity required, the private equity firm will make an assessment of their expected cash flows to ensure that the investment meets their objectives.

Step 7: Does the structure work from a cash flow perspective?

3–71 The final step is to ensure that all sources of funding can be reasonably expected to be properly serviced in terms of interest and capital repayments. Cash generation capability needs to be strong to reduce the debt burden, particularly where cash flow senior debt lending has been used. Cash flow lending, unlike asset finance providers who do not have a repayment profile, require their debt to be repaid. Past experience shows that months 9 to 18 post investment are normally the periods of greatest cash stress and sensitivity.

3.5 Key points

3.5.1 Corporate valuation

3–72
- The discounted cash flow model explicitly or implicitly underpins all private equity firms' analysis of value. The private equity firm is focused on the cash flows it can expect to receive from its involvement.
- Earnings based valuations are used for two reasons:
  — Discounted cash flow models are only prepared for three to five years, and cannot be reliably extended in fast growing companies; and
  — Earnings should reflect cash flow.

Key points

- Earnings based calculations are based on an assessment of future maintainable profits which should equate to cash flow generation and profit multiples.
- Profit multiplies used are principally EBIT and EBITDA multiplies to remove the distortions created by differing financial structures, accounting policies and tax positions.
- Asset based valuations are unusual in private equity transactions as private equity firms are focused on cash returns and not the underlying net worth of the assets.

3.5.2 Role of the funding instruments

- Senior debt structures for cash flow lenders vary substantially during the economic cycle, and are based on the ability of the business to generate profits and cash and not the underlying assets.   3–73
- Asset based funders are based around confidential invoice discounting.
- Cash flow lenders covenants are often more comprehensive as they need to identify early weaknesses in the ability of the business to generate forecast profits and cash.
- Asset based finance has fewer covenants focused solely on the quality of the collateral, and has the added advantage of not having a repayment profile.
- Mezzanine finance ranks behind senior debt but ahead of equity capital, it should be viewed as an expensive form of senior debt.
- Equity is the other funding; it represents risk capital and is usually structured by private equity firms as "expensive debt" in the form of preference shares or loan stock, with little value attributed to the ordinary shares.
- Management will receive a disproportionate amount of equity compared to their investment. Additional equity may also be available through ratchets, which if used are most commonly linked to exit values.

3.5.3 Structuring a private equity investment

- Private equity firms assess investment opportunities by reference to their expected cash flows. Investment opportunities are compared by calculating the IRR of those cash flows.   3–74
- Entry prices and exit values have the greatest impact on the profits and investment returns made by private equity firms.
- The principal steps in structuring a deal are:

- Is the acquisition price reasonable?
- What is the "cash flow" debt capacity?
- Is the debt capacity greater with asset based finance?
- Will the funding structure support any mezzanine?
- What is the total equity funding required?
- Does the investment generate the required returns for equity?
- Does the structure work from a cash flow perspective?

Chapter 4

Tax Relief for Equity Investment by Individuals

4.1 Introduction

Whatever the media perception of private equity, successive governments have pursued a policy of using tax breaks to encourage investment in private trading companies with a view to encouraging the creation of jobs, wealth and innovation. Although the legislation provisions are not separated in this way, there are two discernible themes within the legislative framework. One is the encouragement of private investment generally through certain special tax reliefs for equity investment, and the other is to promote equity investment by management. However, recently, the reliefs for investors have become much more restricted. **4–01**

4.2 Entrepreneurs Relief

In 2008 Taper Relief was abolished and replaced by Entrepreneurs Relief. A summary of the criteria outlining the rules to qualify for the first £5 million of gains to be taxed at an effective rate of ten per cent are set out below. It applies to disposals of qualifying business assets by individuals. The main assets to qualify are as follows: **4–02**

- Shares or securities in a trading company where the holder is an employee or officer of the company/group and provided that certain conditions are met; in particular a five per cent minimum holding of ordinary shares and voting rights in the company and one year holding period prior to disposal;
- Whole or part of a continuing business, carried on by an individual either on his own/her own or in partnership for a period of one year to the disposal;
- Assets used by a business undertaken by a sole trader, or by partners which has now come to an end provided that they were used as business assets at the time of cessation (and subject to some further conditions);

Tax Relief for Equity Investment by Individuals

- Qualifying holiday lettings; and
- Disposals of business assets by trustees may also attract Entrepreneurs Relief provided certain conditions are met. The claim must be made jointly with the qualifying beneficiary, as this will use up all or part of that individual's £5 million lifetime limit.

4.3 Tax reliefs for equity investment—EIS and VCT overview

4–03 The Enterprise Investment Scheme ("EIS") and Venture Capital Trusts have been in existence for some years, but in 2006 and 2007 changes restricted the scope of qualifying investment which will probably limit investment to small high risk trading companies. The EIS applies where a direct investment is made into unquoted trading companies. Further reliefs are available where an indirect investment is made by investing in such companies through a listed fund vehicle known as a venture capital trust ("VCT"). The reliefs available in each case comprise a mixture of upfront income tax relief, a capital gains tax exemption on the ultimate sale of the investment and also the possibility of deferring tax on capital gains already realised by rolling over gains into an EIS or VCT investment.

The reliefs are intended to attract more investment by individuals and not just to fill the "equity gap". Unquoted companies are generally smaller than quoted companies and therefore more prone to fail in a recession. Moreover, since by definition the shares are unmarketable, there is no quick escape from an impending collapse. The risks are great, but then so are the rewards for choosing successful companies—as the record of many venture capitalists testifies.

4–04 With effect from April 6, 2007 further restrictions were applied as well as the reduction of the gross assets test to £7 million before and £8 million after. For VCT funds raised after April 5, 2007 and for EIS subscriptions made after enactment of the Finance Act 2007 an investment does not qualify under VCT or EIS unless it has taken no more than £2 million under both schemes plus the Corporate Venturing Scheme ("CVS") in the 12 months ending on the date of the relevant investment. Furthermore, a new restriction was imposed to the effect that a company raising money under such schemes must have fewer than 50 employees on the date on which the relevant shares and securities are issued (except for VCT funds raised prior to April 6, 2006).

4.4 Qualifying companies

4–05 The focus of the tax reliefs is on "qualifying companies", a creature of statutory definition which is broadly the same for both EIS and VCTs. For EIS purposes the investment made by the individual must be in a qualifying company. A VCT

Qualifying companies

must invest a certain proportion of its assets into qualifying companies in order to quality as a VCT.

4–06 A qualifying company is an unquoted company but not necessarily a UK resident company. Companies listed on the Alternative Investment Market ("AIM") are unquoted for this purpose. It must exist to carry on one or more qualifying trades wholly or mainly in the UK, although it may be a holding company with the qualifying trade being carried on by its qualifying subsidiary or subsidiaries. It is anticipated that this year's Finance Act will change this definition so that the issuing company must have a permanent establishment in the UK. The definition of a qualifying trade is a negative one which prohibits certain activities being carried on to any substantial extent, which is broadly interpreted to mean not exceeding 20 per cent of the total activities. These activities have been selected to exclude trades regarded by HMRC as tainted (e.g. land dealing and share dealing) and to exclude activities which can prudently be pursued without significant risk. Thus prohibited activities include finance, hiring, leasing, licensing, insurance or selling goods other than on terms normally applicable to wholesale or retail trading in those goods.

4–07 One of the aims of these reliefs is to encourage investment in young high-technology companies. Such companies often earn their revenues from licensing their products (e.g. computer software) rather than outright sales. In practice, the result may be that such companies do not satisfy the qualifying company test because of the receipt of significant licensing revenues. The government has sought to address this issue by providing that the licensing of own created intellectual property is not a non-qualifying activity.

The money raised by the qualifying company must be used for the purposes of its trade within a specified time. Using monies to acquire a trading business and assets satisfies this test. As a result of recent changes, using monies to acquire shares in a company will satisfy the test provided that the qualifying trade is carried on by a direct 90 per cent subsidiary of the investee company. However, changes were announced in the 2007 budget to permit the qualifying trade to be carried on by 100 per cent subsidiaries of direct 90 per cent subsidiaries or 90 per cent subsidiaries of direct 100 per cent subsidiaries (with effect from April 6, 2007).

4–08 Another important condition for a qualifying company is that it must not control another company except for a closely defined qualifying subsidiary, nor must it be under the control of another company (or of another company and its connected persons). The definition of control used for this latter test for the purposes of EIS is not the same as that for VCT investments and is less widely drawn. In practice this test often means that for EIS purposes a company will not be a qualifying company if one of its investors comprises a company. For VCT investments the main point is to ensure that the investment by the VCT itself does not cause this test to be breached.

4–09 For EIS purposes, the conditions for a qualifying company must be met for a period of three years from the investment in the company or, if later, from the commencement of a qualifying trade by the company. For VCT investments the conditions must be satisfied for the period during which the investment is held by the VCT.

4.5 Enterprise Investment Scheme

4–10 The aim of this scheme is to give tax reliefs to individuals who are genuine outsiders and who are providing equity funds to a qualifying company for use in its trade on a medium-term basis. The tax reliefs available for a qualifying investment are an upfront income tax relief at the lower rate of tax on the amount subscribed up to a maximum of £500,000 in any tax year. At current rates of tax (2010/11) this relief is worth a maximum of £100,000. In addition, any gain arising on the shares on disposal after three years is exempt provided the income tax relief has not been withdrawn in the meantime. Subject to the same proviso any loss sustained on disposal may be eligible for relief against capital gains or income.

4–11 Since the aim of the scheme is to attract funds for investment in a company the shares acquired must be subscribed for (rather than acquired from another shareholder) and they must be the lowest ranking ordinary shares, without preferential rights to dividends or repayment in a winding-up and must not be redeemable (eligible shares). The funds have to be provided on a medium-term basis so that the conditions for retaining the relief require that there is no disposal of the shares for three years and for this period (subject to certain limited exceptions) the investor must not receive any value from the company, widely defined to extend beyond repayment of share capital to include many kinds of benefit.

4–12 Since the equity capital subscribed is intended to be incremental and not substitute capital, there must be no repayment of any of its share capital by the company for a period of three years. This can be a further impediment to venture capital investment in a qualifying company in that any venture capitalist will usually require a redemption of the redeemable components of its investment within less than three years. If the redeemable component has been advanced by way of loan capital then this particular problem does not arise.

The investor must be a genuine outsider which means neither he/she nor his/her associates must be an employee of the company (or one of its subsidiaries) nor must they own over 30 per cent of the ordinary share capital, the share capital and loan capital, or voting power.

4–13 While there is a general prohibition on employees of the company obtaining relief, an exception is made for unpaid directors and for paid directors provided that their remuneration is reasonable and that when they make the investment they have never been previously connected with the company nor have they ever been employees in the trade carried on by the company ("business angels"). It is essential that a paid director is issued with the shares in respect of which relief is to be claimed before he becomes a director. This provision is aimed at denying EIS relief to managers in a genuine MBO who take over the business in which they previously worked. However it does not catch professional managers who are brought into the management team on the buy-out. They could be entitled to EIS relief on amounts subscribed for shares provided the funds are used for the purpose of a qualifying trade of the company or a subsidiary and not simply for the purpose of acquiring the shares in the target company. Under EIS a repayment of any loan to an EIS shareholder within three years would result in loss of relief.

The EIS focuses on high risk situations but is generally viewed by fund managers as being not particularly generous in its front-end tax relief. This latter point is resulting in a trend amongst investors towards capital gearing with a small amount invested in equity share capital and a much larger amount advanced as a loan. The ability to receive a repayment of the loan when funds permit is valued much more highly than income tax relief at the lower rate which would be available on the amount of the loan if it were invested in eligible shares. The tight definition of control in defining qualifying companies and the bar on repayment of share capital for three years makes it difficult for venture capital companies to be involved in qualifying companies for EIS purposes. **4–14**

4.6 EIS deferral relief

A chargeable gain of any description realised by an individual from the disposal of an asset can be deferred by subscribing for eligible shares in a qualifying company. This is known as EIS deferral relief. There is no requirement that the shares also qualify for income tax relief (i.e. no £500,000 limit) and it is of no consequence if the individual is connected with the company for EIS purposes, i.e. the investor does not have to be a genuine outsider. **4–15**

The deferral relief is available where an individual makes a qualifying investment. The conditions that must be met for a qualifying investment are: **4–16**

- the EIS shares must normally be issued fully paid up for cash during the period beginning one year before and ending three years after the date of the disposal which produced the chargeable gain to be deferred;
- the company must be a qualifying company under EIS rules;
- the subscription of the EIS shares is made for bona fide commercial reasons and not for tax avoidance purposes;

- the individual making the EIS investment must be resident or ordinarily resident in the UK both when the gain accrued and when the EIS shares were subscribed for;
- the relief must be claimed and the individual must specify the amount of the relief which is being claimed, the maximum amount being the amount of the individual's qualifying expenditure on the EIS shares. This enables, if the individual so chooses, part of the original gain to fall into the charge to capital gains tax so that the individual's annual exemption may be utilised (the annual exemption for the 2006/07 tax year is £8,800).

4–17 The amount of the deferred gain is postponed and is not deducted from the cost of the EIS shares. This prevents the deferred gain from becoming exempt from CGT after the EIS shares have been held for three years. The deferred gain is triggered by any one of the following events:

- a disposal of the EIS shares by the individual to which the deferral relief is attributable (other than by an inter-spouse disposal in which case the spouse takes the place of the individual investor);
- the individual becomes non-resident within three years after the issue of the EIS shares (although a period of non-residence of up to three years whilst working abroad in an office or employment is permitted, provided the EIS shares are not sold during this time);
- the shares ceasing to be eligible shares or the company ceasing to be a qualifying company.

4.7 Venture capital trusts

4–18 A VCT is a company designed to encourage indirect investment (through the VCT) into qualifying companies by means of substantial tax breaks for the VCT and its shareholders. In order to obtain and retain the status as a VCT, there are a number of stringent HMRC requirements which must be satisfied.

4–19 The main conditions that a company must satisfy in order to be an approved VCT are that:

- its income for its most recent accounting period must have been wholly or mainly derived from shares or securities;
- at least 70 per cent of its investments (by value) throughout that period must have been "qualifying holdings"—that is, newly issued shares or securities in qualifying companies. In addition to the conditions referred to in 4.2, the companies in which investments are made must have gross assets of no more than £7 million (immediately before the VCT investment) and no

more than £8 million (immediately after the investment) (these limits were £15 million and £16 million respectively for funds raised prior to April 6, 2006). Broadly speaking only the first £1 million per year invested by a VCT into a company will form part of its qualifying holdings;

- at least 30 per cent of its qualifying holdings must, throughout that period, have been holdings of eligible shares—that is, ordinary shares with no preferential rights to dividends or to the company's assets on its winding-up and no right to be redeemed;
- at no time in that period must its holding in any company (other than another VCT) have represented more than 15 per cent of its investments;
- throughout that period its ordinary shares must have been listed on the London Stock Exchange; and
- it must not have retained more than 15 per cent of the income it derived in that period from shares or securities.

The individuals who acquire ordinary shares in the VCT are offered generous tax reliefs. Income tax relief is given at up to 30 per cent on an amount subscribed for new eligible shares in a VCT up to a maximum of £200,000 per annum. The shares must be retained for five years otherwise the relief is withdrawn. **4–20**

Dividends received on ordinary shares in a VCT will not be regarded as income for income tax purposes where the shares were acquired (whether by way of purchase or subscription) within the £200,000 annual permissible limit in any year. The dividend must be paid out of profits earned while the company was a VCT. **4–21**

Any gain accruing on disposal of ordinary shares in a VCT acquired within the permissible limit of £200,000 for any year of assessment will not be chargeable provided that the VCT maintained its status throughout the period of ownership. No loss relief is available if a loss is sustained. This relief applies whether the shares are purchased or subscribed for and irrespective of whether the shares are eligible shares. **4–22**

4.8 Interest relief

An individual can obtain tax relief for interest paid on money borrowed to invest in the ordinary share capital of a close company (but not if the investment is also the subject of a claim for EIS relief). A close company is one that is controlled by five or fewer participators or by directors who are participators. In determining control the interests of close relatives and trustees of a family trust are aggregated so that most family companies fall within the definition. There is no requirement for the company to be a qualifying company or an unquoted company. **4–23**

Tax Relief for Equity Investment by Individuals

4–24 The further conditions for relief are that:

(1) the borrowing must be by way of loan, not overdraft;

(2) the money must be applied in acquiring ordinary shares in the close company or making a loan to it for the purpose of its business or that of an associated company;

(3) from the date of the investment to the date when the interest is paid:

    (a) throughout the whole of its accounting period the company must not be a close investment holding company; a trading company and a holding company of a trading group are not such a company;

    (b) the investor must have worked for the greater part of his time in the actual management or conduct of the company, or an associated company; and

    (c) the investor must not have recovered any capital from the company except where such recovery has operated to reduce the qualifying amount of the loan;

(4) as an alternative to (3)(b), when the interest is paid the investor and his associates must own more than five per cent of the ordinary share capital of the company.

4–25 Two important extensions of the basic statutory rules have added enormously to the appeal of this relief. HMRC will allow a claim for relief in respect of an individual's interest costs of investing in a close company where the company ceases to be a close company but all the other conditions for relief continue to be met. This means that in the context of a management buy-out, managers may invest in a company before the venture capitalist and provided it is then a close company they may obtain tax relief on the interest paid on their personal borrowings to fund the investment. The relief is not then forfeited on interest paid, after the investment by the venture capitalist opens up the company.

4–26 A challenge to this entitlement to relief in a case where the company was not trading at the time of the manager's investment was rejected by the court on the grounds that a trading company existed for the purpose of carrying on a trade but was not required to carry on such a trade in any particular accounting period.

4–27 A loan for the acquisition of shares in a close company is one of the few remaining situations where interest paid without limit can be deducted from income. Some wealthy individuals prefer to borrow for this purpose to release capital for alternative investment which will earn a net return higher than the net cost of borrowing. A re-investor claiming re-investment relief might take this view. However, a claim for EIS denies interest relief to the investor.

4.9 Special relief for capital losses against income

Where a UK resident or ordinarily resident investor in ordinary shares in an unquoted qualifying trading company suffers a loss on the disposal of his shares, the loss may be relieved against the investor's income of the same year of assessment or the preceding year. The shares must have been subscribed for by the investor or by a spouse who then transferred the shares, inter vivos, during his or her lifetime. **4–28**

The disposal of the shares must be: **4–29**

- an arm's length bargain for full consideration; or
- a distribution in a winding-up of the company; or
- a deemed disposal as a result of a claim to the inspector of taxes that the shares have become of negligible value.

4.10 Business property relief for inheritance tax purposes

Inheritance Tax ("IHT") has been described as a voluntary tax paid only by the ignorant, the victims of misfortune and the uncommonly dutiful. This description owes a lot to the generous reliefs available, not least business property relief. The relief allows a reduction in value of relevant business property when an occasion for charging inheritance tax arises, such as on a transfer of assets to a discretionary settlement, or on a death. **4–30**

There are currently two rates of relief: 100 per cent and 50 per cent. So far as property comprising shares in an unquoted company is concerned, the maximum rate of relief is available. The maximum rate of relief is also available for any securities in an unquoted company which by themselves or together with any other unquoted shares (taking into account any unquoted shares or securities held by a spouse) give the holder control of the company. Quoted shares and securities attract the lower (50 per cent) rate of business property relief if they give the holder control of the company. **4–31**

There is no stipulation that the company must be a qualifying company as that term applies for EIS, although it must be a trading company. A shareholding in a company which is engaged in land or share dealing (other than as a market maker) or in making or holding investments is not relevant business property. Entitlement to the relief requires that the shares have been held for at least two years and that they are not subject to a contract for sale at the date when they fall to be valued for inheritance tax purposes. **4–32**

4–33 IHT is payable at 40 per cent on estates in excess of the nil rate band (£325,000 from April 2009) and at half of this rate for lifetime chargeable transfers. To the extent that the assets chargeable to IHT represent relevant business property eligible for the maximum rate of business property relief, the saving in tax is 40 per cent (or, as the case may be, 20 per cent) of the value of that property without any limit. Thus, the cosseted investor who has had tax relief on the interest on money borrowed to invest in a close company, who rolls over his gain on disposal using EIS reinvestment relief and retains his resultant shareholding in a qualifying company, will die happy in the knowledge that death, the great avoider, will wash out the latent gain on his shareholding. Also, business property relief will shelter his relevant business property from any charge to inheritance tax.

4.11 Management shares

4–34 In 2003, Pt 7 of the Income Tax (Earnings and Pensions) Act introduced a new and wide-ranging anti-avoidance regime to prevent what HM Revenue and Customs perceived to be avoidance of income tax and national insurance. Essentially the regime is intended to prevent employees acquiring equity benefits at less than market value without incurring an income tax charge (where shares are "readily convertible assets", which can arise, inter alia, where they are either traded or are shortly to be realised, income tax and national insurance can be collected through PAYE). In order to prevent avoidance income tax charges can also arise where "employment related securities" are the subject of conversion, artificial increases or reductions in value or post acquisition benefits. The boundary between share rights which fall foul of Pt 7 and ratchet provisions that HM Revenue and Customs are willing to accept as not giving rise to a charge to income is seven years.

4–35 One useful development since 2000 has been the introduction of the Enterprise Management Incentive scheme share options. A more flexible form of share options, an employee can hold £120,000 worth of qualifying options which when granted at market value and exercised in qualifying circumstances do not trigger any liability to income tax or national insurance.

4.12 Key points

4–36
- Tax reliefs available under EIS for a qualifying investment are an upfront income tax relief at the lower rate of tax on the amount subscribed up to a maximum of £500,000 in any tax year. In addition any gain arising on the shares on disposal after three years is exempt provided the income tax relief has not been withdrawn in the meantime.
  - Tax on gains can be deferred by reinvesting the gains in unquoted qualifying trading companies so as to qualify for EIS deferral relief.

Key points

- Investments for the purposes of venture capital trusts must be in a small qualifying company, that is one whose net assets do not exceed £7 million before the VCTs investment and do not exceed £8 million after the VCTs investment. The VCT is limited to an investment of £1 million in each tax year in any particular qualifying company.
- Individuals can obtain tax relief for interest paid on money borrowed to invest the ordinary share capital of a close company so long as that individual does not also claim EIS relief.
- The VCT and EIS reliefs have recently become much more restricted.

Chapter 5

Share Capital

5.1 Introduction

A "share" of a company suggests ownership of part of the assets of that company. In the case of ordinary shares (or the equity) this is commercially likely to be the case. However, this is not always so. For example, where a person is entitled to preference shares, then he/she is unlikely to be entitled to participation in the dividends or return of capital other than up to a fixed amount. A share is often described as a "bundle of rights", accompanied by an obligation to pay for such rights. Strictly, a company is a separate legal person. It is the company which owns its assets. A shareholder by virtue of his shares has rights as against the company and the other shareholders but is not as such a legal owner of the company's assets. Depending on the rights attached to his/her shares, a shareholder will have a right to share in the surplus (if any) on a winding-up. Accordingly if the company becomes more valuable, then the value of the shares increases. If the company fails, the shares are usually worthless. Shares represent a shareholder's stake in the company. Rights attached to a share cannot be determined by its general description, because the rights are set out in the articles of association of the company. Different classes of shares will usually have different rights as to dividends, voting and capital. Inevitably any investment of venture capital or private equity in a company will require a restructuring of share capital. It is essential therefore that advisors understand fully the principles of the legislation surrounding the share capital of a company.

5–01

5.2 Maintenance of capital

Each share in an English company has a nominal value; that is to say, a monetary value in its name. For example, you may see an ordinary share of 25p, or a preference share of £1. There is no reason why there cannot be different nominal amounts attached to different classes of share—or nominal values in different currencies. The only restriction is that, if the company is a public limited company, it must have at least the authorised minimum (presently £50,000) in shares

5–02

Share Capital

denominated in sterling (or the prescribed euro equivalent). Many jurisdictions (for example in the USA) do not have the concept of nominal value.

The nominal value does not represent the actual worth of a share nor does it automatically change as the company prospers or ails. For example, a listed company may have an ordinary share of 10p which is presently being traded at 5p, 50p or £5 and changes minute to minute. Its nominal value remains 10p throughout. The main relevance of nominal value arises when a new share is allotted by a company. At this time, a price is agreed with the company for the new shares. That price may be payable in full on allotment or at later stages (special rules apply if the company is a Plc). But the price cannot be less than the nominal value—there is however no restriction on agreeing a price greater than nominal value.

5–03 As part of the principle of maintenance of capital, a shareholder will be required, in the case of a limited company, to pay the nominal amount of his share and any greater amount agreed at which the share was allotted. The amount greater than nominal value is called share premium. This can be regarded as a liability attached to the holding of shares in the company. The share capital can be regarded as the permanent capital of the company, subject to the special rules as to reduction, redemption and purchase of own shares by the company. Alterations of share capital can only be made within the strict procedures laid down in the Companies Act 2006 ("CA 2006"). The principle of the maintenance of the company's capital is a general one. Pennycuick J. in *Ridge Securities Ltd v IRC* [1964] 1 All E.R. 275 said:

> "The corporators may take assets out of the company by way of dividend or, with leave of the court, by way of reduction or in a winding up. They may of course acquire them for full consideration. They cannot take assets out of the company by way of voluntary disposition, however described and if they attempt to do so, the disposition is ultra vires the company."

5–04 Lord Watson in *Trevor v Whitworth* (1887) 12 A.C. 409, summarised the position as follows:

> "Paid up capital may be diminished or lost in the course of the company's trading; that is a result which no legislation can prevent; but the persons who deal with, and give credit to a limited company, can actually rely upon the fact that the company is trading with a certain amount of capital already paid, as well as upon the responsibility of its members for the capital remaining at call; and they are entitled to assume that no part of the capital which has been paid into the coffers of the company have been subsequently paid out, except in the legitimate course of its business."

5–05 The principle as can be seen from the above dictum has its origins in the protection of creditors (and is therefore often enforced by a company acting through its liquidator). Nevertheless it is equally effective to preserve a company's assets for its shareholders for the time being.

Maintenance of capital

The principle of maintenance of capital derives from the nature of limited liability when the liability is limited by shares (as will be the case for almost all venture capital companies). In such a company, the liability of the company itself is unlimited—it is liable to its last penny to pay its creditors and costs of liquidation. It is the liability of its members which is limited. If the company fails, a member is liable to pay the amount, if any, unpaid on the shares. If the shares are fully paid (as is usually the case in venture capital situations) the member (whether manager or venture capitalist) has no further liability and, if the creditors, etc are not met, that is the consequence of limited liability. Of course, if a shareholder has chosen to go on the hook, for example by giving a personal guarantee to the bank, the shareholder will be liable. And the insolvency legislation can, in certain circumstances, attach liabilities to directors or shadow directors. But in these cases, the person is liable as a guarantor or as director, not because he or she was a shareholder.

Accordingly, the amount paid to the company for shares defines the extent of the risk taken by the members and, therefore, the cover available to creditors. The principle of maintenance of capital is designed to support this by saying that the amount put at risk must stay at risk—it cannot simply be paid back to the members, leaving the creditors without even that level of risk capital in the business.

5.2.1 Consideration for issue of shares

It follows from the principle of maintenance of capital that a company limited by shares cannot issue shares which will be fully paid at a discount, that is, for a money consideration less than their nominal value and any premium agreed at the time of allotment (see *Ooregum Gold Mining Company of India v Roper* [1892] A.C. 125). If this were not so, a company could easily mislead creditors as to its true capital value by simply referring to its nominal capital without mentioning that a part of this capital is not represented by assets. Any attempt by the company to issue shares fully paid at a discount was ultra vires. If shares were issued for a non-cash consideration, the court would not enquire into the adequacy of the consideration, unless the consideration was, on the fact of it, not equivalent to the nominal value of the shares (*Theatrical Trust Ltd, Chapman's Case, Re* [1895] 1 Ch. 771). In this case the court would require a valuation of the consideration and, if this was less than the nominal value of the shares, the same consequences would follow as in the case of any issue of shares for cash at a discount. **5–06**

These common law principles were largely codified and extended by companies legislation—currently in CA 1985 ss.99–116 (and broadly restated in CA 2006 Pt 17 Ch.5—payment for shares). CA 2006 s.582 provides that an allottee may pay for shares allotted to him by the company in money or in money's worth. It is sometimes the case that shares may be allotted to a person in consideration for services he has performed for the company. This is prohibited in public companies **5–07**

Share Capital

(CA 2006 s.584, where shares must be paid up in cash). Where shares are issued in contravention of this prohibition, the shareholder has to pay the company the nominal value of the shares and any premium on them, together with interest. Section 586 prohibits a public company from allotting shares unless paid up at least to one quarter of its nominal value and the whole of any premium on it.

5–08 Where shares are issued at a premium to the nominal value the amount of the premium must usually be transferred to the share premium account, which is treated, with minor exceptions, as capital for the purposes of the maintenance of capital principal (s.610). This applies whether the shares are issued for cash or otherwise. There are certain specific exceptions to this in s.610(2) which permits the application of the share premium for any of the following:

- writing off preliminary expenses; or
- writing off the expenses of, or commission paid or discount allowed on, any issues of shares or debentures.

5.2.2 Corporate gifts

5–09 The inability of shareholders to extract capital from their companies has led to more sophisticated attempts to achieve this. A straightforward breach of the maintenance of capital principle is the corporate gift to shareholders but the cases have also thrown up excessive interest payments (*Ridge Securities Ltd v IRC* [1964] 1 All E.R. 275); "dressed up" remuneration reclassified by the court as a repayment of capital to shareholders (*Halt Garage Ltd, Re* [1982] 3 All E.R. 1016) and sale of property at an undervalue also held to be a return of capital at least where the company had no distributable reserves (*Aveling Barford Ltd v Perion Ltd* [1989] B.C.L.C. 626). The objection to such transactions is that they are prejudicial to the interest of minority shareholders and/or creditors. There are a number of possible objections. For example a transfer of assets to a member at below market value may amount to an unlawful return of capital (ss.845–847) or it may involve a breach of the directors' general duties. It may also contravene insolvency law.

5.2.3 Ordinary course of business

5–10 The principle of maintenance of capital does not apply to losses resulting from transactions in the ordinary course of business. Therefore there is nothing to prevent a shareholder selling an asset or buying an asset from a company for full consideration, a wholly arm's length transaction (*Ridge Securities Ltd v IRC*). This of course must be approved in most cases where the shareholder is also a director or an associate of a director or where the company shares are quoted, but

5.2.4 Dispositions out of profits available for distribution

The maintenance of capital principle is further reinforced by the provisions of ss.263–281 relating to distribution (which includes cash dividends), which are effectively restated in CA 2006 Pt 23 (ss.829–853). The effect of these is that, not only is a company prohibited from making a distribution to shareholders out of unrealised profits, but s.830 provides that a company may not make a distribution except out of profits "available for the purpose". These are defined as its accumulated, realised profits, so far as not previously utilised by distribution or capitalisation, less its accumulated, realised losses so far as not previously written off in a reduction or re-organisation of capital duly made. It should, however, also be appreciated that it is not sufficient simply to apply the statutory tests but the directors must have regard to the company's best interests generally. For example, if they paid a dividend in an imprudent manner without regard to the future solvency of the business or to its cash requirements, they could still be liable. Moreover liability may arise under the Insolvency Act 1986 s.238 (transactions at an undervalue) if at the time of payment the company was insolvent and there were no grounds for believing the dividend payment would benefit the company, and the company goes into liquidation. In addition, as we will see, an equity investor or the bank is likely to impose restrictions on the payment of dividends. **5-11**

Also because of the use of the word "accumulated" in relation to profits and losses, the profit for any particular year becomes irrelevant, but the profit and loss account is to be regarded as a continuous account. A company must therefore make good its previous losses before paying a dividend or alternatively apply to the court for a reduction of capital, and so cancel the loss. **5-12**

Dividend level

It would appear from the definition of available profits that a private company may pay a dividend equal to its entire net realised profits, even where there has occurred an unrealised loss. That may be so, but the company is still subject to the general principle that it may not, except in accordance with the proper procedures, reduce its capital. A public company may not make a distribution to the extent that the distribution would reduce its net assets (taking account of provisions expected to occur) below the aggregate of its called up capital, non-distributable reserves and net unrealised profits (s.831). However, a public company which is an "investment company" (as defined) may make a distribution out of its accumulated, realised revenue profits so far as not previously utilised by distribution by capitalisation, less **5-13** its accumulated revenue losses (whether realised or unrealised), so far as not previously written off in a reduction or re-organisation of capital duly made to the extent that the distribution does not reduce the value of its assets as stated in its accounts to less than one and a half times the amount of its liabilities (s.832). Profits are recognised as realised only when realised in the form of cash or other assets the ultimate cash realisation of which can be assessed with reasonable certainty.

5–14 Where a company distributes a non-cash asset to shareholders and the amount at which that asset was stated in the company's accounts included an unrealised profit, that profit is to be treated as a realised profit for the purposes of determining the validity of the distribution (s.846). This provision is often used to enable the subsidiary to sell an asset to its parent company at its book value (for example its acquisition cost) even though its market value is higher, provided also that the maintenance of capital principle is not thereby infringed. CA 2006 ss.845–846 specifically permit companies with distributable profits to transfer assets at book value (despite its market value being higher) without this being treated as a distribution. It is thought that a sale of an asset to a member at an undervalue amounts to a "distribution" to the extent of the undervalue (*Aveling Barford Ltd v Perion Ltd*). It is arguable that the transfer of the asset may also lawfully be achieved by the subsidiary declaring a dividend in an amount equal to the book value to be satisfied by a distribution in specie of the assets. This principle relies upon s.836, which provides that the amount of a distribution, which may lawfully be made, is to be determined by reference to the amounts at which various items are stated in the company's accounts, that is, their book value.

Distribution defined

5–15 A "distribution" is defined as "every description of distribution of the company's assets to its members whether in cash or otherwise" (s.829(1)). "Distribution" however does not include:

- an issue of bonus shares;
- the redemption or purchase of any of the company's own shares out of capital or out of unrealised profits (in accordance with Pt 18 Chs 3, 4 or 5);
- the reduction of share capital in one of the ways permitted; and
- the distribution of assets on winding-up.

There are a number of ways in which the assets of a company are diminished and the assets of the shareholder increased (either in amount or value) which do not fit comfortably within this definition and which, nevertheless, appear to fall within s.829. For example, a loan agreement between a subsidiary and its parent, pursuant to which the subsidiary is obliged to make interest payments to the parent, which to the knowledge of both parties, substantially exceed the market rate (*Ridge Securities Ltd v IRC*). Is the assumption by the subsidiary of the liability to make the payment on entering into the agreement a distribution or is each interest payment (to the extent that it exceeds market rate) a distribution? It is thought, assuming the loan to be intra vires, that payment of interest cannot be a distribution as it is the discharge of a lawful liability; the assumption of the initial liability must be the distribution and the measure must be the resulting reduction in the net asset value of the subsidiary. The same applies to a guarantee entered into by a subsidiary in favour of its parent, in circumstances in which it is almost bound to be called (*Rolled Steel Products (Holdings) Ltd v British Steel Corp* [1984] B.C.L.C. 466, which was described as a gratuitous disposition of the company's property). In *Aveling Barford Ltd v Perion Ltd* [1989] B.C.L.C. 626 it was held that a sale at an undervalue from one company to a sister company could be a distribution. The gratuity element, therefore, need not flow directly to the members.

Moreover, what of the situation where the parent has the ability to diminish the subsidiary's assets without any intervention by the subsidiary? Suppose the parent has granted its subsidiary some revocable licence which is vital to the subsidiary's business (for example, intellectual property rights or the use of advantageously situated premises). The revocation of the licence might cause a disastrous diminution in the value of the subsidiary's net assets, including goodwill, and a corresponding increase in the parent's net assets. Is that a distribution? If the subsidiary has colluded in a transaction benefiting the parent, there should be little difficulty in finding an act by the subsidiary which amounts to a distribution. But if that is not the case, then is there a distribution? Probably not as the subsidiary itself has done nothing.   **5–16**

The provisions of ss.829–853 are without prejudice to any enactment or rule of law, such as the maintenance of capital principle, restricting a company's ability lawfully to make a distribution (s.851). Consequently, if annual accounts are drawn up showing profits available for distribution and trading conditions then deteriorate so that the profit is lost, it is not lawful to pay a dividend merely because s.836 provides for the amount of a distribution which may be made to be determined by reference to the company's accounts. If by virtue of the subsequent adverse trading, the dividend would come out of capital, it is ultra vires and void and on general principles can be recovered from the recipient shareholder and from anyone else into whose hand it subsequently comes, whether or not he/she is aware of the legality (s.847(1), (2)). If a dividend is paid in contravention of ss.829–853 but does not breach any other rule of law, e.g. a dividend paid out of revenue profits of a year without making good the losses of previous years (see *Ammonia Soda Company Ltd v Chamberlain* [1918] 1 Ch. 266), its value (or equivalent value) can only be recovered from the recipient shareholder if he knows, or has reasonable grounds to believe that he is being paid unlawfully (s.847(1), (2)). The directors will face a liability for breaching the statutory code.   **5–17**

5–18 Section 836 provides that distributions shall be determined by reference to the company's accounts. The relevant accounts will normally be the last audited annual accounts. However, subsequent interim accounts may be used instead if the proposed distribution would contravene the relevant section if the last annual accounts were used. If the interim accounts are used, it must be possible to make a reasonable judgement from them as to the amount of the following items: profits, losses, assets, liabilities, provisions, share capital and reserves (s.839(1)). Special rules apply to public companies.

Where a company makes a gratuitous disposition to its shareholders at a time when its debts equal or exceed its assets, it makes the disposition out of share capital and the result would be, if a disposition were valid, to render the company insolvent or more insolvent than it already was. It is not surprising therefore that such a disposition is invalid. It is ultra vires in the sense of unlawful (that it is not permitted by company law) and the company can recover property transferred according to the rules of recoverability discussed above. Lindley L.J. in *George Newman & Co, Re* [1895] 1 Ch. 674 said:

> "To make presents out of profits is one thing but to make them out of capital or out of money borrowed by the company is a very different matter. Such money cannot be lawfully divided amongst the shareholders themselves."

5.2.5 Prohibition on giving of financial assistance

5–19 Financial assistance has its origins in the integrity and preservation of a company's assets for the protection of its creditors and is therefore a direct relative of the maintenance of capital principle. It is also designed to keep separate the assets and liabilities (and therefore the creditors) of the company (or its subsidiaries) on the one hand and its shareholders or would-be shareholders on the other so that the capital meant to be used to meet the creditors of the company is not simply used to assist dealings in its shares. There is no definition of financial assistance but CA 2006 s.677(1) (formerly CA 1985 s.152(1)) sets out a number of different heads of financial assistance:

- by way of gift;
- by way of guarantee, security or indemnity, other than with regard to the indemnifiers own neglect or default, or by way of release or waiver;
- by way of loan or any other agreement whereby any of the obligations of the person giving the assistance are to be fulfilled when any obligation of another party remains unfulfilled, or by way of the novation or the assignment of rights under a loan or such other agreement;
- any other financial assistance given by a company whereby its net assets are reduced to a material extent or it has no net assets.

Maintenance of capital

On October 1, 2008, CA 1985 ss.151 to 153 (financial assistance provisions) and ss.155 to 188 (whitewash procedure) were repealed in so far as they applied to the giving of financial assistance by a private company for the purpose of the acquisition of shares in itself or another private company. The repeal related to financial assistance given on or after October 1, 2008. **5–20**

The financial assistance provisions on public companies remain.

In a buy-out the acquisition finance lenders will look to the target group's assets for security to support Newco's borrowings as Newco will be a shell company with no assets of its own (other than the shares in the target company). Usually, the lenders will require a guarantee by the target company (and members of the target group) of Newco's borrowings supported by security over some or all of the target company's or relevant group member's assets. In addition, Newco's borrowings are often serviced by way of upstreaming monies from the target group. If this is done by loan as opposed to financial assistance it will also constitute financial assistance. Further, the payment of transaction costs, the repayment of existing indebtedness or the giving of releases or group re-organisations in connection with a buy-out can also be financial assistance. Traditionally these were whitewashed. **5–21**

Even though there has been a partial prohibition of financial assistance, directors should be aware of the following. **5–22**

- *Directors' duties* Duties under CA 2006 should clearly be considered. A good practice is for the directors to record in the board minutes their reasons for deciding that the company should give financial assistance and a ratifying shareholders resolution should be obtained.
- *Capacity* A check should be made of the company's articles to ensure the company has the relevant authorities. If a company has been incorporated (from July 21, 1948 to December 2, 1981) with Table A articles as provided in the Companies Act 1948, art.10 will prohibit the giving of financial assistance and this should be changed.
- *Insolvency issues* If a company is on the verge of insolvency and it is not in the creditors' interests then the directors will be in breach of their duties to the company in giving financial assistance.
- *Unlawful reduction of capital* The directors will still need to consider, and then decide and minute whether the giving of financial assistance reduces the company's net assets. For example, where a company gives a guarantee and security for the acquisition debt, the directors need to consider whether a provision should be made in the accounts (in other words, a reduction of net assets) because the guarantee or security is likely to be called.

5–23 The granting of security or guarantee by members of the target group, which constitutes financial assistance, will be a condition precedent to the advancing of the financing to complete the buy-out. Following the buy-out, the boards are likely to be reconstituted and it therefore must be considered as to who is to approve the finance documents to be entered into by the target group companies. The lenders will require this approval immediately before closing but if the directors are not to be directors after closing they will be reluctant to do so. The answer is for the target group companies to be reconstituted prior to closing. The seller may be reluctant because of a fear of losing control. However as owner of the target company until closing, it can always appoint and remove directors if necessary. In practice this reconstitution takes place on the same day as closing.

5–24 Best practice dictates that a shareholder resolution be obtained to approve the giving of financial assistance. As the giving of security and guarantees are a condition precedent, the seller will be the legal shareholder at the time, and so the seller will be required to pass the appropriate resolutions. Sellers are often reluctant to do so but usually agree if Newco agrees to produce the documents and unwind the amendments if the deal does not proceed.

5.2.6 Insolvency

5–25 If a company makes a gift or contribution to its shareholders at a time when it is insolvent, the liquidator or administrator is likely to seek to recover the cash paid away or assets transferred by bringing an action under the Insolvency Act 1986 s.238 and either the liquidator, the administrator or a creditor may be able to bring about such recovery under s.423 of that Act. Section 238 provides that where a company makes a gift or enters into a transaction at an undervalue (and the gift or transaction does not fall within an exemption for genuine business transactions carried out in good faith in the reasonable belief that the transaction will benefit the company) within two years before the onset of insolvency or after the presentation of a petition for an administration order and (in the case of the two-yearly time limit) at a time when the company is unable to pay its debts or becomes so in consequence of the gift or the transaction, the gift or transaction is voidable and, upon an application by the liquidator or administrator, the court may make an order avoiding it and may make whatever further order it thinks fit for the restoration of the position to what it would otherwise have been. Section 423 provides that, where inter alia, a company makes a gift or enters into a transaction at an undervalue, the courts can, on the application of the liquidator or administrator, or (with leave of the court) the victim of the transaction (for example a creditor), make such order as it thinks fit for restoring the position to what it would otherwise have been, if the court is satisfied that the gift or transaction was entered into by the company for the purpose of defeating creditors. Unlike the case under s.238, it is not necessary for s.423 that the company is insolvent at the time or became insolvent as a consequence of the transaction. It is hoped that where the purchase of assets has been negotiated on an arm's length basis that the court would not regard the purchase as being at an undervalue, even if it is subsequently realised (perhaps with the benefit of hindsight) that the price was significantly lower than the market price.

5.2.7 Corporate capacity

A gratuitous disposition by a company, whether to its shareholders or to third parties, which is outside the company's objects and powers is ultra vires in the sense of beyond its corporate capacity. The avoidance of such dispositions and the invalidation of transactions not entered into on commercial terms or otherwise not intended to benefit the company was the most common use of the ultra vires doctrine in its last years. A gratuitous disposition which would otherwise be outside the company's objects and powers is not brought within them merely by being dressed up as something within those objects and powers, e.g. as remuneration or interest (*Halt Garage, Re; Ridge Securities v IRC*). To be intra vires a gratuitous disposition which is within an express object within the memorandum cannot be ultra vires regardless of the purpose for which it is effect (*Horsley & Weight Ltd, Re* [1982] Ch. 442). Furthermore, where a power in the memorandum to make a gratuitous disposition is as a matter of express or implied construction merely incidental to the attainment of the company's main objects, an exercise of the power for an unauthorised purpose will usually be intra vires, because it is capable of being performed as reasonably incidental to the attainment of authorised purposes. The express or implied limitation will be regarded as imposing a limit on the authority of the directors, but not on the company's corporate capacity (*Charterbridge Corp v Lloyds Bank Ltd* [1970] Ch. 62). Consequently, a gratuitous disposition to shareholders which is within the company's corporate capacity but is decided upon by the directors for a purpose not authorised by the memorandum will be intra vires if unanimously consented to by the shareholders, unless it involves a fraud on the company's creditors (usually because the company is insolvent at the time or becomes so as a result of the gratuitous disposition). Subject to any provision in the articles, this will also be the case if such gratuitous disposition is subsequently ratified by an ordinary resolution of the general meeting unless this involves a fraud on the minority shareholders or on the creditors. **5–26**

The practical importance of ultra vires diminished once CA 2006 became fully implemented. New companies now have unrestricted objects and powers unless their articles specifically choose to limit them. It is anticipated that most new companies will not do so, and that many existing companies may opt for unrestricted objects by changing their constitutions.

A gratuitous disposition to shareholders which is beyond the company's corporate capacity is void and therefore not binding on the company (not being the company's act) and being incapable of conferring rights on a third party. However, **5–27**

Share Capital

CA 2006 s.39 provides that the validity of an act done by a company may not be questioned on the grounds of lack of capacity by reason of anything in the company's constitution. The effect of this is that neither the company nor the other party to a transaction can avoid liability on the ground that the company lacked capacity to enter into it. This is without prejudice to the members' rights to bring proceedings to restrain an act beyond the company's corporate capacity in which the company is not yet bound or to the directors' duty to observe the limitations in the constitution. Nor will s.39 prevent a company from recovering property or being compensated for any profit forgone or loss incurred where a director of the company or its holding company or any person connected or companies associated with him is a party to a transaction with the company and the board of directors exceed any limitation on the company's corporate capacity or their powers as directors under the company's constitution (CA 2006 s.195). Where the transaction is entered into not by the board but by an agent or representative of the company CA 2006 s.195 will apply on the basis that the board have exceeded their authority by delegating such power to the agent. The transaction is voidable unless restitution of any money or asset is no longer possible, the company is indemnified for any loss or damage, third-party rights have been acquired for value and without notice of the limitation being breached, or the transaction is ratified in general meeting by ordinary resolution (if the directors have exceeded their powers) or special resolution (if the directors have exceeded the company's corporate capacity) or otherwise as appropriate. Whether a director who has entered into the transaction can be relieved by special resolution will depend on whether an improper advantage has been obtained at the expense of the company. If this is the case any attempt to give relief by shareholders' resolution (unless it is unanimous) will be invalid as constituting a fraud on the minority. Whether or not the transaction is avoided, the director who is a party to the transaction or the connected person or associated company and any director who authorised the transaction is liable to account to the company for any gain made or loss or damage incurred as a result of the transaction. Consequently, any property which is the subject matter of a gratuitous disposition by a company to any shareholder who is a director, relative of a director or a company controlled by a director can be recovered unless one of the exceptions applies, or the company can be compensated for any profit forgone or loss incurred.

5–28 The validity of an act which is ultra vires in the sense of unlawful, e.g. a return of capital to shareholders, a distribution out of unrealised profits or the giving of financial assistance is not affected by CA 1985 s.39. It is and remains wholly void with the consequences, e.g. as to recoverability, discussed above.

5.2.8 Directors' fiduciary duties

5–29 It is the duty of the directors to observe not only the limits of the company's corporate capacity but also such further limits placed on their powers by the

Maintenance of capital

articles, e.g. that they should only bind the company to gratuitous transactions which are incidental to and benefit the company's main business. It applies in particular, but is not confined, to gratuitous dispositions by shareholders. Within the limits of such power the directors must act in the best interests of the company or, from October 1, 2007, in a way that in their opinion promotes the success of the company for the benefit of its members as a whole. Their duties in this respect are owed to the company and not to individual shareholders or creditors. If they are guilty of impropriety, for example paying a dividend out of capital or in selling the company's assets at an undervalue (*Pavlides v Jensen* [1956] Ch. 565) the company can recover from them any profit forgone or loss incurred by the company resulting from the impropriety or negligence. The company's right to such compensation in the case of acts outside the directors' powers or the company's corporate capacity is preserved by s.195(4). A director will be liable to account to the company for any gain made directly or indirectly from it, and to indemnify the company for any loss or damage resulting from the transaction.

An act which is either ultra vires the company in the sense of beyond its corporate capacity or intra vires the company but beyond the powers of the directors can be validly authorised or ratified by the company, which can at the same time (though is not bound to) relieve the directors of the personal liability they would otherwise incur. Authority or ratification and relief from liability would generally be granted by an ordinary resolution of the company in general meetings. But in the case of an act which is ultra vires, ratification must be by special resolution, which in itself does not affect the liability of the directors. However, if the breach of duty involves a fraud on minority shareholders, e.g. directors who are also controlling shareholders making a gift to themselves out of the company's assets, the passing of a resolution in a general meeting absolving them from liability which is procured by their votes is of no effect (unless presumably, unanimous) and therefore they should abstain from voting. Furthermore, the authority or ratification of the general meeting will be of no effect if the company has lost its profits and its share capital, so that it is dealing either with its loan capital or is actually insolvent, or even if the company is of doubtful solvency. **5–30**

Apart from the right to redress from the delinquent directors, the company has alternative remedies in the case of transactions by the directors which involve a breach of their duties. Before the transaction is carried out, but at the time when it is threatened, the company can seek an injunction to restrain it. After a transaction is carried out, it is voidable (but not void) and so can be adopted or avoided by the company.

5.3 Shareholders

The word "shareholder" is not defined in CA 2006. The legislation refers to "members". Section 112 of the Act defines a member of a company as a person **5–31**

Share Capital

who agrees to become a member and whose name is registered in the company's register of members. The importance therefore of physically entering the details of any person in the register cannot be emphasised enough.

5.3.1 Register of members

5–32 Detailed rules with regard to the register of members are set out in CA 2006 s.113. The information to be entered on the register of a company having a share capital is:

- the names and addresses of the member;
- the date on which each person was registered as a member;
- the date at which any person ceased to be a member;
- a statement of the shares held by each member, distinguishing each share by its number (so long as the share has a number) and by its class (so long as the company has more than one class);
- the amount paid or agreed to be considered as paid on the shares of each member.

The date on which a company's register is made up can be of critical importance if, for any reason, it is necessary to show that a particular person was a shareholder (as opposed to being the beneficial owner of a share) on a certain date.

5.3.2 Agreement to become a member

5–33 Agreement to become a member is essential to membership (CA 2006 s.112) though the agreement need not take any specific form unless prescribed by the articles, which is rarely the case. Consent can be agreed in various ways such as agreement to an allotment of shares by the company, agreement to the transfer of shares by an existing member (having been presented by the transferee to the company for registration), or by conduct where a shareholder acts in such a way to indicate ownership of the shares etc.

5.3.3 Who can be a member?

5–34 A company may hold shares in another company. However, a company cannot subscribe for or purchase its own shares and therefore cannot become a member of itself subject to the following exceptions:

- the acquisition by the company of its own fully paid shares other than for valuable consideration;

Shareholders

- the redemption or purchase of shares;
- (for certain public companies only) holding up to ten per cent of the issued share capital of the company in treasury;
- the purchase of shares in pursuance of a court order;
- the forfeiture of shares, or the acceptance of shares surrendered in pursuance of the articles, for failure to pay any sum payable in respect of the shares.

In most such cases, the shares are immediately cancelled.

A bankrupt may continue to be a shareholder even once the beneficial interest in his/her shares has vested in the trustee in bankruptcy, unless the articles provide otherwise. He/she must however vote as directed by the trustee in the same way as any shareholder holding the shares as beneficial owner and it will often be the trustee in bankruptcy who is entitled to the dividends. Since agreement is required of a person before he/she becomes a member of a company, a personal representative or trustee in bankruptcy cannot automatically become a member when the beneficial interest in shares vests in him/her. **5–35**

However it is not necessary for a personal representative to become a member since a transfer shall be valid as if he/she was a member at the time it is executed. The personal representative can transfer the shares therefore without ever being registered him/herself. This is an advantage for him/her since, if he/she became a member, he/she would be liable personally for any calls on the shares, whereas if he/she is not registered as a member he/she will only be liable to the extent of the deceased's assets in his/her hands. Similarly, the trustee in bankruptcy has a statutory power to transfer the bankrupt's shares pursuant to the Insolvency Act 1986 s.314 and Sch.5 without first becoming registered as a member and so avoiding personal calls.

Regulations 30 and 31 of Table A 1985 provide, if adopted, that both personal representatives and trustees in bankruptcy are entitled to all rights, including dividends, of a shareholder even if they are not registered as such, with the exception of the right to attend or vote at any meeting of the company or class of shares. Regulation 38, however, provides that they must be notified of such meetings once they have provided the company with an address. **5–36**

A partnership may be registered as a member under its partnership name. Persons who lack contractual capacity may become shareholders with full rights subject to the general rules of contract. Persons under 18, for example, may become members unless the articles specifically prevent it. However, it is not wise to have shares registered in the name of minors, particularly if a sale is contemplated. Trusts (with adult or corporate trustees) should be used.

5.4 Types of shares

5–37 A company can create classes of shares with differing rights, such as preference shares, deferred shares, redeemable shares and non-voting shares. There is no limit to the number of different classes that can be created.

5.4.1 Ordinary shares

5–38 A company will always have ordinary shares. These are sometimes known as "equity shares". CA 2006 s.548 defines "equity share capital" as:

> "in relation to a company its issued capital excluding any part of that capital which, neither as respects dividends nor as respects capital, carries any right to participate beyond a specified amount in a distribution."

Any other classes of shares in a company, e.g. preference shares or deferred shares will always be in contrast to the rights attaching to ordinary shares.

The rights attaching to the ordinary shares are as determined in the articles of association. However it is usual that ordinary shareholders will receive dividends, though after preference shareholders (if any). It is also to be expected that a full right to vote will be granted to ordinary shareholders. But despite that, almost any number of variations on the ordinary shares can be made by the articles. It is possible for a company to have more than one class of ordinary shares. Therefore you may have some ordinary shares of nominal value £1 and others of 50p, the shares ranking pari passu for all purposes. Or it may have shares which are equivalent regarding dividends and payment of capital but have different voting rights. So for example, an "A" ordinary share may have two votes per share and a "B" ordinary share may have no voting rights at all. In a typical venture capital investment, the management would hold the ordinary shares, which would attract one vote per share but which would only receive dividends or provide a return on capital after those received by the investors. Set out in para.5–39 is the standard clause in the articles regarding the rights attaching to the ordinary shares to be held by the managers.

5–39 The ordinary shares shall entitle the holders of them to the following rights:

    (1)   As regards dividend:

After making all necessary provisions for payment in any financial year of the preference dividend and the preferred dividend (including arrears [*NB: defined as arrears of dividend payments and any interest on them*] of each of the same in respect of any period) and for redemption of the preference shares, the company shall apply any profits which the directors resolve thereafter to distribute in any such year in the following order and priority:

[(a) first, in paying to the holders of the ordinary shares pari passu a non-cumulative dividend at the same rate per share as the amount of the preferred dividend (excluding any arrears of the same) paid in the same year;] and
(b) secondly in paying any balance of such profits to the holders of the preferred ordinary shares, and the ordinary shares pari passu and pro rata to the number of such shares held by each of them;

(Management sometimes request a "catch-up" dividend in priority to any additional dividends paid to preferred ordinary shareholders and ordinary shareholders pro rata to their holdings, i.e. the right to receive a dividend per ordinary share equating to the return received by the investor on its share having the same subscription value. Para.(a) is an example of such a catch-up dividend.)

(2) As regards capital:

On a return of assets on a liquidation, reduction of capital or otherwise, the holders of the ordinary shares shall, subject to the rights of the holders of the preference shares and the preferred ordinary shares, be entitled (in proportion to the number of ordinary shares held by each of them) to be paid out of the surplus assets of the company remaining after payment of its liabilities an amount equal to the subscription price for the ordinary shares together with a sum equal to any arrears on accruals of unpaid dividends on them; thereafter the ordinary shares shall rank pari passu in all respects with the preferred ordinary shares.

(3) As regards voting in general meetings:

The holders of the ordinary shares shall be entitled to receive notice of and to attend and vote at general meetings of the company; on a show of hands every holder of ordinary shares who (being an individual) is present in person or by proxy or (being a corporation) is present by a duly authorised representative or by proxy shall have one vote and on a poll every holder of ordinary shares so present shall have one vote for each ordinary share held by him.

5.4.2 Preferred ordinary shares

These shares are likely to be the shares issued to the investors. Again the rights attaching to the preferred ordinary shares are as determined in the articles of association. However because this is the equity held by the investors, they are likely to be preferred regarding dividends and a return of capital to the ordinary shares but to rank after the preference shares which will provide the bulk of the

5–40

Share Capital

investors' investment being made, although it is quite usual nowadays to see this bulk element in the form of loan notes, which are debt and not part of the share capital at all. The preferred ordinary shares will probably attract only one vote per share though they are likely to be given a number of class rights in order to protect the investment (see Ch.10). These shares are in fact just as likely to be known as "A" ordinary shares or something else. The only purpose is to distinguish them from management's shares and the rights attached to those shares. An investor's equity shares usually have the following rights:

- priority over other ordinary shares possibly by both a fixed dividend and a participating dividend linked to profits;
- dividends pari passu with other ordinary shares after these shares have received the same rate of dividend as the "preferred ordinary shares" sometimes, but not always, after a catch up dividend;
- priority over other ordinary shares on a return of capital on a winding-up to the subscription price and any arrears or accrual of unpaid dividend;
- shares to rank pari passu in a distribution of surplus assets on a winding-up after other ordinary shares have received the same repayment of capital as the preferred ordinary shares;
- possibly a conversion on a one for one basis into ordinary shares at the option of the holder of the preferred ordinary shares (this is an administrative convenience to simplify matters on a sale or flotation of the company);
- one vote per share with veto on specified matters though it is not uncommon to see weighted voting rights attached to the preferred ordinary shares which enhance their vote (say to 75 per cent of the total) to give them control in certain circumstances (e.g. if a dividend is late). This enhancement can have tax and accounting implications for the investors, especially if there is only one investor, or if the investors are connected.

5–41 The dividends payable on the preferred ordinary shares will be determined by the return required, by the amount of the investment being made and the structuring required to achieve this. However it is not uncommon for the preferred ordinary shares to provide a participating dividend determined as a percentage of the net profits (often with an offset of the fixed dividend on the class so that in effect the company pays the higher and not both). There is no universal approach. It all depends on how the venture capitalist has constructed his investment model to deliver his target internal rate of return. Sometimes dividends may accrue from the date of issue but at other times they may only become payable at the end of a period, or if there has not been a sale or flotation which would otherwise have returned capital to the investor. It is essential to the investor that he gets his return and he will structure it in such a way as to ensure this. For this reason, the rate often increases over time to increase the pressure for an exit.

The participating dividend is usually payable by reference to the profit as shown in the audited consolidated accounts for the relevant financial year of the company and is expressed to be payable by a pre-specified date after the relevant year end. Consideration should be given as to what should happen in the case of a sale or flotation occurring in the course of any financial year. An accrual based on management accounts is the usual solution.

In order to ensure that the parent company is able to satisfy its dividend schedule, the investors will wish to ensure that each of the subsidiaries distribute all its profits available for distribution. **5–42**

> "The company shall take all lawful steps available to it to procure that each of its subsidiaries which has profits available for distribution shall from time to time declare and pay to the company such dividends as are necessary to permit lawful and prompt payment by the company of the preference dividend, the preferred ordinary dividend and the participating dividend [and to ensure that the company is able to redeem the preference shares (and, if applicable, the preferred ordinary shares) in each case in accordance with these articles], such steps to include (without limitation), the preparation of such interim or initial accounts (complying with ss.838 and 839 of the Act) of the company and each of its subsidiaries by reference to which profits available for distribution might fall to be calculated".

The investors will wish also to ensure that the dividends will be paid on the dates due without the need for a recommendation of the directors. If not paid it will then become a debt due and payable in priority to any other dividend. (This is a mixed blessing in that if payment is not made (probably because the company is having a difficult time) as a debt of the company it will be shown in the balance sheet, which may jeopardise the company even further in the eyes of customers or suppliers.) **5–43**

5.4.3 Preference shares

The Companies Acts contain no definition of preference shares but the term is generally used to denote those shares which confer on their holders the right to receive dividends and/or to participate in a return of capital in priority to the holders of ordinary shares. Conventional preference shares are essentially fixed income producing shares with no capital growth prospects. The dividend entitlement is fixed either as a percentage of the amount paid upon the share or a sum of money per share. Voting rights are usually limited, both in terms of transactions or events (for example a winding-up) and circumstances (for example when preference dividends which are cumulative are in arrears). The name given to a class of preference share will suggest some of the more important rights attached to a share, for example a "cumulative convertible redeemable preference share". **5–44**

Preference shares are often used in private equity transactions as a form of "soft loan" to produce a more acceptable gearing ratio and so encourage external lending to the investee company. Unlike loan interest, dividends may only be paid if there are sufficient distributable reserves available. If not, the investor's return rolls up in the form of cumulative dividends until such time as circumstances permit them to be paid. In contract missed interest or capital repayments relating to loans will usually constitute an "event of default" with the result that even if the loan is not called in by the lender there may be implications for other creditors of the company who hold the benefit of cross default claims and whose indebtedness may therefore be accelerated.

5–45 The question of whether a company should issue preference shares or take loan finance is often discussed at length. Provision in the form of loan finance, particularly if secured but even if not is safer for a financier than subscription for preference shares because the loan agreement will contain a number of events of default which will allow him to prevent further drawdowns of his loan. In addition if the company goes into liquidation, a provider of loan finance will rank as an unsecured creditor but will still rank ahead of a holder of preference shares who will only receive a dividend if and when all creditors of the company have been paid. If preference shares are used the company's balance sheet will as a result be less highly geared and appear more solid to potential customers and suppliers.

In addition the use of preference shares may enable the management team to have a disproportionately large percentage of the voting capital when compared to the amount of money being invested by the management, and will also ensure that the ordinary shares subscribed by management and the institutional investors have the same price. This provides an opportunity for the management team to earn a similarly disproportionate percentage of any exit proceeds if the company is sold or floated. This is attractive to the managers and acts as an incentive to maximise the return to the venture capitalist.

5–46 There are a number of additional advantages, particularly to management, in issuing preference shares:

- dividends may only be paid if out of available profits. This gives preference shares more flexibility, though there will be a provision that if profits are available they will be used to pay the preference dividend, and so preventing management from building up reserves;
- preference shares will not adversely affect the capital gearing ratio, the prime benefit of which is the ability to borrow more. This however may not be possible if the company is paying high servicing costs on its shares and borrowings.

5–47 Most investors are keen to ensure that the investee company does not become a subsidiary for accounting and is thereby carried on their balance sheet. This may be of relevance both to the issuing company and to the investor.

Types of shares

Preference shares in the equity share capital?

If preference shares have uncapped dividend or return of capital rights, however **5–48** remote, as to either dividends or capital, then they will be "equity share capital" as defined in the CA 1985 s.744. In addition, any such type of preference shares will be treated as "equity securities" for pre-emption purposes and so be included within the statutory pre-emption procedure on the issue of new shares. It does not matter that the shares may be convertible into ordinary shares, which does not necessarily make them part of the equity share capital.

However, if the preference shares participate in a winding-up as if they are ordinary shares this may make them part of the equity share capital. The problem can be avoided by putting a cap on the liquidation entitlement of the shares. A number of other consequences are:

- Should the issuer wish to take advantage of the merger relief provisions of CA 2006 s.612 the shares issued on a company acquisition must be equity share capital.
- If the company is subject to the City Code on Takeover and Mergers ("the Code"), the Code will apply to the offer for preference shares. Moreover, if an offer is made for the company's ordinary shares a comparable offer will have to be made for the preference shares (the Code r.14).

Cumulative shares

Where preference shares carry a fixed preferential dividend it is important to **5–49** know whether or not it is intended to be cumulative, i.e. if a dividend is not paid in that year it accumulates until it is paid by that body corporate. These are shares of which the right to a dividend if not paid in one year due to lack of profits in that year, accumulates until profits are sufficient. The accumulated dividends must then be paid in priority to any distribution to other shareholders. The preference shares are presumed to be cumulative (*Henry v Great Northern Railway Co* (1857) 44 E.R. 858). However, the presumption can be rebutted in the articles where for example the preference shareholders are "entitled out of the net profits of each year to a preferential dividend" (*Staples v Eastman Photographic Materials Co* [1896] 2 Ch. 303). Below is a typical article setting out the dividend obligations:

> "The profits of the company available for distribution shall be applied first in paying to the holders of the preference shares as a class prior to any dividend being paid in respect of any shares of any other class a fixed cumulative dividend in cash (the 'preference dividend') of an amount equal to [ ] per cent of the aggregate amount paid up or credited as paid up on the preference shares for the time being in issue."

Share Capital

5–50 A company can only pay a distribution if it has sufficient profits available for distribution (CA 2006 s.830), determined by reference to the accounts of the company. If a company pays more by way of dividend than can be justified by reference to the accounts, the company may have made an unlawful reduction of capital. If the preference shareholder knew or had reasonable grounds to believe that the payment was unlawful, then he may be liable to repay such part as was unlawful. In addition it may put the company in breach of financing agreements entered into by the company.

A dividend can become payable in a number of different ways which will be dependent on the drafting:

- automatically on pre-determined dates in each year, provided that the company has profits available for distribution. The shareholder cannot sue therefore if the company has no profits available but the dividend, otherwise, will become a debt due to the shareholder on the date specified. The directors' discretion is removed;
- by the directors resolving to pay a preference dividend. However if the company fails to do so, the shareholder will normally have no recourse as no debt will be due;
- by resolution of the shareholders of the company. This is unusual as the preference shareholders will not wish the ordinary shareholders to have control over the payment of the dividend.

Winding-up

5–51 The rights attaching to the preference shares should make it clear that on a winding-up, the preference shareholders should receive arrears of dividend in preference to amounts due to the ordinary shareholders. The draftsmen should also take care to ensure that all arrears of dividend are paid. A preference shareholder may have no right to a dividend unless it has been declared. If a period of time elapses since the last dividend without a new declaration, the dividend available for the intervening period will not become due. Even if the articles provide for payment of arrears of preferential dividend due at the date of winding-up, arrears of undeclared dividend will not be paid on a winding-up (*Roberts and Cooper Ltd, Re* [1929] 2 Ch. 383). A number of commentators believe this to be wrong as it ignores the express intention of the articles. However, it is suggested that preference share rights should provide for the payment of arrears "whether declared or not".

Non-cumulative

5–52 These shares as the name suggests do not carry an accumulation right. If no dividend is distributed, then the lost dividend is not made up in subsequent years.

Therefore if the dividends are non-cumulative the right to any distribution is dependent upon the profit of a particular year. It is very rare for investors' preference shares to be non-cumulative.

Participating

Shares of this type carry the right to a dividend at a nominated rate (e.g. six per cent) together with a right to participate in a further distribution if there remains any surplus of profits after a dividend at a nominated rate (e.g. ten per cent) has been paid to ordinary shareholders. There is a presumption that preference shares are not participating, and therefore an express term must be included in the articles for this to be the case (*Will v United Lankat Plantations Co* [1914] A.C. 11). It is very rare for investors' preference shares to be participating. 5–53

Capital rights

Unless otherwise provided in the articles: 5–54

- the preference shareholders do not have a priority to other shareholders on a winding-up. For this reason, it is usual to provide that they do;
- a preference shareholder does not have a right to any surplus assets in a return of capital above the amount required to return to the preference shareholders;
- the preference shareholders are only entitled to receive the par value of their shares and not any premium element (*Driffield Gas Light Co, Re* [1898] 1 Ch. 451). As a result the articles should specify that the preference shareholders will receive the full issue price (i.e. nominal value plus premium).

One unresolved issue is whether the ordinary shareholders can manipulate matters to ensure the ordinary shareholders receive a maximum share of the assets in detriment to the preference shareholders. The ordinary shareholders may pay themselves a dividend equal to the distributable profits immediately prior to the liquidation and thereby prevent it being distributed to the preference shareholder. However this may give rise to a claim under CA 2006 s.994 as being "unfairly prejudicial" to a minority.

Preference shareholders may also have priority over other shares in relation to the return of capital in a winding-up or on a reduction of capital. The cases are to be reviewed independently of each other and no inference should be drawn that a priority in one of these areas gives a shareholder any priority in the other. In fact the opposite is true and if the terms of issue are silent on any point, whether it be 5–55 the right to dividends or to a return of capital or voting, then the presumption is that all the shareholders shall rank equally in that respect.

In *Scottish Insurance Companies Ltd v Wilsons and Clyde Coal Co Ltd* [1949] A.C. 462, it was held that where the terms of issue of a class of preference shares gave the holders an express right to have their capital repaid in priority to the ordinary shareholders in the winding-up or reduction of capital, there was no inherent or residual right for them to participate in the surplus assets remaining after the ordinary shareholders had also had their capital returned.

The importance of clearly stating the rights on the face of the articles cannot be exaggerated.

Voting rights

5–56 It is quite common for preference shares to have no voting rights at general meetings or to be given a vote on certain matters occurring for example if the preference dividend is in arrears. However voting rights will arise if the preference share rights are varied or removed. These rights will be exercisable at separate class meetings. In addition, preference shareholders are likely to have voting rights at general meetings:

- when the preference dividend is in arrears for more than a specified period;
- if redemption has failed to take place on the agreed dates;
- if a resolution is proposed to wind up the company.

Sometimes investors will seek votes on their preference shares if there is a breach of the investment agreement. It is thought that if this is the case the investment agreement should be filed at Companies House (CA 2006 s.26).

5–57 Set out below is an example of an article that provides holders of the preference shares with voting rights upon the happening of certain events.

As regards voting in general meetings:

(a) the holders of the preference shares shall be entitled to receive notice of, and to attend at, general meetings of the company but shall not in respect of their holdings of such shares be entitled to vote upon any resolution unless:

(i) there shall have been any arrears [*NB: defined as arrears of dividends*] for more than [two months] on the date of the notice convening the meeting; or

Types of shares

(ii) the advisors to the company may try to ensure that this will not trigger where the company is unable to pay a dividend because there are no profits available (*Bradford Investments Plc, Re* (1990) B.C.C. 740). The investors may resist this, as such an underperformance of the investment may be the very situation in which the preference votes (or the threat of them) are most useful.

(iii) the company, on any of the redemption dates under sub-para.[ ] below of this art.[ ], shall have failed or been unable to redeem all or any of the preference shares falling to be redeemed on any such redemption date; or

(iv) the resolution is one which directly or indirectly varies, modifies, alters or abrogates any of the rights, privileges, limitations or restrictions attaching to the preference shares [or preferred ordinary shares]; or

(v) the resolution is for the winding-up of the company, the reduction of share capital, the approval of the giving of financial assistance or the purchase by it of any of its shares; or

(vi) there shall have occurred a breach by the company [or any of the members or directors] of any of the provisions of these articles or the investment agreement provided that the holders of the preference shares shall cease in respect of their holding of such shares to be entitled to vote upon any resolution upon such breach being remedied to the satisfaction of a majority of the holders of the preference shares;

(b) when entitled to vote pursuant to sub-para.(i) above, every holder of preference shares who (being an individual) is present in person or by proxy or (being a corporation) is present by a duly authorised representative or by proxy, shall have one vote on a show of hands and on a poll every holder of preference shares so present shall have one vote for each preference share held by him.

Care should be taken in determining what voting rights should be provided on the right to vote being exercised. Perhaps one vote per share or perhaps the preference shareholders as a class should be able to cast votes equal to say 75 per cent of votes cast on a poll. This will enable investors to pass special resolutions and assist a swift reconstruction. However, it will obviously raise the problem of subsidiary status and consolidation which needs to be considered. Where the company is performing badly and such a "disaster clause" is being invoked it may be undesirable for the preference shareholder to have the company as a subsidiary undertaking. Care should also be taken by the draftsmen to ensure that the voting rights are removed once the matter giving rise to the voting rights has been corrected.

5–58

Redeemable shares

It is very common for preference shares to be redeemable. If a preference share is not redeemable, the issuing company can only remove the preference shares by

5–59

Share Capital

using one of the other procedures available under CA 2006 such as purchase of own shares or reduction of capital.

In addition, there are specific rules to deal with premiums payable on redemptions (CA 2006 s.687). If the premium represents an amount in excess of that which was paid on initial subscription, then excess "profit" must be funded out of distributable reserves. If the shares were issued at a premium, in addition to the nominal value, the investee company can redeem the premium out of the proceeds of the new issue up to an amount equal to whichever is the lesser of the aggregate of the premiums received by the company on the issue of the shares to be redeemed and the current amount of the company's share premium account. It is always possible to redeem the shares at any price wholly out of distributable profits.

5–60 Section 684 allows a company limited by shares or a company limited by guarantee and having a share capital, if authorised by its articles, to issue shares which are, or at the option of the company or the shareholder are liable to be, redeemed. They can be redeemed in one or more tranches over a period of time. It is not possible to issue redeemable shares unless there are other shares of the company which are not redeemable (s.684(4)). Redeemable shares may only be redeemed if they are fully paid. It is not clear whether the payment must be made in cash or can be paid in kind. To avoid difficulty the articles should say explicitly that payment should be paid in cash. This is in any event the better view of the section.

5–61 Subject to an exception in the case of private companies, the shares must be redeemed either out of distributable profits or out of the proceeds of a new issue of shares made for the purposes of redemption (s.687). Where any shares of the company are redeemed or purchased wholly out of the profits of the company, the amount by which the company's issued share capital is to be diminished on cancellation of the shares redeemed or purchased is transferred to a reserve which is called "the capital redemption reserve". No stamp duty is payable on the redemption. The cancellation will reduce the issued share capital but leave the authorised share capital as it was. The capital redemption reserve is non-distributable but may be applied for a capitalisation issue. If the company is a private company it may also make a payment out of capital to redeem shares if it is authorised to do so by its articles. Broadly, the procedure for use of capital (in CA 2006 ss.713 to 723) is as follows:

(1) As at a date not more than 90 days prior to the statutory declaration, the company must draw up a balance sheet (which need not be audited) showing assets, liabilities and distributable reserves (if any). In a group situation, the balance sheet is the individual balance sheet of the company planning the redemption and not the group balance sheet.

(2) The directors make a statutory declaration of solvency in the prescribed form (companies form no.173) and which identifies the shares to be

Types of shares

redeemed and the amount of capital to be used to redeem them—which is broadly the difference between the total redemption price and the distributable reserves. Reserves must be used up first. The amount of capital to be used is known as the "permissible capital payment".

(3) A report from the auditors is attached confirming the calculation of the permissible capital payment and stating that the auditors believe that the directors' view on solvency is reasonable.

(4) On the same day as (or within seven days after) the statutory declaration is made, a shareholders meeting is held to pass the necessary special resolution to approve the use of capital. A statutory written resolution may alternatively be used.

(5) Within seven days of the passing of the special resolution:

 (a) the resolution, statutory declaration and auditors' report are filed at Companies House;
 (b) an advertisement of the intention to use capital is issued in the London Gazette or Edinburgh Gazette as appropriate; and
 (c) a similar advertisement is published in a national newspaper.

(6) The company waits until 35 days have elapsed from the passing of the special resolution to allow for any objection to court.

(7) Assuming none, the redemption completes (if at all) between day 36 and day 49 after the special resolution is passed.

5–62 The importance of the Insolvency Act 1986 s.76 should not be overlooked. If capital is used, and the company goes into insolvent liquidation within 12 months of completion, then the shareholders whose shares were redeemed out of capital are liable to repay up to the amount paid to them out of capital (i.e. the permissible capital payment) or, if less, the amount required to pay the creditors and the costs of liquidation. It does not matter how unforeseeable was the event which caused the company to collapse or how reasonable the decision to use capital to fund the redemption was at the time. The shareholder has no defence. The directors who made the statutory declaration share the same liability but, in their case, there is a defence if the director can show that he or she had reasonable grounds for forming the opinions set out in the declaration.

The extra hassle of using capital for a redemption and the Insolvency Act risk mean that this is rarely seen in venture capital transactions.

5–63 If the company fails to meet its obligations to redeem the preference shares on the due dates the company will not be liable in damages for such failure (CA 2006 s.735). A court will not grant an order for specific performance if the company can show that it is unable to meet the cost from distributable profits. However:

Share Capital

- A preference shareholder may be able to obtain an injunction to prevent payment of dividends to shareholders until the preference shares have been redeemed.

- The court may force the company to redeem the preference shares once it has sufficient profits (*Holders Investment Trust Ltd, Re* [1971] 2 All E.R. 289).

In para.5–64 is a typical article for the redemption of preference shares.

5–64 As regards redemption, the preference shares shall, subject to the Act, be redeemed on and subject to the following terms and conditions:

(a) Subject to the right of the company to redeem the preference shares in accordance with sub-para.(c), the preference shares shall be redeemed by the company pro rata to the number of preference shares held by each holder of them in the numbers and on the dates given in the table below or, if earlier ([at the option of each holder of preference shares] and in respect or all the preference shares held by such holder then unredeemed and outstanding), on a sale or listing [or on a breach by the company [or any of the members or directors]] of any of the provisions of these articles or the investment agreement:

Redemption Date

   [ ]   [ ]

-----------------------------[ ]

----------------------------[ ]

----------------------------[ ]

(b) If the company shall fail or be unable to redeem all or any of the preference shares falling to be redeemed on any redemption date in accordance with sub-para.(a) of this art.[ ] then the rate of the preference dividend on all of the preference shares overdue for redemption shall be increased with effect from the date on which such preference shares were due for redemption from [ ] per cent to [ ] per cent until such preference shares are redeemed;

[(c) The company may [at any time] by giving not less than 14 days' notice in writing to the holders of preference shares redeem the whole or any part of the preference shares then outstanding pro rata to the number of shares held by each of them; [if part only of the preference shares are redeemed by the company pursuant to this sub-para.(c), the numbers of preference shares to be redeemed on any subsequent redemption dates under sub-para.(a) shall be adjusted by reducing the number of shares to be redeemed on each such redemption date by the aggregate number of shares redeemed in accordance with this sub-para.(c) divided by the number of such redemption dates;]

(d) On each redemption date, each registered holder of preference shares to be redeemed shall deliver to the company at its registered office the share certificates for such preference shares and thereupon the company shall pay to such holder (or in the case of joint holders, the holder whose name stands first in the register of members in respect of such shares) the amount due to him in respect of such redemption and shall issue a new share certificate in respect of any unredeemed preference shares comprised in the certificate delivered by him;

(e) As a condition of the redemption, there shall be paid on each preference share redeemed the subscription price for such share together with a sum equal to any arrears in respect of such preference share calculated down to the relevant redemption date and whether declared or not; and

(f) The receipt of the registered holder (or, in the case of joint holders, the holder whose name stands first in the register of members) for the time being of any preference shares being redeemed for the monies payable on redemption of such shares shall constitute an absolute discharge to the company in respect thereof.

Points on redemption

A number of points are worth making with regard to para.5–64. 5–65

- It is usual for the date or dates by which a redemption should be made (the long stop date) to be set out. This does not prevent earlier redemptions at the request of the investee company (subject to availability of distributable reserves) provided that such rights are specified in the articles. For administrative convenience there is usually a minimum number that can be redeemed at any one time.

- The amount payable on redemption must be clearly set out, and cannot be discretionary.

- It may be appropriate to accelerate the obligation of the investee company to redeem if an event of default occurs which would trigger the enfranchisement of the preference shares. As drafted above, a breach of the investment agreement or articles would potentially trigger a redemption. This is likely to be too wide and indeed very unfair. In fact, the value of such a provision will depend on the availability of distributable reserves which may be rare in such circumstances.

5.4.4 Deferred shares

5–66 These shares will only appear in the share structure if they have a role in the operation of the ratchet (see Ch.10). They will either be introduced at the outset of a transaction with a view to being converted into equity if the company does not achieve its targets, or they may result from the investors' shares converting into deferred shares as the management's shareholding ratchets up as a result of high achievement. Conversion is an alternative to redemption and may be more appropriate if there are insufficient distributable reserves available at the relevant time.

As would be expected because deferred shares are merely a device to achieve a reduction in capital, deferred shares will not have any dividend or voting rights and will only obtain a return on capital after meeting the repayment entitlement on all other share capital. They may be redeemable at a nominal amount which allows the balance sheet to be tidied up at a later stage without going through the buy-in procedure or a reduction of capital.

5.4.5 Employees' shares

5–67 Where a company makes special arrangements with shares held by its employees, this will not normally create a separate class of shares; employees will simply hold ordinary, preference or other shares like any other holders, but subject to added conditions which will apply to them as members of a scheme rather than holders of the particular share. Even so, the holder of the shares may be regarded as falling into a separate class for some purposes, e.g. a scheme of arrangement in CA 2006 ss.895–900.

In CA 2006 s.1166 provides a definition of the term "employees' share scheme". For the purposes of the Act, such a scheme is one for encouraging or enabling the holding of shares or debentures in the company by or for the benefit of:

- the bona fide employees or former employees of the company, its subsidiary or holding company, or a subsidiary of the company's holding company; or
- the spouses, civil partners, surviving spouses, surviving civil partners, or children or step-children under the age of 18 of such employees or former employees.

5–68 In various places, the CA 2006 makes special provision for shares held under an employees' share scheme. For example:

- Allotment of new equity shares pursuant to an employees' share scheme does not require shareholder approval under CA 2006 s.549.

Types of shares

- An allotment of equity shares for cash must only be made on a basis which gives pre-emption rights to existing equity shareholders but this rule does not apply to an allotment for the purposes of an employees' share scheme.

The CA 2006 does not address the position of employees' shares or an individual employee leaving the company's employment. Detailed provisions about an employee's participation in a share scheme or when he ceases to be an employee will be contained in the company's articles and under terms of the scheme or issue itself. Share purchase plans and share option plans can be an attractive method of providing incentives for and remunerating management and employees. There is a large number of potential schemes which can be adopted, some of which carry beneficial tax reliefs for participants. In the case of certain of these HMRC-approved schemes, the way in which a participant can be required to dispose of shares on ceasing to be an employee is limited by the applicable legislation. The various types of scheme are considered more fully in Ch.11. **5–69**

5.5 Sale preference

The investors will be keen to ensure that in the event of a sale at a time when the business has not achieved its targets it will receive its investment before any money is paid to the other shareholders. The following may appear: **5–70**

> In the event of a sale at an aggregate price which would result in the holders of the preference shares, and the preferred ordinary shares receiving less than the subscription price on such shares by way of sale and/or redemption and the amount of any arrears and accruals and other amounts due or owing thereon, the total of all and any cash received in respect of the shares that are the subject of the sale shall be reallocated between the holders of such shares so as to ensure the following order of application of the aggregate sale proceeds as follows:
>
> (a) first, in paying to the holders of any preference shares that are unredeemed and outstanding the subscription price on all such shares together with all arrears and accruals (whether deemed or not) and other amounts due or owing on them;
> (b) secondly, in paying to the holders of the preferred ordinary shares the subscription price on each of such shares together with all arrears and other amounts due or owing on them; and
> (c) thirdly, in paying the balance pro rata to the holders of the ordinary shares.

As is to be expected a clause such as this can be very contentious but it is unlikely that an investor will proceed without it.

5.6 Key points

- Basic principles of share capital are: **5–71**
  — Shares in a private company may be paid for in money or money's worth.

Share Capital

- — Where shares are issued at a premium, the amount of the premium must be transferred to the share premium account.
  - — A company can only make a distribution out of profits available for the purpose.
  - — Sophisticated attempts to deliver gifts to shareholders are likely to breach the maintenance of capital rules.
  - — Any gift or contribution to shareholders when the company is insolvent is likely to be recovered by a liquidator.
- A "member" of a company is someone whose name is registered in the company's register of members.
- An issue of preference shares as opposed to loan finance has a number of advantages for a company and for management in that:
  - — it may allow management to have a disproportionately large percentage of the voting capital;
  - — dividends will only be payable out of profits;
  - — preference shares will not affect the capital gearing ratio.
- If the shares are not to be cumulative then it must be expressly stated, otherwise they will be assumed to be so.
- If the shares are to be redeemed the following should be noted:
  - — the long-stop dates by which the redemptions should be made should be set out;
  - — in certain circumstances consider accelerating the redemptions;
  - — generally shares may be redeemed only out of distributable profits or proceeds of a fresh issue made for the purpose;
  - — a private company may use capital to redeem shares if its reserves are inadequate. Use of capital involves extra procedure and exposes the shareholder to a risk of clawback if the company goes into insolvent liquidation within 12 months.

Chapter 6

Managing the Transaction

6.1 Introduction

A typical investment may have four separate phases: 6–01

(1) the preparatory phase;

(2) the offer phase—until such time as agreement has been reached in principle on price and major commercial terms;

(3) the document phase—when the terms agreed in the offer phase are turned into a legally binding document;

(4) the completion phase.

6.2 The preparatory phase

The phase starts in the boardroom when the directors form the opinion that for 6–02 whatever reason the company requires an injection of capital. Bank finance may be too expensive or simply not available and the board determines to use the company's equity to secure financing. A committee of the board may be formed to pursue the introduction of private equity. It is at this stage that the board or the committee will consider whether they should seek preliminary advice from their lawyers, accountants and other professional advisors. The likelihood is that their first port of call will be to their accountants who will advise them on the preparation of a business plan and will guide them on the private equity institution most suited to their needs. In some cases the lawyer may be the first contact. He may be prepared to take on the corporate finance accountant role or alternatively he may prefer to introduce a corporate finance accountant to advise the board.

All too often however, the lawyer plays a very little part at this stage. If the lawyer does have a role it can often be in preparing the company for the investment. Before an investor makes an investment he will instruct a firm of accountants to prepare a due diligence report on the company, and his lawyers will be instructed to prepare a legal report. A legal audit at an early stage by the company's lawyers, therefore, may help to exclude any difficulties that otherwise may occur and become apparent at a later time.

In order to avoid delays in negotiating or completing the investment, the company should gather together, in advance, all material that will reasonably be expected to be required by an investor for the purposes of their due diligence, or by the company to ensure the correctness of the warranties that will be given. In Ch.7 there is a list of the kind of information that the solicitors to the investor are likely to request and an indication of the areas that accountants are likely to cover. If it has not previously been prepared it is likely to cause delay. Also, the information may disclose a problem which requires attention. Becoming aware of such a problem too late will only cause delay and embarrassment. The amount of time consumed in gathering such information should not be underestimated. In particular, the company should not only make enquiries of its employees but also of any professional advisors such as auditors, solicitors and pension consultants.

6.3 The offer phase

6–03 The business plan will have been submitted to a small number of private equity houses (or banks if the transaction can be achieved on debt alone) who will have met the management team and visited the business. They will have decided in principle whether they want to invest in the company and will have submitted an offer to the company or to the accountants or intermediary acting for them. The role of the intermediary is to elicit the best possible offer and he may return to the investor on several occasions to improve on their terms.

It is important at this stage that the board and their advisors determine the fundamental requirements, other than cost, that they are setting out to achieve and lay down the parameters before any offers are received. In particular, for example, the management must decide the role they wish the investor to play once the investment has been made. Generally private equity investors will not act as a bank lender would be expected to act. They will be more hands on in protecting and growing their investment. In addition they can bring expertise to the board that is often not there.

6–04 There will inevitably be some disruption to the business during this process. Frequent numbers of grey-suited men will be found parading through the warehouse. Staff morale may be affected and rumours may abound. Every effort should obviously be made to contain the disruption. The speed of the process is essential.

The greater the number of investors approached, the greater the risk of the proposed matter becoming public knowledge. It is therefore important that the proposed investment be kept confidential. Ideally therefore, from the outset, each prospective investor should be asked to execute a confidentiality agreement before any confidential information about the company is released.

By the end of the offer phase the company will have agreed a price and the amount of the share capital being released along with other commercial terms. This will be documented in an offer letter from the investor to the company. By signing such a letter, the parties will have a moral commitment but it will be expressed to be non-legally binding. Non-legally binding heads of agreement can be as brief or as detailed as the parties require. Generally they will contain financial details of the proposed investment, followed by a long list of conditions to be satisfied before the investment is made, including the obtaining of a satisfactory due diligence report. Apart from agreeing the financial and commercial terms there is often little point discussing the remainder of the offer letter which will be standard to the investor and the industry. **6–05**

At this point in time exclusivity has not been granted to any of the parties. From a legal perspective it is therefore very important to make the most of a strong bargaining position by agreeing as many key terms as possible. Clearly areas such as warranties and indemnities are unlikely to be agreed but there are a large number of key issues in the document that can be agreed saving time and costs later and ensuring a better deal for the management and/or the vendor before exclusivity is granted.

6.4 Transaction management

Private equity transactions are different from other commercial transactions. When buying and selling businesses, the vendor and the purchaser will not continue to deal with each other after the completion. Partly as a result of this, the transaction can and often does become aggressive and unpleasant with each party stubbornly arguing his corner. In private equity transactions, no matter how difficult the bargaining between the investor and the board, once the deal is completed the investors need to work closely with the management in order to further develop the company. A smooth and efficient negotiation and completion will set the relationship between the management and the investor off to a good start. In addition, a private equity transaction, or more particularly, a MBO with all its different facets can be one of the most difficult transactions that a lawyer will undertake. Managing the transaction is therefore very important. Set out below are guidelines to assist in the transaction management of a MBO or MBI. These principles can be adapted to other simpler forms of transactions. **6–06**

6.4.1 Timetable

It is very tempting when the accountants, the directors and the investors have been in negotiations for a long time and those negotiations have come to a satisfactory **6–07** conclusion to assure the management that there are only a small number of legal details to sort out before the transaction is completed and the company will receive its desired funding.

Whilst understanding that the transaction needs to be done quickly, for many numerous and varied commercial reasons, the management should also be made aware of the amount of time that will need to be devoted to the legal process. To set a deadline of three weeks for example to complete a large management buy-out is not sensible and is bound to have the consequence that the management team will be frustrated and angry when the transaction finally completes at least some six weeks later. However it is acknowledged that there are some transactions which need to be done very quickly for obvious commercial reasons, in particular a receivership buy-out from a receiver. Nonetheless, it is important to consider at the outset whether the tight deadline really is essential.

6–08 Often deadlines which are set without the input of the lawyers and which the parties clearly believe to be unachievable will simply be ignored and the consequence will be that there are in fact no deadlines at all. From a lawyer's point of view it can be very frustrating to receive an exquisitely prepared timetable and action list from a merchant banker or financial advisor into which the lawyer has had no input.

A timetable should therefore be justifiable and one which all parties recognise as justifiable. As a result it is worthwhile spending a certain amount of time analysing what needs to be done when drawing up the timetable but at the same time one must be sufficiently flexible to cater for issues arising during the legal process which no-one had anticipated and which will upset the timetable. Externally imposed deadlines are more effective than self-imposed ones and even something as trivial as a key player's holiday can sometimes be the trigger to get the transaction done on time, despite the grumblings that will occur. However, in the author's view it is always better to be honest about the timetable and the project leader should work hard at encouraging everyone to buy in.

6.4.2 What is transaction management?

6–09 The management of a private equity transaction is the process that is established in order to utilise the appropriate resources within or outside your own organisation in order to bring about the successful conclusion of a management buy-out or buy-in. The most important part of project management is to ensure that the right people are on the bus. Too often the selection of members of the buy-out team is controlled less by the skill that is required and more by the "who is available". You should always ensure that, as the leader of the transaction, you play a significant part in the selection process. Having the wrong people on board can make the transaction much more difficult than it need be.

Transaction management

The legal team you bring together will almost certainly have come from different **6–10** departments in your organisation and perhaps even different sites. This in itself brings some interesting challenges, for example:

- team members will only report to you for their work on the buy-out but will report to their departmental partner or manager for other work, who may have different priorities;
- the team is less likely to have stability over a protracted period due to changes in priority of the members or their departmental partner;
- often team members don't know each other and, as a result of unfamiliarity, there can often be immediate barriers. They will be hesitant to share information and opinions openly;
- the limited timescale means there is little time for coaching.

Success in transaction management is not achieved only by using the right tools and techniques. It is achieved by giving time to lead the team and overcoming these areas of potential difficulty. This will then reduce the risk of failure.

6.4.3 Transaction leadership

Project managing the buy-out is a complex role. The transaction manager is **6–11** involved in a changing environment where his primary purpose is to achieve a successful outcome of the transaction. At the same time it is a temporary management role with specific responsibilities that are linked only to the deal. Therefore he/she has to create a balance between the demands and needs of the client, the transaction, the organisation and the transaction team.

The transaction manager must do everything that he believes is necessary to achieve the desired outcome. He is the hub around which the deal operates. It is not a recipe for a quiet life. The transaction manager knows his own organisation and the people with whom he is expecting to work and might expect opposition, conflict, etc. Of course from his own organisation he should always expect full co-operation, enthusiastic support, and plenty of helpful advice. The reality tends to be somewhere in between. In addition if the transaction manager has not been assigned full-time to the role he must balance the time between deal activities during the buy-out and his other responsibilities. This can test a project manager's ability as a time manager and may influence members of the legal team who are in a similar situation. The main characteristics and roles of a transaction manager are:

- responsibility for achieving a successful outcome;
- pleasing the client;

Managing the Transaction

- proven skills in the use of project tools and techniques;
- proven team leadership skills;
- authority to secure resources internally and externally;
- the ability to cut through hierarchical boundaries to get things done;
- an ability to work with the unknown and the unpredictable;
- regarded sometimes with distrust by many of those not involved.

6–12 When a transaction manager brings the core team together they may not have worked with each other before or even know each other. In addition, the transaction manager is an unknown entity to them, if he has not worked with them before and they expect him to build the group into a team. This is therefore a complicated process but is made easier by a clear sense of direction and good leadership. Everyone should know why they are in the team and that they have been selected by the transaction leadership. They will all have experience and skills that are considered relevant to the transaction. The objective is to gather together their abilities, creativity and efforts to take the transaction to closing. A successful team consists of a carefully designed mixture of the right skills and personalities who are able to work together without conflict. They are likely to have been selected because the leadership value and respect their ability to deliver the right technical skills and to deliver a good service under pressure.

These elements demand and extend leadership skills beyond those normally associated with the fixed team leadership role. If the transaction manager is unable to bring along the team with him the position can quickly turn into a lonely one. It is essential therefore that he gets total support and guidance at all times from the deal leader (lead partner).

6.4.4 Lead partner

6–13 The lead partner takes the ultimate responsibility for delivery of the transaction. The responsibilities include:

- selecting the transaction manager;
- scoping the transaction;
- ensuring the proper resources are assigned to the transaction;
- overseeing the deal process and procedures, budgets and controls;
- approval of status reports, milestone reports and risk management reports.

In addition the lead partner will be the lead negotiator on the acquisition documentation and possibly on the equity documentation.

6.4.5 Transaction manager

The transaction manager is responsible for the project work from the initial kick-off through to completion. Responsibilities should include:

- selecting the core due diligence and negotiating team with the lead partner;
- scoping the due diligence and identifying the greatest risks;
- planning and scoping the work involved in the buy-out and the resources required;
- identifying and managing the risks;
- allocating and securing the appropriate resources;
- monitoring on a daily basis the progress of the buy-out in conjunction with the milestone plan;
- solving problems that interfere with the progress or ensure that they are raised early and the right people are solving them;
- controlling costs;
- leading the transaction team;
- preparing status reports and risk assessment or management reports with the approval of the lead partner.

Both the transaction manager and the lead partner need to demonstrate leadership qualities. There are no common characteristics that make an effective leader. The core of the issue is how the transaction manager uses his/her skills to influence the behaviour of people to achieve the successful outcome of the transaction. One type of leadership is to tell people what to do using a "you will" approach. The other extreme is the democratic approach, where information is shared; the manager consults widely and asks people to do the work using a "will you" approach. In reality a good manager will adopt a style that is often subconsciously directed by the situation and environment in which he/she operates, the type of work and its priority of urgency and the way the team act in the environment.

There is no particular right style in how to operate. The manager's skill is the ability to recognise what approach is appropriate at any particular time in order to get the achieved results.

To achieve the desired objectives the manager must use some particular skills to ensure the transaction is completed on time to the quality desired; create co-ordination between the team members and develop team work; and support individual team members and develop their skills.

Managing the Transaction

Keeping a balance between each of these tasks occupies much of the manager's time. The actions a manager takes at each stage of the project are focused and maintain this balance, adopting a range of styles according to the prevailing situation. However, the manager always needs to be aware that there is not just him/her and the team but there is also a client.

6–16 A manager spends much of the time as a transaction manager directed on inner tasks, bringing focus to the transaction, developing and maintaining good team work and making sure that the right skills are in the team. He/she also spends time with the client, understanding their needs and expectations, using their skills when appropriate and keeping them informed of progress.

Establishing the client's requirements very early in the deal is essential. They can influence the transaction at any time with serious consequences to timing and to the legal costs being incurred.

The three essential dimensions of transaction management and leadership are:

(1) identifying, managing and communicating with your client throughout the buy-out;

(2) managing the buy-out once the legal process has started. No other advisor is in a better position than the lawyer to do this;

(3) managing his/her own performance, the team and his client.

Success with your transaction is directly related to balancing the time and effort the manager gives to each of these dimensions from the start.

6.4.6 Managing performance

6–17 The transaction manager must demonstrate throughout the project that he/she is concerned about the performance of everyone involved with the transaction.

The transaction manager is responsible for delivering the results expected by the client and evaluating his/her own performance regularly will help improve the way the job is undertaken. A transaction such as a buy-out requires effective team work. If the team is not well co-ordinated the transaction work suffers and the transaction can become reactive and at worst move from crisis to crisis without clear leadership. This is always made more difficult in a transaction because team members are likely to come from different departments or even other sites. The transaction manager must make an effort early in the transaction to understand the team members and their working environment. Set out below is a checklist for the transaction manager to manage his/her own performance:

Transaction management

- assess own performance continuously;
- pay particular attention to helping and supporting team members;
- coach individual team members when opportunities arise;
- respond promptly to personal issues raised;
- demonstrate continued enthusiasm for the project;
- examine management of time;
- evaluate attention to detail;
- seek external help when appropriate;
- avoid making promises that cannot be met;
- communicate often and clearly with the team;
- establish clear responsibilities for work and delivery times;
- encourage good communication within the team and with their own managers or partners;
- recognise team effort and high performance;
- look after the team interests at all times in the interest of the transaction;
- avoid being reactive by:
  — keeping the client regularly informed of progress;
  — involving them in important decisions;
  — encouraging the team to maintain good communications with you, in order that you can liaise with the client.

6.4.7 Scoping the transaction

At the outset of every private equity transaction the team leader should spend time with his/her client carefully scoping the transaction and the requirements of the client. This will be manifested in a carefully drafted engagement letter setting out the expectations of the client, including resources, clear responsibilities, communications, project brief, timing, documentation and scope of work, and fees. Far too many lawyers will immerse themselves in a transaction without a clear path of the milestones that are necessary to achieve the desired outcome. Progressing the transaction without establishing a clear and focused plan that meets the client's needs is like leaving Basingstoke to go to Macclesfield without looking at the map. You will get there but not without a certain amount of trauma. Client expectations directly relate to client satisfaction. There are degrees of satisfaction relating to the extent to which your client perceives you understand their expectations. Falling short of these expectations leads to an unhappy client. The

6–18

Managing the Transaction

aim is a delighted client by providing all the expected results to an acceptable quality and standard. Fall short on the quality or performance standards and you will inevitably create a complaining client. Spending more time at the outset visiting the targets, understanding their business, properly scoping the transaction and setting up effective communication lines will always be rewarded.

6–19 Effective lines of communication between all parties is essential to help a deal run smoothly. Advisors need to be given the necessary information about the proposed deal as quickly as possible. Much information can be obtained from the business plan and accountants' report but the investors' lawyers rely on the investors to provide them with a detailed insight into the business, the objectives of the investor and the important issues.

It is very important that the lawyers and the directors set up a direct line of communication with the key members of the team to that they can obtain quickly all necessary information about the business. The board have the unenviable task of continuing to run the business while also trying to get the deal done. It is therefore important that their time is not wasted in unproductive meetings on issues which can be dealt with over the phone by one member of the board.

6.4.8 Preparation of the documentation

6–20 There will be pressure on the lawyers to produce documentation quickly. This should be resisted. Documents should only be produced when the investors' or purchasers' lawyers fully understand the transaction. Documents produced at too early a stage can slow a transaction and create unnecessary problems. The investor should not proceed with drafting or negotiating the definitive agreement until they have a reasonable understanding of the group, its business, any particular assets of importance, and its trading relationships. The legal advisors will understandably be reluctant to undertake this work at such an early stage if their fees are contingent upon the success of the transaction. To obtain this understanding, the investor will have commissioned a due diligence report, the results of which may cause him to wish to renegotiate the terms or even withdraw. In addition the investor's lawyers will have sent out their own questionnaire or "shopping list" of legal issues. Ideally the investor's lawyers would wish to wait for the outcome of this due diligence report before preparing the first draft, in order to take account of any points raised by the investigations. This is the procedure generally adopted in the US. In practice however, the investor's lawyer will be hurried into producing a first draft and any points raised in the investigations will be added later. The company will be pressing to receive the document. However, most importantly, it is tactically undesirable for the agreement to be sent to the other side before it has been considered fully by, and amended to reflect fully the concerns of, the investor.

Transaction management

Criticism for a delayed completion is often laid at the feet of the banks. By nature they are more cautious than private equity investors and should therefore be involved at an early stage to establish the parameters. The bank's requirements often cause the deal to be dismantled and reassembled, if they have been involved at too late a stage. However, it is sometimes necessary to take a strong line with the banks (if that is commercially possible) to ensure that they do not overstep their role. As the investors will often have a pre-existing relationship with the banks, and may even introduce them, they can help smooth the process. If at all possible, the banks should be brought into the legal discussions early and their requirements spelled out and agreed explicitly. As the deadline gets closer, concessions often have to be made just to put the funding in place so that the deal can be done.

6–21

The increasingly common scenario is that the business is being sold through an auction process and the sale and purchase agreement is generated by the vendor, pressurising the buyer to finalise the document before exclusivity is granted. In most cases, though not ideal, the purchaser will accept this process in order not to upset the vendor but will revisit the contract (if possible) following the completion of all its due diligence and upon being granted exclusivity.

6.4.9 Executing the transaction

Ensuring effective communication

Communication in a buy-out is the glue that holds everything together. A buy-out is one of the most complicated legal transactions that a lawyer can undertake, poor communication is a major source of conflict and slippage and frustration, so serious attention should be given to communication at the start of the transaction. Ask yourself:

6–22

- who needs to know;
- what do they need to know;
- how much do they need to know;
- how often must they be informed.

Establish distribution lists as appropriate but avoid generating large volumes of paper that few will ever read. The focal point for all communication is the transaction manager. He must decide the ground rules that will be imposed on everyone involved to get prompt feedback of the prevailing situation with the work in progress. Effective monitoring and tracking of the transaction is dependent on good communication in the team, between the transaction manager and his team and his client. He needs prompt feedback about:

6–23

- current progress of the active tasks;
- problems encountered with the work;
- problems anticipated with work waiting to be done;
- technical difficulties being encountered.

The transaction manager should have a continuous awareness of what is happening and what is due to happen next. He should promptly identify any problems that will interfere or harm progress. A number of tools can be utilised to help in this area.

6.4.10 Reporting and update system

6–24 A useful tool for management of the transaction is a reporting and update system. Given that a transaction may involve banks, accountants, actuaries, pension fund trustees, surveyors, etc, it is a good discipline for all concerned to be required to report at least once a week or more frequently, if the timetable is compressed, on the progress they have made and the remaining steps which need to be taken. Someone needs to co-ordinate this, and that person must be identified and agreed upon from the outset. The most appropriate person for this is the transaction manager, though sometimes it is done by the investor. If the co-ordination is to be done by the investor or by an intermediary then it must be done in close consultation with the lawyers. At this stage, the transaction usually revolves around documents which the lawyers produce. Internally, the corporate lawyers working on the transaction should call frequent meetings of those lawyers working on the transaction such as property, banking, intellectual property, pensions and employment lawyers. This achieves numerous purposes but probably most importantly helps to drive the transaction forward and at the same time can highlight problem areas at an early stage. When acting for the investor it is often useful to invite him occasionally to the meeting, in order to monitor progress. If he chooses not to attend a "trouble shooter" email can be produced immediately after the meeting highlighting any problems. This can be in addition to or instead of the status reports referred to below.

Milestone schedule

6–25 A milestone schedule is very useful in monitoring all the significant events that are due to occur during the execution of the deal. It is a signal of a clearly defined point in the transaction that indicates that something special should have occurred to enable the deal to happen. It is therefore an instrument of control placing target points in the transaction schedule for certain events to be signed off as completed. Examples of common events in a buy-out would be:

Transaction management

- completion of accounting due diligence;
- completion of commercial due diligence;
- completion of legal due diligence;
- investment committee approval of the private equity house;
- investment committee approval of the bank;
- vendor board meeting approving the sale;
- agree new chairman, etc.

The transaction manager must be aware of each milestone. He should see them as marker posts showing the route to the finishing line. Where possible he should control the milestones and work to prevent slippage.

Status report

6–26 The client will expect to receive regular status reports. Decide the frequency of these. In practice, such reports are administrative headaches for many people and they will avoid these reports if necessary. Others will write a note or a few lines that are of little value. Some people are delighted to spend a whole afternoon compiling a thorough and detailed report on everything they have done. Long reports are often only scanned and not digested, with key issues being lost. A transaction manager should ask what is needed to clearly define the current status of the transaction. A transaction manager will require sub-reports produced by members of the team. He must inform them how he wants these reports and how frequently. At any point in the transaction the manager will need to know:

- what has been completed;
- what has not been completed and why;
- what is being done about the incomplete work;
- what problems remain unresolved;
- what needs to be done about these unsolved problems;
- what difficulties are anticipated in the work waiting to be done?

Meeting schedule

6–27 The transaction manager should determine what meetings are essential to complete the transaction. Meetings are a continuous problem during a transaction.

Managing the Transaction

Avoid "all parties" meetings if possible. There is no more certain way to run up costs than to convene everyone to a meeting in order to thrash out the issues. There is a tendency in some transactions to resolve every problem by getting everyone together—a particular trait of corporate financiers who have little role in the production of documentation and believe they can best control the process by getting every man and his dog together in the same room. This is generally inefficient and expensive.

Nevertheless there are times when an "all parties" meeting is necessary if only to knock heads together because the transaction is not progressing. Encourage everyone to come to such a meeting with an open mind in order to find solutions. If an "all parties" meeting is necessary it should have a carefully structured agenda with times for the arrival of parties who are not needed for the whole meeting.

6–28 More importantly it is a test of the ability of the lead partner and the transaction partner as to how they control these meetings. When they have identified problems they should also identify the best persons to resolve those problems. This may or may not involve lawyers and the lead partner and transaction partner should make that judgement. There are different types of meetings to serve different purposes and the transaction partner can play a significant role in determining the most appropriate type of meeting:

- one-to-one meetings with the client;
- one-to-one meetings with your team members;
- project-progress meetings with the team;
- problem-solving meetings (with or without lawyers);
- project-review meetings with the client;
- all-partners meetings.

All of these are at different frequencies throughout the transaction but you should not convene the meeting unless you have a good reason and a clear purpose.

6–29 No meeting should be convened unless it has a proper agenda which has been circulated beforehand and the parties attending it can come prepared. Far too many meetings degenerate into a reading of documents which ought to have been read previously. One should not be afraid to stand down meetings if people are not ready, and the lawyer should gain the support of the client to this action.

Meetings should not be held until documents have been prepared, circulated and commented upon in writing. The main issues can then be determined and the meeting concern itself only with those few issues. Generally a meeting in which everyone goes through the document page by page is a disaster.

Transaction management

Risk assessment

There are risks involved in every transaction and risk management is the process of **6–30** identifying them and containing them (where appropriate) to ensure the success of the transaction. The leader will have undertaken a risk assessment exercise at the outset of the transaction, particularly if the firm's fees are contingent upon a successful outcome—it's amazing how much more sophisticated risk assessment becomes when fees are at stake. However a risk assessment undertaken at the outset is of limited value—at that stage the purchaser is generally relying on information provided by the vendor which is only slightly more sophisticated than the language of estate agents. More valuable risk assessment only becomes apparent towards the end of the various due diligence exercises being undertaken.

Following the delivery of the due diligence report it is often appropriate to produce a risk assessment report to be delivered to the client. Many of these issues will have been covered extensively in the due diligence report, however this is the time that the transaction manager can really deliver value by helping the team to focus on the real issues by using his in-depth understanding of the business. He should call the team together and hold a brainstorming session to identify as many risks as possible—i.e. things that could go wrong and hinder or stop the progress of the transaction. At the same time the transaction manager should identify the impact of the risk on the project. The probability of occurrence should be graded on a scale of one to nine where one is low—most unlikely to happen—and nine is high—very likely to happen.

At the same time the impact on the transaction, if it does happen, should also be **6–31** graded so that a high would have significant effect; may cause the loss of the transaction or would be costly to rectify. Medium risk should be less serious but perhaps with a small cost while a low impact may affect timing but with little effect on costs.

		IMPACT ON THE PROJECT		
P R O B A B I L I T Y		LOW	MEDIUM	HIGH
	7–9	medium	high	unacceptable
	4–6	low	high	unacceptable
	1–3	low	medium	high

Once the risk assessment schedule has been produced the manager is in a position to discuss with the client the actions that need to be taken to resolve the issues.

Managing the Transaction

Negotiation of the agreement

6–32 The draftsman has a considerable advantage, in that he/she will know the document very well and it will have been produced from a precedent draft to suit the needs of his/her client. The other party needs to consider not only everything that is included, but also what has been omitted. It is important therefore that the party receiving the draft does not succumb to being called to a meeting too quickly. Unless there is extreme urgency, before agreeing to a meeting, the lawyers, the client and other professional advisors should have adequate time to meet and discuss their respective points. It is important that the lawyer understands the client's feelings on certain points, the strength of his bargaining position, the parameters within which he/she will negotiate as well as the real schedule.

If the party receiving the documents finds them totally unreasonable then a useful tactic is for the client to raise the issues directly with the other party before the agreement is negotiated. This emphasises the seriousness of the issues being raised.

6–33 Different investors have different ways of operating, and the lawyer needs to understand the approach taken by the investors. Certain investors, once they have confidence in their lawyer, will allow them to negotiate the document by giving them a list of "deal-breakers". This can often mean that the transaction will develop more smoothly. Often the lawyer can deal directly with the other party's lawyers to negotiate the majority of the document leaving the "deal-breakers" to be dealt with at an all-parties meeting. Other investors prefer their lawyers to argue every point, allowing themselves the opportunity to concede points and therefore maintain the harmonious relationship with the board.

In the writer's opinion if there are no major problems it is usually most efficient for the first meeting to be between lawyers only. Most of the comments can usually be cleared up this way while at the same time identifying a list of issues that require the clients' input. It is futile for people without the knowledge or the authority to negotiate these issues. At the end of such a meeting it is to be hoped that there will be a small list of points that can be settled at a subsequent all-parties meeting.

Managing time

6–34 The main objective in undertaking the buy-out is to achieve a successful outcome which is generally interpreted as delivering the right result on time and to an agreed fee. Although this may require the lead partner to make changes to the scope of the transaction, the whole process is dependent upon time. Many of the difficulties encountered in managing a buy-out are caused by time management getting out of

Transaction management

control and time in lawyers' offices is money. Some people are very skilled at organising and managing how they use time effectively. Unfortunately many are not so organised and the work output is extremely vulnerable with poor time management. The transaction manager therefore has a direct interest in how everyone working in even the smallest part of the project is using the time allocated to their actual work. A good manager can influence how time is used, avoiding unnecessary work, duplication of effort and ensure attention is given to prioritising the work. Time is a most valuable resource which, if lost or misplaced, is gone forever. It is therefore a constraint and the manager must demonstrate and encourage everyone involved to use effective time management principles to maximise this resource. One area of the deal that does require management is when each draft of the main agreements are produced. One of the failings of the advancement in technology is the ease with which new drafts are produced. However, if issues have not been agreed, producing new drafts will only add to the burden of work and consequentially to the tensions between all parties. It is beyond the remit of this book to discuss time management at length. However one of the most useful tools to keep a careful check on all parts of the transaction is the checklist.

Checklist

The most essential document in the legal process is the preparation of a list of documents and action checklist. This should be drawn up at the beginning of the transaction, and continuously updated. All issues which need to be dealt with should be itemised including legal, financial, commercial and due diligence issues. It should also form the basis of the completion checklist. The person responsible for the progressing of each issue should be marked beside it. The checklist should be reviewed regularly and should be added to and revised following the results of the reporting and update system referred to above. A specimen checklist is set out at the end of this chapter. **6–35**

6.5 International transactions

Managing international transactions are always more challenging because of different cultures and expectations. There are a number of consistent issues that arise that should be addressed. **6–36**

Rules on conflicts of interest vary according to jurisdictions and these should be checked carefully. **6–37**

Differences in languages should not be underestimated and you should ensure that you have effective translators on the team. **6–38**

Fee structures will vary. For example, some jurisdictions do not allow lawyers on a success or contingency fee basis which is something that certain institutional **6–39** clients in the UK have come to expect. You should also make sure that you take into account both local notarial fees and local taxes.

6–40 Understanding timing issues is also important: local holidays, the use of notaries, valuation procedures, setting up new companies, etc.

6–41 It is very important to have engagement letters in place with all cross-border lawyers. These should set out the details of the transaction, the client identity, objectives of the assignment, the score of the assignment (e.g. tax, due diligence, regulating, drafting, negotiation, etc) local regulatory requirements, shareholder approvals, consents, form of reports or weekly briefings or presentations, indemnities and limitations on liability, timing, the team, fees, etc.

6–42 The language used in the documentation is clearly important. English is often used but local laws may require specific documents to be in the relevant local language. Very often the main document (an "umbrella" or "framework" agreement) will be in English and covered by English or New York law, while documents implementing the acquisition are under local law. Ensure the umbrella agreement is reviewed by local lawyers to ensure there are no inconsistencies with the local documentation.

6–43 Clearly advances in technology can assist when undertaking cross-border transactions. The establishment of a project website can assist in co-ordination of the project and help create a virtual deal room. This can include practical information (contract lists, email addresses, public holidays, advice on notaries, etc), contractual documents, due diligence instructions, pro forma reports, etc.

6.6 The completion phase

6–44 The document phase will be concluded by the signing of the agreements. Despite the common view, completion meetings do not have to last for 24 hours. Generally a completion meeting which goes on for such time is symptomatic of a transaction that has not been well managed. Lawyers should resist the client's temptation to get everyone together for a completion meeting when a transaction is not yet ready. There is a huge cost disadvantage with such a meeting. If the parties are not properly prepared for completion, one will find for example, property lawyers, banking lawyers and tax lawyers sitting around until 3am waiting for the point when their input is needed. It is not realistic obviously for them to go away and come back at such a time.

Nevertheless completion meetings can sometimes be unavoidably lengthy. Care should be taken not to summon parties too early if the meeting is likely to be prolonged. It is important to keep everyone fully informed of progress and that frequent time estimates are given. This is particularly the case with people who

The completion phase

have not been part of the deal making process but who are obviously vital to the business as it is important that they feel part of the process and recognise the significance of what they are signing. A short oral guide to the legal completion process provided by the lawyers at the outset can assist their understanding and can reduce the tension and bad tempers which can often occur.

Costs are always a problem in a private equity transaction. This is, in particular, **6–45** because the costs will be paid by the company into which the investment is made. In addition a certain level of professional fees will be assumed by the investor in the projections prepared with the help of the company, often without reference to the professionals. Anything above those assumptions will be resisted.

It is becoming more common for lawyers to be asked for estimates and even fixed or capped quotations. This is difficult to provide in any private equity transaction and even more so in a MBO. This is because there are so many parties involved, each with their own lawyers and each with their own agendas, hidden or otherwise, which can assist or protract the negotiations.

Effective management of the legal process can have a dramatic effect on legal **6–46** fees. The actual production of a document is often the cheapest part. It is usually the meetings and the telephone negotiating that takes time and here, effective management of the transaction can be significant. If timetables are properly prepared and if all-party meetings are not relied on to solve the problem, the lawyers' time can be budgeted very well. Consider whether it is really necessary to have fresh drafts of all the documents every time a few changes are made. The waste of paper is appalling and the time spent in preparing, marking them up, photocopying and distributing them all has to be paid for.

6.7 Pro forma checklist

Part I LIST OF DOCUMENTS   6–47

Acquisition documents (management buy-out/buy-in only)

Document		Party responsible for production	Status of draft (No)
42	Confirm satisfaction of conditions precedent [specify]		
43	Acquisition agreement		
44	Vendor share certificates		
45	Indemnity for lost share certificates from vendors to Newco		
46	Waiver/consents re: pre-emption rights		

Managing the Transaction

47 Executed stock transfer forms

Transferor Transferee Share Type

[   ] [   ] [   ]

[   ] [   ] [   ]

48 Resignations of outgoing directors and secretary of target

[   ] director

[   ] director

[   ] secretary

49 Resignations of outgoing directors and secretary of subsidiary

[   ] director

[   ] director

[   ] secretary

50 Written resignations of auditors of target and subsidiary

51 Deed of tax indemnity

52 Disclosure letter (and bundle)

53 Board minutes of vendors and [guarantors] approving the acquisition and execution of acquisition documents

54 Board minutes of Newco approving the acquisition and execution of acquisition documents

55 Board minutes of Target

56 EGM minutes and resolutions of Target

57 Board minutes of subsidiary

58 EGM minutes and resolutions subsidiary

59 Certificate of title/report on title to the following properties:

[   ]

[   ]

[   ]

60 Powers of attorney

61 Letters of undertaking re: completion monies

62 Certificates of incorporation and change of name of target

63 Certificates of incorporation and change of name of subsidiary

Pro forma checklist

64 Statutory books of target
65 Share certificate book of target
66 Share certificate book of subsidiary
67 Documentation in relation to the release of any charges, guarantees [specify]
68 Completion statement re: transfer of monies
69 Completion agenda

Equity documents

70 Confirmation that the conditions precedent are satisfied [specify]
71 Investment agreement
72 New articles of association
73 Disclosure letter (and bundle)
74 Confirm keyman insurance cover is in place
75 Letter from brokers confirming general insurances in place
76 Powers of attorney (if required) for:

  [   ]

  [   ]

  [   ]

77 Signing authorities for investors:

  [   ]

  [   ]

  [   ]

78 Share certificates for investors
79   1   Various reports addressed to the investors as follows:

  Accounts report
  Environmental report
  Surveyor's report
  Employment report
  Pensions report
  Certificate on title
  Form 123: re-increase in authorised share capital—Form 88(2)
  Form 88(2): return allotment of shares—Form 288
  Form 288 for resigning and new directors

Form 225(1): Notice of change of accounting reference date
Form 287 (change of registered office)
Others.

2 Registration of relevant security at Land Registry
3 Stamping of property transfer documents
4 Stamping of stock transfer forms
5 Completion of registered members and statutory books of the company
6 Restrictive Trade Practices Act registrations with the OFT
7 Notices to employees, suppliers customers, etc.
8 Bible
9 Prepare a list of original documents and filing arrangements

6–48 Part II CHECKLIST OF ISSUES TO BE ATTENDED TO (TAILOR TO THE TRANSACTION)

Action   *Responsibility   Comment*

1 Employees

1.1 List key employees

1.2 Are any employees to be asked to enter into standard form contracts of employment (contain any restrictive covenants whether before or immediately after completion)

1.3 Consider

    (a) keyman insurance
    (b) directors' liability insurance

2 Directors

2.1 Interests of directors or of connected persons:

    (a) identify persons and interest;
    (b) do articles permit or will permit relevant interest;
    (c) declarations of interest (CA 1985 s.317);
    (d) provisions in articles relating to ability to vote and counting in quorum;
    (e) in relation to relevant public company whether any transaction is with a related party for purposes of the London Stock Exchange;

Pro forma checklist

- (f) Substantial property transactions (CA 1985 ss.320–322);
- (g) Credit transactions (CA 1985 s.330);
- (h) Disclosure of directors' interests in securities (CA 1985 Pt IV and s.324).

2.2 Consider whether any director has:

- (a) at any time has been adjudged bankrupt in the UK or elsewhere;
- (b) at any time been party to a deed of arrangement or made any other form of composition with creditors;
- (c) any unsatisfied judgment outstanding against him/her;
- (d) been a director of any company or any body corporate which was liquidated (other than a voluntary winding-up) or had a receiver appointed while the individual was a director or within six months before he/she ceased to be one.

2.3 Consider source of funding for directors' investment

(NB: a directors' questionnaire should be sent to each of the directors which will cover many of the above matters. Though these matters are of some delicacy they confirm with the London Stock Exchange enquiries which though not formally relevant to a venture capital investment could be material to any intending investor and may avoid last-minute embarrassment or scandal.)

3 *Approvals or Licences Responsibility*   *Time for obtaining*   *Comment*

Governmental
Tax (specify)
Trade marks licences
Financial Services Act
Trade associations joint venture arrangements

4 *Investigations/due diligence to be made*

Accounting due diligence
Legal due diligence
Intellectual property due diligence

Environmental matters
Property due diligence
Other

5 *Miscellaneous*

VAT registration
Data protection registration

6.8 Key points

6–49
- In order to avoid delays the company's lawyers should gather together early the information that will be required by the investor. Try to anticipate problems.
- Take transaction management seriously, properly scope the transaction and ensure all members of the team understand their roles.
- Remember that in a venture capital transaction the parties will continue to work together after the documents have been signed. No matter how difficult the bargaining is, try to maintain a harmonious relationship with the other side and their lawyers.
- If a timetable is prepared, make sure that everyone who is to participate in it has an opportunity to comment on it. Ensure that it is realistic.
- Prepare a checklist of matters to be attended to and update it regularly.
- Ensure that meetings are planned properly:
  — decide who is to be present, circulate the agenda and any relevant information in advance;
  — ensure that all, and only the people necessary are present. Make sure the meeting is necessary;
  — agree time limits in advance and start on time;
  — plan the agenda carefully, allocating specific amounts of time to each item; include time to establish the aims of the meeting, ensure effective discussion, reach conclusions and agree the actions necessary; and
  — decide whether minutes or a summary is necessary, if so make them concise and definite, and include reference to who is to do what and when.

Chapter 7

Management Due Diligence

Paul Quinn, The Quinn Partnership

7.1 Introduction

Management due diligence is the focused and balanced enquiry into the capability, background, experience and style of an individual or team of individuals who are to participate in an investment scenario. It is a process designed to identify the risk that a management team may bring to an investment. It is relatively new to the due diligence family as an accepted, full, important and robust process. Management due diligence is different to human due diligence, which is understanding the culture of an organisation and the roles, capabilities and attitudes of its people. Management due diligence focuses on the key drivers of the business, which are so key to the growth of a private equity business, in particular a mid-market private equity business. 7–01

7.1.1 The impact of economic recession

The recent economic recession gave management due diligence practitioners, as well as investors, the time to review and consider the purpose, approach and desired output of management due diligence. Many practitioners have learned significant lessons from the response of investment houses. Such lessons should not be ignored by investors and lenders alike. Turning to organisations and individuals who have turned to the practice to shore up holes in their revenues from other services may turn out to be a retrograde step and care should be advised in choosing from such a pool. 7–02

Indeed, during this time, private equity houses who were not making new investments focused upon the performance issues within their investment portfolio and began to evaluate the management capability requirements of businesses that had previously received investment in what was now a very different business climate.

Never was it more true regarding the assumption that those qualities within the team that brought them to this point in the life of the business, were unlikely to be the ones that took the business to its next version of existence.

Boards, directors and chairmen were reviewed and scrutinised against an often more demanding backdrop and economic climate. Even those businesses that were perceived as performing well began to feel a sense of scrutiny in anticipation of a potential negative impact or opportunity brought by such a market. The strategy of businesses in many cases had been displaced by challenging changes in direction; business survival dominating the board agenda and a more ruthless review of cost base, market pursuit and, inevitably, management suitability.

7–03 So what impact has such a backdrop had upon management due diligence practice?

Firstly, for most, the rationale for management due diligence became viewed as far more robust amongst lenders as well as investors. The credit and investment committee perspective within these financial institutions was to ask more challenging questions of those who presented cases for lending and investment. Executives and case officers needed to more profoundly anticipate the focus upon management motivation, dynamics, capability and readiness for deliverability of the proposed business plan.

Succession issues and the implication of "cash-out" deals were not left to assumptions made by case officers—too often the case in the rosier years of positive market influences.

Providers of management due diligence have had to revisit their reports and notes, identifying where the "volume" around issues should have been higher, where executive capability was overtaken by the difficulty of winning revenue, and where optimistic enthusiasts and benevolent CEOs were reluctant to take tough decisions swiftly and early.

With regard to reporting structures and output design, many leadership and sales models have been complemented by replacement frameworks and more explicit descriptions and graphics displaying risk indices and anticipated executive shelf life, post completion.

However, as the competition for deal winning and career pressure begins to mount, there is already the detection of requests for short-cutting and pressured timetables from advisors eager to kick start deal activity within the sector.

What is pleasing to see, though, is the resolve to address issues with fundamentally sharp and informed data and perspective extruded through professional and thorough diligence processes.

Introduction

7.1.2 Shaping the approach to management due diligence

The depth and breadth of approach to management due diligence is determined 7–04
by a number of factors:

- the structure of the investment;
- the specifics of the proposed business plan under consideration;
- the circumstances of the investment;
- the historical relationships between the team and the new investors;
- the historical relationships within a management team;
- the time available;
- the aggressiveness of the investment strategy of the VC;
- the maturity of the investment director;
- the policy of the investment committee.

The purpose of this aspect of due diligence is often poorly communicated and probably the least palatable from the point of view of a management team who feel a sense of personal scrutiny is underway in a more explicit manner than they have felt so far in the transaction process. Consequently, the professional advisor, investment director and practitioner should ensure that the principle of management due diligence is introduced in a skilled manner. Last-minute positioning of this will incite even the most trusting and placid individuals to show their fighting spirit. This is particularly the case in tougher economic times. Management teams should expect a review of existing internal management processes to evidence the suitability of their approach. Internal regimes of performance management should be expected to be reviewed and for some closer board review post completion.

7.2 Managing expectations

Those private equity professionals not familiar with management due diligence 7–05
need to gain an understanding of best practice and not make too many assumptions when positioning the process with a team or vendor. Many different transaction scenarios will subtly shift the emphasis placed on certain aspects of the process and if the transaction and relationships between parties within it are to be maintained, then it is critical that:

- the commitment to using management due diligence is introduced as early as possible;

- the language chosen by investment directors is a true reflection of what their providers wish to be used and utilised consistently;
- the time commitment is fully understood and communicated;
- the purpose is properly communicated using professional and appropriate wording;
- management teams engage and appreciate the potential benefits as well as threats—this reaction is quite critical since management response is keenly anticipated.

Our advice is that any provider that is engaged should be given as much notice as possible and that some guidance be given from the provider as to what should be communicated to the team. Ideally, specific questions should be answered by the provider.

The best providers of management due diligence have typically experienced the different responses and the frequently asked questions and are far more equipped to allay fears and explain methodology than investment directors.

Those that receive funding might expect to build a stronger constructive relationship with many of the diligence partners that can support them through delivery of the next phases of the business plan—particularly where issues have been genuinely highlighted.

7.3 Problems

7–06 It would be unrealistic to expect that members of a management team being asked to participate in management due diligence processes simply comply without some sensitivities being introduced.

From being asked to provide a list of potential referees, to being interviewed about their career, to undergoing some form of profiling and formal assessment process, it is inevitable that, for some, this will not be comfortable and at its extreme some will react quite emotively.

Rather than lighting the blue touch paper and standing back—which may suit some investment directors—there is more benefit to be gained by managing this process of communication proactively.

For management teams, the advice is simple: accept that a private equity investor will want to know more about you before handing over those millions and he or she will form a judgement by your response to the idea of process as much as to the process itself. Shifting to a different investor will be unlikely to avoid management due diligence, especially if your reason for doing so becomes known. Investment directors are entitled to wonder what it is that teams are hiding if they hear too much protesting.

A stronger agenda of co-operation and longer term advisory engagement between those that identify issues in the management structure, capability maps and broader planning around resourcing the delivery of the business plan, and those members of the team that are the subjects of this scrutiny and advice, is being encouraged by investing organisations where possible. It will not always be a welcomed partnership.

7.4 Rounded best practice

This has developed over the past ten years or so. Essentially, senior level recruitment and selection practices have provided some processes that underpin most approaches to management due diligence. Some more sophisticated approaches that have been more traditionally HR driven have made to migrate with varying levels of success. A lack of understanding of the private equity agenda and the context of a transaction means that whilst traditional HR practitioners might satisfy the demands of the methodology, they struggle to answer the key questions that investors expected to be answered.

7–07

The pragmatics of exclusivity which can restrict access to individuals often caught up in the pull and push of an investor driven, vendor defended and advisor managed timetable can be difficult. This has acted as a barrier to management due diligence historically and it is only recently that time and attention are being built into a transaction's due diligence timetable.

Essentially, whatever methodology is employed, the aim is to generate explicit visibility about the level of risk that exists around the human capital associated with the investment.

The most valuable approaches step beyond the diagnostic descriptions of risk and offer opinions and options as to how risk might be managed and mitigated within the lifetime of the investment. They adhere to pre-completion practicalities, but should aim to provide insight which can be used not just to help get the deal over the line when it comes to completion, but also to focus on life in the portfolio and how best to shape up for exit. Their advice should help structure the management team to maximise those exit options that are possible and understand those that aren't.

There is a greater expectation that management due diligence will offer a more advisory and robust strategic plan of action than mere diagnostics. Fee structures may be reviewed and a longer lasting relationship between provider and management team should be encouraged and positioned at the outset where possible.

7.5 Deal structures

7–08 MBOs, MBIs, development capital deals, buy and build, secondary buy-outs; all have inherent risks that relate to the capability of individuals, the blend of a team and the dynamics that can be expected in the course of investment. Some deal structures are unlikely to feature in the short term as they did before a more challenging economic climate.

Different private equity investors adopt different styles and a change of investor will not necessarily mean that the need for management due diligence has waned. The challenges that lie ahead will also change in terms of the demands that individuals face in the new era of investment. Teams that have taken a business successfully to one level may not be appropriate to face the next level of challenge. This is particularly accurate when factoring in any individual capital gain that has been achieved which may affect motivation to drive the business forward.

Whilst there is a lot of focus on articulating capability, there is an increasing focus upon motivation of an individual to succeed. Whilst referencing an individual can give some insight into what has motivated them historically, it is unlikely, on its own, to give a more in-depth, raw view on motivational personality factors or a more topical note of somebody's current financial horizon. In that instance, profiling generates a more significant gauge.

It is worth looking at the various management due diligence tools that tend to be used in investment led management.

7.6 Covert intelligence operations

7–09 Whilst it should be mentioned, undercover surveillance and more covert investigation is unlikely to be utilised in transaction scenarios. Business espionage has not typically been used in the small or mid-market private equity investment. Perhaps it might be more utilised as investors and lenders evaluate its value in very specific circumstances.

7.7 Legal and financial searches and checks

7–10 Some basic identity checks have to be conducted as a matter of law and financial pre-requisite, others will be optional. These will include:

- identity validation;
- credit history checks;

Legal and financial searches and checks

- academic qualification validation;
- professional membership checks;
- basic career history validation;
- directors check;
- criminal records check.

For some of these, evidence of the individual's written consent will be required.

7.8 Referencing

Referencing is the term given to the process by which former colleagues, contacts and peers of a member of the management team are contacted and questioned with regard to their performance in previous roles in their career. It is one of a number of possible approaches used when attempting to capture an accurate view of the suitability of an individual taking a role within a company which is the subject of investment. **7–11**

Whilst accepted as the obvious minimum level of diligence in recruitment or investment, it is still surprising to see it done poorly or not at all in both areas. Recruiters can face a conflict between placement of individuals and thorough objective probing of referees. Equally, investment directors can sometimes hear what they want to hear when a career changing opportunity needs to move quickly to completion.

The private equity market was already open to conducting traditional referencing activity which has been more commonly accepted as minimum base-line management due diligence practice. Specifically, referees are:

- those with whom the individual being referenced has previously worked;
- a balance of those that the individual reported into, worked alongside or managed;
- the chairman of a company they worked in;
- investors they have worked with;
- the vendor of the current business.

The referees will be a mix of those names provided by the individual themselves but should include a selection of names that have not been provided by the individual. It is common for some research to be conducted in order to uncover the names of relevant individuals not provided by the candidate. **7–12**

Management Due Diligence

Best professional practice should be courteous and alert the individual being referenced to the fact that this process is going on. It may or may not include a list of the names being provided to the candidate for their information.

There are some risks around not providing this list to the referenced candidate:

- there may be market sensitivities that the reference taker is not aware of that can jeopardise the transaction;
- the candidate may be unwittingly compromised and may feel alienated by the process;
- confidentialities can be breached.

7–13 However, referencing is not always conducted by third parties and is often undertaken by investment directors and executives themselves—particularly if they have or their firm has links with prospective referees.

Some of this preliminary referencing activity can be undertaken early on in the qualification of an investment opportunity to guide the thinking of the private equity house as to whether there are any issues they can gain early sight of and consequently reflect in any offer letter that might be submitted.

Referencing of management teams is, in the main, designed to:

- verify factual elements of an individual's previous background and employment history;
- authenticate achievements that an individual claims as their own;
- verify the path of career development including reasons for leaving previous employment;
- uncover any elements of an individual's background that might increase deal risk if they are involved in the transaction;
- gather a view on their suitability for the demands of the business plan;
- gather a view on elements of the personal brand of management adopted by the individual in their role;
- help give an understanding of the suitability of the individual for the role for which they will be given responsibility under the proposed investment;
- explore any specific issues thought relevant by the private equity house.

7–14 The value of referencing a team may not always be strong. For instance, in a team who have been employed in a business for a long time, the value of referencing is limited to a nominal factual check since the shelf-life of any views acquired will be typically limited. In such cases, the most relevant and valuable references may well be gleaned from commercial due diligence which should aim to gather valuable customer views on these individuals.

Character referencing should be avoided. It tends to constitute a subjective, biased fan-club of the individual and does not tend to provide a balanced, business relevant account. Individuals who provide character references are missing the point of the process and perhaps its purpose may need further explanation.

7.9 Outputs of referencing activity

Reference reports tend to be descriptive accounts of the telephone conversations that the interviewer has conducted. Some are no more than transcriptions of the conversation and provide little in the way of value for the investment director other than he can say to the investment committee that referencing on the individual has been conducted. **7–15**

More valuable reports relate the conversation to broader business issues or articulate consistent themes that build some critical mass around pertinent issues. They may also give weighting to differing or competing views that emerge.

7.10 Profiling management teams and structured interviews

Increasingly more widespread in private equity due diligence is a combined methodology of interviewing with the aid of some personality related profile. Provided the tools are sophisticated enough and that they are used by experienced individuals, this approach can offer a perceived robustness as well as a greater level of perceptive insight into team dynamics and individual style than referencing alone. **7–16**

The added advantage is that the individual responsible for reporting the outputs from a process actually meets the individual they are commenting upon and can therefore broaden the feedback based upon that experience.

Tools such as personality questionnaires are commonly used in selection processes as well as internally within corporate organisations. They work on the basis of analysing an individual's response to a series of questions utilising statistical processes and essentially distilling those responses into psychological traits. Those interested in the details can further research psychometric papers for themselves. The profile generated is then a reference point for part of the discussion in a more structured interview with the individual member of the management team. **7–17**

The effectiveness of this process is dependent upon the skill and capability of the interviewer and not the accuracy of the personality profile. A skilled interviewer will identify an inaccurate profile and will test the validity of it through the interview and other aspects of diligence.

In reality, the profile is a tool in the same way that a CV is a tool. You wouldn't rely on either as a sole indicator of suitability.

Management teams, advisors and vendors—as well as practitioners—can make the mistake of focusing too readily on the profile or the profiling methodology when forming their opinions as to the benefits of this approach to management due diligence. There is common misunderstanding as to how the tools are used.

Interviews tend to be structured and typically cover:

- career history of the individual;
- clarification of his or her role;
- discussion of the individual's management style and approach;
- business issues;
- aspirations;
- motivation;
- approach to building relationships;
- ability to manage stakeholders;
- specific team dynamics, e.g. between the proposed CEO and FD in a MBO.

7.11 Outputs of profiling and interviews

7–18 Reports tend to generate feedback at a number of levels:

- reports outlining the level of risk associated with individuals;
- an overview of issues arising from team blend against business plan;
- constructive suggestions regarding the development needs of the executives;
- advice concerning scoping of the role of an appropriate chairman;
- the identification of matters that might hinder exit options;
- specific concerns within the initial scope of the work can be addressed.

Feedback can at its most extreme level identify any "red flags" around individuals who have not shown themselves to be "fit for purpose" or appropriate for the challenge that lies ahead in the investment. By continuing in their proposed role, they significantly increase the risk associated with the investment and make it unlikely that they will fulfil their contribution successfully within the suggested period involvement of the investor conducting the diligence.

Most feedback is balanced yet it is important that in working with degrees of risk the practitioner does not give bland, on the fence views on a team. Firm opinion is essential and "best advice" protects integrity and ultimately drives value. Written reports can depersonalise feedback to the team or individuals that if they came directly from the proposed investor, might otherwise de-rail relationships and threaten the smooth running of the transaction. Reports can prompt discussions and are in themselves useful tools for investors looking to maintain a positive relationship, but raise some delicate or sensitive issues.

7.12 Evaluating the chairman in management due diligence

Management due diligence should also incorporate an assessment of the suitability of the proposed chairman to the investment. It may be that the experience of a seasoned chairman together with his track record within private equity transactions makes him a sure-fire bet for the paper evaluations and challenges of an investment or credit committee. However, his personal style may be a recipe for disaster for the CEO and management team. Practical issues such as the breadth of other commitments within his own portfolio may make him a less accessible resource than the CEO needs.

7–19

Equally, the mentoring abilities of chairmen vary considerably. Many senior executives come to the end of their executive career and perceive that a portfolio of non-executive directorships will give them a living and allow them to enjoy semi-retirement with the prospect of a large capital gain. But few have anticipated this in advance and made the provision to learn about the role and their own shortcomings.

The evaluation of the suitability of a chairman together with a statutory review of how effectively a board is performing on an annual basis is emerging as the new phase of private equity focus.

7.13 Conclusion

Essentially, there are many nuances that are often associated with proposed investments that have an impact upon management due diligence activity. The history of the business proposition and how it has come to the attention of the investors can have a practical impact upon the scope of management due diligence that is envisaged. It is worth noting that the views of what level and depth of activity is appropriate will vary considerably!

7–20

Management Due Diligence

Vendors' views will be different to those of investors; the incumbent team's view will not always be conducive to smooth process: a function of personality of the individuals as well as to do with practical issues about the disruption that the process brings to the day job! But most of all, it is typically the fact that teams and individuals feel they are being scrutinised that makes management due diligence both sensitive and the most intimate aspect of the broader spectrum of due diligence and this sets a challenging context for all parties. Communication and positioning of the rationale for conducting this aspect of management due diligence is critical.

Be aware: how management teams carry themselves through this process of due diligence tells as much about them as any other procedure that might attach itself to the practice. Investment directors should be conscious to gather feedback in this area since it will give a degree of guidance as to what will be witnessed in the boardroom on future occasions.

There is a maturing view of the role of management due diligence in the private equity market that looks as though it will be placed fairly and squarely at the centre of transaction processes for future investments. The cautiousness that exists in the market—particularly when audit trails are examined in the future—is driving a need to ensure that the capabilities, motivation and related issues are addressed in a constructive, mature and durable process to ensure as much visibility of those issues is gathered prior to the decision to invest.

Chapter 8

Due Diligence

8.1 Introduction

There is very little statutory protection for a purchaser of a company or an investor in a business, although common law remedies may entitle them to damages and/or to treat the contract as rescinded for the torts of deceit or misrepresentation. In theory, contractual protection can be obtained from the provision of warranties and/or indemnities by vendors or the investee company and its existing shareholders. However, in practice, in pursuing a warranty and/or an indemnity claim, an investor may only succeed in damaging its investment further. Moreover, any warranties and/or indemnities obtained from individuals will only be as good as the net worth of those individuals, who may also have had the foresight to transfer their assets away from the domain of a possible claim. Even if the warrantors have the funds to satisfy a claim, damages may not be an adequate remedy, particularly if the subject matter of the claim is the damage of reputation or goodwill of the business concerned or the loss of an important customer that would have significantly increased the company's revenue. In addition to these uncertainties, bringing a claim is expensive and time consuming and most claims will be subject to time limits, financial thresholds and lots of other limitations and restrictions.

8–01

As a result of the limited statutory and common law protection provided to an investor, the principle of caveat emptor ("let the buyer beware") will apply in the case of an investment in a business or company. Immediately upon the private equity house making its investment, the value of its investment will be affected by all the targets company's actual and potential liabilities and obligations, whether or not they were disclosed at the time of the investment.

Hence, the principal purpose of due diligence is to obtain sufficient information about the target company or business, including its critical success factors and its strengths and weaknesses, to enable the investor to decide whether or not to proceed with the investment and, if so, on what terms. It is effectively an audit of the target company's affairs. Any information obtained from due diligence which casts doubt on the value of the target company or business or reveals a potential risk for the investor gives the investor the opportunity not to proceed with the investment, to negotiate a fairer price or seek reinforced warranty, indemnity or other contractual protection. Due diligence is not a substitute for contractual protection, but assists in determining which contractual protection is required (for example, testing the accuracy and completeness of the warranties) and what risks the investor may choose to avoid completely. In short it is a useful bargaining tool. It puts the buyer in a better position to assess the risks and rewards of the purchase and to seek to renegotiate the terms of the purchase where appropriate.

Because the due diligence exercise is broad in scope (as will be seen below) it is imperative that efficient project or transaction management tools are employed both to avoid duplication and an inefficient use of time but also to ensure proper communication takes place between all the parties.

8–02 The disclosure process overlaps with, but is separate from, the due diligence process. Due diligence is principally a form of investigation to enable the purchaser to determine whether it wishes to continue with the negotiations and proceed with the purchase or whether there are deficiencies/unexpected liabilities in or problems arising out of the target company or business which make it decide not to proceed. It also provides the purchaser with information to enable its lawyers to tailor the acquisition agreement and warranties to the target company or business to ensure that appropriate contractual comfort about the state and condition of the target company or business is obtained.

Although the disclosure process assists in the eliciting of information useful to the due diligence process, it should not generally be regarded as a substitute for it. Due diligence is a process which goes beyond the mere acceptance and receipt of disclosure material against standard commercial type warranties. It should comprise a thorough investigation of all key aspects of the target company or business (including its assets, liabilities and prospects) not all of which will be covered, either at all or comprehensively, by the warranties (e.g. prospects, environmental liabilities, property).

Commonly, a significant amount of the information provided for due diligence will (depending on the scope of the warranties) be incorporated into and/or be relevant to the subsequent disclosure process. Hence familiarity with the due diligence material will assist in the disclosure process.

8.2 Use of due diligence in private equity transactions

8.2.1 Investment/acquisition

8–03 Generally due diligence is undertaken by private equity houses taking an equity stake in a company or investing to enable a Newco to acquire a target company or business.

Use of due diligence in private equity transactions

Increasingly, target companies or businesses are offered for sale by way of an auction process. Here, advisors to private equity houses bidding for such targets are often asked to produce "preliminary" due diligence reports based on a brief review of documentation that has been placed in a data room by the vendor. This is usually just a snapshot that will help the private equity house to determine whether it wishes to participate in the auction and, if so, to determine its offer price. It is however very limited as a due diligence exercise. Often it is seen as a box ticking exercise to demonstrate to the vendor the keenness of the private equity house to go forward in the auction process. Once the private equity house has reached the final stages of the auction process, it will invariably follow this up with a more exhaustive due diligence exercise.

8.2.2 Investor exits: pre-sale planning

Pre-sale planning by the departing private equity house within a 6 to 12 month period prior to an exit can assist in helping all the vendors to maximise their sale proceeds. A purchaser is likely to subject the investee company to intensive research. It is always sensible to be ahead of the game by undertaking a review of key areas in the business as part of the pre-sale planning process and therefore address any issues and pitfalls before they become pricing issues. A purchaser will often look to reduce the price of a business where there are serious issues that have not been addressed or alternatively one that has grown too quickly where its administration has not kept pace. **8–04**

Pre-sale due diligence need not be a full due diligence exercise such as the one undertaken when the private equity house made the original investment, but should address problem areas in the business, perhaps focused on industry specific issues. For example, if the business is reliant on a number of key customer contracts, a pre-sale review can identify weaknesses with any of those contracts which may give a purchaser a reason to reduce the price. Or, if a company is particularly reliant on its property portfolio, and if a full title investigation was undertaken at the time of the original investment, a title review can be limited to properties purchased by the investee company since then.

The due diligence should aim to provide the shareholders with solutions to each of the problems identified. For example: **8–05**

- to instruct its lawyers or other advisors to remedy the problem. This will obviously involve an upfront cost but may avoid uncertainty or delay in the sale or a reduction in price;
- the private equity house may forewarn bidders of the problem by including details in the information memorandum on a "take it or leave it" basis at a time when bidders are competing on price. Once taken into account, it is

then almost impossible to use this as a price negotiating tactic. It is also more difficult for bidders to seek contractual protection on the issue;

- the investor may choose to do nothing but at least it can prepare itself for the argument it is bound to have, that the price should be reduced.

8.2.3 Investor exits: auctions and vendor due diligence

8–06 When exiting from an investment, private equity houses will often undertake an auction process in order to maximise the consideration. Although the private equity house is unlikely to have had day-to-day management control, it may well dictate the auction process because of its greater experience and its desire to ensure that management remain focused on running the business. Probably, the most efficient way of delivering the same information to a number of potential purchasers is through a data room and the management team will be asked to deliver key information to prepare this. Whilst this involves significant upfront time and effort, it has the advantage of minimising the disruption to management (who will wish to avoid responding to a duplication of requests for information) and ensuring the vendors are in greater control of the process.

8–07 In some cases, the shareholders may request that, in addition to making the data room available, a legal due diligence report is prepared by the company's lawyers to be made available to potential purchasers. This can have the following benefits:

- the preparation of the report can alert the vendors to pitfalls, as discussed above, which can be addressed at an early stage, rather than beginning negotiations on the defensive if the purchaser becomes aware of the problem first;
- the report can provide a summary of much of the information contained in the data room in an eligible and accessible form; and
- the report can then be addressed to the successful bidder at completion, although it is likely that it will want additional work undertaken (as, for example, the report is a snapshot of the target at the time it was prepared and can become out of date relatively quickly).

8.3 Types and manner of due diligence

8–08 The extent of the due diligence undertaken by the investor will depend largely on the time available, how comfortable it feels about the business and cost. Commercial and business due diligence looks at wider issues such as the market in which the business operates, production, sales, insurances, research and development, management, the

Types and manner of due diligence

competition, key strengths and weaknesses etc. The principal types of due diligence that are most commonly undertaken are as follows:

Financial/accounting due diligence (See further s.8.7.) The House of Lords ruled in the case of *Caparo Industries v Dickman* [1990] 2 W.L.R. 358, that auditors owed duties only to the company itself and not to its present and future shareholders or lenders. This narrow approach to auditors' liability (confirmed by the decisions in *Anthony v Wright* (1994) and *Galoo v Bright Grahame Murray* [1995] 1 All E.R. 16) has emphasised the need for a prudent investor to instruct an independent firm of accountants to investigate the target company's financial position.

Commercial/market due diligence This will typically concentrate on the particular sector or market in which the investee or target business operates and its customer base, etc. It is often undertaken by external consultants.

Property/environmental due diligence For example, valuation or surveys may be commissioned and environmental audits undertaken. The extent of these will depend on the nature of the business and the importance of the properties. Title issues will usually be addressed as part of the legal due diligence.

Other specialist due diligence For example: actuarial advice if the target company has a final salary pension scheme; insurance advice on the adequacy of cover; reviews of key intellectual property by trade mark or patent agents; a review of the targets information technology requirements.

Legal due diligence Hence, a due diligence exercise will involve a multi-disciplinary team comprising the investor, the investment bankers, lawyers, accountants, insurance brokers/risk managers, actuarial consultants and any other specialists who may be required. The legal due diligence team will consist of lawyers specialising in various areas, including environment, property, employment, pensions, litigation, tax and intellectual property.

With such large teams, there needs to be a clear demarcation of responsibilities between the various team members. These should be documented in the respective advisor's engagement letter and one person should be appointed to co-ordinate the various strands of due diligence.

8.4 The lawyers' role

The lawyers should play a key role in the multi-disciplinary due diligence team, **8–09** often heading the team and taking the lead in identifying the risk and liability aspects of the investment. Where a large number of professionals are involved, it is important to clarify what the reporting lines are and who is acting for and reporting to whom. For example, will foreign lawyers or trademark agents report to the investor or the lawyers? Communication is all-important. It is not simply a lawyers' exercise and, if it is to be of any value, it should be taken seriously.

Where the investment has cross-border aspects, and the group has companies in different jurisdictions, the investor's lead lawyer should co-ordinate the legal due diligence to be conducted in the various countries involved. In order to do this he should prepare a master due diligence checklist and, in consultation with the local counsel, tailor the checklist to reflect the local laws, custom and practice. There will be local customs determining the extent of due diligence in different countries. This needs to be considered but also it may need to be restricted.

The lead lawyers should co-ordinate the preparation of the due diligence memoranda by the various local counsel and should in addition co-ordinate the timely communication of pertinent information and, in particular, potential risks to the investor and those responsible for negotiating and drafting the purchase or investment agreements. Any relevant information should be delivered on an "as received basis", rather than waiting until the due diligence exercise has been completed.

After the first draft of a report is produced, it is useful to sit down with the management and the investors to consider the issues with them before producing a final draft.

8.5 Due diligence process

8–10 The primary purpose of the due diligence process is to obtain sufficient information about the target's business to enable the purchaser (or other parties with an interest in the transaction) to decide whether the proposed acquisition represents a sound commercial investment. In effect it is an audit of the target's affairs—legal, business, financial and increasingly that of management or leadership (in mid-market transactions the role of management to grow the business is paramount)—aiming to obtain as complete an understanding of the business as possible, including its key performance indicators, strengths and weaknesses.

Whilst the process in which due diligence is undertaken will vary, it would generally involve some or all of the following:

- review of publicly available information;
- inspection of books and records;
- preparation of questionnaires (these should be properly scoped) and a review and analysis of those responses;
- site visits; and
- (importantly) interviews with management, customers and/or suppliers.

8.6 Impact of due diligence on warranty claims: *Infiniteland and Aviss v Artisan*

The Court of Appeal case *Infiniteland and Aviss v Artisan Contracting and Artisan (UK) Plc* [2005] EWCA Civ 758; [2006] 1 B.C.L.C. 632 highlights the importance of the interaction between the due diligence process, disclosure, the drafting of the share purchase agreement and the ability of the purchaser to make a successful claim for breach of warranty.

8–11

The case involved the sale by Artisan Contracting Limited of a number of companies including Bickerton Construction Limited to Infiniteland Limited. Soon after the sale Bickerton's business failed and it was placed in voluntary liquidation.

At some point prior to the sale, Artisan had injected approximately £1 million into Bickerton. Infiniteland sought to make a claim under the accounts warranty and a warranty on the accuracy of the disclosure letter. The accounts showed a trading profit of over £500,000 when in fact there was a loss of about the same amount, the difference being the result of the cash injection.

Artisan, whilst admitting that the cash injection was not properly shown in the accounts, argued that the team advising the purchaser knew about it as a result of their enquiries. Infiniteland had instructed its accountants to carry out financial due diligence on the target, and its accountant had full and free access to the books and records of Bickerton. One of the queries they raised related to the cash injection. In evidence, the accountants confirmed that they had received a full explanation from Bickerton and understood the nature of the credit and how it affected the accounts. However the accountants did not pass on the information to Infiniteland as they believed Infiniteland's financial advisor had already discussed the point with Artisan.

Infiniteland argued that the £1 million cash injection was not properly reflected in the accounts.

The share purchase agreement included a clause that provided that:

8–12

> "the rights and remedies of the purchaser in respect of any breach of the warranties shall not be affected by any investigation made by it or on its behalf into the affairs of any target companies (except to the extent that such investigation gives the purchaser actual knowledge of the relevant facts and circumstances)".

The wording in brackets turned out to be critical. The court held that it was clear that Infiniteland's accountants knew about the £1 million injection and therefore knew that in so far as the accounts gave the impression of a trading profit of approximately £500,000 this impression was misleading.

The court went on to say that where a purchaser chooses to act through an agent for any specific purpose of an acquisition, the actual knowledge of the agent so far as it is knowledge within the aspect for the purpose for which the agent is acting must be treated as the knowledge of the purchaser. As Infiniteland's accountants were acting as the agent of the purchaser in investigating the financial affairs of Bickerton, knowledge acquired by them in that capacity was deemed to be the knowledge of the purchaser. Therefore it was determined that while there had been a breach of warranty, the express provision of the agreement deprived Infiniteland of any remedy that it would otherwise have for that breach.

8.7 Accountancy due diligence

8–13 On a typical acquisition or investment, the purchaser or investor will usually instruct accountants to prepare a report (known as an "accountant's report") on the financial aspects of the target company or business. The contents of such a report will generally be crucial to the investor in deciding whether to proceed with an investment. In view of the expense of an accountant's report, an investor will not instruct its reporting accountants to prepare a report until there is agreement on the principal terms of its investment, though in more aggressive environments this is not always the case.

Scope of accountant's report

Financial due diligence is not the equivalent of an audit of the target company or business and the resulting report will usually make that fact clear. Further it will not typically independently verify the assets and liabilities of the target company or business nor make an in-depth examination of its systems of internal control. Generally, financial due diligence will focus on those areas of the financial affairs of the target company or business that are material to the purchaser's decision to acquire, so that the purchaser can assess the financial risks and opportunities of the acquisition and whether, given those risks and opportunities, the target company or business will fit well into the purchaser's strategy. Financial due diligence can also assist the purchaser to assess potential growth, to understand and quantify the potential synergies between the target company or business and the purchaser's existing operations (if any), to assess the impact of the acquisition on the purchaser's performance statistics and to identify the best acquisition and financing structures.

Part of the accountant's investigations will usually be a review of the audited accounts relating to the target company or business and, in certain cases, the related audit working papers. In practice, access will not be given to working papers unless an appropriate "indemnity" letter (often referred to as a "hold harmless letter") has been given to the target auditors. Essentially this contains a commitment from the purchaser or vendor to indemnify the auditors for any claims that arise as a result of such access being given. They are often widely drafted and should be reviewed carefully.

It is desirable to meet the accountants before drawing up the terms of reference in order to establish a realistic schedule (a full investigation can take several weeks), agree costs and highlight particular areas of concern to the investor. The investor will be keen to ensure that whilst the investigation is as full as possible; its accountants do not waste time and money in duplicating investigations that may be undertaken by other advisors. The normal objective of accountants' investigations is to obtain specific financial, commercial and administrative information regarding the target, including the following: **8–14**

- the constitution and structure of the company: capital structure, shareholders, unusual share rights, legal structure of the group and its history;
- the current position regarding the assets and liabilities to be acquired: summary of the latest net asset position, review of the financial position including any financing arrangements, working capital requirements, contingent liabilities and leasing commitments;
- the up-to-date trading position: summary and discussion of the last five years' profit and loss accounts, an assessment of the performance and explanation of trends;
- business: brief history and description of the current business, its principal activities and methods of operation, including sales and marketing policies; details of domestic and foreign suppliers and customers, including dependence on major suppliers and customers and alternative sources of supply; analysis of turnover and profits by principal activity, review of the business sector including details of major competitors and market share; economic, legislative and other external factors affecting the group;
- the management structure: review of organisation of the accounts department, accounting systems and controls and management information systems, details of directors and senior managers and their terms, recruitment and training policy, employees and their benefit arrangements, trade union and collective agreements and pension schemes;
- accounting policies: summary of accounting policies and discussion of complicated or unusual ones;
- a report on the company's tax affairs;
- a summary of the objectives of management, discussion and assessment of profit and cash flow forecasts, together with underlying assumptions, for the current accounting period;
- various miscellaneous areas such as a review of premises, equipment and insurances;

- an indication of likely impact on customers, suppliers and employees of an acquisition (where relevant) and any other points for concern.

Where the purchaser is a listed company or a company whose shares are traded on AIM (or a subsidiary undertaking of any such company) depending on the size of the acquisition, it may need to give shareholders certain financial information about the merged group. The purchasers' accountants will need to review the figures of the target company or business in order to provide this information.

8–15 The accountant's report is normally prepared in draft and issued to the investor for comment prior to it being finalised. It should also be issued to the management of the company as they will undoubtedly have helpful comments to make on the report. Moreover they will be asked in the investment agreement to warrant any facts contained in the report. It is also becoming common for the accountants preparing the report to ask the managers to warrant to the accountants the representations made to them for the purposes of the report. This is often by way of a side letter which the managers are asked to sign at the completion of the report, but before the final report is delivered. Potentially, therefore, if there is a claim under the report the managers could face a claim not just from the investors but also from the accountants. In fact, in reality the investors are more likely to sue the accountants than the managers, who will have limited funds, but more importantly because it is not good for future business to be seen suing your own management teams. If the accountants are sued they will almost certainly join the managers in an action. It is therefore better to deal with this at the outset of the transaction with the investors, who can in turn make it clear to the accountants undertaking the due diligence that this is not acceptable. If the accountants are persistent, at the very least the letter should be subject to all the limitations that have been agreed in the investment agreement.

Limitation of accountant's liability

8–16 In recent years accountants have been on the receiving end of a spiralling number of legal claims in their role as auditors. This increasingly litigious environment has seriously restricted the availability of professional indemnity insurance, and even where such insurance is available it is becoming prohibitively expensive.

This trend is now affecting the private equity market because accountants, anxious to limit their exposure, want to limit their liability for due diligence reports too. This has caused a certain amount of friction between the banks, the private equity houses and the accounting firms (particularly when the attempt by the accountants to impose a limitation for a particular due diligence report did not emerge until the run up to completion—a fundamental issue at a crucial time). Undoubtedly, this approach simply caused the entrenchment of the banks and the

Accountancy due diligence

private equity houses about what they required. However, if the accountants' liability is unlimited, then it would seem likely that the quality of the report will reflect this, with accountants being more likely to hedge their advice and include a number of unnecessary caveats in their reports. If liability is limited to a meaningful extent then they will be less inclined to water down their advice.

Where accountants seek to impose limitations, it is advisable that the investors' lawyers review the document and, even more importantly, that it is done before the mandate is given in order to have any chance of making sensible changes. From a legal point of view however, limitation of liability for a due diligence report does pose some complex questions. For example, if the due diligence report is addressed to the various banks and private equity houses backing the transaction with a single limit of liability, how does the limitation apply in practice between the beneficiaries of the report? In addition how is the conduct (and the cost) of the claim to be addressed? These issues will need to be addressed in the inter-creditor arrangements and possibly in the syndication arrangements between the private equity houses. **8–17**

In 1998, the BVCA reached a memorandum of understanding with the large accounting practices relating to limitation of liability and proportionality provisions in due diligence for private equity transactions. The memorandum is not legally binding but provides a framework of reference. For deals of less than £10 million, liability will be limited to the transaction value, for transactions of between £10 million and £25 million the liability will be £10 million plus one-third by which the transaction value exceeds £10 million and for transactions over £25 million generally £25 million will be agreed as a cap.

8.8 Legal due diligence

Through this process, the investor will wish to ascertain, so far as is possible, the nature and the value of the assets and liabilities in which it is investing and that the company has good title to the assets free from any third-party rights. In understanding the company's business from a legal perspective, the due diligence will: **8–18**

- provide the investor with the information necessary to allow an informed investment decision;
- identify, and enable the investor to understand, and where possible quantify, the risks and liabilities associated with the investee business;
- alert the purchaser at an early stage to any consents that are required (e.g. shareholder, third-party or regulatory consents);
- place the investor in a better position to negotiate or adjust the cost of the investment and adjust or tailor the representations, warranties or indemnities to be obtained;

Due Diligence

- help the investor to understand the impact of disclosures; and
- help the purchaser/investor to plan the integration of the target business following the acquisition. The knowledge obtained from due diligence can be integrated to that plan.

8.8.1 Scoping the report

8–19 It will be necessary to scope the due diligence in some detail in order to prepare the type of report the investor wants. Some of this will be dictated by the size of the transaction and therefore costs, for example is it looking for a list of documents, a review of significant legal issues or concentration on any particular issues? A debt provider in particular will be most concerned at the quality of his security, as opposed to an investor who is concerned about the ability of the business to grow. It is necessary to have a general discussion about the principal areas of risk and sensitivity for the investor. It will probably be impossible as a result of both time constraints and cost limitations to look at all documents disclosed with the same level of detail.

8–20 It is therefore important to understand what is important in order to prioritise that review. The purchaser will need to identify the main risks and liability inherent in the industry in which the target company operates. It is important therefore that the legal advisors draw on their industry expertise where they can, to consider the normal risks in the industry, the reputation of the target company in the industry, and any knowledge of the selling management team, etc. This includes understanding the nature of the target business and the relative value to the investor of different parts of the business which could be affected by the documents being reviewed. It will be helpful to consider the documents with the investor before the review commences in order that it can give a steer on which are key documents. At the original scoping meeting the following should be agreed:

- the scope and focus of the work;
- the materiality thresholds, to exclude immaterial issues from the report;
- the areas of specialist advice required, e.g. tax, pensions, etc;
- the approach to be taken in the report—its form, its length and the approach to the executive summary;
- a timetable for the steps leading to the issue of the final report;
- the limitations on the due diligence; and
- the costs.

Costs of due diligence particularly in large firms, with a plethora of specialist departments, can be very expensive.

8.8.2 Purchaser information requests

The obvious starting point for legal due diligence is to request information from the company and its advisors. Before a company is willing to give any information to an investor or its advisors it will generally require a satisfactory confidentiality agreement. 8–21

The precise extent of the information required will obviously be dependent upon the nature of the investment. However, it is likely to fall into some or all of the following categories: 8–22

- Constitution. Memorandum and articles and other constitutional documents (these should be reviewed to determine the company's power to consummate the transaction, for any potential impediments to the investment (including any rights of first refusal); details of share capital and of shares under option, statutory books (inquiry should be made to verify that all the company's shares were duly authorised and validly issued, and fully paid); minutes of directors and shareholders' meetings (to include a review of the validity of directors' appointments, proper authorisation of material contracts including purchase of own shares, etc)).

- Accounts. Reports and audited accounts for the past three years and subsequent unaudited and management accounts.

- Licences. Details of any licences and consents obtained or acquired for carrying on the business; any reports or correspondence relating to any infringement of such licences.

- Funding. Details of all borrowings, finance and invoice discounting facilities, a schedule of all indebtedness owed by the company or its subsidiaries, and early pre-payment fees, instruments evidencing indebtedness, all security agreements, guarantees, letters of credit and performance bonds, etc.

- Litigation. Particulars of any pending or threatened legal proceedings or arbitrations or prosecutions, or governmental investigations (where the company sells or distributes products that are or may involve significant product liability exposure, more detailed investigation into the likelihood and magnitude of the actual and potential risks is advisable).

- Employees. Names and addresses, ages, dates from which continuous employment began, salaries and other entitlements to remuneration; normal working hours, notice entitlement and job grade; the terms of employment of, and the fees paid to, all directors and senior executives and information as to other employees' standard terms and the conditions of employment, written statement of particular terms, offer letters, company rules and disciplinary and grievance procedure, details of any trade union or any other collective agreements and codes of conduct or practice, details of any bonus schemes, death or disability benefit schemes; any written employment manual or their literature regarding terms and conditions of employment, agreements with present or former employees with regard to confidentiality and/or non-competition; details of all employee share option schemes, current options and exercise terms; health and safety policies, entitlements to tied-staff accommodation, employment litigation.

- Pensions. Details of all current and proposed schemes, of employees in the scheme, copies of the latest actuarial valuations and the annual report for the vendor's or, if different, target company's scheme, employer's contribution rates, any proposed alterations, details of ex-gratis or unapproved schemes, copies of the relevant tax authorities' approvals.

- Contracts and trading arrangements. Details of material capital commitments, standard terms of trading, major agreements with suppliers and customers, contracts entered into other than in the ordinary course of business, details of agreements, arrangements which are or should be notified to the Commission of the European Communities, details of any joint venture or agency or distribution agreements and membership of any trade association. Details of standard forms used in connection with the sale of the company's products, all written agreements with regard to advertising, promotion, all documents creating any express or implied warranties.

- Insurance. Particulars of all insurances and any insurance claims outstanding; review of historical liability insurance policies under which claims could still be made (for example, employers' liability insurance).

- Information technology. Identify all elements of the computer system used by the target: is shared access to the system required? Who owns copyright to the software? Who wrote it? Were they employees or consultants? What were the terms of their contract? Are there any restrictions in the software licences? Will the disposal fall foul of any restrictions? Does any other part of the group provide assets or services and are these to continue? Does the computer system comply with EC regulations? Does the company own copyright in its website design? Are there any disaster recovery arrangements or ongoing support arrangements? Are there any recurring technical problems with the system? Does the company have access to the source code and software licences? Are there any disputes between the company and any third parties with regard to the use of the licences?

- Assets. Schedule of all material equipment indicating the nature and ownership of such equipment and the material terms of any finance and operating leases or hire purchase agreements.

- Property. Details of all properties owned or used, nature of title, principal terms and rent of any leases, tenancies, licences, book and current values and any mortgages, charges or encumbrances affecting the property, any reports on properties, schedule of investors.

Legal due diligence

- Environmental and health and safety. What is the nature of the company's business and processes? What environmental impact do they have? How does the company deal with waste, and other emissions? Are any permits or licences to conduct the company's business required? Are they maintained? Have they been revoked or challenged? What is the condition of the site? Are any hazardous substances stored at the site? Has the site been operated in compliance with environmental audit? Does the company have statutory health and safety risk assessments? Review all health and safety records and logbooks. Does the record of injuries and illnesses indicate a problem with health and safety? Obtain all correspondence with the health and safety authorities. Is the person in charge of health and safety employed by the company?

- Intellectual property. Details of all UK and foreign patents, registered designs and copyrights, trademarks and trading and claimants' names and other intellectual property rights and know how, evidence of title to them, details of challenges to them.

8.8.3 Independent verification methods

A certain amount of information may be obtained or verified from checking public records or from legal opinions given by the legal advisor to the company. **8–23**

Company searches

For UK companies, a search at the Companies Registry is important. It will show a company's constitutional documents, annual accounts, share capital, directors and secretary, registered office, charges over its assets, liquidation, receivership, dissolution and administration. There is no guarantee that the company search is correct, for example, a company may fail to file the necessary returns which would show its true position. Hence, the warrantors should be asked to warrant such information. **8–24**

Where the vendor is a non-UK company appropriate investigations and searches will need to be undertaken in the relevant country.

These searches should be repeated as close as possible to the exchange of contracts.

Statutory books and records

It is also essential that the result of the search at the Companies Registry is compared with the information contained in the company's statutory books, **8–25** which normally comprise a register of allotment, transfers, directors and secretaries, directors' interests, members and charges. The company should also maintain minute books for both directors' and shareholders' meetings.

The lawyers should endeavour to establish title to the relevant shares. This can be traced by entries in the register of allotments and/or transfers in the register of members together with either the original application forms, where the shares have been allotted, or duly stamped transfer forms where shares have been transferred with the share certificates relating to the shares sold. If an allotment required, for example, a resolution of the shareholders (for example to disapply statutory pre-emption rights or to grant the directors authority to allot the shares), the minute books should contain the relevant minutes and relevant resolutions should appear on the company's record at the Companies Registry.

Credit agency searches

8–26 Credit agency searches can be approached to obtain information about a target company's credit-worthiness. This information will nearly always be more up-to-date than that obtainable from a search at the Companies Registry.

Bankruptcy search

8–27 A bankruptcy search should be undertaken in relation to each of the directors of the company to determine whether any petition in bankruptcy, receiving order in bankruptcy or deed of arrangement has been registered.

Legal opinions

8–28 Legal opinions given by the company's lawyers may serve as a substitute for some matters that would otherwise be subject to the investor's due diligence review. A request for this may arise where information is not readily available, or cannot be made available in relation to a legal matter such as a piece of litigation. They should generally be limited to legal as opposed to factual or commercial matters. They may include the company's constitution, capitalisation and ownership, approvals and consents, and whether completion will violate applicable laws.

Reliance on a legal opinion from the company's lawyers in place of the investor's own due diligence shifts the burden to the opinion giver with respect to the matters covered. It is, however, not common in this country to give a legal opinion and they are not given readily. It may be reasonable to require a legal opinion where the company in which the investment is to be made has a number of foreign subsidiaries. The company's lawyer in the relevant jurisdiction may be asked

Legal due diligence

to confirm that the company validly exists and is in good standing with the relevant authorities, and to confirm constitutional matters relating to the company. However, the investor's lawyer should consult local counsel before launching a US-style legal opinion request.

8.8.4 Review of materials

Having agreed with the client the principal areas upon which due diligence should focus, issued its questionnaire and received materials in response, the lawyers will normally do the following: 8–29

- identify and index all relevant documents which come within the scope of the review or which are or may be material;
- prepare an outline of the principal provisions of that documentation, noting any provisions which may be material, unusual or of special interest to the client—for example, indemnity provisions, restrictive covenants, any termination, repurchase, buy-out or other similar provisions (including penalties), confidentiality provisions, change of control provisions etc;
- consider whether any specific agreement may be affected by any other part of the due diligence exercise;
- consider whether there are reasons to doubt the effectiveness or enforceability of any of the agreements, for example under competition laws, EEC legislation or the Unfair Contract Terms Act 1977;
- consider omissions to any agreement, i.e. terms that are usual in the type of contract that is being reviewed and have not been included; and
- analyse potential liabilities and exposures identified.

8.9 Specific areas of legal due diligence

It is worth commenting on a few of the specialist areas of legal due diligence.

8.9.1 Employees

An important area of due diligence relates to employees. The employment terms of all employees need to be checked carefully and in particular the service agreements of the directors and other key staff. Areas which will need to be looked at include the length of notice required to terminate the agreement and the level of benefits provided. As a minimum most investors would wish to ascertain with regard to the employees: 8–30

- employee salaries and other emoluments;
- entitlements to participate in any bonus or profit sharing/or share option scheme;
- restrictive covenants in the employment contracts particularly with regard to directors or senior management;
- whether or not there is an even age spread so as to ensure the company will not be subject to many retirements;
- whether or not the company has been operating discriminating practices;
- binding collective agreements;
- whether health and safety measures meet with legal requirements.

In the UK where a purchaser is buying a business the liability for employees will be automatically assumed by the purchaser and cannot be excluded. Any major review of large numbers of employees is often limited to key employees. The purchaser will be keen for a review and advice on termination provisions and restrictive covenants so that the purchaser can understand the position if key employees leave. The purchaser will also want to know details of the contract of any unwanted employee he/she is forced to take (for example, termination provisions, costs of dismissal, enforceability of any restraints).

8.9.2 Data protection

8–31 The impact of data protection in corporate transactions is often overlooked. However, in particular, for many companies a customer database is often one (if not the) most valuable asset of the business and a failure to transfer this customer information lawfully to a purchaser could result in it having to incur considerable costs in overhauling its data processing activities in order to achieve compliance with the Data Protection Act.

One point for a vendor is that when disclosing employment records to a potential purchaser, either through a data room or otherwise, he should ensure that he is fully compliant with the Act in the disclosing of personal data. In order to comply with the Act he may have to limit the personal data which is disclosed or ensure that the personal data is given as anonymously as possible and also impose contractual conditions on the purchaser's access to and use of such data.

In order to determine whether data protection is an issue to a business a key question should be asked at the outset: does the target deal with individuals as customers, that is, is the purchaser acquiring a customer database? If so, then there may immediately be compliance issues surrounding information provision, data accuracy, retention and security issues and possibly international transfer issues if it is a multi-national company.

Specific areas of legal due diligence

Obviously the nature of the target's business and its uses of data will determine the level of risk to be attributed to the data protection aspects of the corporate transaction. For example, a customer focused retail operation is more likely to embrace data protection issues than a sale of a large manufacturing operation that deals mainly with corporate customers.

A purchaser during its due diligence process should ask the following questions in order to fully understand the required level of compliance for the target. **8–32**

- Has it notified the Information Commissioner that it is a data controller under the Act?
- Is any kind of data protection statement or privacy policy currently used for the purpose of informing individuals of the uses and disclosures made of their personal data?
- What procedures or policies are adopted to ensure that the personal data is maintained and kept up-to-date?
- Does the target have any procedures or policies in place that will protect the confidentiality of personal data?
- Does the company share its information with any other subsidiaries in the group or associated companies or even through any joint venture operations?
- How does the company deal with requests from individuals to be provided with information about personal data held by them?
- Does the target give individuals the opportunity to remove themselves from the database or opt out of marketing related communications?
- Has the company received any notices of non-compliance with the Act from the commissioner or letters of complaint from an individual?

8.9.3 Pensions

The investor will need to check out the company's pension schemes and the level and security of funding that the schemes require. The type of information which will be required includes: **8–33**

- the nature of the company's present pension arrangements for employees of the company;
- whether the scheme is a final salary scheme or a money purchase scheme—far greater due diligence is required where there are final salary schemes, due to the significant liabilities that they can impose on a company. Normally, detailed actuarial advice will be necessary;

Due Diligence

- whether it is insured or self-administered, contracted-in or contracted-out of the State Earnings Related Pension Scheme ("SERPS") and the level of benefits provided and the amount of the ongoing costs.

Apart from these inquiries, the investor should also seek from the company the following documentation:

- up-to-date copies of the trust deed and rules, all amending deeds and resolutions;
- a copy of the latest actuarial valuation of any final salary scheme;
- a list of the scheme's members and those who are likely to become members during the course of the next 12 months on completing service or age qualifications;
- a copy of the latest scheme booklet;
- copies of any deeds of appointment of trustees;
- any deed of adherence by which the company to be sold agrees to be bound by the scheme;
- evidence of the scheme's exempt approved tax status; and
- if appropriate, a copy of the contracting-out certificate covering the employer.

8.9.4 Property

8–34 It is important to establish at an early stage how important the freehold and leasehold properties are to the operations of the company. In order to do this, a list of properties and very brief details should be obtained from the company.

Although property may not be a major asset of the business, it could prove to be a substantial liability especially if there are environmental liabilities or it is a leasehold property which has a potential dilapidations claim. The investor therefore will require a thorough investigation to be made. Obviously, documents of title should be inspected but in addition a physical inspection of the property should be made where a valuable or important property is being acquired. A formal survey and valuation report by a surveyor may be desirable. An investigation by the investor's lawyers or a certificate of title will not include a valuation or a physical inspection of the relevant property. The surveyor may be asked in addition not simply to value the property but also to carry out a structural survey. Even where time for completion is short, this exercise can be carried out in a limited form. An inspection by a professional can provide essential information. If bank finance is being put in at the same time, the banks often require valuations and surveys. There will usually be a disclaimer in the surveyors' report that they are not responsible to anyone other than the lenders.

Specific areas of legal due diligence

With regard to the title to the properties, the investor can consider one or more of the following possibilities: **8–35**

- the company's lawyers are requested to provide the investor with a certificate of title to the effect that the company has good and marketable title;
- the investor's lawyers carry out a full investigation of title and report to the investor. A consequence of this is that the company will only be willing to give the most basic warranties; or
- if the properties are not of any particular importance, to carry out no investigations and to rely totally on property warranties for protection.

The choice will be dependent on a number of factors, including cost and the time available. Full investigation will be appropriate where the value of the company or business is based on the value of its properties or where they are fundamental to the business and damages for breach of warranty would not be sufficient compensation. Conversely, where there are a number of short leasehold properties of which none are significant for the carrying on of the business then it would be normal to proceed without a full investigation.

Certificate of title

A certificate of title given by the company's lawyers can have a significant advantage where time is of the essence and where the company's lawyers have acted for the company on the purchase of the freehold or leasehold properties which are the subject of the certificates. Nevertheless, in practice, the company's lawyers will frequently seek to reduce their exposure by negotiating the certificate of title as much as possible, so that it becomes of limited use. Moreover, the certificate may not give the investor guidance on certain issues, such as the quality and commercial aspect of leases on which the investor may still seek advice from its own lawyers. A certificate is not sensitive to the characteristics of the property which may, of course, be important to the investor. Certificates draw no conclusions and offer no interpretation. They are just statements of fact. The certification will not necessarily tell the investor what is really important, as a certifying lawyer cannot be given the opportunity to discuss with the investor why it is entering into the transaction. Also, the schedule to the certificate of title often becomes the equivalent of the disclosure letter—only it is worse from a timing point of view. The investor will often obtain the information too late in the day, as there is no channel for the certifying lawyer to warn the investor of a problem at the moment he notices it. The consequence is that the investor's lawyers are often then asked at very short notice to review the disclosures. **8–36**

Where a certificate of title is given, the main course of action for any breach will be against the company's lawyers. The investor's advisors will wish to ensure that **8–37** the company's lawyers have adequate PI insurance and of sufficient calibre. Day-to-day property work of large companies can often be undertaken by small local firms. Such firms may not have specialists capable of handling the transaction. The investor therefore should request that the warrantors also warrant the certificate of title. More specifically, the company's lawyers' certificate will depend to a large extent on replies to enquiries made of the company, and it is sensible therefore that the investor should require the accuracy of those replies to be warranted. In addition, if there are any specific disclaimers in the certificate relating to matters of fact, then these can be warranted. The certificates given may require updating at the date on which they are to be relied upon, i.e. in relation to searches, etc.

8–38 The disadvantage with warranties is, of course, last-minute disclosures undermining their effect. Also, with property warranties, there is usually an argument about their currency. A title defect would only come to light upon the company trying to mortgage or dispose of the property. A twelve year cover is often requested and the position compromised at six years. It is possible to have different time periods for different types of property warranty as well, e.g. those matters which would take longer to come to light, such as "good and marketable title" and "freedom from encumbrances" could be warranted for longer than warranties as to replies to enquiries. Also, warranties themselves are often watered down to such an extent that the investor cannot rely upon them. Where rack-rent leasehold properties are concerned, a halfway house between a full investigation and warranties is to arrange for the investor's lawyers to read the leases. If this course is taken then the investor's lawyers should obtain the leases as early as possible, as it does take some time to carry out this exercise.

Title investigations

8–39 If the investor wishes to instruct his lawyers to investigate title then the investigation will include the carrying out of all the usual property searches and pre-contract enquiries as if the transaction were a normal conveyancing matter. If there are a large number of properties then a sampling exercise is often undertaken.

Title to leasehold and freehold property will be deduced to the investor's lawyers in the usual way depending on whether the property is registered or unregistered. In the case of registered land, office copy entries will be obtained from the Land Registry. In the case of unregistered land, an abstract of title or more likely certified copies of the title deeds should be inspected. If the property is leasehold, a certified copy of the lease and any documents supplemental to it will need to be inspected. Pre-contract enquiries of the company and pre-completion searches should be carried out before completion of the investment. These will include the usual searches of the local authority, Land Charges Registry, Local Land Charges Registry, Land Registry and Companies Registry. The local authority search will

Specific areas of legal due diligence

show information in the planning registers (including planning charges, compulsory purchase notices and enforcement or stop notices) maintenance of roads, road schemes, statutory or informal notices under Public Health Acts, Housing Acts, Highways Acts, listed buildings details, tree preservation orders, etc.

The Land Registry searches will reveal details of easements, restrictive and other covenants and encumbrances, as well as charges. A legal charge should be registered at the Land Registry if it is to be binding (as well as at Companies House). Registration at Companies House alone is generally considered to be insufficient. There may be additional searches required depending on the type of property and where it is located, such as Coal Authority, Network Rail and Environmental Agency searches. There are other more specific searches that may be required such as establishing the position and depth of underground trains in London, or in Cornwall whether the property is affected by mining for tin. **8–40**

Leasehold issues

In the case of leasehold property, the investor may inherit continuing as well as future liabilities for breaches of the covenants in the lease. It is necessary therefore that an investigation be made to ensure that the landlord has not commenced forfeiture proceedings, and that there is no outstanding liability for dilapidations arising from a breach of the repairing covenants, that the payment of the rent is up-to-date and that no major service charge payments are overdue or anticipated. **8–41**

It is also necessary to determine whether the company has a lease (normally giving it security of tenure under Part II of the Landlord and Tenant Act 1954) or merely a licence which can be terminated more easily and does not give any security of tenure to the licensee. It is often very difficult to distinguish between a lease and a licence, regardless of its description as one or the other. If exclusive possession is granted to the occupant, who has remained in occupation for in excess of six months for the purposes of business, it may be a protected lease.

If the investment is for the purposes of acquiring a business rather than the company being sold, an assignment of the lease will be necessary. In almost all cases there will be a requirement for the landlord's consent to be obtained before a market-rent lease can be assigned. Covenants against sub-letting or sharing possession also need to be checked. **8–42**

Once it legitimately assigns the lease, then unless the tenant has entered into an authorised guarantee agreement, its responsibility under the lease will cease. An authorised guarantee is a mechanism by which a tenant guarantees the obligations of its immediate assignee and it is normal market practice for a landlord to require an authorised guarantee to be given as a condition of granting consent to an assignment. Once that assignee has disposed of its interest, then it is at this stage that the tenant is released. While s.19(1) of the Landlord and Tenant Act 1927 still remains, most market-rent leases granted after January 1, 1996 contain detailed provisions specifying the criteria which a tenant must satisfy in order to be able to assign its lease. In relation to leases existing prior to the Act, then the old privity contract rules are preserved, although there are certain limitations on landlords in relation to notification and collection of rent arrears and changes in the lease terms.

8–43 Provided that there is no bar against assignment, it will be implied at law (if not expressed) that the landlord's consent is not to be unreasonably withheld (Landlord and Tenant Act 1927, s.19(1)). A common problem however is that the schedule to which the investor and the purchaser wish to work is much tighter than that to which a landlord will work. The landlord must consider an application for consent to assign and may be liable to the vendor in damages if the vendor suffers loss through the landlord's unreasonable delay in considering the application. However the landlord will normally require references, accounts and other financial information. Where a purchaser is setting up a new company, that company will have no proven track record. The landlord may look for additional security such as a guarantee from a parent company or rent deposit or even personal guarantees from the directors of the purchaser. Furthermore, particularly since January 1, 1996, a landlord may seek to make the consent conditional on all subsisting breaches of the tenant's covenants in the lease being rectified.

If bank finance is required, a lender should be alerted to the fact that some leases contain a prohibition on charging the property, or require the landlord's consent (usually not to be unreasonably withheld) to be obtained before any charge is granted.

As with obtaining landlord's consent to assignment, timing can be a problem if a landlord's prior consent is needed to any property being charged. A lender may decide to exclude a particular property from the initial security and defer charging that property until the necessary consent has been obtained, placing an obligation on the company to procure that consent.

8–44 Because of the original tenant liability rules which make a tenant liable during the whole of the term of its lease, it is necessary to check whether the company has held any market-rent leases before the Act came into force. Although the protections in the Act mitigate some of the hardships of the previous rules, the former tenants can still be required to take the original lease back where the former tenants are defaulting. The landlord will look to the deepest pocket to meet these liabilities and any investor should be aware of this potential contingent liability. As time passes, the exposure will reduce as more leases become subject to the new law. The investor will, however, need to check that no authorised guarantee agreements have been entered into.

The investor's lawyer will also be anxious to check the rent review position. The profitability of the business can be radically affected by an adverse rent review. It is important that rent review clauses in any lease are examined by a lawyer specialising in commercial property and the contractual relationship between the parties carefully checked.

Following the investigations, the investor's lawyers should be able to report on whether there is good marketable title to the relevant property, whether there are mortgages, charges, or third party rights affecting the property, whether there are outstanding disputes with regards to the property and whether the property is served by all the usual mains services and the roads are maintained at the public expense. If the property is leasehold the investor's lawyers should also confirm that the landlord's title is satisfactory, that the appropriate consents have been obtained for assignment, that the last receipt for rent was not qualified and that there are no material breaches of covenants or restrictions in the lease which prevent the use of the property and that there are no unusual or onerous covenants. **8–45**

8.9.5 Environmental due diligence

Environmental law is a rapidly changing area. As a result when making an investment that will be in place for a period of up to ten years the investor must bear in mind that the law is likely to change considerably over that period. However, more than ever in the past, there is a real risk of assuming environmental liabilities. These liabilities may be civil, criminal or statutory clean-up liabilities, and it is possible for all three types to arise from a single situation. Many of the criminal liabilities are strict liability offences where no guilty intent is required and, to make matters worse, the main environmental (and health and safety) statutes contain directors' and officers' liability provisions. The effect of this is that criminal liability can attach to controlling individuals of a body corporate if it commits an offence, as well as to the body corporate itself. **8–46**

It is obvious that if a business has to pay fines, clean-up costs and damages to neighbouring businesses as a result of pollution it has caused, it will be less profitable. It is less obvious that liability can also attach to a business as a consequence of pollution caused by others, either because it owns, occupies or controls a polluted site, or because it has acquired someone else's liability contractually. It is surprisingly easy to breach environmental law, particularly in the area of waste offences, and prosecutions can and do result from relatively trivial incidents where the degree of culpability is low. Companies no longer have a choice but to take these matters seriously. Therefore, those who lend money to them must also take them seriously. A prime requirement for investors is comfort—they do not want any surprises. Companies should therefore consider taking responsibility for instigating environmental due diligence prior to an investment. In any event more and more funders require the investing company to pay for an environmental due diligence report as a condition of any funding.

Due Diligence

8–47 There are several reasons why environmental liabilities are so much more relevant to investments today. These are as follows.

- Increased regulation. Controls over activities which can affect the environment are increasing and becoming more sophisticated. The ambit of control has also broadened to cover non-industrial activities such as intensive livestock production.

- Administrative changes. There have been a number of developments in the administration of pollution control which are designed to make enforcement more effective, most notably the creation of the Environment Agency and the Scottish Environmental Protection Agency in 1996. The regulation of the water environment, waste management and the most polluting and complex industrial processes is now carried out by these bodies in England, Wales and Scotland and is more centralised and consistent than previously.

- European legislation. Directives which establish Europe-wide standards for the main polluting industries are already in place, but increasingly measures to push environmental issues into the hearts of the commercial world are being proposed. A European directive on environmental liability is expected to come into force within a few years.

- Insurance. Cover for pollution and contamination has vanished from most policies, and where it remains it is for sudden and unexpected incidents only. If environmental cover is needed, particularly if it is to extend to gradual pollution, it must be written back in, at additional cost, and the underwriters will normally require detailed investigations to enable them to judge the risk and set a premium.

- Public scrutiny. Public opinion has become notoriously "green" in the last few years and the increasing focus on corporate governance will ensure that environmental issues remain high profile.

8–48 A further important reason for the emergence of environmental due diligence has been the growing awareness of the limitations inherent in the normal means of protecting a purchaser or a lender or investor against risks, i.e. the taking of warranties and indemnities. The shortcomings of relying on warranties or indemnities are:

- Extent of the damages. Warranties and indemnities are only as good as the credit-worthiness of the vendor. Damages for pollution can be extensive and an ability to sue for breach of warranty is of little use if the vendor has gone into liquidation or has insufficient assets to cover the loss.

- Delays in discovery. It is often very difficult to demonstrate when the pollution occurred. Where the new owners carry out some of the same processes involving the same raw materials and discharges, the discovery,

Specific areas of legal due diligence

some time after completion of the transaction, of a pollution problem, may lead to argument as to whether it occurred before or after completion.

- The difficulty of accurate assessment. Warranties and indemnities, even where given, may not reflect the true environmental position of the property. These may be given by senior management who are located many miles away from the site and have only a limited amount of knowledge as to the environmental practices at that site.

An environmental due diligence exercise is a study carried out to determine the extent and the nature of the risk involved in investing in a company and becoming responsible for its liabilities. The degree of sophistication of the study will vary from case to case and depend on a range of factors: **8–49**

- the nature of the processes carried on (presently and historically) at the site, the raw materials used and by-products and waste products produced;
- the value of the investment;
- the compliance records of the processes operated at the premises;
- any proposals for future use of the site;
- previous uses of the site;
- the environmental sensitivity of the site and its surroundings;
- the timescale of the transaction.

Environmental due diligence will usually begin with a legal investigation by the investors' lawyer. It will start by establishing the credentials of the operations and by examining each aspect in the context of the requirements of the regulatory agency. More and more information is becoming available to the public. Copies of applications for consents and the consents themselves together with all supporting information are placed on public registers. Details of enforcement actions are also a matter of public record, and most other environmental information held by regulatory authorities, even if not actually on a public register, is publicly available as a consequence of European directives and conventions on access to environmental information. The next few years are likely to see the increasing introduction of standards for environmental reporting to which companies will have to adhere. **8–50**

Documents supplied by the vendor should be examined from the perspective of environmental liability. Further checks should be made by examining information that is publicly available. The process of data gathering is facilitated nowadays by the ready availability, at modest cost, of information garnered from regulators, historic maps and other sources and packaged by an environmental data provider. Such searches are no real substitute for an environmental audit conducted by an **8–51** experienced environmental professional, but they offer a quick and cheap means of obtaining useful information on which to base a decision as to what further investigations are necessary.

The licences, consents and permissions which the company holds and which regulate the impact its operations have on the environment should be checked to ensure that they are current and that the conditions in them are being complied with. Licences may include upgrading requirements with significant capital expenditure implications.

8–52 Officials from the regulatory bodies can be asked to comment on environmental performance. Their replies may reveal past enforcement procedures, or a cautious comment may suggest that future enforcement action is contemplated. Personal interviews may be conducted, or questionnaires submitted to the staff of the company, to obtain as comprehensive a picture as possible of the likelihood of environmental liabilities being incurred.

8–53 Possibly as a result of this investigation, the employment of a specialist environmental scientist to ascertain the extent of the problem may be required. If environmental consultants are brought in, the level of sophistication of their work can vary enormously. A desk study screening process may be conducted by an experienced individual with knowledge of the property and the risks associated with the industry. This may be adequate for residential and certain commercial properties but is usually not sufficient for reviewing environmental risks associated with industrial properties. This will require a site visit, a review of relevant records, interviews with owners and operators of the site as well as regulatory officials. If it is clear that the process is clean and that management is environmentally aware, nothing more may be required. On the other hand, the full facts may not be discovered until the consultant performs a detailed investigation, including the taking of samples from the site. In a straightforward acquisition, the benefit of environmental due diligence would likely be used to adjust the acquisition price or tailor the warranties. If there is an issue that cannot be resolved within the timescale of the transaction, such as land contamination requiring detailed investigation or the absence of a permit that is required under environmental law, it may be appropriate to deal with it by means of a retention or indemnity. In the case of an indemnity, it should be remembered that it will only afford partial protection against criminal liabilities since criminal penalties cannot be indemnified against for reasons of public policy.

8–54 There are a couple of areas where attention is needed if investors or lenders are not to be put at direct risk of incurring environmental liability. First, liability can attach to knowing permitters as well as to causers of water pollution and land contamination, i.e. to those who know about a pollution situation, have the power to do something about it and fail to exercise that power. Care should therefore be taken when drafting investment agreements and facility documents not to give the funders this combination of knowledge and control, e.g. by requiring the company to report major pollution incidents and giving the funders the right to step in and take action if the company does not. The risk is theoretical and probably small, but is best avoided.

Secondly, the aforementioned directors' and officers' liability provisions in the legislation may mean that representatives of the funders (and particularly any special director) are personally at risk if they are so closely involved in the day-to-day business of the company that they could be said to have consented or connived in the commission of its offences, or allowed them to happen through their neglect. This is generally more of an issue when a company is experiencing financial difficulties and the investors are trying to avoid insolvency during or immediately post investment. **8–55**

The benefit of carrying out a due diligence exercise for the purposes of an investment is different from an acquisition. It may assist in obtaining insurance, with the insured being able to fix a premium in the light of the information revealed by the due diligence exercise. However, the information may be used not to negotiate better terms, but to provide a substantial amount of knowledge for the future management of the site, and to enable the drawing up of an environmental compliance programme. The value of an investment will depend not only on inherited liabilities, but on a full assessment of future liabilities. It is quite likely that the directors will not have considered fully the potential environmental liabilities until forced to do so when seeking debt funding or investment in the company. **8–56**

The investors will always be conscious of the need to achieve a clean exit from the company in a few years' time. When the due diligence exercise is underway, it is therefore as well to consider whether any issues that arise could be an impediment to a future share sale or floatation or other exit strategy. This may be a particular concern if new legislation is expected, perhaps as a result of a European directive that is only in draft form, which is likely to impose additional costs or liabilities on the company.

8.10 Due diligence in public to private transactions

In addition to obligations contained in service agreements, articles of association, the Code, the UKLA model code, etc, the directors have a general common law duty to act in the best interests of the company of which they are directors. Confidential information is vendor/target company property and should not be disclosed without board authority. However, it will be necessary for a certain amount of information to be provided to a private equity house to get the ball rolling. The art from a vendor's point of view is to provide only what is in the public domain together with management's own personal views and reflections and to be careful not to provide "corporate" information, plans, etc. **8–57**

8.11 Vendor issues on due diligence

8.11.1 Confidentiality and staggered provision of information

8–58 Although a vendor will normally require the investor to enter into a confidentiality agreement before handing over information pursuant to a due diligence questionnaire, when acting for the company or the vendor it should always be borne in mind that the best way to protect confidential information is by non-disclosure of it. A vendor with its advisors should therefore consider how and when to disclose to the purchaser any sensitive agreements and claims. Sometimes it may be necessary to hold back key agreements until the acquisition or investment is near completion. Obviously this is more important when the purchaser is a trade competitor.

When an acquisition involves a listed company or a company whose shares are traded under AIM (or a subsidiary-undertaking of any such company) consideration should be given as to whether the information to be handed over by the vendor as part of the due diligence exercise constitutes the recipient an "insider" or gives rise to market abuse issues. If so, appropriate warnings should be given.

8.11.2 Preparation by the vendor/investee company

8–59 A company proposing to be sold or seeking investment should check that it is in the best possible condition to facilitate the sale/investment on the best possible terms. The company needs to consider in advance what information will be required by a prospective purchaser or investor, what problems there are that would cause concern to them, and whether the sale/investment will itself give rise to problems.

Collection of information

8–60 In order to avoid delays in negotiating or completing the transaction, a company should ideally gather together in advance all material that is commonly required by a prospective purchaser/investor, to ensure the correctness of warranties that are likely to be sought. Section 8.8.2 provides a list of the kind of information that a purchaser's or investor's lawyers are likely to request and s.8.7 provides an indication of the areas that accountants would be likely to investigate. Whether or not the lawyers make such a request or there is ultimately an accountant's investigation, it is likely that most of that material will be required by the investor before completion of the transaction, or needed for consideration by the company and its advisors in connection with warranties and related disclosure. If the information is required and has not previously been prepared, it is likely to cause delay. Moreover, there may not be sufficient time to prepare and check the information

Vendor issues on due diligence

properly which may cause a problem which could have been resolved if identified earlier or could give rise to resulting liabilities under warranties.

Controlling the progress

The company may want to control the manner in which information is made available in order to minimise damage to the business. Generally, many of the concerns expressed in this section will not be appropriate to an investment, save that the company will still be concerned to maintain confidentiality, though it will be satisfactory to achieve this by way of a simple agreement. A company will, for obvious reasons, be more relaxed about releasing information to a private equity house rather than a trade purchaser, though it is always worth checking whether the private equity house has any competitor companies in its portfolio. This section is therefore included to assist a vendor in controlling the process of selling a business where confidentiality is very important. However some of the suggestions may be good practice in an investment situation. **8–61**

Subject to any regulatory consents and requirements (for example the City Code on Takeovers and Mergers and possible confidentiality obligations to customers and suppliers), the vendor will recognise that he must provide some information to an investor or a possible purchaser. The extent and the timing of that information disclosure will depend upon the negotiating position of the party and also on third-party considerations. The first step before any information is made available to a potential investor or purchaser, is to set out carefully the basis upon which that information is being provided. This will involve a confidentiality agreement requiring, in summary, that information provided will be: **8–62**

- kept confidential and used only for assessing the prospective transaction; and
- returned at the request of the vendor.

In the case of an unscrupulous purchaser or investor, the delivery of information can disadvantage the vendor or the company. Damages will seldom be sufficient and it is essential that the agreement provides the company or the vendor with as clear and smooth a path to injunctive relief as possible. The draftsmen of confidentiality agreements should therefore take particular care in relation to the definition of confidential information, the parties and also whom it is hoped to bind. It is not possible to bind someone who is not a party to the agreement directly, but as regards the employees or advisors of the recipient, the recipient may be asked to procure that they will observe the obligation of confidentiality. **8–63**

Although confidentiality agreements are essential and useful they should not be relied upon to provide complete protection.

Due Diligence

In addition the vendor or the company should try to control the process. This is of particular importance where the vendor is selling a business as opposed to inviting investment. A typical process would be as follows.

Information memorandum

8–64 The vendor/company and its advisors prepare an information memorandum about the company or business to be sold which provides information about its history, development, some limited financial information, markets and the market share, premises, plant and machinery, management and staff, etc. This will be a selling document and is likely to contain outline information, and would only be made available once a confidentiality agreement had been entered into. It will usually contain a disclaimer and health warning, for example:

> *"This document has been produced by [the Vendor] in connection with its proposed sale of [ ]. This document and the information contained in it are confidential and are made available subject to and on the terms contained in the confidentiality letter between [ ] and [ ] on [ ].*
>
> *No reliance may be placed for any purpose whatsoever on the information contained in this document or in its completeness. No representation or warranty expressed or implied is given by the vendor [company] or any of its directors or its advisors as to the accuracy of the information or opinions contained in this document and no liability is accepted by any of them for any such information or opinion. In particular, for reasons of commercial sensitivity, information on certain matters has not been included in this memorandum.*
>
> *Each confidential purchaser should make its own independent assessment of the merits or otherwise of acquiring [ ] or its activities and should take its own professional advice."*

Data room

8–65 Once indicative offers have been received on the basis of the information memorandum, the vendor/company may make further information available in the form of a data room. This will allow the prospective purchasers access to prepared files or documents for a limited time.

The contents of the data room should be prepared with the help of the company's lawyers and should be designed to answer the sort of inquiries which the purchaser/investor and their lawyers would be expected to raise, subject to leaving out any commercially sensitive information.

Data room rules will be prepared which will set out the times when the data room will be open, whether information contained in the data room can be photocopied or removed, and any other rules thought necessary by the vendor to the smooth running of the data room.

Vendor issues on due diligence

It should be sufficient from the information contained in the data room for the purchaser to provide a more realistic price that it is prepared to pay for the business.

Information requests

An alternative or additional step to a data room is to invite and respond to requests for information. This is, for reasons discussed earlier, the most common approach on an investment. Purchasers will often prefer to send their own information requests, however, where there are a number of purchasers bidding for the business, the vendor should seek to exert some control over this process by providing set information which can be supplemented by any further requests from the purchaser. 8–66

Throughout the information disclosure process, vendors of the company should avoid making false or misleading statements which may not only constitute misrepresentation or fraud under common law but may also be a criminal offence under the Financial Services and Markets Act 2000.

8.11.3 Investigation of problems

When the information has been collected and arranged, it should reveal whether or not there are any problems which are likely to be of concern to a prospective purchaser or investor, or cause delay or embarrassment. It may also reveal ways in which the group or the business could be more favourably presented. The following particular points often require attention. 8–67

Outstanding litigation or tax dispute

If there is any outstanding litigation or a tax dispute, it should be resolved before the investment. Either could considerably depress the value of the company and in turn affect the size and terms of the investment offer and/or have to be covered by an indemnity from the directors. 8–68

Records

Corporate and other statutory records of family companies or subsidiaries in groups are often not properly completed and up-to-date. Much potential embarrassment and difficulty can be avoided if these are written up and the group companies' files at the Companies Registry are in order. It is also important to ensure that all certificates for shares being sold and shared in subsidiaries are available, as are all title deeds and other documents in relation to properties. 8–69

Due Diligence

Third-party consents

8–70 It is important to identify what third-party consents will be required for the transaction. There are many circumstances where approvals would be required from third parties before an investment could be made:

- governmental grants may be repayable on a change of ownership of a business or a company unless the Department for Business, Enterprise and Regulatory Reform agrees otherwise;
- consent may be required by virtue of membership of the company or business of a commodity exchange, self-regulatory organisation or other trade association to the transfer of the company or business;
- HM Revenue and Customs clearances may be required on a number of matters. The most common are Capital Gains Tax Act 1979 ("CGTA"), s.88 (capital gains tax rollover), ICTA 1988, s.707 (capital conciliation of tax advantages from certain transactions in securities), ICTA 1988, s.776 (artificial transactions in land);
- loan or debenture stock or facilities agreements of the company may prohibit the change of control of a company, without the consent of the bank or the loan stock or debenture holders. Consent for change of control may be required by other agreements, such as joint venture agreements, major contracts with suppliers and customers, licences, etc;
- the memorandum and articles of association of a company may require specific third-party shareholder approvals or consents to be obtained before any acquisition or disposal of its shares or business. For example, any pre-emption rights may have to be waived by the shareholders of a company.

Balance sheet

8–71 Are the accounting policies used by the group consistent and are they in accordance with generally accepted accounting principles? Consideration should be given—especially if it is thought that the sale price would be based on the net assets shown by the audited balance sheet or that there would be a completion balance sheet prepared using the same accounting principles—to whether generally accepted accounting principles would allow assets or liabilities to be treated more favourably, or whether it would be desirable to transfer out some assets which are not essential to the group before the balance sheet date, such as patents, trademarks, etc, which are normally used by the group. Sometimes the management of the group has been taking an extremely conservative view of assessments of contingent liabilities and greater provisions have been made than were necessary. Certain assets may have been written down excessively so that, although they may have a considerable market value, they have a low or nil value in the balance sheet, and special account should be taken of them in the price negotiation. Sometimes, assets or liabilities are even in the wrong company's balance sheet.

Tax or other reconstructions

Where the investment is for the purposes of an acquisition a vendor is likely to want to minimise tax and to consider whether any action should be taken prior to the entry into arrangements with any purchaser and, or at the time of the sale, which could mitigate tax liabilities. These may have to be explained to any prospective purchaser at the start of any negotiations. **8–72**

Properties

A particular case where time may be saved later through advance preparation by the company arises where any freehold or leasehold property forms such an important part of the company or business that any investor is likely to require some investigation of title. Searches normally undertaken in such an investigation may take several weeks to obtain; the investor will be unlikely to instruct the lawyers to commence an investigation until at least an agreement in principle has been reached. It may be appropriate, therefore, to instruct lawyers who historically have dealt with the property work of the company to commence preparation of certificates of title for the relevant properties or at least make searches (in particular local authority searches) the replies to which could be given to the investor's lawyers. Consideration should also be given to whether an environmental due diligence report should be sought prior to a sale, or more likely prior to an investment. **8–73**

8.12 The due diligence report

Once the review has been completed the work must be presented to the client. In the interests of speed and to obtain feedback from the client and answer any questions from the client this can be done by way of an oral presentation focusing on the key issues and ensuring that the relevant experts are present to field any difficult questions. It is likely however that this will be followed by a written presentation addressed to both the investors and the bank. The main part that the funders will focus on is the executive summary. It is useful to remember that the report is intended for non-lawyers and so should not be written in legal jargon. **8–74**

A useful exercise is to provide interim reports either by email or conference call to identify any issues at an early stage. This can also have the advantage of saving a lot of time from being wasted if deal breakers are discovered early.

8.13 Post completion audit

8–75 A lot of information has been collected in a due diligence exercise which can be lost if a process is not implemented to review the acquisition process and assess the integration of the new business. Post acquisition audits should therefore be considered within six months of closing. The purpose is to ensure that all recommendations from the reports have been implemented, that the businesses have been integrated and that a warranty review has taken place to identify any potential warranty claims.

Chapter 9

Investment Agreement

9.1 Introduction

Investment agreements for private equity transactions can be drafted in all shapes and sizes, from a simple letter to a far more comprehensive subscription and shareholders' agreement which, with supporting documentation, can run to hundreds of pages. There is nothing more frustrating from an advisor's point of view or that of the client than a poorly prepared document taken directly from the word processor of a law firm that does not reflect the commercial understanding between the parties. Poor preparation at the commencement of a transaction will result in higher costs as well as raising the temperature levels of principals and advisors. The lawyer preparing the first draft of the document should spend time with his client trying to understand the transaction and the purpose of his document. The smaller the investment being made, the less acceptable it is to produce a large unwieldy investment document. Quite simply, a small investment cannot justify large legal costs. Equally it serves little purpose producing a document too early in the process or at least until the due diligence process has been completed. Meetings on a document that are not bespoke to the transaction are generally fruitless and should be resisted. **9–01**

Most lawyers have standard form precedents prepared from the investor's point of view, since it is the investor's solicitors who normally initiate the document, but experienced investment lawyers have a fairly clear idea of what is acceptable. Although it is not intended that the first draft should make concessions which have not been requested, it can be counter-productive and time consuming to produce too harsh a document. At the same time, an experienced lawyer will recognise at all times that, unlike the negotiation of a sale and purchase agreement, the parties are setting out as business partners and hope to remain so. It is important therefore that the lawyers work hard to maintain the goodwill between the parties and that the negotiations are conducted amicably. **9–02**

The main purpose of the investment document is to record the commercial terms of the arrangement between the investors and the investee company and its management, and to outline clearly the control provisions that the investors will require.

A typical investment agreement will set out the details of the parties involved, define the main terms used, outline the mechanics of the investment and detail arrangements for protecting the investors' interests. These arrangements will include the warranting of the information provided to the investors prior to the investment, as well as both positive and negative controls over the operations of the company following the investment.

Set out below is a discussion of some of the more relevant clauses that should be included in the agreement.

9.2 Conditions

9–03 Before making an investment, the investors will need to be satisfied that certain matters or obligations have been fulfilled. The investor will not proceed until these matters have been completed to its satisfaction. It is unlikely that a straightforward investment in a private company will require a separate exchange and completion. This has the advantage that there is no need to negotiate the terms under which the business would be conducted between signing and completion, though if the investment is for the purposes of an acquisition it is possible that third-party consents or approvals will be required for the sale. If that is the case an investor will not give an unconditional commitment to fund the acquisition until all necessary approvals have been obtained and the conditions to the investment have been satisfied. If there is to be a simultaneous signing and completion, these matters will be included in the agreement by way of checklist only. Some of the matters are more important than others, and the investor will always reserve the right to proceed if certain conditions set out in the checklist have not been fully satisfied at the time set for completion.

9–04 A clause similar to the following is likely to be included.

> 1.1 This agreement and all the obligations of the parties hereunder are conditional upon the following taking place to the satisfaction of the investor[s] (or being waived by the investor[s] as to whole or part by notice in writing to the company):
>
> > (a) the passing of the necessary directors' and shareholders' resolutions in the agreed form at a duly convened board meeting and an extraordinary general meeting convened at short notice to increase the share capital of the company, authorise the allotment of the new shares and adopt the new articles;
> > (b) banking facilities and working capital being made available to the company on terms and in amount satisfactory to the investor[s];

Conditions

Additional financing may come from various sources depending predominantly on the security available and the amount required. This may include straightforward bank finance by way of loan or overdraft or alternative finance such as mezzanine, invoice discounting or leasing;

(c) the delivery to the investor[s] of the accountants' report, the commercial report, the accounts, the management accounts, the legal report, the business plan and the certificates of title;

The investor will wish to ascertain, so far as possible, the nature and value of the assets and liabilities of the company in which he/she is investing and that the company has good title to the assets free from third-party rights. He/she will also wish to understand more about the business and the market in which it operates. The process by which an investor satisfies itself on these points is often described as "due diligence". The documents referred to in (c) are all part of the due diligence exercise undertaken by the investors. Chapter 8 deals more fully with the purpose of each document;

(d) the delivery to the investor[s] of the directors' questionnaires;

It is becoming increasingly common to request that the directors complete questionnaires addressed to the investors. These will request information in relation to criminal convictions, bankruptcy, directors' disqualifications and are similar to the sort of questions that a director will be obliged to answer on a flotation. If a possible exit route for an investor is flotation it may eliminate a later problem. Occasionally flotations do not proceed because a key director is not acceptable to the Stock Exchange. In addition, an investor will often ask for a net asset statement from a director. This serves two purposes. If the director is being asked to subscribe alongside the investor it will illustrate whether he/she has funds available. Secondly, it will identify the net worth of the individuals which may become relevant if the directors have given warranties and the investor wishes to pursue a warranty claim. As well as being a condition precedent to the agreement, it is also likely that the directors will be asked to warrant the questionnaire and in some cases, if they have been together for a long time, the questionnaire given by each of the other managers, though this should always be resisted;

(e) the receipt by the investor[s] of references satisfactory to the investor[s] on each of the managers/directors;

These will include personal and business references and will have been taken at an early stage by the investor;

(f) keyman insurance having been effected with an insurance company of good repute for the benefit of the company on the life and health of [ ] for a period of not less than [5] years in the sum of £[ ] on such terms as shall be approved by the investor[s] [and the company having effected directors' and officers' liability insurance with effect

Investment Agreement

from completion in respect of the investor director with an insurance company of good repute, on terms approved by the investor[s];

Putting in place keyman insurance can take longer than is first anticipated and should be addressed very early in the transaction. If not in place by the agreed date for completion, investors will often accept an undertaking that it is put in place as soon as possible. For obvious reasons this is not advisable, and a temporary cover note at the very least should be obtained. If new banking arrangements are being put in place, as in a MBO, or the bank is being asked to increase its exposure, then the bank will also insist on keyman insurance. The purpose of keyman insurance is to provide financial support at a critical time and thereby enable the company to attract a suitable replacement "key" manager following the death of the subject of the keyman. A private equity house will wish to see keyman insurance in place for this reason. However, a bank is likely to want to see the proceeds of the insurance used to repay its loan. It often results in the absurd situation whereby the company takes out two policies, one for the company and one for the bank.

Directors' and officers' risks arise in several forms—allegations of breach of statutory duties (of which there are many) or breach of common law duties. Insurers agree to meet risk in the form of "Wrongful Act". This is usually defined on a wide basis to include actual or alleged misfeasance, fraudulent or wrongful trading, breach of trust, breach of warranty or authority, breach of duty, neglect, error or omissions, mis-statement, misleading statement or other acts wrongfully committed or attempted or any matter claimed against them solely by reason of their capacities as directors or officers.

The policy will be underwritten to meet "loss" including such sums as the insured are legally liable to pay for reason of any wrongful act including awards of damages and costs made against the insured together with any legal costs, charges and expenses incurred by the insured in the defence of any legal action that is commenced or threatened in a court or civil or criminal jurisdiction at first instance or on appeal. Any fines, penalties, punitive, or exemplary damages and other specific areas will be uninsured.

The insurance will not cover legal costs relating to some matters. These might include the loss of, destruction of, or damage to any material property, personal guarantees or indemnities and pollution or contamination;

(g) the managers having subscribed in cash for the ordinary shares at [£1] per share set opposite their respective names in column 2 of Sch.1 Pt I;

[(h) the due execution and exchange of the sale agreement and the satisfaction of all conditions precedent to completion thereof in accordance with its terms so that the sale agreement has become and

Conditions

remains unconditional save for payment for the consideration monies has not been rescinded and the investor[s] are satisfied that it will be completed in accordance with its terms and that the investor[s] have approved all and any documentation proposed to be entered into in connection therewith;]

This clause will be required where the investment being made is to assist the company to make an acquisition. The investor will be concerned to know that he will only be committed to providing his investment once all parties have exchanged contracts and are committed to completion subject to the provision of the finance;

(i) the investor[s] being satisfied that there has been no breach of the representation, warranties and undertakings set out herein which has or may have a material adverse effect upon the financial position or prospects of the company and/or the business.

The investor will wish to make it clear that if there is a material and detrimental change to the financial plight of the company it will not continue to make available the promised funds.

Interpretation

Set out below are the meanings of some of the defined terms used in para.9–04. **9–05**

"the accountants report"	the report on the company (and the subsidiaries) prepared by [ ] and dated [ ] in the agreed form;
"the accounts"	the audited accounts of the [company/each of the group's companies] for the year ended on the accounts date [and the consolidated audited accounts of the group's companies] in the agreed form;
"the accounts date"	[ ];
"the board"	the board of directors of the company as constituted from time to time;
"the business"	the business of [ ];
"the business plan"	the business plan for the company (and the subsidiaries) in a form satisfactory to the investor[s] and in the agreed form;
"the certificates of title"	the certificates of title in relation to each of the properties provided by the company's solicitors to the investor[s] in the agreed form;
"the directors' questionnaire"	a questionnaire in the agreed form completed by each of the directors and addressed to the investor[s] containing information concerning their qualifications as directors of the company;
"the group's companies"	the company and the subsidiaries of the company at the date of this agreement (references to a group company shall be construed accordingly);

"the legal report"	the legal report dated [ ] addressed to the investor[s] and prepared by the [investor's] solicitors in the agreed form;
"the management accounts"	the management accounts of [the company/group companies] for the period of [ ] months ended on [ ] in the agreed form [*NB: normally from the accounts date to completion or the end of the month prior to completion*];
"the new articles"	the new articles of association of the company to be adopted on completion, in the agreed form or any articles of association of the company the time being adopted or amended with the consent of the investor[s] and references to "an article" shall be construed accordingly;
"the new shares"	the [ ] ordinary shares, [ ] preference shares and the [ ] preferred ordinary shares proposed to be subscribed by the investors[s] pursuant to this agreement;
"ordinary shares"	ordinary shares of [£1] each in the capital of the company having the rights set out in the new articles;
"preference shares"	[cumulative, convertible redeemable] preference shares of [£1] in the capital of the company having the rights set out in the new articles;
"preferred ordinary shares"	preferred ordinary shares of [£1] each in the capital of the company having the rights set out in the new articles;
"the properties"	the properties as detailed in Sch.[ ];
"the warranties"	the warranties, representations and undertaking set out in cl.[ ] and Sch.[ ] (references to a warranty being to any of them).

9.3 Mechanics of investment

9–06 Once the commercial terms of the offer have been agreed with the investor, this clause will be non-contentious. The purpose of the investment is to put the company in funds in order to achieve the objectives agreed with the investor and set out in the business plan. The funding arrangements therefore are generally straightforward and will not involve, for example, consideration securities as may be the case in a sale and purchase, though the investor will choose to put its funds in on different bases, e.g. equity shares, preference shares, secure or unsecured convertible loan stock (see Ch.5).

Mechanics of investment

2.1 Subject to cl.1.1 [*NB: the previous clause setting out the conditions to the investment*] the investor[s] applies for the allotment and issue to it at completion and the company agrees to allot at completion to the investor[s] or [its/their] trustee[s], nominee or custodian[s] those new shares [and loan notes] set out opposite their names in Sch.[ ], Pt [ ].

2.2 Each of the managers hereby waives all and any rights of pre-emption whether contained in the new articles or otherwise to which he is entitled and which might prevent the allotment and issue of the new shares at completion in accordance with the terms hereof.

2.3 Completion of the subscription by the investor[s] shall take place at the offices of the investor['s][s'] solicitors on the date of this agreement immediately following its exchange [simultaneously with completion of the sale agreement] (or at such other place and time as the company and the investor[s] may agree) when:

   (a) the investor[s] shall deliver to the company, or as it may direct, the sum of £[ ] by [a town clearing cheque/telegraphic transfer];
   (b) a board meeting shall be convened at which the company shall:

      (i) issue new shares credited as fully paid to the investor[s] and enter [its/their] name (or the name of [its/their] trustee, nominee or custodian) in the register of members in respect thereof;
      [(ii) issue the loan notes credited as fully paid up at par to the investor[s] and enter the investor[s] in the register of loan note holders to be maintained by the company;]

A very important consideration to the company when choosing an investor will be whether he/she is prepared to dig into his/her pockets for further rounds of finance in order to develop the business further, or even to keep the receiver from the door. If further financing is identified from the outset as being required the company will try to commit the investor to making the funds available on request. Understandably, the investor will wish to make such a commitment flexible. If it is anticipated from the outset that further funding will be required it is likely to be made available only when agreed milestones are satisfied. **9–07**

9.4 Warranties

Following the investment, the company will remain liable for all potential and actual liabilities and obligations. Now, however, the investor will bear the risk for a substantial part of those liabilities as a result of becoming a shareholder. There is limited statutory protection for a prospective investor in a company, although common law remedies may entitle it to damages and it may be entitled to treat the contract as discharged or rescinded for the torts of deceit or misrepresentation. **9–08**

Subject to this, the principle of caveat emptor ("let the buyer beware") applies. Some liability, however, can attach to the making of false pre-contractual representations, whether oral or written, which induce the investor to enter into the contract. Because the measure of damages for deceit and misrepresentations can differ from that for breach of warranty, it is normal in an investment agreement to exclude liability for representations made before the contract is signed by including a confirmation by the investor that it has not relied upon any representations or warranties other than those referred to in the agreement, and so restricting its remedies to those based on the contract.

The investors acknowledge to the warrantors that they have relied on no warranties or representations whatsoever other than the warranties.

9–09 Such a clause will only be enforceable if it satisfies the test of reasonableness under the Unfair Contract Terms Act 1977. Where the parties are businessmen, advised by professionals, it would be unlikely that the party relying on the exclusion could not demonstrate reasonableness. However, if the misrepresentation is fraudulent, a disclaimer of responsibility will not be effective. Section 397 of the Financial Services and Markets Act 2000 provides that a person who knowingly provides a misleading forecast or makes a misleading statement or conceals any material facts to induce another person to enter an agreement is guilty of an offence punishable by fine or imprisonment. The directors therefore cannot simply wash their hands of statements made to institutions. To mitigate the benefits of the limited protection given to the investor, it has become customary to ask the company and the executive directors to bear much of the risk by giving warranties and indemnities. The investors, in considering whether to make an investment, will have made numerous visits to the site or sites from which the company operates, and will have been provided with much information. In addition, the investors will have approached a number of specialist advisors to produce various reports. Reporting accountants will have been asked to prepare an accounts report on the financial status of the company and the profit and cash flow projections anticipated by the board. A specialist conversant with the industry may be asked to produce a commercial report ratifying the commercial objectives. A business plan will have been prepared by the management and the legal advisors may prepare a legal report on the constitution and trading contracts entered into by the company. In addition there may be reports from surveyors, insurance brokers, environmental advisors, actuaries, etc. The investment will be made on the assumption that such information is complete and accurate. In order to be assured that this is correct, the investor will ask for a number of warranties or representations to be given. In particular, the company will be asked to warrant all the facts contained in such reports. This serves two main functions: the first is to extract disclosures so that any "skeletons" are known to the investors prior to making their investment; and the second is to provide a means of redress in the event that matters turn out not to be as they have been warranted.

9.4.1 Liability under the warranties

Acquisition agreement warranties

Putting aside issues that arise from a vendor retaining a stake in the target or reinvesting some of its proceeds in Newco, the ideal solution for Newco/the private equity house is to ensure the fullest warranties are given by the vendor of the target company or business. The assumption will be that the target company or business is being acquired at a full price, assuming that the expected inherent value is in fact properly contained within the target company or business acquired, that it has got what it ought to have and has not got what it should not have. Management teams, if they are minority shareholders in the new venture, will be expected to warrant on the same basis as the vendors. Management teams are unlikely to be receiving any or any significant part of the sale proceeds and therefore will quite properly restrict the warranties they are providing save where they are fairly within their control (personal statements about themselves); or in respect of which it is reasonable to give integrity-based confirmation (business plan, experts' reports, acquisition agreement warranties, etc).

The approach taken will broadly depend on the type of private equity deal that is being negotiated.

Institutional buy-outs/MBI

The common and distinct factors in these situations are usually that the private equity house will be driving the process because it will have a significant majority shareholding in Newco and the private equity house will not be acquiring the benefit of assistance from incumbent management.

The private equity house will insist (usually successfully) on receiving a full set of warranties and indemnities as with any standard acquisition agreement.

If in any IBO or MBI there are incumbent managers taking a stake in Newco the vendor may request any of the following.

- A general disclosure of all matters within the actual or constructive knowledge of such management.
- Warranties or indemnities from incumbent managers to cover any liabilities which the vendor may incur where such management have or ought to have knowledge of these matters. This will not be acceptable to Newco or the private equity house.

Investment Agreement

- Limitation of all warranties by reference to the actual knowledge of a limited number of employees retained by the vendor. Again this will not be acceptable to Newco or the private equity house.

- Limitation of all warranties by reference to the actual or constructive knowledge of the private equity house (that is matters disclosed in the accountant's report, the legal due diligence report, etc; even if these have not been shown to the vendor). This is sometimes given but undesirable if only because the private equity house is unlikely to realise the full impact of some of that information until they have been in the business for a period of time. The usual compromise is some form of confirmation from Newco/the private equity house to the effect that it is not effectively "warehousing" matters which it knows or suspects are breaches of warranties in respect of which it intends to bring claims immediately after completion.

Management buy-outs

9–12 In a buy-out, a lead participant in the purchase process will be the buy-out team and the vendor will contend that the team will or ought to have knowledge of that which they are acquiring. The same arguments arise as to who is receiving the value and who should bear the risk, etc; but logic does not always prevail and the debates can become quite heated. In general the following approach should be taken by the lawyers acting for Newco/management.

- A general exclusion of warranty liability in the acquisition agreement in respect of anything within management's knowledge should be resisted.

- If needs be, the private equity house cannot object in principle to the vendor seeking some comfort from management that they are not aware of breaches of warranty provided that this is limited to actual knowledge on the part of the management team. Anything wider than that such as knowledge after due and careful enquiry or a form of constructive knowledge is unreasonable. Management will often quite rightly ask the question "What's in it for me?" However management's lawyers should not have a problem with a basic concept that anything that is within the actual knowledge of the management team should be brought to the attention of the vendors.

- Management should risk giving any form of warranty to the vendor that they have disclosed to the vendor everything they should have disclosed about the target company or business. Whilst they may prefer to discuss matters and help they should not go so far as to give contractual commitment in this regard.

In addition the vendor will ask management to consider the warranties to be given by the vendors. If so a provision should be sought by management's lawyers that (in the absence of fraud or deliberate non-disclosure) the vendor will not sue the management for information given/omitted to be given. This can either be included in the acquisition agreement or in a side letter from the vendor to management. Failure to do this will leave management exposed to claims in negligence. The lawyers to the private equity house will also be supportive of this argument as they will not wish their management to be involved in any litigation at a time when they are to be focused on the operating business.

The private equity house, even a MBO, will want as good a set of warranties as is reasonably obtainable from the vendor because it is incorrect to accept a vendor's suggestion that the management team ought to give comfort to the private equity house in the areas in respect of which it has or ought to have knowledge and that warranties from a management team will compliment where limited warranties have been given by a vendor. Management warranties and vendor warranties are not reverse sides of the same coin. Liability, enforceability and commercial considerations are significantly different. Vendor warranties will be backed up by the considerable consideration that the vendors will be taking away from the table whereas management warranties will have much less value. At the same time it is also inconceivable that a private equity house will sue a management team in the absence of fraud or a very real desire to set some form of example. **9–13**

Investment agreement warranties

The warranties in the investment agreement will be given by the company and possibly by the directors, depending on the strength of their negotiating position. If a claim had to be made under the warranties by the investor, then this would obviously harm the company in which the investor has now become a shareholder. The investor will therefore prefer the executive directors who are familiar with the company's business to provide the warranties. Nevertheless, the investors will face an uphill struggle in asking the directors or senior managers to provide warranties. Unlike a sale, where warranties will be given by the vendors, the directors or managers will not feel any immediate or direct benefit in their pockets that would encourage them to provide such warranties. In addition, in practice, the directors or managers will be unlikely to have sufficient resources to meet any potential warranty claims and would therefore demand relatively low limits on their liability. Though it is increasingly common for directors/shareholders to partially exit on a new investment being made and thereby release some cash. This is likely to be an extremely contentious area. The investor, however, despite these difficulties, will usually include warranties given by the directors if only to "concentrate their minds" on the disclosures to be given to the investors. The argument will therefore focus upon the limitations to those warranties. Whereas damages for deceit or misrepresentation aim to place the investor in the position it would have been had there been no deceit or misrepresentation, and do not compensate it for any losses of bargain, the aim in awarding damages for breach of warranties (like other breaches of contract), is to place the investor in the position it would have been had **9–14**

Investment Agreement

the contract been performed. The measure of damages will be the difference between the value of the share subscribed for by the investor at the time of completion with all the warranties fulfilled and their actual value at that time given the breach of warranty. However, the parties may adopt a different measure of damages under the terms of the agreement itself. Whatever the measure of damages, the warrantors will wish to limit the liability in the company's case to the level of investment made by the investor but in the case of the directors to a much more reasonable level, possibly determined as a multiple of salary. In view of the potential liability imposed by the warranties, which, no matter how healthy the company is, will (or should) seriously concern any director being asked to give them, the legal advisors to the company and the directors will attempt to limit the liability as much as possible.

9–15 (1) The warrantors shall not be liable by way of damages or otherwise howsoever in respect of any breach of the warranties if:

(a) the warrantors shall have been given written notice by the investor of a specific breach of a or claim under any warranty (which notice shall state the full details of the event or circumstances giving rise to the breach or claim, the basis on which the investor is making a claim against the warrantors and the total amount of liability which results):

(i) in so far as any such liability relates to taxation, prior to the [sixth] anniversary of completion;
(ii) in relation to any other liability, prior to the [second] anniversary of completion; and

(b) proceedings shall have been commenced and served upon the investor in connection with such breach or claim against the warrantors within six months from the date of giving notice to the warrantors as aforesaid.

Limitations

9–16 The normal period of limitation within which an action must be brought is six years, unless the document is a deed, in which case the period is twelve years. It is usual to agree a period of two or three years in respect of the warranties and six or seven years for taxation matters. The rationale is that two or three audits of the company should identify most defects which existed at completion but as the statutory limitation period for taxation matters is six years from the end of the relevant accountancy period a six-year period should apply to such matters. As well as imposing a time limit for claims, another purpose of this clause is to ensure that the investor cannot maintain an open position by giving a general notice of claims at the end of the period. The warrantors can require any claim to be made in sufficiently specific terms to ensure that it is made in good faith.

(2) The maximum aggregate liability of the warrantors for breaches of the warranties shall be £[ ]. **9–17**

The warrantors will seek a ceiling on their liability under the warranties. This is usually fixed at the amount of the investment being made. This may not always be appropriate and the investor should consider any funds introduced to the business, for example in order to repay loans, or to be introduced upon the happening of certain events.

(3) No liability shall in any event arise in respect of any claim for breach of the warranties unless the liability arising from such claim:

   (a) amounts to £[ ] or more in respect of any single claim; and
   (b) together with aggregate of all other single claims of any amount arising from any other breach of the warranties amounts to £[ ] or more;

but if such liabilities shall exceed the amounts set out in paras (a) and (b) above (subject to the other provisions hereof), the warrantors shall only be liable for the excess and not for the whole of such liabilities.

To avoid trivial claims, the warrantors will usually require that claims cannot be brought unless they exceed a minimum level. From the investor's point of view there is no real justification for accepting this except that in practice he/she is unlikely to pursue minor claims. There is no consistent view as to whether, once the minimum level is exceeded, the claim should relate to the full amount or the excess only. **9–18**

One point that the investor should be aware of, however, is that if he agreed to a de minimis clause, he/she should apply any amendments to the warranties so that they only apply to "material" matters. If this was accepted it would provide the warrantors with a double margin of error.

(4) The investor shall reimburse to the warrantors an amount equal to any such paid by the warrantors under any of the warranties which is subsequently recovered or paid to the investor, [ ] [or] the company or any of them by a third party. **9–19**

(5) In the event that the investor or the company shall be in receipt of any claim which might constitute or give rise to a breach of any of the warranties the investor shall as soon as reasonably practicable notify the warrantors giving full details as far as practicable and shall not settle or compromise any such claim or make any admission of liability without the prior written consent of the warrantors. If so requested by the warrantors, the investor shall, and shall procure that the company shall, take all reasonable steps to avoid, resist, appeal, compromise or defend any claim and any adjudication in respect thereof for this purpose take all appropriate proceedings in the name of the company.

Investment Agreement

> If so requested by the warrantors, the investor shall take all appropriate proceedings in the name of the company (or procure that the same are taken) and the warrantors shall be allowed to have the conduct of any negotiations, proceedings or appeals in respect of or arising from any claim against the company which might give rise to a claim for a breach of the warranties.

The warrantors will be keen to ensure that they have the conduct of any claim in order to minimise the potential liability. The investor's main concern will be to ensure that ceding such control does not cause the company operational difficulties and in particular does not damage relations with a favoured customer.

9–20
> (6) Where a breach of any of the warranties shall be in respect of a matter where the company shall be insured against any loss for damage arising therefrom, the investor shall not make any claim against the warrantors for breach of any such warranty without first procuring that the company shall make a claim against its insurers for compensation for the loss or damage suffered and thereafter any claim against the warrantors shall be limited (in addition to all other limitations on the warrantors' liability elsewhere referred to herein) to the amount by which the amount of the loss or damage suffered by the investor as a result of such breach shall exceed the compensation paid by the said insurers to the company.

The warrantors will be keen to ensure that the investors do not make a claim where the matter would be covered by insurance taken out by the company.

> (7) No liability shall attach to the warrantors in respect of a breach of the warranties contained herein to the extent that:
>
> (a) any such breach or claim occurs as a result of any legislation not in force at the date hereof which takes effect retrospectively;
>
> (b) any such breach or claim is attributable to, or arises from any voluntary act, omission, transaction or arrangement or carried out by either the investor, the company or their respective successors in title from time to time or any associated company of any of the foregoing at any time after completion;
>
> (c) any allowance, provision or reserve has been made in the accounts in respect of the matter to which such breach or claim relates.

The warrantors will wish to ensure that they are not liable to a claim where provisions have been made in the accounts or it is a result of matters or actions outside their control.

9–21
> (8) No breach of the warranties shall in any event give rise to a right on the part of the investor to rescind or terminate this agreement following completion. The sole remedy of the investor in respect of any breach of the warranties shall be in damages.

The essential requirement of rescission is that the parties should be capable of being restored to their original position. This will often not be possible once completion of the investment has taken place. Rescission can however be a significant remedy where there is a delay between exchange and completion.

Possibly the most contentious limitation will be the financial limit for a breach of warranty imposed on the manager or directors. The investor will wish the warranties to be joint and several, and up to the aggregate of the investment being made by the investor. As a result, the investor can recover against any of the warrantors. The sued warrantor can obtain a right to a contribution from the other warrantors pursuant to the Civil Liability (Contribution) Act 1978 which allows the court to determine a just and equitable basis for allocating the liability amongst the warrantors. The ultimate effect therefore of joint and several liability, is to shift to the warrantors the burden that a warrantor may not be traceable or able to meet his/her share of the liability. The warrantors may consider having a separate agreement amongst themselves determining how liability should be apportioned. This is often considered where the warrantors' positions are not straightforward, for example where shares are held by a trust. The court will apply such an agreement in actions for contributions brought by one warrantor against the others. A trustee warrantor is unlikely to be able to accept joint and several liability as it could not put itself in a position where it may be liable in excess of funds under its trusteeship. In recent years market practice has moved and several liability is generally accepted as the norm. In fact joint and several liability can work against any investor where he/she wishes to bring a claim against one manager who then insists on joining the other manager into the action to the detriment of the business. The different bases of liability are set out below.

Several liability

Where two or more warrantors agree to be liable on a several basis, each separately promises something to the investor. Liability is cumulative, and if one warrantor discharges his/her obligations to the investor the others are not released from their obligations. A warrantor cannot claim as of right any contribution from co-warrantors where his/her obligation is several. **9–22**

Joint liability

Where warrantors agree to be jointly liable to the investor, they give one joint promise to do one thing. Liability is not cumulative and performance by one warrantor will satisfy the obligations of all. **9–23**

Joint and several liability

Where two or more warrantors agree to be jointly and severally liable to the investor, they jointly promise to do something and also separately promise to do **9–24** the same thing. Liability is not cumulative, and performance by one warrantor discharges the liability of the others.

Distinction between joint and joint and several liability

9–25 The principal aim of the investor in seeking the performance of one obligation by two or more warrantors is to enable him to elect to sue one warrantor for the whole amount of any debt promised or for damages in respect of any obligation breached (leaving the party sued to recover contributions to his/her liability from the other warrantors), or to sue all the warrantors together as he/she thinks fit. The risk of one warrantor failing to meet the proportionate part of his/her liability therefore falls on the warrantor not the investor.

It is important to ensure that an obligation given by more than one person is expressly on a joint and several basis. In the absence of appropriate "words of severance", (e.g. "the warrantors agree" denoting joint liability; "the warrantors agree for themselves and for either of them" denoting joint and several liability) liability is presumed to be joint. Certain technical common law rules made joint liability unfavourable to the investor. Although the principal disadvantages have been removed by statute, one disadvantage remains: on the death of a joint promissory, his/her liability passes to his/her surviving joint promissorys. In contrast, under joint and several liability such liability passes to the estate of the deceased. An ability to sue the estates of deceased promissorys and not just surviving promissorys is obviously important to the investor if the deceased promissory is the only one having sufficient assets to satisfy a judgment.

Proportionate liability

9–26 Warrantors will usually attempt to ensure that liability for warranties and under the deed of indemnity is on a several basis and also stipulates a maximum amount for which each warrantor will be liable in respect of any claim, usually pro rata to the number of shares sold by him/her. The warrantors are thereby avoiding the risk of one warrantor failing to meet his/her proportionate part of the total liability. Without this maximum liability, several liability is of no use to the warrantor, as otherwise the investor could sue each of the warrantors for its total loss.

The directors will at least want to reduce the financial limits to a more sensible level, possibly a multiple of salary. If the purpose of the warranties is to concentrate the minds of the directors then arguably this will achieve the same purpose, and perhaps even more so than an outlandish figure that bears little resemblance to the net worth of the warrantor. Proving a breach of warranty is always difficult. Investors do not like to sue their own management teams—it is not good for business. If the breach is sufficient to damage the business they will deal with it by replacing the

Warranties

management team unless the management have fraudulently or wilfully misled them and in that case they will not require the benefit of the warranties but can sue under the Financial Services and Markets Act 2000.

9–27 The purpose of the warranties should simply be to focus the directors' attentions and provide a considerable body of information about the company. Other parts of the documentation will provide for ways of removing the directors and transferring their shares at little cost. However these all assume that the director will leave the company. It is not common but there are situations where the director stays with the company but he/she is forced to transfer his/her shares in satisfaction of a warranty claim. For example:

If a claim is made for a breach of any of the warranties against the managers and the managers and the investors shall agree such claim, or failing agreement a court of competent jurisdiction shall award final judgment in respect of the claim, the claim shall be satisfied in cash and if the investors should so require by notice in writing to the managers within seven days of such agreement or final judgment, by the transfer to the investors (pro rata to their shareholding) of any shares in the company issued to the managers equal in value to the amount of the agreed claim. For these purposes the valuation of the shares shall be the market value as defined in the new articles.

Warranty and indemnity insurance

9–28 Warranty and indemnity insurance can sometimes play a role in private equity transactions particularly when an institutional investor is exiting and the burden of providing warranty cover falls on the management. It is worth spending a few moments here explaining how such policies operate upon investors and management seeking an exit. Specialist insurers will provide indemnity for "damages" and costs and any warranty proceedings brought against the directors, the parent company or shareholders as a result of the sale of their business assets.

Historically, many vendors' policies were being sought by vendors at the request of the purchaser who then became loss payee under the vendor's policy, or had the benefit of the vendors' policy assigned to him/her. However, purchasers were sometimes concerned that the vendors' policy might be avoided as a result of fraud by the vendor and the purchaser would then receive no indemnity.

To deal with this concern the purchaser could buy a "Purchaser's Fraud Policy" that would pay the purchaser's claim in those cases where he had proved his/her loss but did not recover as an assignee of the vendor's policy as that had been avoided by subscribing insurers due to fraud by the vendor.

9–29 Share/asset agreements often incorporate the following (simplified) structures:

Investment Agreement

(1) venture capitalist (holding 90 per cent of the share capital) and management team (holding 10 per cent of the share capital) are to sell their company;

(2) purchase price for the target company: £100 million;

(3) warranties and tax indemnity to be given by the management team vendors;

(4) venture capitalist vendor refusing/unable to give any warranties or accept liability under the tax indemnity;

(5) management team wish to limit their liability under the warranties and tax indemnity in the sale agreement to £10 million (their "share" of the purchase price) or less;

(6) purchaser requires "security" for entire transaction value of £100 million and asks for the management team's liability in the sale agreement to be £100 million;

(7) management team only prepared to be "personally responsible" for £10 million, but will accept liability under the sale agreement for £100 million and take out insurance for the entire £100 million if there is an undertaking in the sale agreement from the purchaser;

EITHER:

(a) not to enforce the judgment debt against the management team beyond £10 million in the situation where the vendor's policy does not respond for any reason:

OR:

(b) not to enforce the judgment debt against the management team at all in the situation where the vendor's policy does not respond for any reason.

Some purchasers' solicitors felt that by using one of these structures there was no insurable interest for the vendors to insure under the vendors' policy and therefore the vendors' policy would be void and the assignment of the vendor's policy would therefore become worthless. Insurers are entitled to require proof of an insurable interest at the time of loss in all indemnity insurances. The event against which liability insurers are obliged to provide indemnity is the establishment and ascertainment of the liability of the assured by judgment, settlement or award (*Post Office v Norwich Union* [1967] 2 Q.B. 363; *Bradley v Eagle Star* [1989] A.C. 957). The insured is therefore entitled to an indemnity regardless of whether he has paid or can pay the amount of the judgment.

9–30 The definition of "loss" in the vendor's policy reflects the effect of the *Post Office v Norwich Union* and *Bradley v Eagle Star* cases. Accordingly, an insured under such a policy would be entitled to indemnity under the policy upon the making of a judgment or award for assessed damages for breach of warranty against him. The "Limitations on the Warrantors' Liability" do not impact on the liability of the insured which provides the basis for the judgment or award but merely restrict the extent of the enforcement of any such judgment or award to the amount recoverable from insurers. The provisions are therefore regulating the extent to which the insured can be required to make payments against the established and ascertained liability but as payment against liability is irrelevant to the insured's entitlement to indemnity under the vendor's policy, it must follow that the provisions are irrelevant to the question of whether the insured has an insurable interest and to the entitlement of the insured to an indemnity. The provisions do not negate or restrict the insured's liability to the purchaser and provide no defence on the merits or on quantum to the purchaser's claim. If the purchaser can prove his/her case, a judgment or award for assessed damages will be made against the insured and as at the date of the loss (i.e. the making of the judgment or award), the fact that there is a judgment or award for assessed damages against the insured will be sufficient to satisfy the requirements that the insured should have an insurable interest at the date of loss and to satisfy the indemnity principle.

It would, of course, always be open to the insurers to argue that the above approach to the "Limitations on the Warrantors' Liability" is an artificial approach and that the substantive reality when one looks at the package as a whole is that the personal liability of the insured is excluded. However the considered view is that the "Limitations on the Warrantors' Liability" are no more than that—limitations on the liability of the warrantor which, rather than being expressed, for example, by reference to a fixed figure, are expressed by reference to the extent of the warrantor's rights against its own insurers. The purchaser must have proved its claim and the quantum of its claim for breach of warranty against the insured and the insured must therefore have had a real contractual liability for the amount of the judgment or award. The terms in question are only limiting what the insured has to pay in respect of that established and ascertained liability. **9–31**

9.4.2 Investor's knowledge

The investor is likely to seek the inclusion of a clause similar to the following: **9–32**

> The rights and remedies of the investor[s] in respect of any breach of any of the warranties shall not be affected by completion, any investigation made by or on behalf of any of the investor[s] into the affairs of the company or any other event or matter whatsoever which otherwise might have attested such rights and remedies except a specific and duly authorised written waiver or release.

However, a Court of Appeal case (*Eurocopy Plc v Teesdale* [1992] B.C.L.C. 1067), suggests that there is a risk that a purchaser (in that case) or an investor will be deprived of a remedy for breach of warranty where it is aware of the breach **9–33** following a disclosure, or otherwise, and despite any provisions in the investment agreement, that no actual or constructive knowledge on the part of the investor would prejudice a claim. This was a Court of Appeal decision not on the substantive issues, and merely established that there was an arguable case, but it does mean that purchasers and investors alike should be cautious about relying on warranties if they have actual knowledge of breach at the time the contract is made.

Despite the *Eurocopy* case, a clause similar to the above is almost always included. In practice the investor's advisors will argue that though they have been given access to much information, they may not realise its impact or import until later when they understand the business. Any request therefore by the company's lawyers asking the investor to confirm at completion that they do not have or are not aware of a warranty claim is likely to be rejected.

9–34   The investors will also be keen to prevent the directors joining the company in any warranty claim brought against a director and as a result damaging their investment. A clause similar to the following will be included:

> Any information supplied by the company [or the subsidiaries] or its agents, representatives or advisors to the directors or their agents, representatives or advisors in connection with, or which forms the basis of, any of the warranties or the disclosure letter or otherwise in relation to the business and affairs of the company [or its subsidiaries] (whether before or after the date hereof) shall not be treated as a representation, warranty or guarantee of the accuracy thereof by the company [or the subsidiaries] to the directors and shall not constitute a defence to any claim by the investor[s] under the warranties and each of the directors hereby irrevocably waives any and all claims against the company [or the subsidiaries] in respect thereof.

The scope of the waiver should be considered carefully and should exclude fraud and wilful misrepresentation.

9.4.3 Scope of the warranties

9–35   Warranties can extend to one page or to dozens of pages and it is a matter of judgment on the part of the investors and their advisors as to what level of risk is involved in order to determine an appropriate level of warranties. The central importance of warranties from the directors to the investor is information. The investor will wish to ensure that the information from the directors and its reporting accountants is reliable. It has no real wish to sue the director and in the absence of fraud or wilful omission is unlikely to do so. The second aspect of warranties from the directors is commitment. Members of the management team who are giving warranties to the investor will inevitably feel uneasy about an extension of their exposure to financial risk. Nevertheless the institutions will feel that the management team, who will previously have had day-to-day control of the affairs of the investee company, can reasonably be expected to know about and therefore warrant the state of those affairs. If the directors are not prepared to make a commitment then the institutions will be nervous about the investment.

The investors will expect a warranty in respect of facts and information contained in the business plan or accountants' report or other reports commissioned for the purposes of the investment. With regard to the business plan and the accountants' report, this will be difficult to refuse since the plan will have been prepared by them and the accountants' report will rely on information provided by them. The warrantors, for their part, will be reluctant to give a warranty extending to matters of opinion. It may be an acceptable solution for the warrantors to warrant the accuracy of all factual information given to the accountants in producing the report and limited to identified information or to facts contained in the report.

All information so far as it contains a statement of fact and does not comprise a statement of opinion contained in or referred to in the accountants' report and/or the business plan is true and accurate in all material respects. None of the warrantors are aware of any fact or matter not disclosed in writing to the investor which may render such information untrue, incorrect or misleading in any material respect.

The projections and forecasts are of course more difficult and the management team should not be allowed to warrant any projections, forecasts or opinions contained in the business plan or the accountants' report. Nevertheless the investor will need to know that there is some substance behind the projections and that they are based upon reasonable assumptions. The following is often a compromise. **9–36**

> All statements of opinion, projections and forecasts set out in the accountants' report and/or the business plan are opinions honestly and reasonably made by the person holding or making them after having due regard to all information of which the warrantors are aware at the date of this Agreement.

The warranties referred to above will be requested whether the investment is for development capital, a MBO or a MBI.

If a MBI, an investor will be unlikely to obtain very much comfort from the new management team and will be forced to rely on warranties which the purchaser can obtain from the vendor as well as those warranties referred to above. In a MBO, the management team, if they have "hands-on" control, will be in a better position to provide a level of historical warranties appropriate to the investment. However, the investor will generally prefer to seek as many warranties as possible from the vendor with the management team filling in the gaps by providing comfort on specific issues within their control and covering areas where the vendor has not obliged by providing a warranty. In addition, the warrantors will be asked to provide a general warranty that they are not aware of any breaches in the acquisition agreement.

Investment Agreement

The investor may, and in a development capital investment will certainly, seek historical warranties that cover the completeness and accuracy of the audited accounts, the payment of taxation, compliance with legal requirements, absence of any material litigation, details of material contracts, events since the accounts date and, in relevant cases, details of intellectual property rights. Whether this list should be extended will depend upon the circumstances of each investment.

Latest accounts

9–37 The investor will almost invariably require warranties to the effect that the latest audited accounts of the company have been prepared in accordance with law, and on a consistent basis in accordance with the accountancy principles generally accepted in the UK, to give a true and fair view of the group or business as at the relevant balance sheet date. It is often suggested that this warranty should be to the effect that the accounts are "true and accurate". In fact the statutory obligation (CA 2006, ss.395, 396) is that the accounts should give a true and fair view of the state of affairs of the company or should be prepared in accordance with international accounting standards. A warranty that the accounts are accurate would be unrealistic.

Warrantors will usually require any warranty about management to be more limited, especially if these are not prepared on the same basis and do not provide for the same adjustments.

Further, specific warranties may be sought with regard to valuation of stock, work in progress, depreciation and revaluation of fixed assets, provisions or revenues for all liabilities, and book debts.

Events since balance sheet date

9–38 It is usual and very important that the investor obtains a warranty that since the balance sheet date of the last audited accounts there have been no material adverse changes in the financial position or prospects of the business or group. This would generally extend to such matters as:

- the business having been carried on in the ordinary course;
- there have been no disposal of assets other than in the ordinary course;
- no unusual or long term (for more than one year) commitments or contracts have been entered into;
- no important customer or source of supply has been lost;
- no changes in the remuneration or terms of employment of the senior executives;
- no shares have been issued or dividends or distributions made.

Warranties

Borrowings

The investor may wish to know that the borrowing powers of any of the group companies as set out in their articles or any agreements have not been exceeded. Further warranties may be sought as to the amount and terms of loan capital and borrowings outstanding, and confirming that no indebtedness is liable to be repaid early, or that there are no circumstances likely to give rise to an enforcement of security. The investor will also wish to be satisfied that in addition to its investment, it has procured sufficient funding to enable it to achieve the forecasts contained in the business plan. The investor will wish to know from the outset that sufficient funds are available because it will not want to find itself being asked to invest further monies or accept a dilution at some later date simply to enable the original project to be completed.

9–39

Insurance

Before putting his money in, the investor will wish to know that all the assets, stock and undertakings of the group are insured either to their full replacement value or more satisfactorily from the warrantors' point of view for amounts reasonably regarded as adequate against risks normally insured against by companies carrying on similar businesses. The investor will also wish to know that the policies are valid and not voidable which they can be for even very small misrepresentations.

9–40

Trading arrangements

The investor will wish to know that there are no material capital commitments or contracts outstanding. The warrantor will want to make sure that the warranty is as precise as possible.

In addition it may be appropriate to gauge the trading risk of the business to obtain a warranty that no more than a certain percentage of the aggregate amount of all the purchases or sales of the business are obtained or made from or to the same supplier or customer. This is likely to have been covered in the accountants' report and may even have been independently verified. Nevertheless the investor will want to know from the management team that they are not aware of anything that will change this.

The investor will also be concerned to know that there are no debts or contracts between the group or any of the management team. The purpose of this is to protect against arrangements which may be in breach of the CA 2006.

Investment Agreement

Legal matters

9–41 *Statutory requirements* The investor will require confirmation that the businesses have been carried on in compliance with all statutory requirements and regulations for the time being in force, and that all necessary consents and licences have been obtained and maintained.

9–42 *Litigation* The investor will inevitably require a warranty in respect of actual or potential litigation or claims. To avoid a deluge of disclosures that may not be of interest to the investor, an exception may be made for actions involving the collection of debts or perhaps up to a certain monetary limit which will eliminate disclosures in relation to debt collection. The investor will also wish to know of any circumstances that are likely to lead to any claim or litigation. The normal compromise is for the warrantors to provide this warranty but limit it to their knowledge.

9–43 *Employment matters* The investor will know very little about the employment record of the company other than what it has gleaned from the accountants' report. Inevitably it will require a warranty that all existing contracts of service with senior employees (usually defined by monetary figures) and consultants have been disclosed, and that there are no other agreements with employees or consultants which cannot be terminated by, say, three-months notice, without giving rise to any claim for compensation. The investor may also require a list of all employees with details of the financial terms of their employment including bonuses and other economic benefits, as well as their ages and terms of employment if it is intended to make the employees redundant in the near future. Warranties will normally be required stating the employer has complied with all statutory obligations, regulations and codes of conduct and practice relevant to employee or trade union relations, etc.

Pensions

9–44 The investor will want to learn as quickly as possible about the pension arrangements made for the employees. In particular, it will wish to confirm that all documents relating to the pensions have been disclosed to the purchaser. As a result of an investigation of the documentation and the scheme, special warranties may be required in some circumstances.

Freehold and leasehold property

9–45 If the property has been the subject of a normal investigation of title by the investor's solicitors then a warranty as to title may not be required. If however, a

Warranties

full investigation is not made or solicitors' certificate of title is obtained then the investor may require the warrantors to warrant title or the accuracy of the certificate of title, bearing in mind that much of the solicitors' investigation will be dependent on the information provided to them by the warrantors.

Further warranties will generally be required to show that the freehold and leasehold properties in the agreement comprise all the premises and land occupied or used in connection with the business and the particulars in the agreement are true and correct. The investor will also seek a warranty that each of the properties complies with all applicable statutory by-laws and that the buildings and other structures are in good and substantial repair, enjoy usual main services and are not subject to any defect or disputes. This will be fiercely contested.

With regard to leasehold properties, warranties may be required to the effect that title of the landlord and any superior landlord was investigated upon acquisition of the lease and found to be satisfactory and the investor will seek confirmation, in respect of all leases, that the rent has been paid and all covenants observed, that the lease continues in force and all licences and consents required from the landlord have been obtained with no rent outstanding.

Assets

The investor will almost always require a warranty that the other assets of the group, including debts due to it, are the absolute property of the group and have not been subject to any assignment, charge, lien or encumbrance, hire purchase, condition of sale or credit sale agreement. This warranty would require disclosure of any retention of title provisions. **9–46**

Intellectual property

Depending upon the nature of the business, a warranty will generally be required about the intellectual property owned by the business; that it is not being infringed or does not infringe the rights of others. **9–47**

Investment costs

Increasingly, investors are looking harder at the total investment costs being incurred as a result of any investment. This can often lead to the investor asking for a warranty that the total investment costs will not exceed the figure contained in the disclosure letter.

This is a very difficult warranty for the management team to give, and should be avoided. All advisors are getting used to giving and reviewing estimates of costs

Investment Agreement

and this issue will need to be addressed during the transaction, but it is extremely unfair to make the management responsible for these costs.

Disclosure letter

9–48 The warranties will be qualified by a formal disclosure letter which will be delivered by the warrantors or their solicitors to the investor or its solicitors at the time of signing the agreement. It is a key document in the investment process. Warranties and disclosures must be considered together. Parties mistakenly often dedicate far more time to the negotiation of warranties than they do to the consideration of the disclosure letter.

The disclosure letter will take the form of a letter from the warrantors to the investor or from the warrantors' solicitors to the investor's solicitors. It is usually divided into two parts, "general disclosures" and "specific disclosures" and will have attached to it copies of the documentation being disclosed known as the "disclosure bundle". Two copies of the disclosure bundle will be prepared, one for the investor and one for retention by the warrantors. They will be identical and each document should be initialled by the other advisors for identification purposes.

9–49 Disclosure letters can be very lengthy and time consuming to produce. The investor will prefer to be fed parts of the disclosure letter as they are produced rather than be delivered the final letter the night before completion is set to take place. The warrantors' advisors may argue that they are only able to produce the letter upon the warranties being agreed. This may alter the final letter but should not stop the process from being started. Any revisions and updates can be easily incorporated.

A number of the warranties may be qualified as to knowledge. This will be defined in the investment agreement and may be restricted to the identification of certain persons. The person from the company's legal team responsible for the co-ordination and gathering of the disclosures must ensure that all relevant personnel have been drawn into the disclosure process.

The disclosure letter will be effective at the date of the agreement but the investor will seek to obtain as early a draft as possible as there is likely to be a large amount of information and documentation which will require digestion, and may result in further investigation or amendments to the agreement by way of requests for indemnities or special provisions or a re-negotiation of the price. No matter how thorough the investor is in his/her due diligence, the first draft disclosure letter nearly always seems to throw up previously undiscovered problems. They may even cause the investor to walk away from the transaction.

9–50 The disclosure letter should be treated as seriously as the investment agreement and the negotiation of the warranties. A certain amount of time will be required to negotiate the disclosure letter in cases where the benefit of the warranty is negated or materially reduced by the extent of the disclosures made. This is common and in essence amounts to re-negotiation of the warranties. For example, where it has been accepted that no investigation of properties should be made by the investor, "all matters contained in the title deeds, public records and apparent from a survey" will render the vast majority of property warranties useless. An individual in the investor's legal team should be given overall responsibility for the disclosure letter and the bundle. There needs to be a clear understanding at the outset about which personnel within the legal team, and indeed other advisors, need to review what documentation. A master bundle should be kept and copies distributed for review. The investor should raise enquiries in relation to the drafts of the disclosure letter and associated documents to ensure that the disclosures are clear and unambiguous and that it fully understands the consequences of accepting them. For example if the disclosure letter provides details of a major dispute, the investor's advisors will wish the disclosure to describe the status of any litigation, as well as any relevant details. The investor will also be keen to ensure that he/she is not burdened with last-minute disclosures, as is often the case. The investor should stand firm and refuse to accept such disclosures.

The warrantors are likely to try to include by reference and by general disclosures as much information as possible. For example, the disclosure of all public information by the company, all documents registered at Companies Registry, all information which the investor may obtain by inspecting books, records to which it is given access by the warrantors, and the contents of all documents attached to, or referred to in the disclosure letter. The investor will generally refuse to allow such disclosures to the extent that it is unable to make a satisfactory check, or has had insufficient time to inspect or read records and documents made available, or has not seen the documents incorporated by reference into the letter. In order to be able to sue for misrepresentation, the investor needs to show that it relied upon the misleading representation and was thereby induced to enter into the contract. **9–51**

On the other hand, the warrantors should be aware of including additional specific information in the form of a disclosure letter if, as is common, the warrantors are being asked to warrant the accuracy of all the information in the disclosure letter.

Disclosure letters are often delivered late and often result in a delay in completion or at the very least a protracted completion meeting. In an attempt to avoid this, a clause similar to the following may be included in the investment agreement in order to highlight the requirements of the investor.

Each disclosure in the disclosure letter shall: **9–52**

- be made with specific reference and shall provide full and precise details of the nature and extent of the particular exemption to the warranties;

- specify the maximum amount of any ascertainable financial liability referred to therein and shall further specify the best possible pre-estimate of the maximum amount of any non-ascertainable or contingent financial liability referred to therein;

- (if it refers to any separate documents) identify precisely the nature of such document and the terms of or provisions in such document which are relied upon, with a copy of the relevant document being attached to the disclosure letter and specified by reference in a documents' schedule to be attached to the disclosure letter;

- constitute a warranty that the matters set forth or referred to therein are true and accurate in all material respects and give a true and fair view of the nature and extent of the exceptions to the warranties or in the case of any pre-estimates of the maximum amount of any non-ascertainable or contingent financial liability that the amount in question represents the best possible pre-estimate of the liability in question having regard to all information then available and after making diligent inquiry.

Any disclosure which fails to comply with any of the foregoing requirements in any respect shall not be effective and the matters stated therein shall be deemed not to be disclosed so that the warranties shall continue to have full effect without qualification by such disclosure.

9–53 This serves the purpose of determining the criteria that is required by the investors for the purposes of a proper disclosure. However, a disclosure that does not satisfy such criteria is deemed not to be sufficient or effective irrespective of whether it is contained in the disclosure letter accepted at completion. The warrantors are unlikely to accept the above as determining whether a disclosure is acceptable or not, their argument being that if the investor accepts the disclosure letter, then he should accept the effectiveness of the disclosures. Nevertheless a clause similar to the above in an early draft of the investment agreement does demonstrate clearly what is required before the investor will accept the disclosures.

Complete disclosures

9–54 It is in the investor's interest that the disclosures are complete so that it can address the issues or negotiate better terms rather than discuss the breach of a warranty at a later stage and have to sue for such breach. It is also in the warrantors' interest to ensure that all disclosures are complete otherwise it will run the risk of a breach of warranty being brought against them. In addition the investor will often request that the disclosures are warranted as true and accurate. Whether this is expressed or not it would not be effective disclosure unless it was a true and accurate disclosure and therefore would not limit liability under the warranty.

Warranties

If a disclosure is not sufficiently precise, the warrantor runs the risk of a court finding a disclosure was not adequate to preclude a claim for breach of warranty (see *Levison v Farin* [1978] 2 All E.R. 1149). This was in the context of a sale and purchase agreement. Mrs Levison sold her dress-making business to one of her competitors, Mrs Farin. The accounts for the year ending December 31, 1972 showed her business to have net assets of £44,000. However, the purchaser knew that the business was making losses which were reducing the new assets. The sale was completed in May 1973. This was five months after the last set of accounts at which time the net assets had reduced by £8,600. The vendor gave the following warranty "save as disclosed ... between 31 December 1972 and the completion date ... there will have been no material adverse change in the overall value of the net assets of the (target company) on the basis of a valuation adopted in the balance sheet allowing for normal trade fluctuations". The court found that there had been a material adverse change in the net assets and that consequently there was a breach of warranty. However, the vendor argued that the purchaser was well aware of the trading position of the company before the agreement was signed and that the target company was losing money. This was as a result of the vendor's illness. The vendor argued that this constituted sufficient disclosure and precluded an action for breach of warranty by the purchaser. The court decided against the vendor and found that there was not adequate disclosure to qualify the warranty. All that was disclosed was "a possible cause of loss, not an actual drop in net asset value". In essence, merely putting the purchaser on an enquiry or making the purchaser aware of certain facts did not constitute adequate disclosure in the context of this warranty.

9–55

As a counter to this, the warrantors will often seek to preclude any later complaints that it has made insufficient disclosure of a matter by including the following provision in the disclosure letter:

9–56

> Where particulars only of a matter as set out or referred to in this letter, or a document is referred to or not attached, or a reference is made to a particular part only of such a document, full particulars of the matter and the full contents of the document are deemed to be disclosed and it is assumed that the purchaser/investor does not require any further particulars.

This will receive some resistance from the investor who will argue that it should have a cause of action unless full disclosure has been made. This begs the question, what is full disclosure, but the investor will argue that the onus will be on the warrantors to determine which disclosures are required by the warranties.

General disclosures

The warrantors are likely to try to include by reference and by general disclosures as much information as possible, for example, the disclosure of all public information by the company, all documents registered at the Companies Registry, all information which the investor may obtain by inspecting books, records to which it

9–57

is given access by the warrantors and the contents of all documents attached to, or referred to in the disclosure letter. The effect of the general disclosures is that the purchaser is deemed to have knowledge of all the matters so disclosed. As a consequence, the golden rule for an investor is that it should not accept a disclosure unless all relevant members of the investor's team have had a full opportunity to review, understand and investigate the relevant disclosures.

I have set out in para.9–58 a summary of the approach often taken by the investor to some of the general disclosures.

Searches at the Companies Registry or other public registries

9–58 The warrantors will often attempt to provide that the investor is deemed to have knowledge of all matters kept on file at the Companies Registry. The investor will often take the stance that just because information is publicly available does not necessarily mean that it is deemed to be disclosed and thereby qualify the warranties. If the investor chooses to accept this disclosure, then the investor's legal team must review carefully the company searches and ensure that the searches are dated as at the date of the disclosure letter or the date agreed in the disclosure letter at which the searches should be reviewed. In the case of an old company, this will obviously impose a considerable burden upon the investor's legal team as there is likely to be a considerable amount of material at the Companies Registry. A compromise solution may be to accept disclosures of entries made at the Registry within, for example, the prior two years.

A similar approach should also be taken to deemed disclosure of any searches of public registers (trade mark searches and searches of non-UK company registries). Again if the investor is willing to accept such disclosures then someone in the investor's legal team must ensure that the relevant records have been reviewed and that any searches are updated at the date provided for in the disclosure letter. If that is not the case, then the searches should be restricted to those actually carried out by the investor.

Similarly, the investor should limit disclosure of property searches to those actually carried out by the investor's advisors.

Inspection of properties

9–59 The warrantors quite often will seek to include a general disclosure that the investor is aware of all matters from an inspection of the real properties. This should be firmly rejected by the investor. Even if a property inspection could be organised, it is unlikely that it could be conducted by all personnel and advisors who might appreciate and understand the impact of what they are viewing.

Warranties

A compromise would be to permit the warrantors to include in the disclosure bundle a copy of any surveyors' report relating to the properties prepared for the investor. This may be irrelevant if the warrantors have successfully resisted giving warranties as to the structure of the properties.

Corporate records

9–60 The warrantors will generally seek to disclose corporate records of the target company group. The approach taken by the investor will be similar to that described above in relation to public searches. Once again, if the disclosure is accepted then the corporate records must be reviewed in detail. If a company is very old, then again any review may be limited to, for example, the prior two years.

Correspondence

9–61 The warrantors may seek to disclose all prior correspondence. There could be a vast amount of correspondence, and it may make nonsense of the warranties. For example, former drafts of the disclosure letter could be described as previous correspondence. If the investor is prepared to accept some form of disclosure then it should be restricted to certain identified correspondence, copies of which are included in the disclosure bundle and agreed between the parties.

Public domain

9–62 The first draft of the disclosure letter often includes a general disclosure of all matters within the public domain. This is extremely broad and would encompass information contained in public registers that would not normally be searched by an investor (for example registers at the Office of Fair Trading) and matters, although in the public domain, of which the investor cannot be expected to be aware, for example, everything that has ever appeared in the local press. This disclosure should be firmly rejected.

Due diligence exercise

9–63 The warrantor will often argue that the investor, as a result of its extensive due diligence, knows as much as or even more about the company than the warrantors themselves. Accordingly the warrantors' advisors will argue that all matters that are discovered in the course of the due diligence investigation should be deemed to be disclosed.

In a sale and purchase agreement, the purchaser would be very reluctant to provide the vendors with a copy of the due diligence report, which has assisted them in determining a price. However, in an investment it is quite likely that the due diligence report will have been made available to the warrantors for their comments. Nevertheless, the report will not have been prepared with a view to qualifying the warranties. The purchaser should respond that a due diligence investigation is not a substitute for a disclosure letter which is the forum that allows the purchaser to ensure that the disclosures are properly reviewed by all relevant personnel. Nevertheless, we have seen earlier that as a result of the *Eurocopy* case there is a risk that the investors would not be able to sue for breach of warranty if it has knowledge of such breach prior to its investment.

Matters contained or referred to in the disclosure bundle

9–64 The purchaser should refuse deemed disclosure matters "referred to" in the disclosure bundle. If something is only referred to, but not contained in the bundle, the matter cannot be said to have been brought to the attention of the investor.

Legal professional privilege

9–65 Some communications between a lawyer and his/her client carry so called legal privilege. A document is privileged if it is given to or by a legal advisor, for the purpose of getting or giving legal advice, and is confidential. Moreover, a document arising in contemplation of or in connection with pending litigation, for example, communications with third parties to obtain evidence for use in litigation, may be legally privileged.

In the course of responding to an investor's due diligence request and delivering documents to the investor as part of the disclosure bundle, the warrantors should be aware of the possible loss of legal professional privilege. The loss of such privilege could mean that the document would no longer be privileged from production during legal proceedings and so could prejudice the company in a dispute.

In some circumstances it may be possible to argue that the warrantor and the investor share a common interest which is not lost by disclosure, but as a general rule, the warrantors should exercise extreme caution before disclosing any document which is likely to be privileged.

The warrantors may need to consider whether full disclosure against the breach of warranty can be made without disclosing the privileged document. If full disclosure cannot be made without disclosing that document, then the warrantor needs to decide whether the benefit of retaining the privilege outweighs the detriment of non-disclosure. Clearly a warrantor who fails to disclose the relevant

Warranties

matter in respect of the warrantors runs the risk of being sued for breach of warranty.

9.5 Investor controls

As well as retrospective comfort that the information provided to the investors is accurate, it is as important that the investor has prospective comfort over the future management of the business to ensure that the investment conforms to the projections given to it by the management and in accordance with the business plan. As a result, investor controls are imposed on management. These are likely to be formal written controls. They are necessary to an investor because: **9–66**

- No matter how substantial the due diligence undertaken by the investors or their advisors has been, the investors are taking a significant risk in a company about which they know only a little and in a management team about whom they know less. To counter this risk they insist upon a prompt and regular supply of information and the ability to take control quickly should the need arise.

- Unless requirements and controls are built into the investment documentation, if the investor has taken only a minority stake (which is quite likely in smaller transactions) he/she will only have the most limited rights which a minority shareholder has under the Companies Act and no more.

- The investee company will not be a public company and therefore will not be subject to detailed disclosure requirements or the protective arm of the Stock Exchange.

- Even if the investor has appointed a director to the board of the investee company that director will be in a minority position and unable to control events through his/her single vote.

- The investor does not have day-to-day involvement with the company and so he/she has neither the knowledge nor the opportunity to be involved in the decision making process.

The simplest way to protect the investor is by formal written positive and negative controls, but, so far as possible, controls that can bite if they are breached.

Controls can be presented to the management as a positive benefit. They can develop good corporate habits and educate the company and its senior managers about the process and systems that will be required in anticipation of an eventual flotation. A good example of this is the use of the audit and remuneration committees. Even in a development capital situation where there is an existing company, that may have been around for some years, corporate affairs may well have been handled in a very ad hoc or disorganised way probably because the company **9–67**

Investment Agreement

may have been dominated by a single entrepreneur used to running his/her own show, or a dominant director used to making decisions informally without proper meetings or consultations. The management teams will essentially be looking to carry on the business in the same manner as prior to the investment without undue interference from the investor.

9–68 The investor should consider the circumstances of the particular investment in determining the parameters of the controls required. Having established the level of the involvement that the investor requires then he/she needs to establish the areas of the business over which particular controls are needed and the decisions in which he/she will wish to be involved. Controls can be split broadly into the following categories:

- management controls;
- financial controls;
- employment controls;
- corporate governance controls; and
- shareholder protections.

9.5.1 Management controls

9–69 It is usual for the investors to have "veto" rights so that the company can only carry out certain transactions with the express approval of the investors. In general these controls will define those decisions that management are able to make on a daily basis without reference to the investors and those decisions which should be reserved to the investor. In particular, these rights will extend to the management of the business, the control of the finances and the employment of senior staff.

The investor is investing large amounts of money and it is impossible to argue that he/she should provide a totally free hand to management to run the business and protect this investment, no matter how much faith he/she has in them. On the other hand, an experienced management team with a proven track record is likely to be given more freedom. It is obviously important to the investor that the business is not wound up or transformed into a different business from that in which he/she is investing, by way of, for example, a major asset purchase or by any other substantial alteration without the investor playing a part in these decisions. Control provisions over management are a way of reserving major decisions to the investor but leaving the executive directors free to run the business without continuous interferences.

The extent of the controls required is likely to vary according to the equity involvement of the management relative to the investors. For example, if the investor is a minority shareholder and the management have a majority shareholding, the extent of these controls may need to be widened, and require the management to bring more decisions to the investors before putting them into practice. Below are some of the management controls that the investor will require.

The approval of the investor is required to: 9–70

- enter into or vary any transaction or arrangement with, or for the benefit of, any of its directors or shareholders or any other person who is a "connected person" with any of its directors or shareholders;
- enter into any partnership or joint venture or arrangement with any other person, firm or company;
- surrender or agree to any material change in the terms of any substantial supply or distribution agreement to which it is from time to time a party;
- enter into either any unusual or onerous contract or any other material or major or long term contract or assume any material liability otherwise than in the ordinary course of business;
- delegate any matters to a committee of its directors;
- deal in any way (including the acquisition or disposal, whether outright or by way of licence or otherwise howsoever) with intellectual property;
- do any act or thing outside the ordinary course of the business carried on by it;
- negotiate or permit a listing of any shares in the company;
- conduct any litigation or arbitration material to the company; save for the collection of debts arising in the ordinary course of the business carried on by the company or any application for an interim injunction or other application (including interim defence) which is urgently required in the best interests of the company in circumstances in which it is not reasonably practicable to obtain prior consent as aforesaid;
- make any material change in the nature of its business as carried on at the date of adoption of the new articles; and
- formulate the group's risk management strategy, health and safety policy and environmental policy.

9.5.2 Financial controls

Financial controls will be included in the agreement to ensure that the investor's 9–71
funds are used for the purposes designated in the business plan or any subsequent

budget controls which are often imposed in matters such as capital expenditure, borrowing, hire purchase lending and similar commitments. Variations from the business plan or agreed expenditure levels will require the investor's consent. These consents not only protect the investor, but benefit the company by instilling tight financial discipline in the business.

The investor may require a list of financial controls to:

- borrow monies (other than by way of its agreed overdraft facility) or accept credit (other than normal trade credit);

- make any payment otherwise than on an arm's length basis;

- enter into or give or permit or suffer to subsist any guarantee of or indemnity or contract of suretyship for or otherwise commit itself in respect of the due payment of money or the performance of any contract, engagement or obligation of any other person or body;

- propose or pay dividend or propose or make any other distribution other than as provided in the new articles or by a subsidiary undertaking to its parent undertaking;

- incur any capital expenditure (including obligations under hire purchase and leasing arrangements) exceeding the amount in the relevant capital expenditure budget referred to in cl.[ ] by £[ ] or (where no items were specified but a general provision made) in relation to any item exceeding £[ ] or in any other way exceed a figure set out in such budget;

- dispose (otherwise than at the time and for the price contained in the relevant capital disposals forecast) of any asset of a capital nature with a book or market value in excess of £[ ];

- [save as contemplated by the financing agreements] mortgage or charge or permit the creation of or suffer to subsist any mortgage charge lien or encumbrance over the whole or any part of its undertaking, property or assets [(other than those mortgages and charges detailed in sch.[ ])];

- make any loan or give any credit (other than normal trade credit);

- enter into any agreement or arrangement for the sale and lease-back of any asset.

9.5.3 Employment controls

9–72 Employment controls are often the most difficult to negotiate because the management have a personal interest in them. The most significant and practical control that an investor can impose is to ensure that each of the directors or management team have a personally significant financial investment in the company.

Investor controls

An investor makes an investment not simply because he/she is confident that the business will project a satisfactory return but also because the investor believes the management can deliver that return. The investor will therefore wish to ensure that his/her management team are focused on making the business a success. He/she will have satisfied him/herself of this by way of due diligence undertaken before the legal contracts are under way. However he/she will also wish to ensure that a number of controls are included in the documents. In addition to the controls already discussed there will be additional controls with regard to the employees.

A number of prohibitions will be included in the agreement which, inter alia, may prevent directors or senior management being changed or new ones appointed without the consent of the investor.

The directors/managers will not without the approval of the investors: **9–73**

- appoint or remove any director (other than as the investor['s][s'] director);

- engage any employee or consultant on terms that either his contract cannot be terminated by a three-month notice or less or his/her emoluments and/or commissions or bonuses are or are likely to be at the rate of £[25,000] per annum or more or increase the emoluments and/or commissions or bonuses of any employee to more than £[25,000] per annum or vary the terms of employment of any employee earning (or so that after such variation he/she will, or is likely to earn) more than £[25,000] per annum;

- increase the total remuneration of any of the directors other than as provided in their service agreements or make any alteration to the terms of their service agreements;

- vary or make or fail to make (where the company or board has a right to make and the investor[s] has requested in writing that the company or board so makes) any binding decisions on the terms of employment and service of any officer or principal employee of the company, increase or vary the salary or other benefits of any such officer or employee, or appoint or dismiss any such officer or employee;

- establish any pension, death or disability or life assurance scheme or any share ownership or share option plan or any shadow share scheme or any employee benefit trust or other profit sharing, bonus or incentive scheme for any of the directors, employees or former directors or employees (or dependants thereof) of any member of the [Group] or vary the terms or rules of any new or existing scheme.

The service contract and the investment agreement will also include controls in the form of restrictive covenants to ensure that while employed the management devote their full attention to making the business a success and do not undertake any other form of work while employed by the Company.

Investment Agreement

9.5.4 Shareholder protections

9–74 Shareholder protections for the purposes of this clause can be described as anti-dilution or anti-leakage provisions.

Anti-dilution provisions are fundamental to preservation of the investor's position as a shareholder. Into this category fall negative controls which prevent the issue of further shares, the re-organisation of share capital or changes to the company's articles of association without the consent of the investor. As a result the percentage in relative value of the investor's shareholding is protected.

Anti-leakage provisions serve a similar function in that they ensure that the business profits are fed through to the company in which the investor has subscribed funds by preventing the establishment of partnerships and the purchase of shares in other companies without the investor's consent.

9–75 The directors/managers will not without the approval of the investors:

- permit or cause to be proposed any alteration to its share capital (including any increase thereof) or the rights attaching to its shares;
- create, allot, issue or redeem any share or loan capital or grant or agree to grant any options for the issue of any share or loan capital, or establish any employees' share option scheme except in accordance with the new articles;
- subscribe or otherwise acquire, or dispose of any shares or any option over shares in the capital of any other company;
- acquire the whole or part of any other business or undertaking (other than the purchase of raw materials and stock in the ordinary course of business);
- permit or cause to be proposed any amendment to its memorandum or articles of association;
- cease or propose to cease to carry on its business or be wound up save where it is insolvent;
- apply or permit its directors to apply to petition to the court for an administration order to be made in respect of the company; and
- make any change to:
  — its auditors;
  — its bankers or the terms of the mandate given to such bankers in relation to its account(s);
  — its accounting reference date.

These provisions go to the core of the protections required by the investors. Most of the veto rights referred to in this section, for practical reasons, provide that such approval may be given on behalf of the investors by any director or other representative nominated by them. However because these restrictions are of such importance, they are often reserved to the investor, particularly where the investor is part of a syndicate.

Importance of enforcement provisions

Enforcement provisions are particularly important where the investor does not have a majority stake. He/she will be content to allow the management to run the business if things are going well but will wish to take more of an involvement if the business begins to slide and their return looks shaky. If the returns required by the investor are not achieved, additional voting rights may be conferred on the investor. This will allow the investor to take effective day-to-day management control of the investee company or to insist on a change of management. It may be done by voting enhancement provisions contained in the articles of association which will trigger if the dividends payable to the investors are in arrears or the redemption schedule is not met. However, it is important that these controls are expressed as a right which the investor can exercise if it so wishes and not as an automatic effect of preference dividend arrears or a failure to redeem. This is because enhanced voting rights may have the effect of making the investee company a subsidiary of the investor, which may not be desirable. Nevertheless the fact that the investor has such a right should be enough to ensure that the investor's views are listened to. 9–76

The company's lawyers will have little success in attempting to remove any of the above controls. However they should be anxious to ensure that such decisions are made expediently. The investor is likely to have made it a condition of the investment that he/she shall be entitled to appoint a non-executive director to the board of the company. A decision which requires considerable thought is, who is to exercise the investor controls? Should it be the investor himself, as a shareholder, or should it be the non-executive director whom the investor may have appointed, or should some control be exercised by the investor and some by his appointed shareholding?

For practical reasons, it is common to provide that such approval may be given on behalf of the investors by any director or other representative nominated by them. Management does not want to be put in a position where business decisions are unnecessarily delayed by the need for a non-executive director to consult at length with his/her appointor. On the other hand, the non-executive director should not be "bounced" into making decisions which will have wide ranging consequences not just for the company but for the financial commitment made by the investor. Where there is a syndicate of investors, some of the more fundamental and constitutional restrictions can often only be approved by the investors and not by the director. In a large investment there may be two directors appointed by 9–77

Investment Agreement

the investors, one appointed by the lead investor and the other appointed by all of the syndication. The investment agreement would provide that certain actions require the consent of both appointees. But thought needs to be given to what happens if the two directors disagree. Some issues can only be decided by shareholders and these controls cannot therefore be vested in the non-executive director. These include:

- matters requiring a special resolution;
- increasing or altering the share capital;
- giving director powers to allot shares;
- appointing or removing auditors; and
- removing a director before the expiration of his/her term of office.

9–78 For matters which are to be decided by the investors, it is necessary to decide how to resolve a disagreement amongst investors. In practice, this is often less of a problem as investors will bear in mind their ability to work together when choosing syndicate members. However, there are a large number of well-publicised investments that demonstrate the potential difficulties. Generally, controls on major business issues such as altering borrowing requirements or making a change to the nature of the company's business are reserved for the investors to decide, while less significant matters (such as hiring and firing staff) are left to the director appointed by the company. It is important to address this matter at the outset of a transaction. Quite often the investor will agree with his/her syndicate partner a number of issues with respect to the management of the investment. This is often achieved by way of a letter between the investors. However, the management will be particularly concerned to know the process upon which decisions are made, and to ensure that they are made quickly and efficiently without restricting the development of the business. In view of this, a clause along the following lines may be included in the agreement.

Relationship between the investors

9–79   1 Notwithstanding that this agreement may provide for the agreement, approval or consent of the investors, the company and the managers shall be entitled to assume (without further enquiry) that any written agreement, approval or consent given by the investors' representative is duly given by the investors' representative for and on behalf of all the investors.

    2 The investors' representative shall be entitled (but not be bound) to give any agreement, approval or consent without reference to any other investor in relation to any matter which in the opinion of the investors' representative is not material to the overall investment made by the investors hereunder.

Investor controls

3 Subject to sub-cl.2, the investors' representative shall be bound to notify the holder of the [preferred ordinary shares] of any request it receives for the giving of such agreement, approval or consent unless such agreement, approval or consent is given by the investors' directors at a meeting of the board of the company. Any such notification shall be in writing and state a time (being reasonable in all the circumstances) within which each holder of [preferred ordinary shares] is to give relevant directions. If the holder of the [preferred ordinary shares] together at the relevant time a majority in number of the preferred ordinary shares direct the investors' representative to give such agreement, approval or consent, the investors' representative shall do so, but not otherwise. For the avoidance of doubt, the investors' directors shall be entitled to give agreements, approval or consents at board meetings without reference back to the holder of the preferred ordinary shares.

4 (a) If any matter or event shall come to the attention of the investors' representative or any of the investors which may give rise to or constitute a material breach of the warranties, the investors' representative or such investor shall notify the investors with a view to arranging a discussion of the action to be taken.

   (b) No claim in respect of a breach of the warranties shall be notified to the warrantors without the prior approval of the investor together holding at the relevant time a majority in number of the [preferred ordinary shares].

   (c) All claims for breach of the warranties shall be co-ordinated by the investor's representative and no investor shall make or pursue any claim unless it has been approved under (b) and is made in conjunction with similar claims by the investors together holding a majority in number of the [preferred ordinary shares].

5 The investors shall indemnify the investors' representative from and against any liabilities, costs and expenses which may be suffered or incurred by it arising out of the operation of this clause (other than as a result of its negligence or wilful default) and as between the investors any liability hereunder shall be shared in proportion to the numbers of preferred ordinary shares held by them at the relevant time.

6 The holder of the preferred ordinary shares together holding a majority in number of the preferred ordinary shares may at any time by notice in writing to the company and to the existing investors' representative, appoint another person approved by the board of the company (such approval not to be unreasonably withheld or delayed) as investors' representative in place of the existing investors' representative for the purpose of this agreement.

9.6 Common issues raised by management

9–80 There are a number of common negotiating points raised by management or their lawyers when negotiating with a private equity house. This section attempts to highlight the main issues. As well as negotiating on behalf of individual management, management's lawyers must also consider the interests of Newco should one of the management team depart and leave the remaining management in place.

9.6.1 Investment agreement

Warranty

9–81 There are a number of arguments which management will commonly raise. Some of the main ones are as follows.

- That historical warranties should not be given by management and the private equity house should seek recourse only from the vendors through the acquisition agreement. Warranties to be given by management therefore should be limited to personal/Newco/business plan type/sweeper acquisition agreement warranties. The private equity house in its attempt to get comfortable with the acquisition may well seek limited warranties covering other areas including management accounts, absence of litigation, current trading, etc.

- Warranties should be given severally and "proportionately" rather than jointly and severally, i.e. a pro rata claim against each manager as opposed to a claim for the whole amount from one manager or a combination of managers. In general a private equity house will accept several liability from managers in relation to most warranties but they may not do so where they are looking to the management as a team, for example, with regard to the business plan.

- Management will look to a warranty cap of typically one to three times salary on the warranties.

- The warranty period should be a reasonable period. Two audits are usually acceptable.

- Management will require a grace period in which to remedy any breaches. There should be a blanket exclusion of trivial claims and also management will want to include as high a figure as possible for aggregate claims.

- Management may attempt to decline to warrant the accuracy of the due diligence reports, particularly where opinions are expressed. It is unreasonable however not to warrant factual information in these reports as being materially accurate.

Common issues raised by management

- That all rights should be exhausted against third parties prior to any warranty claim being enforced against the managers and that the management will be reimbursed (net of tax) if the private equity house/Newco subsequently receives payment from any third party which covers the same subject matter as the claim pursuant to which management have paid out.

- Sometimes management will argue that if there is a successful claim they should have the right to choose whether to satisfy such claim in cash or in shares. The private equity house will normally find this unacceptable. If there is a hole in Newco's funding then they would wish to have access to cash to put it right.

- Confirmation will be required that the vendor is barred from counter-claiming against managers.

Investment agreement restrictive covenants

9–82 Investment agreement and service agreement restrictive covenants should differ because they serve different purposes. The investment agreement restrictive covenants should protect the business at the time of the investment as opposed to the date of the managers' departure and should be more widely drawn with no link to the termination of the managers' service contracts. They should be linked to the length of time which the private equity house expects to remain in the target company or business. This is generally the view in how investment agreement restrictive covenants should be drafted, though it is fair to say this is not always market practice. If the investment agreement restrictive covenants do link to the termination of employment then the management should try to incorporate the following:

- that the covenants should terminate in the event of unfair or wrongful dismissal; or

- that the period should be reduced if the employer is put on garden leave.

Links to service agreements and investment articles

9–83 Management will wish to avoid any links to any other documents as far as possible so that ideally a breach or a material breach of the investment or articles will not lead to summary termination of the managers' service contracts, in term triggering the bad leaver provisions in the articles and resulting in the managers' immediate departure and the sale of shares at a lower subscription price and market value. A private equity house will try to achieve the opposite. If management ultimately are forced to concede, then they should at least ensure that the breaches referred to are specific breaches and not of the agreements as a whole and are material breaches. So for example the breaches could refer to restrictive covenants or breaches of the investor controls.

Investor director/chairman/remuneration committee

9–84
- A management may wish to put a restraint on the number of investor directors which the private equity house may appoint and also to discuss with the private equity house the appointment of the chairman. That is a key appointment and management will wish to be involved in those discussions.

- Management will wish to have a say in who constitutes the remuneration committee and as a minimum should seek impartiality (e.g. independent chairman).

Exit

9–85 Management will wish to resist the private equity house's attempts to fix the investment agreement's terms in which Newco will be floated or sold in due course. Any provisions regarding the giving of warranties by management on an exit should be a statement of intention only.

Obligation of Newco

9–86 When management are not in control of Newco they would not wish to accept obligations to procure that Newco does or does not do certain things as this is not within their ability to ensure. The obligations should instead be to exercise the voters, directors, shareholders, etc.

9.6.2 Articles of association

9–87 There are a number of points that management will wish to consider and negotiate when reviewing the articles of association. These are as follows.

- They will require a free transfer of management shares to family or to a trust for tax planning reasons and to PRs and beneficiaries under their wills. It should be considered carefully how wide the definition permitted transferees should be and the private equity house will insist that any person to whom the shares have been freely transferred must be required to transfer them in any circumstances where the original management shareholder would have been required to do so.

- They will require pre-emption rights and management shares to be offered first to the management then to a warehouse then to the private equity house.

The private equity house may want to participate pro rata with management in respect of bad leaver shares because of the favourable price at which they will be on offer. However the management are likely to argue that the "pot" belongs to the management teams whatever its numbers or make-up. Where the parties end up will depend on the relative bargaining strength.

- Clearly one of the most negotiated areas will be that of good and bad leaver. Management will want the bad leaver definition to include only summary dismissal for misconduct, resignation (possibly only within a certain time period) and possibly under-performance, though that should be heavily negotiated by management. The private equity house may insist that all leavers are bad even within a period of one or two years. The difficult areas are likely to be resignation after an initial period and termination of service contracts by the employer other than for misconduct. Management will try to ensure that any discretionary element of the decision as to who is not a good leaver rests with the remuneration committee as opposed to the private equity house. The main issues that arise when a manager leaves are first of all whether there is an obligation to sell. The private equity house will usually insist on this. The second issue is that of price. Generally anything other than the most generous valuation procedure (that is Newco to be valued as a whole on the basis of a full market P/E ratio and then take the proportion of the equity which leavers' shares represent) is likely to be used as a substantial discount to any foreseeable realistic value.

- The other most argued clauses are those of the drag along/tag along. The managers having put a considerable amount of effort and money into becoming shareholders in the business will want a period of time in which to demonstrate that they can grow the business and obtain a substantial gain. This of course is in the interest of the private equity house, though the private equity house will not wish to have any restriction on its ability to drag more shareholders should it wish to exit the business early for reasons other than agreed at the time of their investment.

9.6.3 Swamping rights

A number of private equity houses who take less than 75 per cent of the equity will want swamping rights, allowing them to take voting control when things go wrong. Private equity houses investing in "captive" funds are likely to insist on these rights instead of taking a majority holding to avoid accounting consolidation issues. **9–88**

The sort of situations in which swamping will apply are as follows.

- Where there has been a breach of the investment agreement/articles by Newco or any of the managers which may be considered likely to have a material and adverse effect on the private equity house's investment in Newco. The private equity house will try to ensure that this is subjective, which lies wholly in its hands, but management's lawyers should negotiate for as specific provisions as possible.

- Where payment of interest on the institutional loan notes is late (usually by more than an appropriate grace period).
- Where Newco has failed to redeem the institutional loan notes on the due dates for redemption.
- Where Newco fails to make a dividend payment on the institutional shares (usually again within a grace period of the due date for payment).
- Where there has been an event of default under the facility agreement or the occurrence of an event which with the passing of time or the granting notice would constitute such an event of default.

To be properly effective, swamping rights need to operate at board as well as at shareholder level. This is usually done by giving the institutional director weighted voting rights in particular circumstances. This would normally be resisted by management and is usually only insisted upon by the private equity house in fairly extreme circumstances.

Service agreements

9–89 The following provisions should be reviewed and checked on behalf of management:

- That the notice periods are acceptable to the managers. Twelve months is common for chief executives and six months for other directors.
- That salary and all benefits are as a manager expects them to be (including pension, car, medical insurance, death in service, bonus, etc).
- With regard to termination provisions ensure that there are appropriate limitations in the circumstances on which Newco can terminate and discuss with management the inclusion of a payment in lieu of notice clause.

9.7 Corporate governance controls

9–90 Corporate governance is a new title for the kind of controls that investors have been insisting upon for years. These are the kind of provisions which are designed to ensure that the investor is kept properly informed about the business. This will be achieved mainly through the appointment of a director from the investor or nominated by the investor. It goes without saying that a relationship needs to develop between the members of the board for its business to succeed. As a result, it is unlikely that the investor will object if the management team seek to include a clause which entitles them at least to be consulted before the investor nominates its appointed director or changes its nominated director. Further controls will expand to providing accounting information on a regular and timely basis and to holding board meetings with a proper agenda and minutes.

The board and the investors' director

(1) All the business of the company (other than day-to-day business) shall be carried on by the board. Board meetings will be held at intervals of not more than [ ] weeks and at least [ ] board meetings will be held in each calendar year.   9–91

(2) The company shall send to the investor[s] and to the investor['s][s'] director (if any):

(a) reasonable advance notice of each meeting of the board and each committee of the board and such notice shall be accompanied by a written agenda specifying the business to be transacted at such meeting (together with all papers to be circulated or presented to the same including (without limitation) the management accounts and financial statements required to be produced and circulated in accordance with cl.[ ]) and the parties agree that no business shall be transacted at any meeting of the board (or committee of the board) save for that specified in the agenda of such meeting unless the investor['s][s'] director shall otherwise agree; and

(b) as soon as practicable after each such meeting a copy of the minutes thereof.

The management team will be asked to supply regular financial information to the investor to enable the investor to monitor the company's performance. It is important for management that this does not become so onerous that it prevents them from attending to the day-to-day business. This can easily occur in smaller companies. At the very least, if that is the case, a period of time should be allowed in which to achieve the new reporting requirements.

Accounts and financial and other information

(1) The company shall prepare management accounts (in a form to be subject to the prior approval of the investor[s]) containing trading and profit and loss accounts, with comparisons to budgets, balance sheets, cash flow statements and forecasts every calendar month and shall make them available to the investor[s] within 21 days after the end of each calendar month   9–92

and the board shall consider such accounts at its next meeting. The first management accounts shall be made available within 21 days after the end of the calendar month in which completion takes place.

(2) The company shall, immediately before the end of each financial year, after consultation with the investor[s], submit to the investor[s] and adopt, subject to the approval of the investor[s] as to form and content, a detailed operating and capital budget and cash flow forecast in respect of the next financial year.

(3) The audited accounts of the company [and audited consolidated accounts of the company and the subsidiaries] in respect of each financial year or accounting period of the company shall be made available to the investor[s] within four months of the end of the accounting period to which such audited accounts relate.

(4) In the event that the company is in breach of any of sub-cll.1, 2 or 3, the company will, forthwith on being so directed by the investor[s] in writing, appoint a suitably qualified accountant/financial controller approved by the investor[s] whose duties shall include the preparation of accounts and information as provided for herein.

(NB: though a breach of these clauses may not be detrimental to the investor, it is a sign of mismanagement and the investor will wish to rectify the situation early before it becomes a large problem. One of the ways of doing this is to put in his own person to satisfy the governance requirements.)

(5) The investors and the investors' director will be entitled to examine the books and accounts of the company and whether or not the investors appoint an investors' director, the company shall supply the investors with all information relating to the business affairs and financial position of the company as the investors may reasonably require.

(6) The investors' director and any representative appointed pursuant to cl.[ ] shall be at liberty from time to time to make full disclosure to the investors and its managers in relation to the business affairs and financial position of the company.

The investor may also insist on the investee company establishing audit and/or remuneration committees. Ideally, these should consist of the non-executive directors only but should at least have some executive input. Having established these committees, it is important that the investors' consent is required if any recommendation of the audit and remuneration committees is not to be followed. There is little benefit in establishing them if their recommendations can simply be ignored. Set out below is an example of some of those matters that may be delegated by the board to such a committee.

Corporate governance controls

Remuneration committee

That the board delegate absolutely to the remuneration committee all those functions, matters and duties specified to be discharged by the remuneration committee as follows: **9–93**

(1) to consider and (in the case of the directors of the company) determine or (in the case of such other employees of the company and its subsidiary companies as the board may from time to time determine) make recommendations to the board concerning all the elements of the remuneration of such persons, including:

   (a) salary;
   (b) performance related payments (including profit-sharing schemes);
   (c) discretionary payments;
   (d) pension contributions;
   (e) benefits in kind;

(2) to consider and (in the case of executive directors of the company) determine or (in the case of such other employees of the company and its subsidiary companies as the board may from time to time determine) make recommendations to the board concerning the other provisions of the service agreements of such persons (in particular, the notice and any notice period);

(3) to advise on and monitor all performance related formulae;

(4) to administer all aspects of any discretionary share option scheme operated by the company from time to time, including (subject always to the rules of any such scheme and any applicable legal or stock exchange requirements):

   (a) the selection of those eligible directors and employees of the company and its subsidiary companies to whom options should be granted or awards made under any such scheme;
   (b) the timing of any such grant or awards;
   (c) the numbers of shares over which options or awards (if any) are to be granted or made;
   (d) the exercise price at which options (if any) are to be granted or shares awarded are to be acquired;
   (e) the imposition of any objective condition which must be complied with before any option (if any) may be exercised or before any award may vest;

(5) to have regard in the performance of the above duties to any published guidelines or recommendations regarding the remuneration of directors of listed companies which the remuneration committee considers relevant or appropriate;

Investment Agreement

- (6) to consider and make recommendations to the board concerning disclosure of details of remuneration packages and structures in addition to those required by law or, if applicable to the company, by the London Stock Exchange; and

- (7) to consider such other matters as may be requested by the board.

Audit committee

9–94 That the board delegate absolutely to the audit committee all those functions, matters and duties specified to be discharged by the audit committee as follows:

- (1) to consider the appointment of the auditors, the audit fee and any questions of resignation or dismissal;

- (2) to discuss with the auditors before the audit commences the nature and scope of the audit;

- (3) to review the half-year and annual financial statements before submission to the board, focusing particularly on:
  - (a) any changes in accounting policy and practices;
  - (b) major judgmental areas;
  - (c) significant adjustments resulting from the audit;
  - (d) the going concern assumption;
  - (e) compliance with accounting standards;
  - (f) compliance with applicable regulatory and legal requirements;

- (4) to discuss problems and reservations arising from the interim and final audits, and any matters the auditors may wish to discuss (in the absence of the executive directors and other management, where necessary);

- (5) to review the auditors' management letter and management response;

- (6) to review the company's statement on internal control systems prior to endorsement by the board;

- (7) (where an internal audit function exists) to review the internal audit programme, ensure co-ordination between the internal and external auditors, and ensure that the internal audit function is adequately resourced and has appropriate standing within the company;

- (8) to consider the major findings of internal investigations and management's response; and

- (9) to consider such other matters as may be requested by the board.

Remedies for breach

The investor controls are prospective protection for the investor in the same way that the warranties seek to give retrospective protection. Suitable remedies for breach of the investor controls are difficult, because in essence a venture capital investment is more akin to a business partnership. Legal remedies, therefore, are very much the last resort. Generally, the options available to an investor are greater non-executive involvement or a change in management. 9–95

The controls included in the documentation mean that a breach will be a breach of contract. One remedy for such a breach which may be effective is to accelerate redemption of any preference shares held by the investor. In the case of a breach of a negative pledge in a loan document, the investor can require the repayment of any loans which it has made to the company. The main contractual remedy for breach is an action for damages, which will require the investor to establish any loss suffered. Unless the management is independently wealthy, any claim for damages by an investor is not likely, from its point of view, to be very satisfactory. It may be possible to obtain an injunction or an order for specific performance in cases where the investor learns of an impending breach.

If the investor is a minority shareholder then, of course, there may be certain circumstances by the possibility of bringing a minority shareholders' action under s.994 of CA 2006. However, this is very difficult and complicated. If successful, the usual order made by the court is that the minority is bought out by the oppressive shareholders. This, of course, presupposes that the other shareholders have the money to do so.

A further remedy open to the investors is to include a term in the service contracts of key management that any breach of the terms of the investment agreement constitutes a breach of the service contract and so allows dismissal without notice or, if considered unreasonable, on a shorter notice period than the agreed term. This coupled with an obligation on the company to enforce the terms of all service contracts, similar to that set out below, are powerful tools to ensure compliance with investor controls. 9–96

The managers (severally to the extent that such provisions contained and referred to herein relate to them severally but not otherwise) and the company undertake to and covenant with the investor[s] that they will observe and perform and be bound by all the provisions on their part to be observed and performed or binding of them under the new articles the acquisition agreement (including all other agreements to be entered into pursuant thereto or consequent upon) the service agreements and the financing agreements (including all other agreements to be entered into pursuant thereto or consequent upon) and this agreement and to inform each of the investor[s] directors forthwith upon their becoming aware of any breach of the same by any person and the company shall at its own expense take such steps as the investor[s] may require in order either to enforce the rights of the company under any such agreement deed or document or to procure that the company shall refrain from taking steps to enforce such rights.

Although the use of a legal remedy may be a last resort, the importance of making a forceful point to management about even minor breaches of investor controls cannot be stressed strongly enough. Unless the feeling is engendered from the outset that the controls are there for a purpose and are to be enforced, the investor will probably find the discipline of the company fading fast. If the management feel that the investor controls will be rigorously enforced, they will continue to work in accordance with them.

9.8 Minority protection

9-97 Often standard form investor controls are inserted into the first draft of the investment agreement or articles of association without contemplating the needs and requirements of the business or the impact of the actual voting percentages held by the management and the investors. Some controls will also be required but there may be occasions where there are adequate unwritten controls so that a full set of restrictions are not necessary.

In any event if the investor has more than 25 per cent of the votes then he can block all special resolutions. Set out below are the thresholds upon which a specified percentage will gain benefit.

9.8.1 Voting power

Percentage of equity held	Remedy
Minority percentage	Apply to a court where conduct of the company is unfairly prejudicial to a member.
5%	Requisition a shareholders' meeting.
10%	Apply to the Secretary of State for investigation where misfeasance is suspected or members have not been kept informed.
	On a take-over where the purchaser has acquired 90 per cent of the shares, the remaining shareholders can require the purchaser to acquire their shares.
15%	Apply to the court to cancel a variation of class rights where the memorandum or articles providing

Minority protection

for such variations to be subject to the consent of a specified proportion of that class or a resolution passed at a class meeting where class rights not contained in the memorandum and the articles do not contain provisions for the variation of the class right (CA 2006 s.633).

25% and more	Block a special resolution.
50% and more	Control.
75%	Vary class rights
	Pass a special resolution.
90%	On a take-over, the purchaser has the right to compulsorily acquire the remaining ten per cent.
95%	Pass a special resolution on short notice.

Therefore matters such as changes to the articles of association could not take place without the investor's consent unless he holds less than 25 per cent of the equity. However, it may be necessary to remember when considering such thresholds that these may change if, for example, the managers have been given the benefit of a ratchet which will result in the dilution of the investors or an employee share scheme is being established. In smaller transactions or in the introduction of development capital, it is quite possible that the investor will take a minority stake. **9–98**

9.8.2 Minority protection rights

In larger investments, the investor is likely to start with a controlling interest in the equity with the management team holding a minority interest. However a ratchet may also have been put in place which will allow the management's share of the equity to increase if certain performance targets have been met. **9–99**

The purpose of this section is to consider the rights that the managers as a class, the individual manager and also the investor may wish to protect as if a minority shareholder. Inevitably, these issues are not exclusive to the investment agreement and are also referred to in Ch.10.

Individual manager

The first protection an individual manager is likely to seek is a favourable service agreement including, in particular, a satisfactory duration of employment. Under s.188 of CA 2006 it is not possible for an individual to have a service agreement which continues for a period in excess of two years, unless the terms **9–100** are first approved by the members in a general meeting. The manager will seek the longest rolling notice period he/she can get away with. However, venture capitalists are more cautious than they used to be at the end of the 1980s and rarely is a rolling notice period longer than 12 months ever granted. Though managers will often pursue a longer notice period, it should be considered whether it is appropriate for a board of directors to agree to commit their company to long notice periods and whether it would be in the best interests of the company.

9–101 The manager will also look to his position as a shareholder of the company and will need to consider the following situations all of which will be addressed in the new articles.

- What will happen to his/her shares if he/she ceases to be an employee? There are dozens of variations in this respect and the final position will come down to the attitude of the investor and the strength of the bargaining position of the manager. If the investment is a development capital investment and the managers already hold shares, the investor will find it difficult imposing obligations on the managers to sell their shares. A number of questions need to be addressed. Should he/she be allowed to keep his/her shares? If he/she is obliged to serve a transfer notice, should the position be altered if he/she is wrongfully or unfairly dismissed? Who should the shares be offered to first, the investor, the other manager or should they be warehoused for incoming managers? From the company's point of view it is preferable that the shares are transferred upon an employee leaving for whatever reason, whether it be a perfectly acceptable reason such as health, or upon dismissal. Problems can obviously be caused by disaffected former employees continuing to hold shares, but also administrative problems can occur if the company is to be sold and a former employee has emigrated overseas without a forwarding address. More important is the price at which the shares should be sold and the factors that should be taken into consideration.

- What will happen to his/her shares on death? Will they pass to his/her estate or will they be treated as if he/she had served a transfer notice? In practice he/she will probably have to accept that a transfer notice is served.

- Should the employee be able to transfer his/her shares or some of them whilst he/she is employed without going through the pre-emption procedures to another member of the management team or to trustees of a family trust. The investor is likely to be more flexible with regard to this.

We have already discussed warranties at some length. As mentioned, the manager will obviously look to limit those warranties as far as possible. He/she will also wish to protect his/her estate by ensuring that any liability will not only expire after an agreed period but also on the death of the manager.

Minority protection

There are also a number of provisions in Table A of CA 1985 as amended by the Companies (Tables A to F) Amendment Regulations 2007, which if not amended or deleted will be incorporated in the new articles. These are referred to in Ch.10.

The management team

One of the more important protections the management team will try to negotiate is that once the capital structure, articles and investment or shareholder agreement have been agreed, it will not be possible for the investor as controlling shareholder to effect a re-organisation of the capital structure of the company without the consent of the management team. The investor may be happy to accept this so long as the company is achieving the projections set out in the business plan but will not take the risk that the management could prevent a refinancing if required. This will normally be addressed by a change in class rights and is discussed at greater length in Ch.10. **9–102**

The management will wish to participate as fully as possible should the investor choose to syndicate any part of his/her investment, but of greater concern to the management will be a decision by the investor to sell all of his/her shareholding to another investor who may take a different attitude with respect to their involvement in the affairs of the company. One, not ideal, but possible, way out is to ask for a call option under which they can require the investor to offer its shareholding in the company to the management team transferring to another investor.

Another way that the management can protect themselves as a class is by entering into an agreement between themselves determining the way in which they will operate in the running of the company. This may deal with such matters as voting at board meetings, consultation before transferring shares, etc.

The investor

As well as warranties, which we have discussed, the investor will look for restrictive covenants in the shareholder agreement under which the managers will undertake for a limited period from the termination of their involvement with the company, that they will not compete with the company or solicit its customers or employees. It will probably be easier to enforce such a covenant where it is contained in the shareholder agreement rather than the service agreement of each manager because a court will look more leniently on the recipient of the covenant where it is given as part of an overall package rather than as part of an employment arrangement. **9–103**

Once the investor has secured the right to appoint one or more directors, it will want to agree the manner in which the board meetings of the company will be conducted.

Investment Agreement

Unlike the case of general meetings, there is no statutory period of notice that needs to be given before a board meeting can be held. Furthermore, Table A provides no guidance on the length of notice required. One important guideline to which the courts have had regard, is the custom and practice of a company with regard to board meetings. Generally, the courts seem reluctant to interfere with the commercial running of a business or company. It will be up to the investor and the management team to agree an appropriate notice period.

Where an institution has a right to appoint more than one director, it will wish to ensure that the presence of any one of its representatives or nominees at the board meeting will confer on that person the same number of votes as would have been available if all of the institution's nominees had been present. However, bearing in mind the veto restrictions referred to earlier, the investor may be relaxed on this point.

Whether or not the chairman is given a casting vote is the subject of negotiation. Bearing in mind again the restrictions referred to earlier, this is unlikely to be contentious.

9.9 Syndication

9–104 Often a lead investor may make the whole investment on the basis that it will subsequently find other investors to whom the investment can be syndicated. In such cases the investment agreement will need to include provisions relevant for multiple investors and to permit the introduction of new investors particularly with a view to ensuring that the warranties, undertakings and restrictions given by the investor apply for the benefit of the new investor. A clause along the lines of the following may be included:

> Notwithstanding anything to the contrary contained herein or in the new articles, the investor[s] shall be entitled at any time after completion to transfer all or any part of the new shares to another investor or investors to the intent and effect that any such investor shall be entitled to the benefit of all such provisions of this agreement and to any new articles as the investor[s] shall require and the managers and the company shall do or procure to be done (insofar as lies within their respective powers) all such matters and things including the execution of all such documents as shall be necessary or which the investor[s] shall reasonably require for the purpose of giving effect to the provisions of this clause.

9–105 The investor will wish to ensure that a transfer of the relevant shares can take place without having to go through the pre-emption procedures. Syndication is likely to take place relatively quickly after completion but in any event, the investor will be unlikely to be able to syndicate his investment after a 12-month period and therefore any transfer allowing for syndication should be restricted to such a period. The investor will be keen to ensure maximum co-operation from the managers. As a result the following may be included.

The company and each of the managers shall co-operate and assist the investor in procuring syndicatees which shall include (without limiting the generality of the foregoing): **9–106**

- instructing their solicitors to assist in the syndication and assisting the investors in the preparation of an information memorandum and any other relevant information; such information memorandum and other relevant information to be made available to potential syndicatees; and

- convening a meeting of the board at which there shall be conducted the business and resolutions passed as contemplated in the pro forma minutes provided to the company by the investor in connection with the syndication.

The management team should also attempt to play as great a part in the process as possible, if only by obtaining consultation rights, bearing in mind the relationship that will develop with the investor. The following should be possible: **9–107**

The investor shall:

- consult with the company regarding the identity of potential syndicatees;

- not supply any information to any potential syndicatee unless such potential syndicatees agree to treat such information as confidential on such terms as the investors shall reasonably determine; and

- procure that each syndicatee shall enter into a deed of adherence (in the agreed form) before completion of its investment and shall deliver to the company a completed copy of such agreement.

One final point to bear in mind is that on any transfer of shares, stamp duty will be attached. This can be avoided by providing for a redemption and subsequent issue of shares to the syndicate.

9.10 Exit

Sooner or later the investors and possibly the management will wish to realise all or part of their investment in the company. For managers and employees, realisation may help repay personal borrowings taken out at the time of the investment or buy-out as well as make a capital gain. For venture capitalists, realisations may be necessary to meet internal rates of return, to pay dividends or find new investment opportunities. For the company, an exit by investing parties may enable new funds to be raised and so continue the expansion of the company. There are **9–108** numerous different forms of exit from liquidation, from repayment of debt and redemption or repurchase of shares, to a sale or flotation or even a MBO. Below is a brief consideration of the most likely exits.

9.10.1 Flotations

9–109 The process of listing a company on the London Stock Exchange was often seen as the ultimate goal of many private company directors. It is the "exit route" more frequently referred to by venture capitalists but, strictly speaking, a flotation should be viewed as a partial exit and as a stepping stone in the development of a company. It allows shareholders to "cash in" some of their investment, often enough to recover the original amount of the investment but it may not initially be a complete sale of the company. There are positive benefits in this partial realisation. It may assist the development of a company and it may provide a "shop window" for the sale of the company.

As an alternative, the Alternative Investment Market ("AIM") was designed for smaller companies. It is an option for companies which are not ready to get a full London Stock Exchange listing, but it is a stepping stone towards that end if desired. AIM enables new equity to be raised and creates a market in the shares of companies that might be unable to get a full listing. Obtaining an AIM quotation and complying with continuing market obligations is generally less costly than the official list although there is some criticism that it is still too high. In addition, considerable tax advantages are available to some AIM shareholders. A major advantage is that there is no need to obtain shareholders' approval for major acquisitions and disposals. It is also the case that the London Stock Exchange does not vet the prospectus, leaving that task to the nominated advisor, so a certain amount of time should be saved.

Some of the specific advantages of a flotation are as follows.

Publicity

9–110 The publicity of a flotation can have an added advantage of making potential and existing customers and suppliers more aware of the company's activities. Obviously, it also does the same for any competitor.

Advertisements are likely to appear in national newspapers, a prospectus will be prepared and a series of factual articles based on information in the prospectus is likely to follow. There is likely to be a series of presentations to journalists with the aim of having features written on the company and once the dealings in the shares start, usually about a week after impact day, there is generally further press comment. The movement of the share price during the first few days of dealing

Exit

is often considered to be news-worthy. The larger the movement—some go down as well as up—the greater the coverage.

Credibility

There is no doubt that public companies have greater credibility than private companies. For some this can simply be achieved by re-registering as a public company, because to many people there is a belief that the status of a "Plc" means that a company's shares are traded. However, the presence of a full listing on the London Stock Exchange does have a far greater benefit than the title Plc. In particular, the ease of access to information will be greater comfort to customers and suppliers. 9–111

It is also worth bearing in mind that the financial strength of a company can be more easily checked once the shares are listed. Not only will the company be required to publish information on a timely basis, services such as Extel will carry up-to-date information and brokers' analysts will report on the company's future prospects.

The flotation process is often seen as a seal of approval, the facts and figures will have been studied in great detail by the sponsor, the broker, the accountants, lawyers and potential investors.

Flexibility for the future

The availability of a market for a minority interest in the company's shares gives tremendous flexibility for the future. Organic growth can be funded by share issues for cash to a wide spectrum of shareholders who individually do not have a great influence over the direction of the company and the status of being a listed company can improve the company's ability to borrow money at attractive rates. 9–112

In addition, acquisitions can be funded by the issue of shares in exchange for shares in the target companies.

The ease of availability of information means that potential bidders for the company have access to more information than should be the case for private companies. This should be seen as an opportunity and not a threat because many public companies are still controlled by the management so any bid would have to be made on a friendly or agreed basis.

Partial exit only

Director shareholders will only be permitted by the sponsor to sell part of their holdings. This will typically be enough to cover personal debts incurred upon 9–113 investing in the company but not enough to reduce their commitment to the company.

This means that the founder shareholders have the opportunity to benefit from the uplift in value in the shares which can be expected after flotation if the company is to be a good investment for those who invest on flotation.

Employee incentives

9–114 The opportunity to buy shares in the company can be an incentive for employees. Many people are now quite sophisticated in their knowledge of investments due to privatisation and the fact that all newspapers have financial pages. Employees should not be forgotten at the time of flotation. They can often take pride in owning shares in the company which adds to job satisfaction.

There are however a number of drawbacks with a flotation which should be considered. These are as follows.

Size of company

9–115 To some extent the choice between a trade sale or flotation is likely to be influenced by absolute size. A credible flotation candidate should have a stock market capitalisation of at least £30 million and the prospect of achieving a substantial increase in value within a relatively short period. Companies with smaller stock values generally receive little or no research coverage by brokers. In addition, their shares are often illiquid, traded only on a "matched-bargain" basis and their share price can be unrepresentative of the underlying value. However, the void below this is now covered by AIM which offers easy access to a broad range of companies because there are no restrictions on capitalisation or the number of shares to be in public hands and there is no requirement for a lengthy trading record. As a result AIM is suitable for high-tech companies with high growth potential.

Process

9–116 The flotation of a company by means of a public offering of shares is a wholly different operation from a trade sale. The job of the financial advisors acting as sponsor in the process is to fulfil on behalf of the future shareholders many of the responsibilities—for example, due diligence—a corporate buyer would himself be able to undertake. The public liabilities associated with the issue of a prospectus are substantial and onerous, and the complexities of a flotation naturally mean that it is a longer process than a trade sale. Typically, a flotation is likely to take around six to seven months from the start through to "impact day".

Regulations

In addition, running a public company is necessarily subject to far more onerous regulations than a private company, though AIM significantly reduces the number of responsibilities. **9–117**

9.10.2 Trade sale

There are a number of advantages of a trade sale which are not achievable on a flotation. **9–118**

Price

The price a trade buyer may pay can be higher than that which is achievable by any other exit route. This will particularly be the case if: **9–119**

- the business is attractive to international buyers who may be prepared to pay premium prices to enter the market; or
- purchasers are prepared to offer more than the business is worth on a stand-alone basis because of the basis of synergies arising from combining the vendor's business with that of the purchaser; or
- the company either supplies products or is involved in markets that are unfamiliar to institutional investors and analysts and where the industry is undergoing rationalisation.

Earn-outs

Often shareholders believe they are missing out on the growth potential of a business by selling too soon. One way around this is to use an "earn-out". **9–120**

Under an earn-out, the sale of a company is completed, the ultimate purchase price is determined by the performance of that company over an agreed period, post completion, usually one to two years depending upon profitability.

The main benefit of an earn-out is that it provides a solution for:

- a willing but optimistic seller who can obtain a share of the upside;
- the purchaser who will not pay upfront for growth which may not be achieved; and
- it motivates and incentivises the seller.

Investment Agreement

However, earn-outs are not a substitute for obtaining the proper price for the business. They do need to be carefully considered as conflicts can arise between the purchaser's objective of obtaining a sustainable level of profits and the vendor's objective to maximise profitability during the earn-out period. Furthermore, the seller will want to retain management control during the earn-out period which can cause friction if the new owners want to begin to manage the business from the date of completion.

Size of transaction

9–121 A trade sale can be a suitable exit route for a business irrespective of its size. Trade sales in fact have no range in value and a transaction can be for £1 upwards.

The realisation

9–122 In brief, all shareholders can sell their shares. This is almost too obvious to be worth stating but a trade sale is an exit mechanism for 100 per cent of the shares whilst a flotation is not.

Tax structuring

9–123 The consideration can be tailored to the individual shareholders' requirements. Often these are driven by tax considerations. The consideration package can be tailor-made and typically will include cash, bank-guaranteed loan notes and shares in the purchaser. This can be a key advantage of a trade sale because taxation may ultimately account for 40 per cent of the gross proceeds. This charge can be mitigated and by careful structuring the net proceeds receivable can be enhanced considerably.

Flexibility

9–124 If there are weaknesses in the trading record or management of a business these can be dealt with as part of the process. The company does not need to satisfy the conditions which are essential if a company is to be floated, such as sound trading record, adequate financial controls, good management, retirement, good prospects, etc. If a buyer can be found, then almost all of these issues can be dealt with by the purchaser.

Control over the process

9–125 With a trade sale the vendor is in control throughout the process and can influence the timing of the sale and who to approach. The vendor does not have to accept the highest or indeed any bid. In contrast, a public company must treat all purchasers equally and sell to the highest bidder to be fair to outside shareholders. This can be an important consideration if there is to be an exit long term following the initial sale of shares in a flotation.

Within the context of the advantages of trade sales, there are also a number of features of the route that need to be dealt with carefully for them not to be drawbacks.

Loss of independence

Trade sales imply a surrender of control to the management of the company acquiring the business. This can give rise to conflict where the vendors are staying on post sale since entrepreneurs who have been used to working for themselves find it difficult to be accountable to anybody else. This could be a particular problem when the MBO team may be unhappy to return to subsidiary status again if frustrations, in this respect, had led to an initial buy-out. **9–126**

However, experienced acquirers usually tend to take great care to ensure that the key people are incentivised to continue to contribute positively to the running of the business.

Confidentiality

Vendors are usually keen to ensure absolute confidentiality regarding the sale of the business to a trade buyer. This is understandable since news of a possible sale can unsettle employees, customers and suppliers of the business. Moreover, if the trade buyer is a competitor, then vendors will be reluctant to provide information which may be necessary to evaluate the business but which is commercially sensitive. Confidentiality can be maintained if the process is carefully handled. **9–127**

Warranties

In a trade sale, the vendors will be required to give warranties regarding the company and its affairs. These are a basis for disclosing pertinent information about the business that the vendor is aware of. If the sale of the company has been properly planned major issues arising out of the due diligence and warranty process will have been anticipated and addressed and should not present a problem to the completion of a deal. However the investors will make it clear at the time of their investment that they are not prepared to give warranties and therefore the burden will fall on the management team. **9–128**

9.10.3 Secondary buy-outs

9–129 An increasing feature of the MBO scene in the mid 1990s was the second-round buy-out, in which one private equity house provides finance to buy out the shares of one of its competitors. Such transactions used to be very rare because buyers and sellers were naturally suspicious that the other side had superior information. The maturing of many fixed-end funds and the current huge appetite for deals have changed this attitude and second-round buy-outs have become much more common.

Conflicts can develop between institutional investors and management shareholders over the timing of an exit. Private equity players usually want a relatively early exit, either to meet the constraints of a time-limited fund or to maximise the internal rate of return ("IRR") on the investment. Management team members, on the other hand, may want to delay an existing order to retain their independence, safeguard their employment, or because they believe further growth in value can be achieved. Such differing time horizons can be extremely difficult to reconcile.

9–130 Management and institutions might also disagree on the price that the company should be sold for. The price expectations of the management may be set by the amount that they need to realise before retiring whereas a private equity house, seeking to crystallise an acceptable return, might be prepared to sell for less. They might disagree, too, on the method of exit. The purchaser will have significant concerns over the lack of warranty cover being provided by the institutional vendor. Current market practice is still that private equity houses will not give warranties, though they will often provide that a small part of their consideration can be locked into a retention fund for a short period. The warranty gap is often filled by warranty and indemnity insurance.

Note also that such disagreements are not necessarily confined to being between management and institutions. Members of the management team may disagree with each other, as might private equity houses in a syndicate. Perhaps the best advice that may be given at the outset is to minimise the number of shareholders, choose co-investors with similar exit objectives and agree the preferred exit strategy early in the MBO discussions.

9.11 Issues arising on buy-outs without private equity

9–131 As private equity houses have moved up market in the size of the investments they make, a vacuum has been left at the small to medium end of the buy-out market which is increasingly filled by a buy-out, financed by specialised lenders such as invoices discounters and other asset-backed lenders or on occasion, by the vendors but without a private equity house. Such buy-outs are often simpler than

Issues arising on buy-outs without private equity

those involving private equity. If there is no institutional equity there is less need to demonstrate the potential for the capital growth by which private equity houses normally make their gains. Equally if there is no private equity house and the funds used to complete the buy-out are wholly or largely secured on debts or other assets, there is often little need for a full commercial and legal due diligence exercise into the target company or business. Furthermore, the lenders documentation is often standard form and doesn't require or allow detailed negotiation.

However the same commercial issues need to be addressed in a buy-out without private equity, though the dynamics are very different, particularly where the managers take equal or largely equal stakes and there is not one manager with a substantial majority interest. The dynamics are different for the following reasons: **9–132**

- There is no "sweet equity". In a buy-out without private equity all shareholders tend to pay the same for their equity interest and management and are not therefore benefiting from the gearing provided by the equity institution paying significantly more for its interest in Newco.
- The aggregate equity and loan investment by shareholders in a buy-out without private equity often does not constitute a significant part of the aggregate consideration required to complete the buy-out.
- Management will normally own 100 per cent of Newco, so a departing manager is likely to have a much greater interest in Newco.
- The objectivity provided by a professional institutional investor is missing. If there are problems with the business and a break down in relations between shareholders the dispute has a greater chance of becoming acrimonious and personal.
- Personal guarantees are often more of an issue in non-private equity backed buy-outs. The managers are often putting their assets at risk in order to complete the buy-out.
- With no private equity house there is unlikely to be anyone involved with "deep pockets". Therefore individual exit arrangements need to be considered differently from a private equity backed buy-out.

Set out below are some of the key commercial issues that managers need to consider when undertaking a transaction not backed by private equity: **9–133**

- Financial return: it is important to establish whether the team are looking for an income return or capital growth or both. If all the managers are to be employed in the business, their income will be by way of salary, but if one or more is not to be employed full-time or contemplates a time when he will not be so employed what their income expectations will be and how these

Investment Agreement

are to be met will have to be determined. Dividends policies may need to be discussed and documented.

- Dismissal of managers: it will be important to discuss with the managers at an early stage whether or not one of them can be dismissed as an employee/director or otherwise excluded from the day-to-day management/control of Newco (and if so on whose instance and with what consequences in particular in relation to the dismissed managers shareholdings.

- Consequences of dismissal/cessation of employment or involvement of the business: it will be important to establish each manager's motivation for participating in the buy-out, whether it is intended to get capital growth or it is intended as a lifestyle business. The motivation for the buy-out is likely to have a bearing on what the managers believe should happen to the shares of the manager who is properly dismissed or who leaves Newco to pursue other interests or leaves Newco by reason of retirement, death or ill health.

9–134 As with a private equity backed buy-out, it would normally be the case that one might expect a leaver to be required to offer his shares for sale to the remaining manager shareholder. It is however possible to conceive circumstances where this need not be the case, e.g. where another manager's contribution is largely financial and the other managers are contributing time and skills rather than assets or cash.

It certainly seems more common in buy-outs without private equity to see vesting schedules which allow leavers to keep all the proportion of their shares once they have remained involved in Newco for a specified period following completion of the buy-out.

Consider why the shares are being kept and therefore whether they should carry all the rights previously attaching to them. If for instance they are being kept for capital growth only it may be appropriate to strip them of certain rights after cessation of employment, such as voting rights or the right to appoint a director or veto rights on operational matters, etc.

It may be that the owners/managers will agree that a leaver can keep some or all of his shares on an exit. If that is the case the lawyer acting for the leaver needs to carefully consider issues relating to the operation of Newco following any leaver's departure and in particular the payment of bonuses and/or increased salary to the remaining managers. Any private equity backed buyer, the payment of dividends, increased salary and bonuses to management usually requires the consent of both the bank lenders and the private equity house. It is therefore hard for the management to extract value from Newco. In a non-private equity backed buy-out there will often be no such restrictions and therefore a leaver who retains a shareholding may be in danger of having the value of his shareholding prejudiced by the payment of bonuses and increased salaries. The managers should be

Issues arising on buy-outs without private equity

advised, therefore, to consider appropriate contractual operational restrictions to cover the issue, the entitlement to an income stream post employment and having enhanced rights to information above the standard of shareholder rights to accounts.

Restricted matters

- The issues in relation to restricted matters are very similar to those relating to the dismissal of a manager. In a two-man quasi partnership company held in equal or almost equal shares, it will be likely that all significant decisions require unanimity. Where one of two managers has a substantial majority, it may be necessary to consider a limited use of restrictive matters which would require the consent of the minority shareholders. **9–135**

- Things are more complicated where there are more than two managers. The managers should be asked to consider a list of restrictive matters to be included in the shareholders' agreement and to consider which of those matters should only be permitted by a unanimous decision and which should be permitted by simple majority.

- One of the key issues to be considered will be the issue of further shares and management dilution. On completion of the buy-out the managers have agreed interests in Newco. In due course some managers may wish to change this (by issuing new shares to raise further new finance for Newco to fund development, or to incentivise junior management or refinance Newco). Clearly any new shares will dilute management's original interests in Newco and management tend to be sensitive about this possibility. Probably the raising of further finance for the issue of shares could be critical to a company's success or survival and accordingly any restrictions should be very carefully considered.

- Restrictions should remain in place even after a shareholder ceases to be employed by or actively involved in Newco. It should also be considered whether management should have entrenched rights—for example to be a director of Newco—and where and how such rights should be entrenched.

Exit issues

In a private equity backed buy-out it is standard for the private equity house to control the exit and often it requires freedom to realise its investment by selling the shares and if necessary forcing management to join in that sale. Management will normally request and be given a right of tag along which prevents the private equity house realising its investment and selling its shares without procuring matching offers by the purchaser for management's shares. **9–136**

Where there is no private equity house an exit can be considered another example of a restricted matter to be dealt with in the shareholders' agreement or more usually the articles of association. The issue for negotiation will be what majority of managers controls the exit.

As with many other issues the answer will depend on the motivation for the managers in undertaking the buy-out. If the buy-out is a lifestyle one, each manager might properly consider that his investment is long term and that accordingly his consent should be required to any exit. By contrast, if an exit was always contemplated then it is likely that they would agree to a majority of the managers controlling the exit.

A further issue to be considered is whether or not the pre-emption provisions cease to apply in the application of any drag along provisions. The traditional private equity house approach has been that managers do not have a right of pre-emption to match any third-party offer which might trigger the drag along provisions (as this is likely to prejudice negotiations with potential purchasers). However, more private equity houses appear to be offering management a first option to match any offer and in a context of a non-private equity buy-out one should at least consider whether any pre-emption rights should override drag along rights so that potential dragged shareholders have a right to match a third-party offer.

9.12 Checklist

9–137 Set out below is a checklist of matters that should be included in the investment agreement or should be addressed as issues relevant to a new investment. These are provided by way of guidance only and the terms will vary according to the transaction.

Checklist

	Yes	No	Comments

1 Parties

1.1 Confirm the company, the directors, the investors and all other shareholders.

1.2 Detail class and number of shares to be issued to each shareholder.

1.3 Detail amount of loan stock (if any) issued to the investor. Provide details of interest terms, payment dates and security obtained.

1.4 Confirm that all relevant money laundering/IMRO guidelines are complied with.

2 Warranties

2.1 Confirm who gives warranties (would usually be management and company).

2.2 Limitation of [three X salary] for each manager or, if higher, amount invested in company by that manager.
[three X salary is suggested as a guide. Consider higher limits for wealthy individuals or managers receiving cash as part of transaction.]

2.3 Joint and several—or several liability.

2.4 Time limit—three months following receipt of two sets of audited accounts following completion (or seven years if any taxation provisions).

2.5 Aggregate de minimis not exceeding £[50,000] before claim made (claim for whole amount and not just excess).

2.6 No limitation for fraud or fraudulent misrepresentation.

2.7 Management waive the right to sue the company.

2.8 Knowledge deemed to include awareness of other manager's knowledge (subject to exclusion in respect of "personal warranties").

Investment Agreement

	Yes	No	Comments

3 Accuracy of information/Warranties

[NB: there is listed below suggested practice for management's warranties. In addition, consider the need for additional warranties concerning the operational management of target in a MBO.]

3.1 Manager's declaration complete and accurate in all material respects.
3.2 No interest of managers in competitors.
3.3 No breach by manager of existing contractual commitments.
3.4 No insider interests of managers and no entitlement to commissions.
3.5 Correct constitutional information on investee company warranted by managers.
3.6 Warranties on accounts or that company has not traded.
3.7 The factual information contained in the accountant's reports, legal due diligence reports and/or commercial reports is true and accurate in all material respects and no material facts have been withheld by the managers from the relevant advisors.
3.8 All opinions in such reports believed to be reasonable after all reasonable and careful enquiry.
3.9 All factual information in the business plan is true and accurate in all material respects.
3.10 No material facts have been omitted from the business plan which would render it inaccurate or misleading.
3.11 Forecasts and projections prepared in good faith after diligent and careful consideration and enquiries and managers know of no reason why they are not fairly stated.
3.12 Assumptions set out on which the forecasts are based are reasonable and realistic and represent all the assumptions on which the forecasts are being prepared.

254

Checklist

	Yes	No	Comments

3.13 There is no information relating to the group which is known to the warrantor at the date of the agreement which the warrantor has not made known to the investors and which could materially and adversely affect the value of the shares if known by a purchaser and vendor of such shares.

3.14 Not aware of any breach of acquisition warranties.

4 Nominated directors and investor representatives

4.1 Entitled to appoint at least one person to the board as non-executive investor director and right to remove and appoint replacement.

4.2 The investor director to have the right to appoint any person as his alternate director.

4.3 Any nominated director, alternate director or attending representative to be entitled to disclose information to investors relating to the group as he/she thinks fit.

4.4 The company to pay to the investors a fee of £[   ] in relation to investor director, to be reviewed annually by the board or index-linked together with all out-of-pocket expenses reasonably incurred.

4.5 Is there an audit and/or remuneration committee and the right of investor director to be appointed to such committee.

4.6 The company to take out and maintain in force for each nominated director an appropriate insurance policy.

5 Management and business

5.1 The company to be obliged to maintain effective and appropriate accounting systems.

Investment Agreement

	Yes	No	Comments
5.2 To produce monthly management accounts (including P1L, balance sheet, cash flow statement, cap. ex. statement and other information requested by the investor) within 21 business days of end of each month together with a report on activities and a comparison with the business plan and/or operating budget. [*NB: usually an initial grace period of three months is acceptable for such systems to be put in place.*]			
5.3 No later than one month before the end of each financial year the company to produce an operating budget (profit and loss account, balance sheets and cash flow forecast) for the next financial year, having obtained investor approval of the amounts for capital and other expenditure, such budget to be adopted before the beginning of the next financial year.			
5.4 The company should prepare and distribute minutes of each board meeting.			
5.5 Within four months of the end of the financial year the company to prepare audited consolidated accounts.			
5.6 The company to provide any other information relating to the business as the investor may from time to time require.			
5.7 The investors to have access to the books and records of the company as they may require.			
5.8 The company to maintain adequate general business insurance.			
5.9 The company to maintain keyman life insurance policies on the lives of [ ] to a value of £[ ] for the benefit of the company.			
5.10 The company to hold at least ten board meetings a year and at least one in every two month period with a minimum ten days notice to the investor director(s) and the provision of copies of all papers required for such meetings. Initial schedule for meetings in first year to be provided within one month of completion.			

Checklist

	Yes	No	Comments

5.11 [There is listed below a comprehensive set of matters for investor consent. Consider whether consent should be required from the investor, or from the investor director. Typically, investor consent will be required for more fundamental matters (e.g. (a) to (k) below), whilst ongoing trading matters will be at the discretion of the investor director. Also consider any specific consents for the transaction (e.g. material supply or distribution agreements)]

Investor veto (either through investor or investor director in writing—see note) over the following items.

(a) Dispose of the whole or a substantial part of the business or assets or make an application for flotation.

(b) Dispose of or form or acquire any subsidiary or business or enter into any partnership or joint venture.

(c) Grant or create any charge, security or incumbrance over any asset.

(d) Declare or pay any dividends.

(e) Make any increase, reduction or other alteration whatsoever to the issued share capital of the company.

(f) Permit any amendment to the Memorandum of Articles of Association of the Company.

(g) Cease to carry on the business of the company, save where the company is insolvent.

(h) Apply for an administration order to be made in respect of the company.

(i) Make any changes in the accounting reference date, accounting policies, auditors or bankers of the company.

(j) Any material change in the nature or scope of the company's business.

Investment Agreement

	Yes	No	Comments

(k) Establish any share incentive, or share option scheme or any bonus, profit sharing, other incentive scheme for directors and/or employees, or vary the terms of any such scheme.

(l) Enter into any contract or assume any liability which is of a long term or unusual nature or enter into any contract which is outside the ordinary course of the business.

(m) Acquire or dispose of assets other than at market value on an arm's length basis.

(n) Grant dispose or acquire any interest in land.

(o) Grant any licence agreement or arrangement concerning any part of the trading names of the company or deal in any way with intellectual property.

(p) Commit to any capital expenditure which is not set out in the annual budget which exceeds [£50,000] (in aggregate with other related capital expenditure) or dispose of any assets of a capital nature, with a book or market value in excess of [£50,000].

(q) Make any loan or grant credit to anyone other than in the normal course of business.

(r) Give any guarantee, indemnity or suretyship unless within the ordinary course of business.

(s) Factor its debts, or borrow money or occur indebtedness other than normal trade credit in the ordinary course of business or in accordance with the annual budget.

(t) Waive or fail to enforce terms of the Sale and Purchase Agreement, or service contracts with its directors or other staff.

(u) Appoint or remove any director, or make any payment to any director of the company or any person connected with a director.

(v) Appoint any sub-committee of the board.

Checklist

	Yes	No	Comments

(w) Establish any pension or life assurance scheme or make any material alteration to the terms of such scheme.

(x) Engage any employee on terms that either his contract cannot be terminated by a three-month notice or less or his emoluments are or are likely to be at the rate of £[50,000] per annum or more or increase the emoluments or vary the terms of employment of any such employee.
[If a remuneration committee is to be established, confirm details of composition of committee and remuneration threshold for referral to committee.]

(y) Conduct any litigation material to the company, save for the collection of debts arising in the ordinary course of the business.

5.12 References in 5.11 to include subsidiaries within the group.

5.13 Investor director consents may also be given by investor in writing.

6 Transfer of shares

6.1 Any transferee to whom shares are transferred must adhere to the subscription agreement.

7 Announcements

7.1 No announcements before or after completion without prior approval of each of the other parties.

7.2 Investors may use information which they receive under the provisions of the agreement to report to their other syndicate investors.

Investment Agreement

	Yes	No	Comments

8 Exit

8.1 Managers agree that they will notify investors of details of any written offer from any third party for the whole or part of the share capital of the company.

8.2 No warranties on sale or listing to be provided by the investor except as to title.

8.3 Listing to extend to all shares.

9 Costs

9.1 All fees including legal fees, accountants' fees, headhunters' fees and stamp duty and expenses incurred by the investors in connection with the agreement to be paid by the company on completion in accordance with agreed fee schedule.

9.2 Investors authorise the payment by the company of the specific fees incurred by the company and the vendors in connection with this agreement on demand on completion in accordance with fee schedule.

9.3 Provisions for collection (and confirmation of amount) of negotiation fee.

10 Service Agreements/Non-Compete

10.1 Obligations on managers to comply with service agreement.

10.2 After termination of employment managers will not solicit or interfere or attempt to entice away employees or customers, or interfere with suppliers for at least [two] years following completion and will not carry on or be interested in any competing business for at least [one] year following termination.

260

Chapter 10

Articles of Association

10.1 Introduction

The articles of association (the articles) represent a contract between the company and its shareholders. A statutory contract which binds the company and its members to the same extent as if they were respectively signed and sealed by each member: **10–01**

Subject to the provisions of this Act, articles, when registered, bind the company and its members to the same extent as if they respectively had been signed and sealed by each member, and contained covenants on the part of each member to observe all the provisions of the articles.

On becoming a shareholder each member to this contract is deemed to have undertaken to observe all provisions contained in the memorandum and articles. On the other hand the investment agreement is a device resorted to by private companies to supplement the basic infrastructure provided by the articles. While the enforceability or otherwise of the articles is subject both to the numerous principles developed by the courts and to the various statutory powers imposed on companies, the shareholder's agreement is regulated by the law of contract. The aim of the articles is to regulate how the company is governed and how power and control is shared between the shareholders and the directors and how the rights of different classes of shareholders operate among themselves.

It is essential when drafting the articles of association that the legal advisors understand the economics of the transaction and the equity deal agreed between the parties. It is probably the most important part of the transaction and as a result the area that should receive the most attention.

The articles are a public document of the company which requires registration at Companies House. The investment agreement generally does not require filing though draftsmen should be careful to ensure that it does not fall within provisions of the Companies Act requiring filing. The Companies Act states that a **10–02** company may alter its articles by special resolution. Any alteration has effect as if originally contained in the articles. The articles cannot be entrenched by a provision stating that they cannot be altered (*Malleson v National Insurance and Guarantee Corp* [1894] 1 Ch. 200). In contrast a shareholder agreement can only be varied with the consent of all parties.

Frequently companies adopt a standard form of articles of association. For new companies, under the Companies Act 2006 Table A is replaced by two forms of model articles—a new radically simplified set of model articles more suited to small private companies and a more extensive form for public companies. However its promoters may adopt such provisions as they wish on incorporation (subject to statute and the common law) and its shareholders can later make alterations. Private equity transactions usually call for a complex share structure, and a number of articles which are common only to an investment of private equity. Hence this leads to a very complex set of articles. We have already considered the need for different classes of shares and the types of shares which are likely to be subscribed for in order to provide equity finance in a venture capital transaction. In the main, this is to facilitate financial engineering so that a comparatively large amount of share capital can be introduced by an investor without diluting management interests in the equity of the investee company to an almost negligible figure. There are various other reasons including the operation of a ratchet, which we will discuss more fully in this chapter.

10.2 *Russell v Northern Bank Development Corp Ltd*

10–03 As we have seen in Ch.9, venture capital is approached from the stand point of a passive investor or "sleeping partner". The investor controls are usually reserved to the investor in order that it can veto any significant changes in an investee company's businesses activities or operational strategies. The appropriate place for inserting the investor controls within the legal documentation is often a matter of some contention and the case of *Russell v Northern Bank Development Corp Ltd* [1992] 3 All E.R. 162, HL has made the decision more complicated. Controls which limit the company's "statutory powers" cannot after *Russell* be imposed on the company itself. Therefore binding the shareholders themselves is vital.

If there are shareholders who are not party to the investment or shareholders' agreement, for example because they are junior managers in a MBO, or there are a large number of small shareholders, then certain controls, such as transfer provisions, must be included in the articles as this is the only way of binding them.

10–04 Controls can appear in the articles of association or in the investment agreement or in both. However, provided that all the shareholders have also executed the investment agreement, the legal effect will be the same between the shareholders whether the controls are contained in the articles of association or in the investment agreement. There are, however, conflicting authorities as to whether a member can enforce the articles generally against another member or whether such a right should be effected through the medium of the company (*Welton v Saffery* [1897] A.C. 299) because the articles would amount to a breach of contract in the same way as a breach of the investment agreement. However, if a company appoints a director under the articles for ten years this term can be reduced by the passing of a special resolution. If the company wishes to remove the director instead, an ordinary resolution pursuant to s.168 of CA 2006 will be sufficient. In either case no liability for breach of contract will occur unless this also results in a breach of a service agreement in which case the director will be eligible for compensation in accordance with the ordinary principles of contract law.

Subject to this qualification, the courts have generally given members the freedom to determine the terms of any shareholder agreement. In *Bushell v Faith* [1970] A.C. 1099, for example, the validity of agreements used to entrench rights which prevented the company from exercising its statutory power was recognised. The shareholder agreement, in this case, which was contained in the articles was designed to entrench the position of a director by an artificial use of extra voting powers where there was a desire to remove him. On a resolution under what is now s.168 of CA 2006, the director was to have "weighted" votes attached to his/her shares which virtually made the passing of an ordinary resolution impossible.

10–05 The vote attached to a share is a right of property which the shareholder is entitled to exercise in his/her own interests and to deal with as he/she thinks fit (*Northern Counties Securities Ltd v Jackson and Steeple Ltd* [1974] 1 W.L.R. 1133). It follows therefore that an agreement between two or more shareholders to co-ordinate their votes is lawful. In contrast to this the companies legislation confers many powers on companies, the most important of which are to alter objects and articles by special resolution, and the power to alter share capital provided there is authority in the articles. The question of whether it is possible to contract-out of these statutory powers was discussed in *Russell v Northern Bank Development Corp Ltd*. A company and all its shareholders entered into a shareholder agreement. One of the clauses provided that, "no further share capital shall be created or issued in the company ... without the written consent of each of the parties hereto". Can one of the shareholders who is a party to that agreement obtain an injunction restraining his co-shareholders from voting in favour of a resolution to increase the share capital? To restrain the company, a co-shareholder, would in effect prevent the exercise of the statutory power conferred on the company under s.617 of CA 2006 to increase its share capital by ordinary resolution. The decision in *Russell* provides a firm and unequivocal answer: there can be no contracting-out by a company in respect of its statutory powers. At the same time the House of Lords sanctioned the making of voting agreements which can have the effect of fettering the exercise of a statutory power. The House therefore made a distinction between an undertaking by a company which restricts its statutory powers to alter its articles or increase its share capital, and an agreement between the shareholders for the time being of a company as to how they will exercise their rights if any such alteration or increase is proposed. The former is void as an unlawful fetter on the company's statutory rights, but the latter is valid.

10–06 As well as voting arrangements, practitioners have found other ways of circumventing the restriction with the effect that, except for those who are poorly advised, the practical effect of the *Russell* case is limited. Rights may be entrenched in articles either by using the concept of separate classes of shares to which are attached the rights which are sought to be protected (and which can only be amended with the separate consent of the holders of the shares of each separate class: CA 2006, s.633), or by increasing the voting power of specific shares in the article which embodies the special rights if and to the extent that a special resolution is proposed to alter that article, and so allowing the protected shareholder to prevent the passing of a special resolution if he/she wishes. Alternatively, the rights could be set out in the memorandum and declared unalterable. In the Court of Appeal, it was held that the fetters on the company's statutory powers rendered the entire agreement void. Fortunately the House of Lords offered a lifeline which should save most existing shareholder agreements by ruling that it was possible to apply the doctrine of severance, and allowed *Russell* to enforce the parts of the agreement that fell into the category of an agreement between shareholders as to how they will exercise their voting rights. At the same time it issued a warning that there is danger in seeking to extend the scope of such agreements beyond their proper sphere, and in particular in making the company itself a party.

Class rights

10–07 Under the typical Newco structure, the investor and management team members are issued with different classes of shares. Management shares are usually "plain vanilla" ordinary shares. Investors usually receive preferred ordinary shares ("A" ordinary shares). Together these will be the equity shares. Separate classes are usually required to reflect the different rights that will attach to the different classes of shares. For example in relation to voting rights and dividends, investors may be seeking a yield from their equity shares in the form of dividends whereas it is unusual for managers to receive dividends prior to exit. In the same way investors often have a priority when Newco has underperformed.

One of the most fundamental controls which an investor requires is a veto over changes to the memorandum and articles of association of the investee company. *Russell*, as we have seen, determines that a company cannot restrict its power to change those articles of association. Therefore a provision in the investment agreement whereby the company covenants not to change its articles of association without the consent of the investor beforehand would not be enforceable. There are obviously other examples of powers which a company cannot fetter its power to change, for example, winding up the company, reducing the share capital, changing the company's name, increasing the authorised share capital, etc.

It seems fairly certain that an agreement between the shareholders themselves not to vote their shares to change the articles of association, reduce share capital, etc, will be enforceable if the company is not a party to that agreement but invariably the investee company is party to the investment agreement. The House of Lords' decision suggests that a severance clause could be inserted in the investment agreement to make it clear that certain controls are not intended to bind the company but only to bind the shareholders which, in effect, would cause the company to comply with the control. But what if not all the shareholders are party to the investment agreement? It could be possible to get a voting covenant from each of the other shareholders but that would be cumbersome and it would be difficult to establish what consideration there would be for such a covenant. The alternative is to insert weighted voting rights in the articles of association so that to pass specific resolutions (for example, amending the articles of association) certain classes of shares will have more than one vote. This effectively ensures that unwanted amendments cannot be passed without the agreement of the holders of those shares.

Alternatively, these controls could be enshrined as class rights. If the controls are put in the articles of association and the investors have their own separate class of shares, the rights contained in this separate class will be class rights. They generally attach to the preference shares or the preferred ordinary shares being the shares held by investors. For any of the particular rights attached to the investor's shares to be incapable of amendment without the consent of the investors, they must amount to "class rights". They can then only be varied in accordance with the provisions of ss.630–634 of CA 2006. Some of the more important points of this section are: **10–08**

(1) different rules will apply depending upon whether the class rights are contained in the articles, the memorandum or the resolution creating the shares and depending whether or not the articles contain provisions relating to the variation of class rights;

(2) depending upon where the class rights are contained and whether the memorandum or articles contain any mechanism for approving a variation of class rights, it is likely that in addition to a special resolution to change the company's articles, an approval of a variation may require:

    (a) the holders of three-quarters in nominal value of the issued shares of the relevant class consenting in writing to the variation or an extraordinary resolution being passed at a separate class meeting consenting to the variation;

    (b) all of the members of the company agreeing to the variation;

(3) the quorum requirements for the class meeting are two persons holding at least one-third in nominal value of the shares of the relevant class, or one person at an adjourned meeting if the first meeting was adjourned because of an insufficient quorum.

10–09 The power to create class rights has not been affected by *Russell*. So for example, the preferred ordinary shares could have attached to them, as a right in the articles of association, the stipulation that the articles of association may not be changed, the share capital reduced, the company wound up, etc, without the consent of the preferred ordinary shareholders. Care however, must be taken to ensure that these rights attach to shares which will be retained by an investor and not to redeemable or convertible shares.

There is continuing debate about what matters should properly be the subject of class rights. On the one hand, dividend rights clearly affect the essence of the shareholders' rights in the shares and are doubtless capable of being class rights. On the other hand, a right to prevent the company from entering into a joint venture or partnership cannot be said to affect the nature and relative rights of the shares themselves but rather the business of the company. There is doubt therefore whether such a control will be a class right. Shareholders are often surprised at the ways in which their position can be changed without there being a variation of their class rights. Other examples are:

- An issue of bonus shares to holders of other shares in the company, which has the effect of increasing their voting power compared to his own will not amount to a class right (*White v Bristol Aeroplane Co Ltd* [1953] Ch. 65).

- An issue of new shares to rank ahead of his/her preference shares will not be a variation of his/her class rights if there was no contractual promise to him/her that such prior ranking shares would not be issued (*Allen v Gold Reefs of West Africa Ltd* [1900] 1 Ch. 656).

10–10 Traditionally in private equity transactions, a long list of matters that were to be regarded as class rights were set out in the document containing the preference share or preferred ordinary share rights, normally the articles. However, more practitioners now consider the better view to be that a fairly narrow range of matters can genuinely be construed as class rights and so a limited list should be contained in the articles and restrictions of the sort that do not affect the share rights should go into the investment agreement since they are highly unlikely to be fetters on the statutory powers of the company. Therefore the company as well as the other parties to the investment agreement undertake to be bound by such restrictions.

Below are fundamental controls required by an investor and drafted as class rights attaching to the shares held by the investor for inclusion in the articles:

Without prejudice to the generality of this article the special rights attached to the preference shares and the preferred ordinary shares shall each be deemed to be varied at any time by any of the following:

(1) an increase, reduction or other alteration in the issued share capital of any member of the group or a variation in the rights attaching to any class thereof, apart from an alteration arising out of a conversion or a redemption of shares under these articles;

(2) the grant of an option to subscribe for shares in any member of the group or the issue of any securities convertible into shares of the company or any of its subsidiaries;

(3) the creation by any member of the group of any mortgage, charge, pledge, lien, encumbrance or other security interest (excluding an interest arising by operation or of law in the ordinary course of business);

(4) the directors permitting the borrowings of the group to exceed the limit imposed by these articles;

(5) the making of any material change (including cessation) in the nature of the business of the group taken as a whole;

(6) the alteration of the memorandum of association of the company or these articles or the passing of any special or extraordinary resolution of the members (or any class of them);

(7) the declaration or payment of any dividend or the making of any other distribution in respect of the profits, assets or reserves of the company or any of its subsidiaries other than the preference and preferred ordinary dividends and any other dividends declared and paid strictly in accordance with these articles;

(8) the institution of any proceedings or the passing of any resolution for the winding-up of any member of the group;

[(a) the removal of an investor director otherwise than in accordance with art.[ ];]

(9) incurring an obligation to do any of the foregoing.

10.3 Minority shareholder protections

Class consents will be included as a matter of course for the benefit of the investor. Management advisors will wish to obtain a limited set of protections for management particularly if together they only represent a minority shareholding in the company. Most investors will not wish to provide management with any form of class rights over and above their statutory rights as to do so would further

10–11

Articles of Association

their controls. The ability of management to secure class rights will depend on the strength of their negotiating position and ultimately their importance to the deal. Without any protection, a shareholder without control of the company will be in a vulnerable position. Some investors are reluctant to provide management with any protection, others will do so providing it does not restrict their ability to refinance the company should the need arise. The clause below includes some limited class protections but allows the investor to refinance without restriction if required. The management are the holders of the ordinary shares.

1 Unless the [finance documents] require the following actions to be taken, the consent of the holders of the ordinary shares [*NB: generally the shares held by management*] as a class shall be required to and accordingly the special rights attached to the ordinary shares shall be deemed to be varied only by:

1.1 any alteration or reduction or increase of the authorised capital or issued capital of the company [(other than any issue of up to [ ] ordinary shares in aggregate to employees of or consultants to any member of the group (or any nominee of any of the same),] in terms of cl.[ ] of the subscription agreement, to which issue the holders of the ordinary shares are hereby deemed to have consented); or

(As a practical point, often the company will wish to provide for shares to be issued to employees at a later date. It is easier to allow for this at the time of the investment).

1.2 the passing of the resolution effecting the amendment of the articles of association of the company; or

1.3 the passing of a resolution for the solvent winding-up of the company; or

1.4 the application by way of capitalisation of any sum in or towards paying up any debenture or debenture stock of the company; or

1.5 the capitalisation by the company of any undistributed profits (whether or not the same are available for distribution and including profits standing to any reserve) or any sum standing to the credit of its share premium account or any capital redemption reserve; or

1.6 the creation or grant of any option or other rights to subscribe for shares in the equity share capital of the company or securities convertible into shares in the equity share capital of the company.

Provided always that without prejudice to any other right available to them under the Act such consent or sanction of the holders of ordinary shares shall not be required in respect of any increase in the authorised share capital of the company or allotment of shares in the capital of the company or the creation or grant of any option or other rights to subscribe for shares or securities convertible into shares in the capital of the company which would otherwise require such consent or sanction of the holders of the ordinary shares pursuant to art.[ ] above or of any alteration to these articles necessary to provide for the rights attaching to any class of shares in the capital of the company which would otherwise require such consent or sanction of the holders of the ordinary shares pursuant to art.[ ] above if such increase, creation, grant or alteration is made in order to facilitate a further investment in the company to the extent only to which it is in the opinion of any member or members holding in aggregate 50 per cent in nominal value of the preferred ordinary shares then in issue the same is necessary to remedy any breach by the company of any covenant to any banker to the company or to prevent such a breach from arising which, in such opinion, but for the allotment would arise.

If the investor is adamant that he/she will not allow class protections to the management, and many investors are, it is worth exploring whether the investors will agree to some of the more fundamental concerns of management being included in the investment agreement. **10–13**

An alternative and more aggressive way of dealing with this is to provide the managers with minority protection rights (either in the investment agreement or in the articles) but to agree that such rights will terminate if the targets set out in the business plan (or within a narrow range of them) are not achieved. This should be more palatable to most investors though many will still regard it as an unnecessary restriction on their contract.

10.4 Share transfer provisions

In most buy-outs the guiding principle is that shares are used by investors to incentivise employees and directors to add value to the business at the exit. The ordinary shares issued to the managers are likely to be cheaper than the equity shares issued to the investor, hence the term "sweet equity". If the projections set out in the business plan are achieved then the upside is great. As a result managers are generally not allowed to transfer their ordinary shares without the consent of the investor, except in certain limited circumstances. At the same time management will have put a lot of due diligence into choosing the investor and will be keen to see the ability of the investor to syndicate limited.

10.4.1 Pre-emption rights

It is normal for articles used in investment capital transactions to include pre-emption rights upon a transfer which are appropriate to private companies. First and foremost, however, the institutional investor will wish to ensure that it can transfer shares within its own group and also that it will be able to syndicate to another investor if necessary without having to go through the pre-emption hurdle. If syndication after the transaction is suggested, management should explore the reasons why. If the reason is insufficient funds and the management are expecting to seek further funding later, perhaps by way of example for **10–14** acquisition, then it may be that the private equity house is an inappropriate choice. Moreover the relationship between the private equity house and management is a partnership and the management have every right to feel comfortable with the purposes of the syndication. Nevertheless the institution is likely to insist on an article allowing syndication:

Any shares (other than any shares in respect of which the holder shall have been required by the directors under these articles to give a transfer notice or shall have been deemed to have given a transfer notice) may at any time be transferred:

(1) by any member being a company (not being in relation to the shares concerned a holder thereof as a trustee of any family trusts) to a member of the same group as the transferor company; or

(2) by a holder of preference shares or preferred ordinary shares which is a fund or by its trustee custodian or nominee:

   (a) to any trustee nominee or custodian for such financial institution and vice versa;
   (b) to any unit holder, shareholder, partner, participant, manager or advisor (or an employee of such manager or advisor) in any such fund;
   (c) to any other fund financial institution managed or advised by the same manager or advisor as the transferor; or
   (d) to any person, company or fund whose business consists of holding securities for investment purposes; or
   (e) to any co-investor or its trustee, nominee or custodian thereof;

(3) to a nominee, custodian or to a member of the same group of any of the persons referred to in sub-paras (a), (b), (c) or (d) of para.(2) of this art.[ ].

10–15 The definition of a fund should include any bank, investment trust or investment company, unit trust, building society, industrial provident or friendly society or any other collective investment scheme (as defined by the FSMA), any investment professional (as defined in art.19(5)(d) of the FSMA (Financial Promotion) Order 2001 (the "FPO")), any high-net-worth company or unincorporated association or high-value trust (as defined in art.49(2)(a)–(c) of the FPO), partnership, limited partnership, pension fund or insurance company or any person who is an authorised person under the FSMA, any subsidiary undertaking or parent undertaking of any of the foregoing and any co-investment scheme in relation to any of the foregoing.

It is unlikely that the investor will be able to syndicate more than 12 months after the transaction even if he/she should wish to do so. The management's lawyers will probably therefore have little difficulty in restricting the syndication provisions to 12 months.

Share transfer provisions

Where transfer provisions are included allowing movement between corporate groups, provisions should also be included to ensure the transfer back to the holding company if ownership of the subsidiary changes to a third party. So, for example, if the original member has left or is leaving the wholly owned group of companies which the transferee is leaving, then the transferee will be obliged to transfer the shares back to the original member and in the event of the transferee failing to execute such a transfer and to present it to the board duly stamped for registration of the transfer, the board may appoint some person to execute (an) instrument(s) of transfer of such shares in favour of the original member and shall thereupon cause the name of such original member to be entered in the register of members of the company as the holder of the shares.

Other matters that are often included in the provisions permitting transfers without triggering the pre-emption clauses are: **10–16**

- where more than 95 per cent of the members agree such a transfer;
- a transfer in consequence of the death or bankruptcy of an individual member to allow for any transfer that such person, if not dead or bankrupt, could undertake;
- to a close relation (but always include a clause providing for the transfer back if such a person ceases to be a privileged relation, for example following a divorce);
- to or within a family trust. This is usually to facilitate tax planning for the managers;
- for the purpose of warehousing. We will see later in the chapter that a departing employee or director will be obliged to sell his/her shares. The investor will be keen to ensure that these shares are held until such time as a replacement for the departing executive has been found and will be used to attract suitable management.

Broadly speaking, having dealt with permitted transfers, any other transfers of shares which are offered for sale, must first be offered to other shareholders before they can be transferred to third parties.

Market value

The market value of shares is usually determined by virtue of a third party having offered to buy them at a specified price, in which case such price then becomes the "sale price". If there is not such a third party available, the board and the proposing transferor will attempt to reach agreement on the sale price. Failing this, final determination of the sale price representing the fair market value of such shares will be made by independent third parties such as auditors or an independent **10–17** accountant or merchant bank. Once the sale price has been determined provisions relating to the transfer of shares usually provide that an "offering-round" procedure begins. The proposing transferor must serve a transfer notice notifying the company of his intention to sell and constituting the company as his agent to offer the shares to the members in priority to a transfer to a third party. There is no fixed sequence and any number of permutations are possible. For example:

- shares may be offered to other members of the same class in priority to all other shareholders of the company; or
- shares may be offered with equity shares to all other equity shareholders pro rata to their total holdings of equity shares in the capital of the company, irrespective of the class of equity concerned; or
- there may be an intervening right for the founders or key members of the management team to pick off the shares before a general offer round; or
- there may be an intervening right for the investor or the board to specify that shares should not be offered round but instead should be "warehoused".

In addition, it is likely that the articles will contain an absolute prohibition on the sale or transfer of shares to someone carrying on business in competition with that carried on by the company and its subsidiaries. From an investor's point of view, this is not always prudent, as it is quite possible that the highest price offered for the shares would come from a rival competitor.

10.4.2 Compulsory transfer notice

10–18 The articles will usually provide that if an executive director or employee ceases to be employed by the investee company then he/she shall be deemed to have served a transfer notice in respect of those shares he/she holds in the capital of the investee company. There are a number of variations to this provision. For example, management may be allowed to keep an increasing proportion of their shares as time elapses from the date of the investment until such cessation occurs. Additionally, compulsory transfer notices may be excluded if cessation of the executive's appointment with the company is a result of:

- wrongful dismissal or redundancy;
- retirement at normal retirement age or due to ill health or disability;
- death; and/or
- if a majority of the non-executive directors and/or the investors sold with the investor's approval.

Share transfer provisions

Generally, however, any negotiation of the compulsory transfer provisions is a negotiation as to price and not as to whether the transfer notice is obligatory or not.

Quite often the investor, in order to ensure the continuing commitment of the managers at least until such time as he/she understands the business, will include a clause preventing a manager from selling his/her shares for an initial period. **10–19**

No transfer notice shall be served in respect of [ordinary shares] until the [third] anniversary of the adoption of the articles other than served in accordance with the art.[ ] (the compulsory transfer provisions) or with the consent of the investor's director.

A strong argument can be made by the investor that not only are they investing in the business but they are also investing in the management who should not be free to walk away prior to the private equity house exiting.

It is not uncommon to see "good and bad leaver" provisions included in the compulsory transfer provisions so that management who walk out or leave the company voluntarily are penalised by receiving an amount equal to whichever is the lower of market value or the amount which they subscribed or par. This will deprive management of any uplift in the market value for a specified period from completion.

Note that a mandatory transfer notice merely obliges a party to offer his/her shares for sale and does not oblige the other shareholders to buy such shares.

Set out below is a fairly common provision found in the articles. **10–20**

1 Compulsory transfers—management shareholders

1.1 In the case of a relevant member (being a person who has acquired shares from a relevant executive) or the relevant executive (defined as an employee, director or consultant of the company or a subsidiary of the company) in relation to a relevant member ceasing to be a relevant executive at any time, then within 12 months after such cessation, the directors may serve notice on such relevant member requiring such relevant member to give a transfer notice (as defined in art.5) in respect of all of the shares held by such relevant member for a price per share of either:

(a) if such relevant member or relevant executive in relation to a relevant member shall have ceased to be a relevant executive in circumstances involving a breach by the relevant executive of his/her service agreement or leaves voluntarily (even if proper notice has been given) except on death, ill health or on retirement age, then the price per share and market value as determined in accordance with art.[ ]; and

(b) if such relevant member or relevant executive in relation to a relevant member shall have ceased to be a relevant executive for any other reason than those reasons specified in para.(a), then the price per share shall be market value as determined in accordance with art.[ ].

In the clause above, the directors have the right to require the relevant executive or relevant member to transfer his/her shares upon a relevant event. In fact it is more usual to see a deemed transfer provision trigger immediately upon the event occurring. In any event, the draftsman should ensure that in addition to this clause there is an "attorney" clause allowing a member of the board to execute the necessary transfer documents should the relevant executive or relevant member fail to do so.

10–21 If this clause is to stand, the relevant executive will be concerned that para.(a) cannot be exercised if he has been wrongfully dismissed. However for the relevant executive to prove wrongful dismissal will be time consuming and costly. His advisor may attempt to include something along the following lines as a compromise.

1 If a transfer notice is served or deemed to be served pursuant to art.[ ] and the relevant executive is not found to be wrongfully dismissed from his employment with the company in breach of any service agreement, the sale price shall be the lower of the par, the subscription price per share and market value.

2 If for the purpose of this article, the directors and the relevant executive cannot agree as to whether or not his/her dismissal was wrongful, the matter shall be determined by a Queen's Counsel experienced in employment law who shall be appointed by agreement between the directors and the relevant executive or, failing agreement on such appointment within seven days of commencing negotiations on such appointment by the Chairman of the Bar Council on the application of either party (the QC). The parties shall jointly instruct the QC and shall submit, so far as possible and as soon as reasonably practicable, an agreed statement of facts or, failing such agreement, their separate statements of fact. The parties shall use their reasonable efforts to ensure that the QC shall give and be able to give his/her determination of whether or not the dismissal was wrongful within 14 days after the dispute has been referred to him/her. Any determination of the QC shall be final and binding on the parties (in the absence of manifest error) and he shall act as expert and not as arbitrator. The costs of the QC shall be [shared between the relevant executive and the company] [borne by the company].

10–22 Often, as can be seen, most of the discussion will revolve around the price to be paid for the shares. The investor will be more likely to look more kindly on employees leaving who are "good leavers". This will be defined as an employee leaving by reasons of death, disability or incapacity. The management's lawyers should extend the same reasons to those of the spouse or immediate family of the employee. Doctor's advice may cause a manager to leave the company either because of his/her own health or that of his/her immediate family. It is difficult for any caring investor to argue against these reasons. Moreover, it is a time above any when the employee will require full value from his/her shares. In addition, an investor will agree to a good leaver being one who has been unfairly dismissed. The management's lawyers should attempt to ensure that this is extended to situations where the company chooses not to renew a fixed-term contract or after proper notice has been given. If the investor accepts that he is likely to exclude termination made summarily, other than on grounds of insanity or illness. Of more concern to the investor will be a desire to prevent a good leaver going to work for a competitor and the investor will be keen to ensure that a proviso to a good leaver definition is included as follows:

> Provided that any relevant executive who, before the relevant transfer of shares pursuant to the transfer notice is employed by or acts as consultant to, or agrees to be employed by or act as consultant to, any competitor of any member of the [group] shall be deemed not to be a [good leaver].

A further concern often raised by the management's lawyers is that the company **10–23** may dispense of the relevant executive's services at a crucial time, either prior to a sale or a listing and as a result the employee will not enjoy the fruits of his/her hard work at the company by sharing in any enhanced premiums paid on a sale or listing. As a compromise, the following may be included:

> If there is a realisation within [six] months after the date of any transfer resulting from death or ill health pursuant to art.[ ] or from a wrongful dismissal pursuant to art.[ ], the holder or holders of the ordinary shares which shall have been transferred pursuant to arts [ ] or [ ] (each a "relevant transfer share") shall upon the realisation receive payment in respect of each relevant transfer share from the person or persons who hold such shares at the time of the realisation of an amount for each relevant transfer share equal to the amount by which the value of the share on the realisation exceeds the price paid to the relevant member or relevant executive in relation to such relevant member on transfer pursuant to arts [ ] or [ ] less any costs incurred on the realisation attributable to the relevant transfer share.
>
> For the purposes of this art.[ ] "Realisation" means the earlier of a sale or listing.

Management's lawyers may argue that six months is too short a period as a sale or listing can often take that long to effect. The corollary to this, however, is that any longer period will detract from the efforts of existing or incoming management who will have worked to increase the value of the company. Because the articles are a contract between the company and its members, as discussed earlier, and the executive having sold his shares will no longer be a member, consideration should be given to whether a clause such as this should be contained in the investment agreement or if that terminates on ceasing to be a shareholder, in a side letter.

Where an employee or director had any form of equity interest prior to the **10–24** buy-out, he will argue that at least a portion of his shareholding should be vested at the date of the buy-out and should not be subjected to mandatory transfer provisions. This is normally the case on a secondary buy-out or a development capital investment.

10.4.3 Warehousing shares and employee benefit trusts

10–25 The pre-emption provisions governing share transfers (within investment and articles of association) need to address the potential consequences of "surplus" shares. This can occur because, when shares become available for transfer, there may be no takers amongst the existing shareholder group. Management may not have the required funds and the private equity house may be unwilling to commit further funds. Because of this, it is common to provide either that the company can effect a buy-back of the shares or that the remaining shareholders can nominate a third party (either an incoming manager or a new investor). In addition the investment articles may also provide that shares be held for the benefit of employees of Newco using an employee benefit trust (commonly referred to as being warehoused).

Warehousing

10–26 It is important to ensure that the articles deal with the transfer into the employee benefit trust, transfers from retiring trustees to new trustees and also transfers from trustees to employees. In addition the articles should be checked to ensure that they allow sufficient time for the shares to be transferred into and held in trust and from the outgoing shareholders point of view that he is not going to have to wait an inordinate length of time until he is paid for his shares.

Employee benefit trusts ("EBTs")

10–27 The EBT can be a friendly purchaser to buy shares back from employees or other shareholders and is often used in conjunction with mandatory transfer provisions contained in investment articles. It is very useful to be utilised where the leaver provisions are required to be operated before a replacement has been identified or before the management team or private equity house feels comfortable enough to give an incoming manager some equity. More generally, an EBT can be very attractive to private companies who wish simply to provide a means of incentivising their employees by equity participation in the company.

10–28 The main advantages of an EBT are:

- the EBT route avoids Newco having to redeem or buy back the shares;

- in certain circumstances Newco can obtain a corporation tax deduction for monies which it donates to enable the trust to buy shares.

Private companies should think carefully before establishing or using an EBT as transactions with EBTs can often have important tax and other implications and these should be very carefully checked out.

10.4.4 Transfer of control

10–29 If the transfer of a "controlling interest" would result from a transfer then it is common to include a clause providing that the proposed transferee should be obliged to extend to all other shareholders an offer to purchase their shares on like terms. There is no fixed definition of "controlling interest" and it varies from case to case. Frequently the figure of 51 per cent or more is found though it is not uncommon to see this clause trigger at a level of 30 per cent or more of voting control. Determining the "controlling interest" is likely to depend on the share structure. If management hold more than 30 per cent but less than 50 per cent then the "controlling interest" is likely to be 30 per cent. One point for negotiation is whether this clause should be subject to the pre-emption arrangements and the shares offered round before selling to a third party. The investor may not like this as it may delay the process and frighten the buyer. However, from the management's point of view it may allow them time to refinance the company should they wish and may provide them an alternative.

Sometimes existing shareholders are exempted from an obligation to make a general offer. This should always be excluded in relation to the investor. Draftsmen should also be careful to exempt the effects of the ratchet as it operates between the shareholders.

10–30 Provision also needs to be included to facilitate the resolving of disputes as to the price to be offered by the offeror. The question is usually left to an independent expert acting at the joint expense of the parties. Disputes will generally arise because of the inclusion of alternative consideration, such as shares, earn-outs or commercial contracts. The independent expert's job will be to determine the true consideration. In determining the value of the shares, equity shares are normally treated on an equal basis and discounts and increments for minority and majority interests respectively are ignored. However, some investors will insist that full account be taken of the fact that management hold a minority interest. If this is the case, the managers' advisors should agree the discount that is to be made in valuing a minority shareholding, which should be recorded in the articles.

Special consideration needs to be given to the preference shares, if the same have not been redeemed or are incapable of redemption because of insufficient distributable reserves. Often the offeror is obliged to purchase the outstanding preference

Articles of Association

shares for a price equal to the amount which the holders would otherwise have received on redemption and therefore including arrears of dividends, etc. This may become a particularly thorny issue where preference shares are being issued to the vendor who then tries to raise the benefits to be received from such shares to those expected by an institution from their shares, a situation in which the institutional investor will draw considerable distinction between his/her preference shares and those of the vendor. The issue can become emotive and it is better to deal with it at the heads of agreement stage.

10–31 Set out below is a typical article.

> 2 Acquisition of control
>
> 2.1 In the event that any person or persons who was or were not a member or members of the company [or entitled to become such] on the date of the adoption of these articles ("the acquiring member") (but excluding any holder for the time being of preference shares or preferred ordinary shares at the date of adoption of these articles or any of its permitted transferees) either alone or in concert (as such expression is defined in the City Code on Takeovers and Mergers) with any other person(s), shall become beneficially entitled to more than [50] per cent of the equity shares [*NB: those shares conferring a right to vote at general meetings*] after the date of adoption of these articles of being so beneficially entitled shall become beneficially entitled to a further [1] per cent he shall forthwith be required by serving notice on the holder of the equity shares that he is so beneficially entitled and thereupon be bound to offer to purchase the remaining equity shares at a price per share ("the acquisition price") equal to the highest price per share paid by the acquiring member of such shares in the company, acquired by him/her.
>
> 2.2 The company shall forthwith give notice to every member other than the acquiring member that he/she may within 28 days from the date of such notice or such longer period as the directors may determine in order to give effect to art.[ ] [*NB: pre-emption provisions*] sell his/her shares to the acquiring member at the acquisition price [*NB: the price shall include any arrears, deficiencies or accruals of dividends*]. Any member may accept such offer by giving notice of his intention to do so to the company accompanied by share certificates for the shares agreed to be sold together with the necessary transfers.
>
> 2.3 The directors may require to be satisfied that the shares acquired by the acquiring member in the period referred to in art.2.1 were acquired bona fide for the consideration stated in the transfer without any deduction rebate or allowance whatsoever to the purchaser and if not so satisfied may require the acquisition price to be determined in accordance with art.[ ] [*NB: this allows for a referral to an independent expert*].

Share transfer provisions

2.4 If the acquiring member shall fail to serve a notice or make an offer in accordance with art.2.1 (or, if and to the extent that the offer is accepted, the acquiring member shall fail to complete the purchase of any shares pursuant to the offer) he (and any member with whom he/she is acting in concert as provided in art.2.1) shall cease to have any rights to vote or to dividend in respect of all the shares held by him/her and the directors may where relevant refuse to register the transfer of the shares acquired by the acquiring member which give rise to the obligations under art.2.1 and may require the acquiring member to serve a transfer notice in accordance with art.[ ] in respect of all or any of the shares held by him/her.

10.4.5 Forced sale provisions

This article will be extremely contentious and fought vehemently by the management's lawyers. However in view of the investor's desire for an exit, it is becoming increasingly common, even if watered down considerably. The investor cannot take the risk that management will block the investor's exit. The investor will be particularly concerned where the employees have been issued with shares. They are also known as "drag along" or "come along" provisions. 10–32

It is likely that a would-be purchaser would wish to acquire the entire share capital of the company. This may well affect the consideration which the purchaser will be prepared to offer for the investee company. Accordingly, the investor will consider including a provision whereby if the institutional investor shareholders wish to accept the offer, the other shareholders should be obliged to follow suit and sell at the same price per share. This may be just about acceptable in a MBO with certain compromises because everyone is aiming for an early exit but is likely to be unacceptable in a development capital investment. It should therefore be dealt with at as early a stage in the transaction as possible. One possible compromise is to set a date when the investor can impose a sale. This provides the investor with an ultimatum if the management and the investor together have not engineered a successful conclusion to their original plans. Another option is to provide that the employee shareholders hold a general meeting upon receiving an offer, at which a simple majority voting in favour of the sale will oblige all the employee shareholders to sell. In addition, the article may be made subject to the pre-emption provisions and thereby allowing the managers to refinance the company. 10–33

1 If [after [a date three to five years ahead]] the majority shareholder(s) of the preferred ordinary shares (for the purposes of this article ("the seller")) having been unable to sell all or any part of his holding of preferred ordinary shares intends to sell all or part of such shares (or any interest in such shares) in accordance with art.[ ] (the shares to be sold by the seller being

Articles of Association

referred to as "selling shares") the seller may give to the company not less than 14 days' notice in advance before selling the selling shares. The notice ("the selling notice") will include details of the selling shares and the proposed price for each selling share to be paid by the proposed purchaser ("the proposed purchaser"), details of the proposed purchaser, the place, date and time of the completion of the proposed purchase being a date not less than 14 days from the date of the selling notice ("completion").

2 Immediately upon receipt of the selling notice, the company shall:

   (a) give notice in writing (a "compulsory sale notice") to each of the members (other than the seller) giving the details contained in the selling notice, inviting them each to sell to the proposed purchaser at completion such proportion of their holdings of ordinary shares as is equal to the proportion which the selling shares bears to the total holding of shares in the equity shares held by the seller (including the selling shares);

   (b) call a separate general meeting of the holders of the ordinary shares to vote upon an ordinary resolution to sell to the proposed purchaser upon the terms set out in the compulsory sale notice. Section 630 of the Act shall apply in regard to the convening and conduct of such meeting.

3 If a majority of the holders of ordinary shares present and voting at the separate general meeting referred to in art.[ ] vote in favour of the resolution referred to in the article, then any member who has been served a compulsory sale notice shall sell all of his/her shares referred to in the compulsory sale notice on the terms contained therein.

10–34 This largely reflects the provisions in the Companies Act but the timescales are contracted and the provisions can be triggered at a lower threshold. Failure of the dissident minority to comply should trigger provisions in the articles empowering the directors to sell shares on their behalf and so ensuring that delivery of the entire issued share capital in the investee company can be guaranteed. Below is a suitable provision.

4 If any of the member(s) ("the defaulting member(s)") fails to comply with the terms of a compulsory sale notice given by him/her, the company shall be constituted by the agent of each defaulting member for the sale of his shares in accordance with the compulsory sale notice (together with all rights then attached thereto) and the directors may authorise some person to execute and deliver on behalf of each defaulting member the necessary transfer(s) and the company may receive the purchase money in trust for each of the defaulting members and cause the proposed purchaser to be registered as the holder of such shares. The receipt by the company of the purchase money, pursuant to such transfers, shall constitute a good and valid discharge to the proposed purchaser (who shall not be bound to see the

application therefore) and after the proposed purchaser has been registered in purported exercise of the aforesaid powers the validity of the proceedings shall not be questioned by any person. The company shall not pay the purchase money to a defaulting member until he/she shall, in respect of the shares being the subject of the compulsory sale notice, have delivered his/her transfers to the company. Provided that all the members comply with each compulsory sale notice, the seller shall sell the selling shares to the proposed purchaser on completion, subject at all times to the seller being able to withdraw the selling notice at any time prior to completion by giving notice to the company to that effect, whereupon each compulsory transfer notice shall cease to have effect.

A further and possibly more acceptable compromise is to trigger the forced sale provisions upon a specified percentage of all equity shareholders agreeing to do so (including 90 per cent of the institutional shareholders).

There is little authority on the enforceability of forced sale provisions however an Australian case has been quoted for authority for the proposition that to be enforceable the drag along article must be absolutely clear (*Gambotto v WCP Ltd* (1995) 182 CLR 432). Even with such an article it is very hard for an investor to sell against the wishes of the management. A management team that is not wholeheartedly on board during a sale process will not find it hard to derail the process by the positions it takes on due diligence, warranty provisions, etc. Management often attempt to negotiate these provisions to allow for a period when the business can't be sold without their consent, or a minimum price is achieved or that they have the opportunity to match the offer. These are generally refused by the investor who will want its exit unfettered.

10.5 Investor director(s)

An institutional investor will have made it a condition of his/her investment that he will be able to appoint a non-executive director to the board. Such right is normally enshrined in the articles by attaching the right to the preferred ordinary shares. It will also extend to the removal or replacement of any such directors. **10–35**

The holders of not less than 50 per cent by nominal amount of the issued preferred ordinary shares may by notice in writing addressed to the company appoint [up to any two people] [one person] an [a] director[s] ["the investor director[s]"] and remove from office any person so appointed and appoint another person in his place.

Inevitably, a fee will be paid by the company for the services of the investor director. This can be agreed after the transaction is completed but if possible **10–36** should be agreed before. If the management team insist on an industry expert being appointed it may be that there will not be time before and the appointment and negotiation of fees will be left until afterwards.

An investor director shall be entitled to all notices and to exercise voting rights and in all other respects as other directors save that:

> (a) [each] investor director shall be entitled to receive an annual fee not exceeding £[ ] together with any VAT thereon (plus all out of pocket expenses) or such higher sum as may from time to time be fixed by the board. Such figure shall be increased on [ ] of each year by a percentage equal to the percentage increase in the Index of Retail Prices (all items) maintained by the Department of Employment in the period to [ ] preceding each such date from the previous;

An investor director should be able to nominate an alternate to be present at board meetings as his substitute.

> (b) any alternate appointed by an investor director need not be approved by the board;

10–37 As a director of the company the investor director owes fiduciary duties to the company which are over and above those of the shareholders appointing him. It is most important therefore that he/she be allowed to disclose any information he/she receives to the shareholder appointing him/her and possibly to the banks.

> (c) an investor director may disclose any information he/she receives as a director of the company to the appointer or any holding company or subsidiary of the appointer or to their agents or professional or investment advisors [or to any party to the finance agreements] or any person who the banks (as defined in the finance agreements) wish to syndicate part of the [finance facilities].

Finally the investor will wish to ensure that this article cannot be modified.

On any resolution to amend or delete this article or to remove any investor director, each preferred ordinary share shall on a poll carry 100 votes.

Directors owe their duties to all of the shareholders and not to any individual shareholder or group of shareholders. In reality an investor director is likely to represent the interests of the institutional investor. Care therefore needs to be taken in drafting to ensure that such directors represent the interests of all shareholders.

10.6 Ratchets

A venture capital transaction may include the use of a ratchet. A ratchet is a tool **10–38** by which investors offer performance related stepped incentives in the form of equity to the management, to ensure all sides the best possible return on their investment.

Ratchets, however, are not as popular as they used to be. One of the reasons for this is that it is easy to become engrossed in technical detail and forget the purpose of the exercise. For the incentive to be effective the management must understand how it operates.

The purpose of a ratchet is to re-distribute the equity cake in the light of certain contingencies within the prescribed timescale. It is important that the objective is understood by everyone at the outset.

10.6.1 Why have ratchets?

There are probably four principal aims of ratchets and invariably the objective **10–39** will be a combination of several of them.

Incentivisation

The most commonly quoted reason for an investor introducing a ratchet is in order **10–40** to incentivise the management team to work even harder to improve the performance of the company. To maximise the growth in value of their shares, an institution will often decide to motivate the management team by offering them a considerable financial incentive over and above their salaries. It is hoped that this will ensure that the managers devote all their energies to maximising both the profit and, eventually, the capital gains on disposal of the business. Ratchets can fall into two broad categories, "carrot" or "stick" ratchets. In the former, management start with a lower equity stake which may rise accordingly to a pre-determined formula, up to a maximum level if particular targets are met, whereas in the latter, management may begin at a higher equity level which remains the same or falls according to performance.

Evaluation

At the outset of a MBO, there is often considerable discussion between the **10–41** investor and the management team about the value of the management's contribution ("the envy ratio"). The management will argue that their own cash and their total commitment as well as the opportunity that they have brought to the investor to considerably enhance their investment is a substantial contribution and should be accounted for in a premium paid by the investor for their shares over and above that paid by the management. Such a premium will generally be introduced by way of preference share capital or loan capital, depending upon market conditions. As a result, the management will have a greater proportion of the equity in relation to their investment.

There is often a large gap between what the management team and the investor believe the business to be worth. This valuation gap can be bridged by introducing a ratchet. The initial equity split would start off at a valuation put on the business by the investors, but if the profit targets or the other performance related targets indicated by the management team in their business plan are realised then they will ratchet upwards to reach their valuation.

Negotiating

10–42 Management teams will look for an added value return in addition to their employment benefits and may feel hard done by if they are unable to agree the principle of a ratchet. Some managers are prepared to accept substantial commission or bonus arrangements to satisfy this added value, but others for whatever reason will insist on a ratchet. It can sometimes be used as a negotiating pawn by the investor.

In particular when investors are competing for the transaction, then the use of a ratchet and the level of equity will often be a key incentive used to win the transaction.

Exit

10–43 Often the management team will be earning good incomes as company executives and there may not be the same ambition among them to drive the company towards an exit which may for instance result in the management becoming the subsidiary of a parent company and therefore reducing their freedom. To induce them away from their present occupation and additionally to drive them towards an exit may require the prospect of a substantial gain that a ratchet can offer.

Performance

10–44 In order for a ratchet to be successful, there must be a method of measuring performance. This can be achieved by measuring either:

Ratchets

- income flow (profit/interest received);
- capital value (this is generally upon realisation); or
- timeframe (when the cash is received).

By far the most popular ratchets are those linked to the value of the company or realisation.

All three of these are key components in the calculation of internal rates of return ("IRRs"). IRRs give a comparison to the investor between the return the investor might reasonably expect to obtain if it invested in a particular company, compared with other investment opportunities.

10.6.2 Internal rates of return ("IRRs")

10–45 IRRs are much more relevant to the fund type of venture capitalist rather than those funded by banks. The reason is that in order to raise funds from pension fund managers or similar, it is very important to show an IRR or a similar measurable return.

In order to understand an IRR, the principles of net present value ("NPV") must be grasped. NPV is the value today of a cash receipt in the future. If a shop offers to sell a clock for £20 payable in 12 months time, what would be the value today of that future sum of £20? The answer is the sum required to be put on deposit to accumulate £20 in 12 months time. If an interest rate of ten per cent is assumed then the figure would be £18.19.

Calculating an IRR is a technique involving setting a discount rate by the investor to achieve a set IRR which when applied to the cash flow to be received by the investor over the life of an investment provides a discounted value for the total amount received over the life of the investment. This value is then subtracted from the original cost of the investment with a view (should the opportunity come up to expectations) to reducing that figure or NPV to zero. A worked example is set out in section 10.6.4.

10–46 Determining the NPV allows the investor to compare the investment opportunity being offered to it against the return it could expect to make by placing the same amount of funds on the money market. NPVs and therefore IRRs take into account the time value of the money received by the investor by discounting future receipts. Taking account of inflation and other factors such as the economic climate, an anticipated return by placing the money on the money markets might be around ten per cent. This investor will then take into account a number of other factors either general or specific to the investment. Taking account of such factors will increase the IRR from 10 per cent to usually between 30 and 40 per cent. These factors are as follows:

- the profit and cash flow forecasts of the company over the life of the investment;
- what type of investment it is. For example, if it is true venture capital or seed capital then it will be high risk, but if it is funds for expansion, then it will be medium to low risk;
- the economic climate and trends within the industry;
- the quality of management;
- the historical stability of the company;
- the likely term of the investment; and
- the size of the investment.

10–47 The IRR is then calculated using a spreadsheet model which, over the investment period, will take account of all cash flow; the cash invested, fees received, interest received, dividends received (including a tax credit), the repayment of loans, the redemption of shares and the notional sale proceeds of the loan outstanding, the balance of preference shares and the equity valuation. The equity valuation will be dependent upon the forecast profit in the year of the investment and the P/E ratio applied.

10.6.3 Mechanics

10–48 Once the IRR has been determined the investor will calculate the total cash flow that it requires over the life of the investment to achieve the IRR and produce a NPV of zero at the end of the investment.

The investor will be hoping to achieve its IRR as a result of a substantial realised capital gain at the exit of the investment and through a preferential dividend and/or loan interest over the period of the investment.

The investor will be careful not to overburden the company in which it is investing with high interest or dividend payments particularly early on and may even structure the investment to provide interest holidays in order to get the investment well established. The structure will be dependent on expected cash flows from the investment.

For example, if a return were likely to come from the realisation of a specific project (launch of a new product or building of hotels or restaurants) the investor would be less likely to look for an income stream but would expect a substantial capital growth on the investment at the realisation of the project.

The investor has a number of options which can range from either providing simply loan finance or subscribing for the various classes of share capital. Set out below is a typical IRR example.

10.6.4 Investment example

An institution invests in Newco by way of £100,000 ordinary shares and £500,000 preference shares. The ordinary shares are 75 per cent of the issued share capital and will not earn dividends. The preference shares carry a ten per cent net coupon and are to be redeemed in five equal instalments commencing on the second anniversary of the deal. An "exit" is assumed in Year 5, at which time the gross capitalisation is expected to be £2 million.

The cash flows for the institution are given in the following table. The IRR is 35 per cent based on a number of assumptions, some of which are highlighted below. The exit value of the ordinary shares of £1,350,000 is calculated as the gross capitalisation of £2 million, less £200,000 preference shares to be repaid, multiplied by 75 per cent (the institutional per cent).

Year	0	1	2	3	4	5
Ords	(100)	–	–	–	1,350	
Prefs	(500)	–	100	100	100	200
Divi's	–	50	50	40	30	20
ACT	–	17	17 13	10	7	
Total cash flow	(600)	67	167	153	140	1,577
DCF $EN 35%	1.000	0.741	0.549	0.407	0.301	0.224
NPV	(600)	50	92	63	42	353

Most IRR calculations accept annual rests for all receipts and payments as an acceptable approximation. In the above example cash flows, the tax credits on dividends are included as institutional receipts. Further, no time lag is assumed between the dividend and the utilisation of the tax credit. This is a common treatment but may not be appropriate in all circumstances.

The single most significant influence on IRR calculations is the assumed exit value and its timing. Because of this it is a common practice to present IRR information in the form of a matrix with "exit year" being one axis and P/E values the other.

IRR should never be used as the sole measure of the feasibility of a transaction or of its cost. The technique can produce spurious results and does not seek to tell you that an investment for a longer period or of a larger amount at a lower IRR is more attractive. That is a matter of judgement.

The introduction of a ratchet inevitably adds a layer of complication to the articles and the tax implications will need to be considered carefully, in particular the employment related securities provisions of the Income Tax (Earnings and Pensions) Act 2003 and the 2003 HMRC/BVCA memoranda of understanding.

10.6.5 Exit ratchet

10–51 The exit ratchet is becoming far more popular than a ratchet based on profits. It is also much simpler to put into practice. In addition, it has the great advantage of forcing a management team to achieve the realisation which may not be the case with a profit ratchet. A profit ratchet is also more easily influenced by management through earlier cost recognition or deferral of income. The intention being to "inflate" the profits in the ratchet calculation year. Otherwise a single year's results could be affected by factors "beyond their control". Thus it would normally be more satisfactory to base the triggers on average profitability over a longer period. The two most common methods of achieving realisations are by way of a trade sale or a flotation.

Trade sale

10–52 This should be fairly straightforward and unless there is deferred or contingent consideration which is dealt with later there should not be any valuation problems.

If the purchaser issues consideration shares or loan notes then the market value of that consideration should be taken as being part of the sale proceeds rather than the part value of the shares or the possible future value of those shares.

Listing

10–53 Here the market capitalisation of the company on a listing is the basis of the exit valuation. While that may sound quite simple, it is often difficult to define very clearly the point at which the valuation is to take place. For example, if the listing is by way of a placing, should the placing price or the price at which dealings commence be used or, because that price is artificial, would the average dealing price during the first dealing day be better?

One of the most practical methods is as follows:

- if a prospectus is or listing particulars are issued then use any issue price or placing place referred to in that document; and
- in any other case such as an introduction, use the best possible estimate that the sponsoring broker can make of the bona fide price at which dealing shall start.

Ratchets

10–54 The means of effecting the ratchet will be either by way of share transfers at set values or by the purchase by the company of some of the institution's shares or by the non-conversion of a different class of share into ordinary shares.

Numerous variants of these types exist and can incorporate both "performance" and "exit" ratchets. The ratchet mechanism, together with the necessary definitions of profitability or exit value, is normally set out in Newco's articles of association.

Newco may issue preferred ordinary shares to the institutional investor which will be converted into ordinary shares at the time of exit, depending on the ratchet mechanism.

10–55 An exit value ratchet might operate on the basis of the following agreed table.

Market capitalisation	Ordinary shares	Value of institutional stake
£m	%	%
up to 20	30	up to 6
20–30	30–20 pro rata	6–6.25
over 30	20	over 6

If the company has on exit a market capitalisation of £22 million, the institution's preferred ordinary shares will convert into 28 per cent of the ordinary share capital worth £6.16 million. There are two features of this sort of ratchet: the institutional shareholding declines with increased exit value, effectively "capping" their return for exit values between £20 million and £30 million, and for an exit range of £25 million to £31.25 million there is no benefit to the institutional investor from an increased exit valuation. A similar table could be constructed for a profit or performance based ratchet.

10.6.6 Valuation difficulties

Early realisation

10–56 If a profit based ratchet is proposed then consider what should happen if there is a realisation before the end of the profit based ratchet period.

In practice, this will probably be dealt with by the fact that if the management team feel the ratchet is going to trigger then they will simply hold out for a better price for those shares than the investor and if this price is not offered then they will simply not sell.

However in some cases the investors are able to force a sale. If that is the case then consider putting in provisions for an early triggering of the ratchet. For example interim accounts could be prepared or an assumption could be made that profits would continue at the same rate as the previous year.

Deferred and contingent consideration

10–57 Particular problems also arise when looking at sales and in particular deferred or contingent consideration on a sale.

Deferred consideration is merely consideration that is received with absolute certainty but at a later date. Contingent consideration is, as it states, contingent upon some future event, for example profits being earned on an earn-out formula. The first of these events will happen, the latter only may happen, but how should they be treated in terms of valuation for an exit ratchet?

With regard to deferred consideration, a NPV based on what is an appropriate discount factor at the time of the exit itself should be applied to produce a net present-day value on the day of the exit itself.

With regard to contingent consideration it is very difficult. It may be best to exclude it entirely and leave it that the contingent element of the consideration, since it is more likely dependent upon the management team's future activity, is excluded from the exit valuation but that all the counterpart consideration is only paid in respect of the management team's share.

Certain investors may find this hard to swallow, but if the contingent element is not too large and since the investors are not usually involved in giving warranties to support the sale price, a fair quid pro quo is that the management team should take the benefit of the contingent consideration.

Warranty claims

10–58 Bearing in mind that a trade sale will inevitably be coupled with warranties and indemnities, what happens if any of these claims are made and how will it affect the ratchet? Provided the investors are not giving warranties then it is probably better left alone. Again, the management take the benefit of the ratchet but also take the risk of warranty claims.

Practical points

10–59 • Make sure that what the investor and the management team wish to achieve is clearly identified and that it is appropriate for the company.

- Do not over-complicate. The effect of this would delay the timetable, increase the costs and produce a ratchet that is unworkable and totally beyond the comprehension of both the investor and the management team, as well as the lawyers and accountants.

- Be wary in situations where there are more than two classes of equity shares. If this happens, make sure it is understood who is to suffer from the dilution if a ratchet works, bearing in mind it must work at somebody's expense.

- Try and make sure that the ratchet is a fairly shallow graph at first so that the management team can get onto the graph reasonably easily but once onto it they need to make considerable effort to get a greater return. In other words, it should be shallow and then become steeper. There is no greater disincentive to a management team than knowing there is a ratchet there that they have spent a long time negotiating but within 12 months realising there is little or no chance of ever gaining anything from it.

- Remember that to both investors and management teams ratchets are often very highly emotional items.

- Acquisitions or disposals will inevitably affect profitability and exit values. Given that institutions will normally have a veto on such future decisions, the prospects of negotiating the ratchet are very strong. However, the outcome of any renegotiation cannot be predicted and is rarely satisfactory for both parties.

- Just as there are problems in defining exit values on flotation or sale, there are also practical difficulties in defining profits for performance related exits. Subsequent changes in amending reference dates, accounting policies, tax rates and the classification of matters which might be regarded as exceptional or extraordinary may all affect the ratchet.

10.7 Miscellaneous

The Companies Act prescribes that Table A shall be adopted unless specifically excluded or modified. It is important therefore that the provisions contained in Table A are considered carefully. **10–60**

- Regulation 39 provides that if the company inadvertently fails to give notice of a general meeting to a director, non-receipt of that notice will not invalidate the proceedings of the meeting. The managers may wish to exclude this provision.

- Table A contains provisions (regs 65–69 inclusive) for the appointment of alternate directors. However, reg.65 provides that a director may appoint another director or a person approved by the board as his/her alternate. The individual manager may prefer to be free to appoint whom he/she likes as his/her alternate assuming that it is acceptable to the investor and the other members of the management team.

- The individual manager is also likely to want the provision relating to rotation of the directors to be removed. These are found in regs 73–77.

- Regulation 88 provides that it shall not be necessary to give notice of a meeting to a director who is absent from the UK [this may not be appropriate and should be confirmed].

Quorum

10–61 The investor may want the articles to provide that a quorum of directors will not be present unless its own nominee director is present, so that effectively no board business can be transacted unless and until the investor's nominee arrives. This is a common request but should not be necessary in view of the extensive restrictions imposed on the activities of the company without the consent of the investor or its director. In any event, if the investor insists on such a provision, management advisors should ensure that the company is not prevented from conducting its business by a relevant part of the quorum simply not turning up. This is achieved by amending the wording to the effect that if a quorum is not present within half an hour of the meeting, it should be adjourned to a date determined by those who are present and those present at the adjourned meeting will form the quorum wherever they are. Also to be considered will be whether notice of the adjourned meeting will have to be given to all directors and what period should elapse before the reconvened meeting.

10.8 Checklist

10–62 Set out on the next page is a checklist of matters that should be included in the Articles of Association of a new investment. These are provided by way of guidance only and the terms will vary according to the transaction.

Checklist

Checklist of matters to be included in the Articles of Association

	Yes	No	Comments

1 Share Capital
- 1.1 Confirm details of all shareholders and classes of shares held.
- 1.2 Separate classes for investor and management.

2 Dividend Rights
- 2.1 State details of any fixed and/or participating dividends receivable by the investor. *[NB: consider use of participating dividends in particular to motivate exit]*
- 2.2 Balance of dividends distributed pari passu only with investors' consent (i.e. no catch-up for management).

3 Return of Capital Rights
- 3.1 Investor to receive all subscription monies and dividends first.
- 3.2 Management to receive subscription monies and dividends second.
- 3.3 Balance distributable pari passu.
- 3.4 Confirm details of any enhanced capital rights for investor.
- 3.5 Please state any details of any ratchet arrangement and attach a worked example.

4 Voting Rights
- 4.1 All equity one vote per share.
- 4.2 Preference shares no votes.
- 4.3 Enhanced voting rights for investor (normally so as to give investor control) on events of default.

5 Conversion Rights
- 5.1 Right for investor to convert to ordinary shares.

Articles of Association

	Yes	No	Comments

6 Redemption of Preference Shares

6.1 Confirm redemption profile and any redemption premiums.
6.2 Facility for company to redeem preference shares early in reverse order of maturity.
6.3 Confirm reason for use of preference shares rather than loan stock.

7 Transfer of a Significant Interest

7.1 Drag along in favour of investor for any transfer resulting in a change of control.
7.2 Any offer for the purchase of over 50 per cent of the company cannot be accepted without an offer being made for 100 per cent.

8 Permitted Transfer of Shares

8.1 Confirm provisions included allowing investor to transfer its shares within its own group of funds or to its investors.
8.2 Permitted transfers for tax planning by management. [Only transfers to close family members. If family trusts included, must be private trusts and subject to investor's approval.]
8.3 All other transfers subject to pre-emption rights.
8.4 Any management shares which become available to be offered to invitees (replacements) first, then to other members pro rata or class by class.

9 Good Leaver/Bad Leaver Provisions

9.1 Check definition of good and bad leavers. Should there be a time period when definitions lapse? How are unfair dismissals and wrongful dismissals dealt with?
9.2 Requirement to offer shares for sale on departure:
    9.2.1   Good leaver: Offer all at market value.
    9.2.2   Bad leaver: Offer all at lower of issue price or market value.

Checklist

	Yes	No	Comments

9.3 Is there any revaluation mechanism in favour of a leaver in the event of an exit within a specified period of time of a deemed transfer. If so, please provide details.

9.4 Is there an obligation for leavers' shares to be offered first to the company or to an employee trust for "warehousing" before offered to other shareholders?

9.5 Confirm that any shares held by family members/trust effectively "clawed back".

10 Miscellaneous

10.1 Confirm that provisions relating to appointment of Investor Director(s) (see Subscription and Shareholders Agreement) also set out in Articles.

10.2 Prohibition on variation or abrogation of class rights without consent of 75 per cent of that class.

10.3 All investors' shares to require class consent for:
 (a) changes in issued or authorised share capital;
 (b) issue of options or other convertible securities or loan notes;
 (c) creation of encumbrances;
 (d) material change to business of group;
 (e) changes to memorandum/articles of association;
 (f) winding-up;
 (g) sale, asset sale or listing;
 (h) change to auditors.

10.4 No class rights to be given to management.
[If the investor is the majority shareholder then no class rights should be given to management holding a minority shareholding over and above those assumed by law]

10.5 Inclusion of borrowing limit.

295

Chapter 11

Directors and Employees

11.1 Introduction

The law of the duties of directors is a wide and evolving area derived from a mixture **11–01** of common law and statute. Historically, the laws governing directors' duties were contained in the Companies Act 1985 and Insolvency Act 1986 together with other legislation and a considerable amount of case law. On November 8, 2006, however, a new Act—the Companies Act 2006—received Royal Assent. The Companies Act 2006 ("CA 2006") repealed and replaced most of the existing statutes in an attempt to codify existing common law principles, and to implement EU directives.

Before the Insolvency Act 1986, the classic statement of the director's duties was that of Roner J. in *City Equitable Fire Insurance Company Ltd, Re* [1925] 1 Ch. 407 in which he said:

> "a director need not exhibit in the performance of his duties a greater degree of skill than may reasonably be expected from a person of his knowledge and experience".

This was a case of power without responsibility. However, this subjective test must now be considered alongside the objective degree of skill expected of directors under the Insolvency Act 1986. Furthermore, there is a definite statutory trend towards increasing the number and severity of corporate offences for which directors are held personally liable.

The CA 2006 codified the existing common law duties of directors to create seven codified duties. These duties are not an exhaustive list, however, and it has been made clear that the existing law remains relevant for the purposes of interpreting the CA 2006.

This chapter also considers some of the more specific provisions that are likely to **11–02** be found in service agreements entered into in venture capital transactions. The service agreement sets out the terms of the director's relationship with the company but will normally be negotiated with the venture capitalist.

Finally, employee participation is considered. The principal purpose of employee participation is to ensure that the company has an incentivised workforce. Employee share ownership can also generate funds but this is likely to be of secondary importance.

11.2 Duties of directors

11–03 Prior to embarking on the expensive and time consuming process of raising venture capital, it is important to determine whether a proposition fits the profile of a typical venture capital investment. In judging the investment fit, there are four important criteria on which a venture fund places emphasis: the management, past performance, future prospects and exit prospects. This section will review each of the key areas in detail.

11.2.1 Who is a director?

11–04 There is no statutory definition of a director. Section 250 of the CA 2006 says merely that "director" includes any person occupying the position of director, by whatever name called. However, for certain purposes the expression "director" includes not only those who have been formally elected to that office but also any other person in accordance with whose directions or instructions the directors of the company are accustomed to act (s.251 of the CA 2006 calls these persons "shadow directors"). A shadow director is a creation of statute—the product of a number of provisions in the Companies and Insolvency Acts which specifically extend the obligations of properly appointed directors to persons who come within the "shadow director" definition. Generally no-one would admit to being a shadow director, but the concept is relevant in several areas of statutory law relating to director's duties, particularly those aimed at controlling conflicts of interest. The CA 2006 distinguishes between directors and shadow directors as not all duties apply to shadow directors. The penalties imposed on directors for "wrongful trading" under the Insolvency Act continue to include shadow directors as the same are defined in the CA 2006.

A venture capitalist may fall into the category of a shadow director, particularly if the company is consolidated in its accounts. A liquidator faced with a shortfall will always consider whether a venture capitalist was a shadow director and therefore responsible for wrongful trading and liable for the debts of the company. The venture capitalist and its appointed director will have considerable input and influence in the director's discussions concerning the financial health of the company. The venture capitalist should therefore ensure that its instructions are not perceived as orders to be followed automatically. This is very difficult when with regard to most decisions the company will not be able to act without the consent of the venture capitalist.

Duties of directors

Directors are often compared with agents, in that when they contract, they do so on behalf of the company, without taking any liability on themselves unless they act outside their powers or expressly accept liability. They are also often compared to trustees, in that directors have duties of good faith towards their companies similar in some respects to the duty of a trustee towards the beneficiaries, and both must apply property under their control for specified purposes. However, there are significant differences between the position of directors and the positions of agents and trustees, and neither analogy provides a satisfactory definition of the nature of the director's role. **11–05**

One important distinction is the difference between directors and employees. A director as such is not an employee of the company. However, if he/she is appointed to some executive post such as managing director, or works full-time or part-time for the company so that he/she is part of its "workforce" (whether or not he/she has a formal service contract) he/she will be an employee of the company and will have additional rights and duties going beyond those of a director pure and simple.

11.2.2 Types of directors

A managing director and a chairman may be designated from one of the members of the board. These offices are not recognised by statute. However, a company's articles of association may appoint one or more of its members to be the managing director or directors of the company on such terms and with such powers as the board thinks fit. His/her powers will be solely based on the terms of the company's articles of association, his/her service contract and any board resolutions appointing him/her. A chairman is appointed by the board and presides over the board according to the company's articles. He/she should ensure proper conduct of meetings and attempt to direct discussions towards a consensus. Some companies' articles may accord a casting vote to the chairman. Additionally the company's directors may include alternate directors, non-executive directors and shadow directors. **11–06**

Executive directors are the senior managers working full-time or part-time for a company usually with a service agreement who have been formally appointed directors. Commonly in a venture capital context they will also be shareholders and as a result of various incentives they will be motivated to ensure the success of the company.

Under a company's articles a director is often entitled to appoint an alternate to act in his place (see for example Table A, reg.65 as amended by Companies (Tables A to F) Amendment Regulations 2007, although note that Table A will be replaced under regulations from a date to be confirmed by new example articles which have yet to be finalised). The appointment of an alternate generally ceases when the appointor ceases to hold office. In the appointor's absence the alternate **11–07** is treated as a director of the company and subject to the same duties and penalties as his/her appointor.

Non-executive directors are directors and not normally employees of the company. They may be appointed to add balance to the board or possibly to represent the interest of particular groups of shareholders. They are generally independent of the company's management and often allocated the task of determining the remuneration of executive management and making recommendations as to appropriate bonus and incentive schemes by participating in remuneration committees but they are not involved in the day-to-day business.

The distinction between executive and non-executive directors is of considerable practical significance. While the terms do not have a precise legal meaning it is typically inferred that executive directors have a full-time managerial role while a non-executive director is likely to be a part-time advisor or consultant, who may well have a monitoring role in relation to the executive director.

11–08 Legally a director is a director, and his/her executive or non-executive status does not affect this. However it may be relevant in a number of circumstances. For example, when the standard of a director's care and skill is in question he/she may be able to argue that a lower level of care and skill is relevant to him/her if he/she is a non-executive. However, this argument is unlikely to apply to a venture capitalist appointed director who will invariably be a sophisticated individual with a financial background who will have significant vetoing powers and his/her decisions will have a crucial influence on the future of the company. In the case of a company obtaining private equity, the venture capitalist will own shares of a particular class in the company which will entitle it to appoint a non-executive director to the board. It is very rare that a venture capitalist will not appoint a director to watch over its interest. The consent of that director, who will usually be a senior employee of the venture capitalist or alternatively someone with experience in the relevant industry sector, may well be required under the company's articles and shareholders' series of stated matters. Such director will also obtain all the company's regular financial statements and have extensive monitoring and vetoing powers.

While such a director is appointed to promote the venture capitalist's interests, he/she must not, of course, allow this relationship with the venture capitalist to interfere with the overriding duty to act in the company's best interest. As a director, as a matter of law, he/she must not safeguard the venture capitalist's interests to the detriment of the company's interests and cannot be compelled by the venture capitalist who appointed him/her to exercise his/her discretion in a particular way. If that director is also a director of the venture capitalist's company he/she may at certain times therefore face an unreasonable conflict of interest.

11.2.3 Duties of directors

The duties of directors can in general be divided into two categories: duties of **11–09** honesty and good faith or fiduciary duties, and duties of care and skill. The duties of honesty and good faith require the director to act in what he believes to be the best interests of the company, to exercise his powers for the particular purposes for which they were conferred and not to put him/herself in a position where his/her ability to do so is restricted or where there is a conflict between his/her duty and some personal interest. In contrast with the fiduciary duties of directors, the standards of care and skill which a director must show are not high. The case law on this subject dates from a time when directors rarely acted in an executive capacity, so that the standards applied have little relevance to the duties of the highly paid fully professional executive director.

In addition to the fiduciary duties and duties of skill and care, there are a number of miscellaneous statutory duties which do not fit easily into either category. We will consider each of these duties separately.

The CA 2006 codifies the principal common law and general equitable directors' duties into seven statutory duties (ss.170–181 of the CA 2006).

This list is not exhaustive and other common law and existing statutory duties **11–10** continue to apply. The codified duties of directors are as follows:

- to act within their powers;
- to promote the success of the company;
- to exercise independent judgement;
- to exercise reasonable care, skill and diligence;
- to avoid conflicts of interest;
- not to accept benefits from third parties;
- to declare interests in any proposed transaction or arrangement with the company.

The case law in relation to the previous common law duties are relevant to the interpretation of the duties under the CA 2006 and details are set out here for reference.

To whom are these duties owed?

The general rule is that directors' duties are owed to the company alone, which **11–11** means to the present and future shareholders of the company and not to any shareholder individually. If a director has failed in his/her duty, the members must look to the board to enforce it on behalf of the company, although if the board fails to take action, the members in a general meeting may resolve that the company does so. A minority shareholder is not usually entitled to sue in the name of the company unless the company's affairs are being or have been conducted in a manner which is unfairly prejudicial to the members or a part of them.

All shareholders will have the right to commence legal proceedings against directors on behalf of the company for negligence, breach of duty or breach of trust. Although this potentially increases the liability of directors, shareholders have to seek the permission of the court to pursue the claim. A two-stage court procedure must be implemented.

11–12
- Stage 1, the applicant must make a prima facie case for granting permission to pursue the claim.
- Stage 2, the court will decide whether to give permission for the action to proceed based on specified factors.

Since directors' duties are owed to the company, the company may ratify the actions of a director who is in breach of his/her duties or who has exceeded his/her authority. There are exceptions to this, the main one being that the company cannot ratify an act which the company itself has no power to do.

Although directors' duties are owed mainly to the company, directors must also have regard to a number of factors. Directors must have regard, though to a lesser extent, to the interests of creditors and employees. The duties that directors owe to creditors are relevant mainly in the context of an insolvency or potential insolvency of the company concerned. In the wider sense referred to above, directors also have responsibilities, going beyond their strict legal duties, to customers, the public and the State.

11–13 In *Kuwait Asia Bank EC v National Mutual Life Nominees Ltd* [1990] 3 W.L.R. 297 the Privy Council held, on an appeal from the New Zealand Court of Appeal, that in the absence of fraud or bad faith, a shareholder or other person who controlled the appointment of a director owed no duty to the company's creditors to ensure that the company acted with diligence. The director became an agent of the company acting in his/her individual capacity as a distinct legal person and was bound to ignore the interests of his/her employer and appointor who accordingly could not be liable, in the absence of fraud or bad faith, for the director's acts either as employer or as principal.

11–14 Under s.172 of the CA 2006, when exercising their duty to promote the success of the company directors will have regard to:

Duties of directors

- the likely consequences of any decision in the long term;
- the interests of the company's employees;
- the need to foster the company's business relationships with suppliers, customers and others;
- the impact of the company's operations on the community and the environment;
- the desirability of the company maintaining a reputation for high standards of business conduct; and
- the need to act fairly as between members of the company.

Fiduciary duties

11–15 *Duty to act in good faith in the interests of the company (including duties towards employees)* A director must exercise his/her powers in good faith and in what he/she considers to be in the interests of the company. This is the primary duty of a director. The test of good faith is subjective, so that if the director honestly believes that he/she is exercising his/her powers in the best interests of the company a court will not consider his/her duty broken merely because, in the court's opinion, his/her actions are not in the interests of the company. The case law surrounding this common law duty is likely to be relevant to the codified duty to promote the success of the company (s.172 of the CA 2006).

Fiduciary duties cannot be reduced to a single set of rules and principles which apply in the same way to all relationships. The scope of this duty, which largely derives from common law, was extended by the CA 2006, which recognised the rights of employees for the first time in English company law. Section 172 of the CA 2006 provides that directors must have regard to the interests of the company's employees in general, as well as the interests of its members. This duty, like directors' other duties, is owed to the company itself and is not enforceable by individual employees. Consequently, only if a company's employees are also shareholders of the company can they in their capacity as shareholders enforce the director's obligation to have regard to the interests of its employees. The precise scope of the duty is unclear, since it does not change the overriding requirement that the directors must act in the best interests of the company as a whole.

11–16 Despite the provisions of s.172 and apart from the exceptional circumstances of a liquidation, the recognised view is that the standard by which the directors should be judged is "the interest of the company as a commercial entity, to be judged in most cases by a reference to the interests of present and future shareholders alone"

11–17 *Duty to use powers for their proper purpose* Directors must exercise their powers only for the purpose for which they were conferred. A director who breaches this duty cannot argue that his/her actions were done in good faith in what he/she honestly believed to be the best interests of the company. If directors act for a collateral or improper purpose then even if their actions meet the subjective test of "good faith" the conduct will be open to challenge. As a result a court will apply a "reasonable man" objective test in this context. It allows the court to make a common sense judgment of the facts surrounding the exercise of the power. In one case, the directors allotted new shares to an intending takeover bidder so that he could outvote two shareholders who had announced that they would reject his offer. Although the company did need new capital at the time, and the directors acted honestly and believed what they were doing was in the interests of the company, it was held that the directors had acted with an improper purpose and the allotment was set aside.

11–18 *Duty not to exceed powers* The directors must not do any act which is unlawful, or outside the company's powers, or outside the powers conferred on the directors by the memorandum and articles of association. This is so even if they are acting honestly, believing that what they are doing is in the best interests of the company. Directors may be personally liable in the same way as trustees if they dispose of the company's property in an unauthorised manner, for example by paying dividends out of capital or by making an illegal loan even if they act in good faith. They may be personally liable on the contract or liable to the company to compensate it for any loss suffered on the contract. It is essential therefore that a director is properly authorised by the board or shareholders before entering into contracts on the company's behalf. In a company with a venture capital shareholder, there will be an investment or shareholder agreement containing a substantial list of items which will require the venture capitalist's consent before executing. This is reflected in the codified duty to act within powers under s.171 of the CA 2006.

Conflicts of interest and duty

11–19 A director must not take advantage of his/her position. Several duties can be grouped under this heading, including the duty not to make a personal profit from his/her position, and a number of statutory provisions designed to eliminate conflicts of interest and abuses by directors of their position.

The general duty to ensure that personal interests are not brought into conflict with those of the company, and to act in the best interests of the company if a conflict occurs, can be regarded as a duty in its own right as well as forming the basis for the other duties mentioned in this section. By way of illustration, consider a director who fails to win a contract for the company and is offered the contract in a private capacity. If the director kept the offer secret and succeeded in persuading the company to release him/her from the contract by pretending to be ill, so that he/she could take up the offer, he/she would be held liable to account to the company for the profit which would be obtained from the contract, on the basis that he/she should not have embarked on a course of conduct which put his/her personal interest in direct conflict with his/her continuing duties as a director of the company.

11–20 If the venture capital transaction involves a MBO, particular care must be taken to avoid conflicts of interest where management are also directors of the company which is to be the subject of the buy-out. Any decisions by the company regarding the proposals should always be taken by the non-management buy-out directors.

This duty is found in s.175 of the CA 2006. A director must avoid a situation where he has or may have a direct or indirect interest that conflicts or may conflict with the interests of the company. Note, however, that this duty does not cover transactions between the company and a director which are dealt with separately. Although the aim is to ensure directors do not benefit personally to the company's disadvantage, the duty does catch circumstances in which the director makes no personal gain.

Other examples of this general duty are set out below.

11–21 *Duty not to make a personal profit* A director is under a duty not to make a profit as a result of his/her directorship, irrespective of whether the company is in any way harmed or could itself have taken advantage of the circumstances. Although the articles of association of a company frequently relax the consequences of a breach of his/her duty, the general rule is that any profit which a director acquires by reason of his/her office belongs to the company and unless the director has disclosed the profit, and obtained the approval of the shareholders in general meeting, he/she must account for the profit to the company.

11–22 Any action on a director's part which is so closely connected with the company's affairs that it can be said to have been done in the course of the performance of his/her duties, or which makes use of any opportunity or special knowledge which has come to him/her as a director, will give rise to the application of this rule if the director profits personally.

In *Regal (Hastings) Ltd v Gulliver* [1942] 1 All E.R. 378, Russell J. said:

> "the directors stand in a fiduciary relationship to the company in regard to the exercise of their power as directors, and having obtained these shares by reason and only by reason of the fact that they were directors of the company and in the course of the execution of that office are accountable for the profits which they have made out of them".

A director who makes a profit which he/she was only able to make by using his/her fiduciary position (the use of information or a business opportunity which was gained in the course of his/her directorship) must therefore account for the profit made to the company.

11–23 Issues of shares by a company can give rise to conflicts of interests for directors. Directors are free to subscribe for or purchase shares in the company of which they are directors, but when their company issues shares, directors are under a duty to obtain an issue price which reflects the market value of the shares at the time of allotment. Consequently, if directors allot shares to themselves at an issue price which is less than the current market value of the shares, they are accountable to the company for the difference as a personal profit obtained by them as a result of the exercise of their power of allotment. Moreover if the directors later sell the shares at a price higher than the market value at the date of allotment, the company can recover from the directors the whole difference between the price realised by the directors and the issue price paid by them (*Parker v McKenna* (1874) 10 Ch. App. 96).

11–24 *Interests in contracts* This, like many of the other duties mentioned in this section, overlaps with the previous duty. Duties relating to directors' interests in contracts are imposed both by statute and by the common law, and are codified in s.177 of the CA 2006.

11–25 Under s.182 of the CA 2006, a director has a duty to disclose to the board the nature of any personal interest which he/she may have in relation to any contract or arrangements involving the company. Disclosure must usually be made at the first board meeting at which the involvement of the company is mentioned, although a director may give general notice that he/she is interested in a particular firm and is to be regarded as interested in any contract which the company may make with that firm. The amount of information to be given will depend on the circumstances, but it has been held that a disclosure must be "full and frank". There is no specific definition of "interested" but it is generally understood to relate to a situation in which a director, or person connected to him, would acquire some financial benefit or advantage from the contract or proposed contract with the company. Failure to disclose will entitle the company to any profit and will render the director liable to a fine. Even if properly disclosed, a contract in which a director is "interested" will be voidable if not made for the company's purposes. The question of whether a director can vote (or be counted in the quorum) on these transactions (and keep any resulting profit) is determined by the company's articles.

11–26 This is captured in s.177 of the CA 2006 albeit with some changes including:

- the extent of the director's interest must be included; (s.177(1)—previously, only the nature of the interest had to be declared);
- the notification must be updated if the director's interest changes prior to entry into the arrangement (no matter how minor the change) (s.177(3));

Duties of directors

- the timing of the notification. Notification no longer has to be given at the first board meeting in which the matter is discussed, the requirement instead being only to notify before the transaction is entered into (s.177(4));
- the manner of notification in that it can be by written or general notice, as well as at a directors' meeting (s.177(2));
- a breach of this duty is enforceable in the same way as any other fiduciary duty owed by the directors, that is with civil not criminal sanctions.

11-27 Whereas s.317 of the 1985 Act dealt with proposed and existing contracts together, the CA 2006 deals with them separately and the duty to declare an interest extends only to proposed contracts (s.177). Declarations of interest in relation to existing contracts are dealt with separately (although on similar terms) under ss.182 to 187 of the CA 2006, but the duty to disclose an interest in an existing contract does not form part of a director's statutory duties.

Directors also have a common law duty to disclose to the shareholders in general meeting any personal interest which they may have in relation to a contract which the company has made or is proposing to make. The articles normally relax the consequences of a breach of this rule, but in the absence of any such provision, the shareholders must specifically ratify the contract or authorise the directors to enter into it. If proper disclosure is not made (or ratification or authorisation is not given) in accordance with these rules, the company may revoke the contract. In such circumstances the company is entitled to claim from the director any profit made by him/her in connection with the contract.

11-28 However, the articles usually provide that as long as a director has disclosed his/her interest to the board, a contract in which he/she is interested may not be revoked by the company and the director will not be liable to account for any profit he/she may have made. The current Table A (in the Companies (Tables A to F) Regulations 1985 (SI 1985/805) as amended by the Companies (Tables A to F) Amendment Regulations 2007, which contains specimen regulations for the management of a company which, with certain amendments, apply to most UK companies) contains a provision to this effect. However, such a provision would not justify the director committing a breach of duty or other default such as failing to give proper advice, concealing material information or imposing an unfair bargain.

11-29 *Directors' service contracts* Section 188 of the CA 2006 is aimed at controlling conflicts of interest.

A company to which the section applies is prohibited from entering into a service contract (i.e. contract of employment) with a director for a period of more than two years unless the company has the right to terminate the contract before the end of that period. Any contract for a term of more than two years must be approved by the shareholders of the company in general meeting and in the case of a director of a holding company, also by a resolution of the holding company. If the shareholders' approval is not obtained, the company will be deemed to be able to terminate the contract by giving reasonable notice to the director.

11–30 Under ss.188–189 and 227–230 of the CA 2006 the law changed to require approval for directors' service contracts with a guaranteed term in excess of two years. Approval is not required if the company is a wholly-owned subsidiary. If approval is not obtained, the company is able to terminate the relevant contract on reasonable notice.

11–31 The CA 2006 (unlike the 1985 Act) defines what is meant by a director's service contract (s.227) and includes:

- contracts of employment with the company or a subsidiary;
- contracts for services (therefore including consultancy agreements); and
- letters of appointment to the office of director.

Also, the CA 2006 requires that copies of every service contract be kept for their duration and for at least one year after they expire. The exemption for contracts for directors working outside the UK and for contracts with less than 12 months to run were not retained. Shareholders also have the right to request a copy of any service contract on payment of a prescribed fee. As in the 1985 Act, these provisions regarding service contracts apply to shadow directors. The restriction in s.311 of the 1985 Act prohibiting companies from paying directors free of income tax or agreeing to vary it in line with changes in such tax was removed by virtue of s.1177 of the CA 2006.

11–32 *Substantial property transactions*   Section 190 of the CA 2006 regulates sales and purchases between a director and his company. It does not apply to a director of a wholly-owned subsidiary or to a director of a company which is not registered under the UK Companies Act (e.g. an overseas subsidiary).

The section prohibits any arrangement between a company and any of its directors, including directors of its holding company, under which the director acquires a substantial non-cash asset or assets from the shareholders of the company in general meeting. The section applies even though the director may be paying the full market price for the assets involved and, like several other sections in the Act designed to control conflicts of interest, it applies not only to directors themselves but also to persons connected with directors. Persons connected with a director include his/her family, partners, any other company of which he/she is a director and trusts of which he/she is a trustee.

The section only applies to transactions where the value of the assets transferred exceeds £100,000 (or, if lower, ten per cent of the company's net assets). Assets worth less than £5,000 are not included. In addition, the section does not apply:

Duties of directors

- if the transaction is between a holding company and its wholly-owned subsidiary or between two wholly-owned subsidiaries of the same holding company (this exception is necessary because of the wide definition of "connected person"); or
- if the company is in liquidation (other than a members' voluntary winding-up); or
- if the director (or a connected person) receives property in his/her capacity as shareholder (e.g. payment of a dividend in kind).

Any transaction which contravenes this provision may be revoked by the company unless the company affirms the transaction in general meeting within a reasonable time, or unless the parties cannot be put back into the exact position they were in before the agreement was made. The offending director will also be liable to account to the company for any loss which the company suffers and for any gain he/she obtains as a result of the transaction. **11–33**

Sections 190–196 of the CA 2006 brought some changes as follows: **11–34**

- the definition of connected persons was extended (ss.252–253 of CA 2006) to include adult (as well as infant) children or step-children of the director, the director's parents, anyone who lives with the director as a partner in an "enduring family relationship", and children and step-children of such a partner up to the age of 18 who live with the director;
- allowing entry into contracts conditional on members' approval and/or holding company members' approval (s.190);
- providing for an aggregation of the value of non-cash assets which form either part of an arrangement or a series of arrangements, when determining whether the relevant financial thresholds have been exceeded (s.190(5)).
- increasing the requisite de minimis threshold from £2,000 to £5,000 (s.191); and
- extending the exceptions to the requirement for members' approval to include:
  — companies in administration (s.193);
  — anything which a director is entitled to under his service contract or for loss of office (s.190(6)); and
  — the acquisition by the company of assets from a person in his character as a member (s.192(a)).

Loans and similar transactions The Act contains significant provisions regulating loans and other similar financial benefits (e.g. guarantees) given to directors by companies. Some of the provisions apply to all companies, whether private or **11–35** public. Others apply only to "relevant companies" (defined as public companies or companies in a group including a public company). Further distinctions are made between, on the one hand, money lending companies and banks and, on the other, companies not in the business of lending.

11–36 Under s.197 of the CA 2006 all companies are prohibited from making loans to their directors, or to directors of their holding companies, and from entering into guarantees or providing security in connection with a loan made by anyone to such a director. Shadow directors are treated in the same way as directors for the purpose of the prohibition (s.223 (1)).

Anti-avoidance provisions prohibit a company from doing indirectly what it is forbidden to do directly.

Other restrictions apply only to relevant companies. They are prohibited from making "quasi loans" to directors or connected persons. A quasi loan is a payment (or an agreement to make a payment) to one person on behalf of another, where the beneficiary is liable to reimburse the payer. Quasi loans therefore include the payment of a director's private debts by the company at his/her request.

Relevant companies are also prohibited from entering into credit transactions, e.g. a sale to a director (or connected person) on deferred payment terms.

11–37 There are a number of important exceptions. Some of these exceptions depend on the purpose for which the financial accommodation is made and many are conditional on the indebtedness of the director or connected person not exceeding a certain amount.

(1) The provisions do not apply where the aggregate amount lent to a director does not exceed £5,000.

(2) A company may provide funds to a director to meet expenses incurred for the purposes of the company or to enable him/her to perform the duties of his/her office. The approval of the shareholders in general meeting is required and if this is not obtained at or before the first annual general meeting after the loan is made, the funds must be repaid to the company within six months of that meeting. There is an upper limit of £10,000 in aggregate on the amount which can be lent under this exception.

(3) Companies whose ordinary business includes lending or giving guarantees may lend to their directors for any purpose provided that:

(a) the loan is made in the ordinary course of the company's business; and
(b) the loan is on normal commercial terms. A recognised bank may lend an unlimited amount to a director under this exception, but other companies may not lend more than £100,000.

Duties of directors

(4) A company may lend up to £100,000 to a director for the purchase or improvement of his home on preferential terms as long as the same facility is available to all the company's employees.

A director who receives a loan in breach of the above provisions is liable to pay the amounts borrowed in full, to account to the company for any gain he/she has made and to indemnify the company for any loss or damage which results from the transaction. Where a relevant company is involved, breach of the provisions also carries criminal penalties. **11–38**

Under ss.197–214 of the CA 2006, the prohibitions under the 1985 Act were replaced with a requirement for members' and (where relevant) holding company members' approval by ordinary resolution (unless the company's articles require different). The wider ranging requirements for approval for: **11–39**

- quasi loans, credit transactions or guarantee or security for them for the benefit of a director or a holding company director; and
- loans, quasi loans, credit transactions or guarantees or security for them for the benefit of any connected persons of a director or a holding company director will apply to public companies and their "associated companies" (s.256) i.e.:
    - any subsidiary of a public company;
    - any holding company of a public company; and
    - any of that holding company's subsidiaries.

There are a number of exemptions (in most cases wider than the existing ones), which for most smaller companies will capture the majority of relevant arrangements with directors, etc. For example, the exemptions cover: **11–40**

- loans and quasi loans in respect of any director and his connected persons of up to £10,000;
- credit transactions in respect of any director and his connected persons of up to £15,000;
- any type of arrangement to meet expenditure on company business up to a maximum of £50,000 in respect of each director and his connected persons;
- loans to fund directors' or holding company directors' defence costs for legal or regulatory proceedings etc—this extends to claims in relation to associated companies; and
- credit transactions in the ordinary course of the company's business.

The CA 2006 also permits subsequent affirmation of loans, quasi loans, credit transactions and related security entered into by the company in breach of such **11–41** provisions. However, in relation to substantial property transactions, such affirmation does not absolve the directors from liability in relation to the breach (who may be liable to account for any gain made and indemnify the company for any loss or damage resulting from the transaction) (see ss.213 and 214 of the CA 2006).

11–42 *Outside involvement*   A director is not prohibited from having outside interests. A non-executive director may accept a directorship in a competing company or even compete on his/her own account, although he/she could not, of course, use the company's property or trade secrets. A director who performed services for the company over and above those stemming simply from his/her position on the board might, however, be under an express or implied duty not to compete.

11–43 *Compensation for loss of office*   Under s.312 of CA 1985, any compensation payable to a director for loss of office must be approved by the company in general meeting although this does not include a bona fide payment by way of damages for breach of contract or a pension in respect of past services (s.316(3)of the 1985 Act).

11–44 Sections 215–222 of CA 2006 deal with payments for loss of office. The new provisions are simpler but have the potential to be equally as restrictive as the provisions under the 1985 Act. The changes include:

- a definition of payment for loss of office including loss of employment and retirement payments;
- the associated changes of the widening of the definition of connected persons; and
- new exemptions for payments in discharge of a existing legal obligation; damages for breach of any legal obligation and settlement/compromise in relation to claims regarding employment and small payments up to £200. This does allow some scope for payments beyond breach of contract which are not currently allowed without members' approval. An example would be a genuine assessment of unfair dismissal damages.

Duties of skill and care

11–45 In contrast with the extensive duties of good faith, which impose a largely negative obligation to do nothing which conflicts with the director's duty to the company, a director has only a limited duty to do anything on the positive side to promote the welfare of the company.

11–46 Like the other duties of directors, the duty is owed to the company, which can sue the director for damages if it suffers any loss as a result of a breach. As is hardly surprising, there are scarcely any recent decisions where a director has been held liable for a breach of this duty.

Duties of directors

In the absence of a service contract obliging him/her to do so, a director is not bound to give continuous attention to the affairs of his company. This is typical for non-executive directors. The duties are of an intermittent nature to be performed at periodic board meetings and meetings of any committee of the board which he/she is on. A director is not bound to attend all such meetings although he/she ought to whenever he/she reasonably can. Again, a greater duty can be imposed by express or implied agreement between the director and the company, as would probably be the case with an executive director.

A director may delegate those of his/her duties normally carried out by employ- **11–47** ees or agents of the company provided he/she ensures that the relevant person is suitably qualified, but in the absence of authority from the company the directors must act collectively as a board and have no general right to delegate their powers. However, the articles usually allow the directors to delegate their powers to a managing or other executive director or to a committee of the directors.

The default of one director does not necessarily impose liability on the others. A director is not generally liable for the acts of other directors and is under no duty to supervise their conduct. However, a director who knows of the conduct in question and who has participated in it to some degree (even if only slightly) or a director who has failed to supervise or enquire when there are suspicious circumstances, may be liable to the company.

The CA 2006 codifies the duty of care and skill in s.174. The statutory duty **11–48** includes both subjective and objective elements (in contrast to the existing common law test which is subjective only). Under the CA 2006, a director must exercise the same standard of care, skill and diligence as would be exercised by a reasonably diligent person with:

- the general knowledge, skill and experience that may reasonably be expected of a person carrying out the same functions as that director; and
- the general knowledge, skill and experience that the director actually has.

Therefore, the more qualified or experienced the director, the greater the statutory standard required.

Miscellaneous statutory duties

A number of statutory duties exist which do not fit easily into the categories either **11–49** of good faith or skill and care.

Fraudulent trading, wrongful trading and misfeasance Of the various miscellaneous statutory duties, the most significant are the provisions relating to fraudulent trading, wrongful trading and misfeasance. These provide creditors with virtually their only practical hope of fixing directors with liability for the debts of the company.

Fraudulent trading occurs when, in the course of winding a company up, it is shown that the business has been carried on with intent to defraud creditors or for any fraudulent purpose (Insolvency Act 1986, s.213). Fraud is not easy to prove. The full criminal standard of proof is required, which largely explains why the section has been used relatively rarely and the offence of "wrongful trading" was introduced. If fraudulent trading is proved, any persons who were knowingly party to the fraud can be made personally liable for any of the debts or liabilities of the company, without limit on their liability. Any person guilty of fraudulent trading also commits a criminal offence punishable by up to seven years' imprisonment or a fine of unlimited amount or both. The criminal penalties apply whether or not the company has been or is being wound up.

11–50 The Insolvency Act introduces a new concept into the law as it affects directors, that of "wrongful trading". The concept of wrongful trading removes the need to prove fraud, is a civil action and therefore requires a lower burden of proof based on a balance of probabilities. Any director who concludes or ought to conclude that there is no "reasonable prospect" of the company avoiding insolvent liquidation must take every step with a view to minimising the potential loss to creditors; and in relation to this obligation the director is deemed to have the general knowledge, skill and experience reasonably expected of a person carrying out these functions as well as the knowledge he/she actually has. The burden on a finance director will be considerable and greater than that on fellow directors in view of the knowledge, skill and experience which he/she can be expected to have or actually has. To avoid problems, good management information and accounts must be available to enable a director to make a proper assessment of the company's liabilities; to encourage the court to make any assessment of the facts on the basis of that record; and to demonstrate diligence. A director should ensure that accounts are filed on time; that potentially voidable transactions are carefully monitored; that regular board meetings are held; and that detailed board minutes are made. A director must monitor actual, contingent and prospective liabilities and asset values (particularly intergroup guarantees, loans and bank security arrangements) so that he/she has accurate and up-to-date financial information. Immediately a director reaches the view that there is a reasonable prospect of potentially insolvent liquidation, he/she should convene a board meeting to consider the situation and resolve to seek independent advice and assistance. If nothing else, this will assist towards a defence that he/she took every step to minimise losses.

It is unlikely that a director can escape liability to resigning, and if a director is found liable he/she may be ordered "to make such contribution to the company's assets as the court thinks proper"; he/she may also be disqualified as "unfit". Instead a director should, when the alarm bells first ring, persuade colleagues to seek independent advice on a unanimous basis. A director cannot wind up a company on his/her own but should make his/her opinion clear to fellow directors and have minuted his assessment of the company's situation. Only then should he/she resign.

The introduction of an additional test of insolvency to the existing "inability to pay debts" test has further increased the burden on directors. Since a company is now deemed to be insolvent if the value of its assets is less than the amount of its liabilities including contingent and prospective liabilities, a director will be on notice that the company cannot avoid insolvent liquidation in some circumstances when this would not otherwise have been the case. When considering the financial position of a company and whether there is no reasonable prospect of it avoiding insolvent liquidations, a director must have regard to the position of the company itself and not that of its group as a whole. **11–51**

Proceedings for misfeasance (wrongful exercise of authority) can be brought against any director, manager or officer of a company in liquidation if he/she has misapplied, retained or become accountable for, any property of the company, or has been guilty of any misfeasance or breach of trust in relation to the company. "Misfeasance" does not necessarily involve moral blame but is meant to cover any misapplication or wrongful retention of the company's property. A director who is in breach of this duty must repay money misapplied or pay compensation.

Allotment of securities

Section 549 of CA 2006 imposes a limitation on the power of the directors to allot "relevant securities". These include shares, rights to subscribe for shares and rights to convert any security into shares. Subscribers' shares and shares allotted in pursuance of an employees' share scheme are excluded. The directors may not allot relevant securities unless they have been authorised by the company in general meeting or by its articles. The articles of a company which is a wholly-owned subsidiary of a holding company will normally give directors this authority. The section requires certain matters to be specified in the authority, including the date when it expires, which must not be more than five years from the time when it is granted (unless, in the case of a private company, an elective resolution has been passed applying s.549 of the Act, in which event the authority may be for a longer, or even an indefinite, period). There are criminal penalties for breaching the section and a director who knowingly and willingly contravenes this section is liable to a fine. Nothing in the section affects the validity of any allotment. **11–52**

The CA 2006 contains similar restrictions on the ability of directors to allot shares or grant rights to subscribe for shares with one material relaxation. For companies that only have one class of shares, the directors will have the ability to allot or grant rights to subscribe for shares without shareholders' approval unless the articles provide otherwise.

Directors and Employees

Miscellaneous offences

11–53 Legislation has created numerous opportunities for directors to commit criminal offences in the course of the administration of a company. Some of these offences are relatively trivial, but the penalties which the courts can impose range from fairly small fines following summary conviction (in a Magistrates' Court) to imprisonment and unlimited fines on conviction and indictment (in a Crown Court with a jury). The usual mechanism the Act employs is to impose a duty, such as the need to file an annual return, and back it up with the sanction that "the company and every officer of the company who is in default shall be liable to a default fine". Failure to file an annual return is however a matter which the Insolvency Act provides that the court should take into account in assessing whether a director is "unfit to be concerned in the management of a company".

Some of the more serious offences, mostly involving fraud or dishonesty, carry severe penalties. For example, a director who publishes a written statement which he/she knows is misleading, false or deceptive, with intent to deceive the company's members or creditors about its affairs, may be sentenced to a lengthy term of imprisonment.

11.2.4 Directors' responsibility for the accounts

11–54 Companies are required to keep proper accounting records. These are records which are sufficient to explain their current transactions and financial position and to enable the directors to prepare an annual profit and loss account and balance sheet to be laid before their shareholders (s.386 of the CA 2006).

The directors of every company are under an obligation to prepare all accounts. Additionally, under s.393 of the CA 2006, directors must not approve the annual accounts of the company unless they are satisfied that they give a true and fair view of the assets, liabilities, financial position and profit or loss of the company (or in the case of group accounts, of the undertakings included in the consolidation). Accordingly, every director should:

- consider the accounts in draft;
- seek explanations of any matters not clear to him/her;
- draw matters which (whether from direct knowledge or otherwise) he/she considers are not being satisfactorily dealt with to the attention of:
  — the Audit Committee (every audit committee should produce minutes which should be circulated to every director; if they are not circulated, he/she should ask to see them);

Duties of directors

— the auditors; and
— the full board (whom he/she could formally request should consult the company's solicitors and/or relevant regulators).

A director may in the last resort have to consult his/her own solicitors (in practice, it will probably be at his/her own expense). **11–55**

If a director is not satisfied after he/she has received explanations and/or advice, his/her sanctions are:

- to have his/her objections formally minuted and to warn what action he/she will take;
- to vote against adoption of the accounts;
- almost certainly in that event, to resign as a director (but this may have adverse consequences for his/her employment, rights under service agreement, shares, etc, unless he/she can successfully argue that he/she has been constructively dismissed) and (subject to this not thereby breaching any duty of confidentiality) to state publicly the reasons for his/her resignation;
- if the accounts have been sent out under s.423 of the CA 2006 or if the accounts have been laid before the shareholders at a general meeting or delivered to the registrar of companies, to consider notifying the DTI with a view to the Secretary of State exercising his/her rights under ss.455 and 456 of the CA 2006. Ultimately this can lead to an application to the court for a declaration that the accounts do not comply with the requirements of the legislation and for an order requiring the directors to prepare revised accounts.

False or misleading statements to auditors

The auditor may require any director of the company to provide it with such information or explanations as it thinks necessary for the performance of its duties as auditors. It is an offence not to comply with any request without delay. Additionally, a director who knowingly or recklessly makes a statement to the auditor that conveys or purports to convey any information or explanations required by the auditor which is misleading, false or deceptive in any material particular. **11–56**

Publication of accounts

The company and every officer who is in default is liable to a fine if the company fails to comply with the provisions concerning the publication of the **11–57** accounts and reports (ss.425(1) and (2) of the CA 2006). There is a similar offence concerning failure to furnish copies on demand (ss.431 and 432 of the CA 2006).

If any of the requirements of ss.434 to 436 of the CA 2006 (requirement for published statutory accounts to be accompanied by auditors' report, requirement to publish statutory group accounts, requirements in relation to the publication of non-statutory accounts) are not complied with, the company and every officer of it who is in default is liable to a fine.

Failure to lay and deliver accounts and reports within the period permitted renders every person who was a director of the company immediately before the end of that period liable to a fine, and, for continued contravention, to a daily default fine. It is a defence for any such person to prove that he/she took all reasonable steps for securing that those requirements would be complied with before the end of that period. There is a similar offence in relation to failure to deliver accounts and reports to the registrar.

Disqualification

11–58 Persistent default in relation to the provision of the companies' legislation requiring the filing of accounts or other documents at Companies House may lead to disqualification as a director for up to five years (Company Directors Disqualification Act 1986, s.3).

Dishonesty or fraud

11–59 Section 17 of the Theft Act 1968 provides that where a person dishonestly, with a view to gain for him/herself or another or with intent to cause loss to another, destroys, defaces, conceals or falsifies any account, record or document made for accounting purposes or, if, in furnishing information for any purpose, produces or makes use of any account, record or document made for accounting purposes which he/she knows to be misleading, false or deceptive in a material particular, he/she is liable to imprisonment.

Liability for dishonest statements in writing by officers of companies is imposed by the Theft Act 1968, s.19.

Criminal liability may also arise where it appears that any business of the company has been carried on with intent to defraud creditors of the company.

11.2.5 Third-party claims

Liability in negligence

Following such cases as *Caparo Industries Plc v Dickman* [1990] 2 W.L.R. 358 and **11–60** *Al-Nakib Investments (Jersey) Ltd v Longcroft* [1990] 1 W.L.R. 1390 (Ch D), the duty of care owed by a director would seem to be owed only to a very limited number of persons. In *Caparo*, accountants were held only to owe a duty of care where a "special relationship" could be found to exist. Such a relationship would, in particular, exist where the accountant was or ought to have been aware that his/her advice and/or the accounts would be made available to and relied upon by a particular person for a particular transaction. In *Al-Nakib*, inaccuracies in a prospectus circulated to shareholders in connection with a rights issue encouraged shareholders and others to enter into various market transactions. The defendant directors were able to obtain the striking out of claims relating to the market transactions since the prospectus had been addressed to the first plaintiff for a particular purpose (the rights issue); no duty of care was found to be owed to anyone except in relation to such losses as flowed from the rights issue. By analogy with *Caparo* and as supported by *Al-Nakib* there is no reason to suppose that a director's duty of care is owed to any wider group of persons. Further confirmation of this position is *Morgan Crucible Co v Hill Samuel & Co Ltd* [1991] B.C.L.C. 178. It was held in the Court of Appeal that a takeover bidder can bring an action for negligence against directors, advisors and accountants. Leave was granted to Morgan Crucible to amend its statement of claim. The Court of Appeal ruling laid down that Morgan Crucible would not be bound to fail in establishing a duty of care owed by the defendants. The feature distinguishing the *Morgan Crucible* claim from *Caparo* was that in *Caparo*, the relevant statements by the auditors had not been given for the purpose for which the plaintiff had relied on them. In *Morgan Crucible* it was arguable that the plaintiff would rely on the statement with a view to deciding to make an increased bid and it was indeed intended that they should rely on them.

Accordingly, leave to amend was given. However, the case was decided only on **11–61** whether a point was arguable and its value as a precedent is limited.

On the basis of the above decisions, unless the director was aware that the accounts in question were being made available to and relied on by a particular group or a particular person for a particular transaction, there is no reason to suppose that a director's duty of care is owed to any wider group of persons.

Deceit

A person is liable in the tort of deceit if he/she makes a false statement (i.e. a **11–62** statement which he/she does not believe to be true) with the intention that it shall be acted upon and it is acted upon. (It should be noted that to avoid liability under this heading the maker of the statement must believe it to be true. If he/she is uncertain whether the statement is true or indifferent as to its truth he/she may be liable in the tort of deceit.)

Liability in deceit does not depend on proof of a duty of care. However, the extent of those to whom liability exists has never been fully worked out. It seems likely that the defendant would only be liable to those whom he/she intended to deceive. If he/she intended to deceive all the world, there could, presumably, be liability to every plaintiff who suffered loss in consequence of the deceit.

11.2.6 Liability for contracts and wrongs of the company

11–63 The general principle of limited liability means that directors are not liable for the debts of the company, or for any of its other acts or omissions. The company is regarded as a legal person in its own right separate from its shareholders and directors. This rule is subject to exceptions, and in certain circumstances a director may be personally liable to third parties.

Contracts

11–64 Where a director enters into a contract on behalf of his company with proper authority to do so, he/she will not be liable to the other party since he/she is merely acting as the company's agent. However directors have been held liable on contracts by which they intended to bind the company and not themselves, and the reason for the director's personal liability has been that on the facts they were held to have contracted personally.

The majority of cases where a director may be liable to the third party arise from circumstances where he/she had no actual authority to make the contract. However, he/she may make himself liable even where he/she does have actual authority, e.g. if he/she expressly guarantees the company's performance or if he/she does not contract in the company's name or on its behalf, and is therefore taken as contracting personally, when the ordinary principles of agency will apply. Section 82 of CA 2006 provides that a director who signs or authorises any cheque, bill of exchange or order for money or goods which does not correctly state the name of the company will be personally liable if the company does not pay (and he/she will also commit a criminal offence).

11–65 Where a director has exceeded his/her actual authority he/she may be liable to the third party for what is known as "breach of warranty of authority". This liability is based on the assumption that the director has warranted to the third party that he/she

Duties of directors

has authority to enter into the contract. If he/she had no such authority because the contract was beyond the powers of either himself, or the board, or the company itself, the company may be able to repudiate the contract and the director will be liable to the third party personally. The measure of damages will be the value which the contract would have had if it had been binding on the company.

In certain circumstances, the company will be bound even though the director has exceeded his/her authority. If this is the case he/she will not be liable to the third party him/herself, but may be liable to the company unless it ratifies his/her breach of duty in having exceeded his/her authority. (Such ratification is not possible where the contract was beyond the powers of the company itself.) The circumstances in which a company will be bound by a contract made by a director acting outside the scope of his/her actual authority are complex. The company will be bound if the director was acting within the scope of his/her "usual" or "apparent" authority. A managing director will have usual authority to make contracts on behalf of the company, but any other director acting on his/her own will not. (Commercial practice is at variance with the law here. An individual director will often be assumed to have power to contract on behalf of the company even if he/she is not a managing director.) An individual director may, however, be "held out" by the company as having authority, for example if the board leads third parties to believe a director has the powers of a managing director. He/she will then have apparent authority to enter into the contract and the company will be bound. **11–66**

Under s.40 of the CA 2006, directors' powers are deemed to be free of any limitation under the memorandum or articles of association which a third party is under no obligation to inspect. The section only applies to the exercise of the "power of the board of directors" (which clearly applies to board decisions but not necessarily to the actions of individual directors), but if a director enters into a contract which has been approved by the board but which is beyond the authority of the directors (e.g. above a borrowing limit in the articles) or beyond the powers of the company itself (e.g. in connection with a business which the company currently has no power to carry on under its memorandum of association), the company will nevertheless be bound by the contract unless the third party actually knew that the director was acting outside the scope of his/her authority or was otherwise not acting in good faith. This principle is restated in s.39 of the CA 2006, but will apply to the exercise of "powers of the directors" (as opposed to "power of the board"). **11–67**

Furthermore if the articles empower its board to enter into certain transactions only if specified conditions are fulfilled, or a specified procedure is followed, a third party who enters into such a transaction with the board of directors is not concerned to ensure that the condition has been fulfilled, and he can enforce the transaction against the company unless he/she knows or suspects that they have not (*Royal British Bank v Turquand* (1856) 6 El. & Bl. 327).

It is also worth noting that where a person enters into a contract on behalf of a company which has not yet been incorporated he/she will be personally liable. Finally a person who is involved in the management of a company while subject to a disqualification order or an undischarged bankrupt is "personally responsible" for all debts and liabilities incurred by the company while he/she is also involved; and any person who, while involved in the management of a company, acts or is willing to act on instructions which he/she knows to be given by such a person is liable for the debts and liabilities incurred by the company while he/she is so acting or willing to act.

Torts

11–68 Torts are civil wrongs, e.g. negligence, nuisance and defamation. The general principle of separate corporate identity means that a director is not liable personally for wrongs done by the company merely because the wrongful act could only have been done on his/her authority. But if it can be proved that he/she was actively involved in committing the wrongful act he/she will be jointly liable with the company.

11.2.7 Relief from liability

11–69 A director who is guilty of a breach of duty may still be relieved of liability in certain circumstances.

Ratification

11–70 A director may be relieved from liability for breach of duty if the matter is fully disclosed to the shareholders and approved either by an ordinary resolution at a general meeting or by their unanimous approval (whether at a meeting or not). The CA 2006 makes it clear that such ratification must not be obtained with the votes of the director and any member "connected" (as defined in ss.252–256) to him/her. Certain breaches of duty cannot be ratified. These are:

- where the director has been guilty of fraud or dishonesty;
- where the act is outside the powers of the company itself or is illegal;
- where the articles require a special procedure to be followed which has not been;
- where the personal rights of members have been infringed (e.g. an improper refusal to register a transfer of a share); or
- where the breach of duty involves the majority of the shareholders depriving the company of money, property or business opportunities at the expense of the minority.

Duties of directors

By the articles

It is common to include in articles a limited form of indemnity. A director cannot be completely protected under the articles, any article (or contract) is void if it exempts or indemnifies any director for liability for negligence, default, breach of duty or breach of trust. The section does, however, allow the company to indemnify a director against costs incurred in either successfully defending himself or obtaining relief from the court. Regulation 118 in Table A gives an indemnity in these terms. **11–71**

Relief by the court

Even if a director has been found in breach of duty or otherwise in default, the court has a discretionary power under s.1157 of CA 2006 to relieve him/her from personal liability if it decides that he/she has acted honestly and reasonably and ought fairly to be excused. Such relief can be given completely or partially but will only be given if "having regard to all the circumstances of the case he ought fairly to be excused". **11–72**

Limitation periods

Under the Limitation Acts an action cannot be brought against a director for breach of duty after six years. This does not apply if the director has been fraudulent or where the director is holding the company's property. **11–73**

11.2.8 Publicity and disclosure

A number of provisions enable the public to find out who the directors of a company are and require directors to disclose certain information. **11–74**

Register of directors

Every company must keep a register of directors (ss.162 and 167 in the CA 2006). The register must specify for each director: full names, any former names, usual residential address, nationality, business occupation, and details of any other UK directorships he/she holds. If the company is a public company or a subsidiary of a public company date of birth must also be given. The Act provides that any directorship held during the previous five years will need to be disclosed (except directorships of dormant companies). Directorships of companies in the same group do not need to be disclosed. The register must be kept at the registered **11–75** office of the company and be open to inspection during business hours to members of the company free of charge. Details of the particulars contained in the register must be filed at Companies House. Any changes among the directors or their particulars must be notified to the Registrar within 14 days. These provisions also apply to the company secretary. The company's file held at Companies House can be inspected by any member of the public at the Companies Registration Offices in London or Cardiff or copies obtained from Companies House online on payment of a fee.

Service contracts

11–76 Copies of directors' service contracts or, if a director's service contract has not been reduced to writing, a memorandum of its terms, must be kept at the registered office, or at some other place authorised by the CA 2006 of which notice has been given to Companies House. Under the CA 2006 these will also have to be kept for a period of 12 months after expiry. Documents to be kept under these provisions are open to inspection by any member of the company. Under the CA 2006, any member may request a copy of a service agreement on payment of a fee.

Business communications

11–77 (Other than in the text or as a signatory) no director's name should be stated on any business communications (including letters, email, etc) unless the names of all the directors are shown.

Interests in shares

11–78 Historically, directors were required to disclose their interests in the company's shares and debentures and the company to maintain registers of such interests.

Salaries

11–79 Companies must make disclosures concerning directors' pay, bonuses and benefits. Section 409 of the CA 2006 requires the aggregate amount of these to be shown in the company's accounts, as well as the aggregate amount of pensions and payments for loss of office made to directors or past directors. The CA 2006 also requires the accounts to show the salary of the chairman of the board and the number of directors in certain "income brackets" set out in the Act. Similar reporting obligations on directors' remuneration and benefits are contained in the CA 2006.

Duties of directors

Material interests

A director's duty to disclose interests in contracts has been mentioned above. Additional provisions in the CA 2006 require disclosure in the company's accounts of transactions in which a director is interested. Transactions which must be disclosed fall into two categories: **11–80**

- a loan or similar transactions or an agreement to enter into such a transaction must be disclosed;
- any other transaction or arrangement with the company (or a subsidiary) in which the director had a direct or indirect material interest; whether an interest is material or not is a matter for the majority of the board (excluding the director concerned) to decide.

The disclosure requirements apply to anyone who was a director of the company at any time during the relevant financial year (i.e. whether or not he/she was a director at the time of the transaction) or was a director of its holding company or was connected with such a director. There are exemptions for minor transactions.

11.2.9 Meetings

The proper forum for the directors to take their decisions is at a board meeting. As mentioned above, directors must act collectively and normally only a managing director will have authority to act on his/her own. The rules for the conduct of board meetings depend first on the articles. Subject to what these say, the directors are, in general, free to meet and regulate their meetings as they think fit. In essence directors' meetings are informal and operate by discussion rather than by debate of formal motions and amendments. The conduct of the meetings is in the hands of the chairman and is, therefore, to some extent a function of his/her individual competence and style. He/she must not stifle discussions, but equally he/she is entitled to direct them and, in the final analysis to curtail them. **11–81**

Notice

Sometimes the articles provide for formal notice of board meetings. In a venture capital transaction the investment agreement may provide for a fixed number of meetings per year, and the notice to be given. If they do not, reasonable notice must be given. What is reasonable notice depends on the circumstances; five minutes may be sufficient if there is nothing to prevent the directors attending. Notice can be oral or written and need only specify the time and place of the meeting and not what is to be discussed, although it is usual to circulate an agenda beforehand together with any accounts or written reports which need **11–82** prior study. A director who wishes to object that the notice that has been given is too short must do so within a reasonable time. In the absence of any provision to the contrary in the articles, any director can call a board meeting and the secretary must call a meeting if requested by one of the directors. Under reg.88 of Table A no notice of a board meeting has to be given to a director who is absent from the UK. This regulation is frequently excluded in articles of a UK company with directors resident overseas. Whatever may be the minimum requirement of the articles for notice, it is clearly desirable, in the case of any substantive item of business, that papers be circulated sufficiently in advance to enable the directors to attend the meeting able to make a reasonable contribution. Directors may, if the articles permit, conduct business by written resolution and/or hold a meeting by telephone.

Quorum

11–83 The quorum is usually specified in the articles. If these incorporate 1985 Table A, the quorum will be two, but it is possible for the articles of a private company to provide for a quorum of one. If the articles do not specify a quorum, the majority of the directors will constitute a quorum, unless the company has established some other practice. A venture capital investor will often require that its director will be part of the quorum. However in view of the extensive restrictions contained in the investment agreement and articles preventing any significant actions being taken without the consent of the venture capitalist or its representative this should not be necessary.

It is sometimes necessary to review whether a quorum is present for the discussion of a particular item of business. If, for instance, a director is interested in a contract to be made by the company, he/she will be prevented from voting on that contract unless the articles provide otherwise. A decision taken by the board when a quorum is not present is invalid, although it can be ratified by a later meeting. If the number of directors of the company falls below the number needed to form a quorum, the articles commonly provide for the directors to meet for the purposes of increasing their number or summoning a general meeting of the shareholders, but not for any other purpose.

Procedure

11–84 The articles normally provide that the directors may elect a chairman and decide the period for which he/she is to hold office. In the absence of the chairman the directors will elect one of their number to take the chair. In most boards, matters are discussed by the directors until they are agreed, when the passing of a resolution becomes a mere formality. If agreement cannot be reached, the chairman must either put the matter to the vote or defer it until the next meeting. Unless the articles provide otherwise, each director is entitled to one vote and a resolution is only passed if a majority of votes are cast in its favour. The chairman of the meeting can vote and the articles will often give him/her a second (casting) vote if the other directors are split equally.

Alternates

Provided that the articles so permit, a director may appoint an alternate director **11–85** (akin to a proxy) to represent him at board meetings and to vote on his/her behalf. For example, reg.65 of 1985 Table A permits a director to appoint another director or any persons approved by resolution of the directors to be his/her alternate. Such an alternate is entitled to receive notice of all board meetings and to attend and vote at those at which his/her appointer is not present and under reg.66 "generally to perform all functions of his appointer as a director in his absence" (so, e.g. he/she would be entitled to attest the affixing of the company seal).

Written resolutions

The articles often provide that a resolution in writing signed by all the directors **11–86** is as effective as a decision taken at a board meeting. Regulation 83 of 1985 Table A contains such a provision.

Minutes

The CA 2006 requires every company to keep minutes of all general meetings **11–87** and directors' meetings in books kept for that purpose under s.248. Failure to comply with this provision is a criminal offence. Minutes will be proof of what was done at a meeting, in the absence of evidence to the contrary.

11.2.10 Disqualification

The courts

The courts have certain powers to disqualify a person from being a director or **11–88** from taking part in the management of a company. A disqualification order can be made, inter alia, in the following circumstances:

- If a person is convicted of an indictable offence connected with forming, managing or winding up a company, or with the receivership or management of its property. An indictable offence is a crime which is classified as being sufficiently serious to be triable before a jury in the Crown Court;

Directors and Employees

- Where a person has persistently failed to comply with requirements under the CA 2006 to file documents at Companies House. A person who is convicted three times in five years of failing to comply with such a requirement will be treated as being persistently in default;

- If in the course of winding up the company it appears that a person has been guilty of fraudulent trading or has otherwise been guilty of fraud or breach of duty;

- Where his conduct makes him "unfit to be concerned in the management of a company". The Insolvency Act specifies a number of matters which should be taken into account in assessing such unfitness. These include any breach of duty in relation to the company, the extent of the directors' responsibility for the causes of the insolvency, for any transaction at an undervalue or any voidable preference (which is presumed in any dealings that the company has with connected persons). A director who is deemed to be unfit shall be disqualified for a period of not less than two years.

A person against whom a disqualification order has been made is prohibited from being a director or liquidator of a company or a receiver or manager of company property, or from in any way being concerned or taking part in the promotion, formation or management of a company (whether directly or indirectly) without the court's consent. A person who contravenes a disqualification order can be sentenced to up to two years' imprisonment.

The articles

11–89 The articles usually provide that a director will cease to hold office in certain events such as his/her becoming bankrupt. The grounds most frequently found are filing to obtain or keep qualification shares (where a director is required to hold shares in his/her company), becoming of unsound mind, being absent from board meetings without permission for more than six months, and resigning. Resignation once given cannot be withdrawn, even if it has not been accepted, and it has been held that where a director gives verbal notice which is accepted at a board meeting he will have validly resigned even if the articles state that written notice must be given.

The law

11–90 Certain individuals are automatically prevented from acting as directors. Section 11 of the Company Directors Disqualification Act 1986 prohibits an undischarged bankrupt from acting as a director or liquidator of a company or from otherwise taking part in the formation or management of a company without the court's consent. Contravention is punishable by up to two years' imprisonment. There are no restrictions on the appointment of foreigners as directors, although a foreign director who intends to come to the UK to work must comply with the immigration rules.

11.2.11 Directors' and officers' liability insurance

Companies have the ability to effect and maintain directors' and officers' liability insurance for the benefit of a director or a director of an associated company in relation to liability attaching to a director in connection with any negligence, default breach of duty or breach of trust by him in relation to the company. **11–91**

Such policies generally provide protection against two types of liability:

- the liabilities of directors for acts committed in their capacity as directors of the company (known as "side A cover"); and
- the liabilities of the company in relation to claims made by directors under indemnities lawfully given by the company to directors (known as "side B cover").

The policies are usually drawn on a "claims-made" basis, so the insurer which is obliged to cover a relevant claim is the one when the claim is first made and not the one "on risk" when the original wrongful act was committed.

Whilst such policies are beneficial to directors, it is important to recognise their limitations. For example: **11–92**

- the premiums can be expensive, so there is always a balance to be drawn between cost of cover and risk;
- the policy will be subject to a financial cap which is available to cover all claims made under the policy in a specified period. The level of cover may prove to be insufficient and if there are claims, the extent of the cover then available is eroded leaving reduced funds for subsequent claims;
- polices will have a number of exclusions—for example, regulatory or criminal fines; bodily injury and property damage; fraudulent, dishonest and criminal acts; acts taken by directors in their personal capacities or in their capacities as shareholders; claims brought by one director against another; claims by the company against a director; the exclusions of certain geographical areas (e.g. the highly litigious United States of America).

Directors and Employees

11.3 Key points

11–93
- The offices of managing director and chairman are not recognised by statute but determined by the board or the company's articles of association.

- Currently directors' duties can be divided into two categories: duties of honesty and good faith and the duties of care and skill. Seven duties are codified under the Companies Act 2006.

- Director's duties are owed to the company, which means to the present and future shareholders and not to an individual shareholder.

- An officer of the company is liable to imprisonment or a fine if he/she misleads the auditors (whether in writing or orally) (s.463 Companies Act 2006).

- Consider taking out a comprehensive insurance policy indemnifying directors in respect of breach of trust, neglect, error, misleading statements, etc.

- It is no longer usual for investors to accept long term service agreements. Much more common is a 12-month rolling term or a fixed term of two years followed by a 12-month rolling term.

- Beware of clauses appearing in the service agreement that allow for termination as a result of a breach of the terms of the investment agreement or another agreement.

- Do not attempt to be too aggressive when drafting restrictive covenants. Better to have an enforceable limited protection than an unenforceable but extensive covenant.

- Most employee share schemes are tax-driven. Take tax advice.

11.4 Service agreements

11–94 The service agreements of the executive directors set out the terms of the directors' personal employment relationship with the company. In a private equity situation they form an extremely important part of the investment package and tend to be negotiated actively between the management and the private equity house directly even though it is the individuals concerned who will be entering into the service agreement with the company. The most contentious areas are always the same and revolve around the financial package, the directors' commitment to the company and certain specific protections for the company, such as the notice period, the protection of confidential information and the imposition of post termination restrictive covenants.

Service agreements

11–95 The service agreements in practice protect both parties. They provide the executives with a feeling of security of employment and, in the event that employment is terminated, financial compensation. This is particularly important where the investors are to obtain a majority shareholding in the company and would have the ability to remove a director under s.168 of the CA 2006. They also provide the executives with an overall package covering salary and other benefits. This may provide executives with a dilemma. In the short term they would obviously like as large a salary as possible, and if they have had to borrow money to invest in a company they will not wish their standard of living to be reduced and would therefore seek to improve their present financial package in order to account for any interest payments at the very least. However, a venture capitalist will remind them that their salary adds to the overall costs of the investment and as a result is a deduction from profit. The ratchet mechanism is geared to the value of the company on exit, and therefore if the executives are too greedy in the short term then they may well regret it in the long term.

In addition the service agreements protect the venture capitalist. The success of the company is determined very much by the quality and commitment of the management, and therefore the venture capitalist will seek to ensure that the management are fully committed and are not able to walk away from the company, without seriously considering a number of possible penalties that will be triggered.

Duration of the employment

11–96 In general venture capitalists are no longer willing to provide long notice periods to managers. Agreements containing a 12-month rolling notice period or a fixed period of two years (followed by a 12-month notice period) as a maximum are much more common.

If longer periods are provided for, then the draftsman must bear in mind ss.188–189 and 227–230 of the CA 2006. In particular, shareholder approval will be required for directors' service agreements with a guaranteed term of more than two years. It should also be considered whether a fixed term (as opposed to a notice period) is in the company's best commercial interests. Unless it is, it may be voidable at the instance of the company.

A typical clause would be as follows:

> The employment shall commence on [ ] and, subject to cl.[ ] (this cross reference is to the clause dealing with summary dismissal), shall continue for a period of [ ] years until 20[ ] and thereafter unless or until terminated by either party giving to the other not less than [ ] months' notice in writing to expire on 20[ ] or at any time thereafter.

11–97 Consideration should also be given, where a rolling notice period is required, to whether a shorter period of notice should be given either by the executive or by the company. However, the existence of a wide disparity between notice periods is unusual.

Termination

11–98 The agreement is likely to have the normal clauses allowing the company to terminate the contract by summary notice in the event that the executive commits a serious offence as set out in those clauses. In a service agreement used in a private equity investment, the investor may also try to include a clause which makes it a matter for summary dismissal where the executive is responsible for a material breach of the investment agreement or of the warranties contained in that agreement. Examples of such a clause would be:

> The company shall have the right to terminate this agreement with immediate effect by summary notice at any time in the event of the executive committing a material breach [of the investment agreement] [cl.D of the investment agreement] OR
>
> The company shall have the right to terminate this agreement with immediate effect by summary notice at any time in the event of the executive committing a material breach of the warranties set out in cl.[ ] and Sch.[ ] of the investment agreement, (where such material breach includes any breach of which the executive was aware at the date of completion of the investment agreement but the executive wilfully failed to disclose the facts and circumstances surrounding or relating to such breach) and the executive shall have no claim against the company in respect of the termination of his employment by the company pursuant to this clause.

11–99 The latter clause is an aggressive position and is generally included to focus the mind of the executive when considering the warranties or in fulfilling his/her duties under the investment agreement. It rubs salt in the wound of an investor if the company has to pay out on a large warranty claim caused by the executive followed by a large compensation claim to remove the executive. Nevertheless, it is often resisted by executives. On a similar theme, some investors seek to include, as a matter for summary dismissal, or at least a reduced notice period, a failure to achieve the projections contained in the business plan or to come within X per cent of their achievement. Again this would normally be resisted by directors.

Garden leave

11–100 This type of provision in a service agreement provides the employer with a way of restraining a director from competing with it after the director has ceased to be actively involved in the business. Where the director informs the employer of his/her wish to leave or join a competitor, the employer may hold the director to the remainder of his/her fixed term (or notice period) and keep him/her "in the garden" (i.e. not provide work and require him/her not to attend work) provided that the employer continues to pay his/her salary and to provide his/her contractual benefits. This is the most effective way of protecting customer connections and confidential information which may become redundant or, at least, less valuable by the time the director joins his/her future employer.

Garden leave is difficult, if not impossible, to enforce without an express contractual right. An example of a garden leave clause is as follows:

> Any time during any period of notice of termination (whether given by the company or the executive) or the balance of any fixed term the company shall be under no obligation for a period not exceeding [six months] to assign any duties to the executive and shall be entitled to exclude him/her from its premises and prohibit contact with the company's customers, suppliers and employees, provided that this shall not affect the executive's entitlement to receive his/her normal salary and other contractual benefits. The executive shall not commence any employment or engagement with any third party during such period and the executive's express and implied obligations under this agreement shall continue as modified by this clause, including but not limited to the implied duty of good faith and fidelity.

The maximum period of garden leave should be specified and should not exceed the period of notice to which the executive is entitled under the agreement or the remainder of any fixed term. However, the company should carefully consider the proposed period of garden leave which it is seeking to impose. Excessive garden leave periods can be challenged by the director and can potentially be reduced by the courts.

By imposing a period of garden leave, the company can prevent the executive having access to confidential information or coming into contact with customers, while ensuring that he/she remains bound by obligations to the company, in particular, the implied obligation of good faith and fidelity that exists in an employment relationship. It would be a breach of his/her duties for the director to work for a competitor as long as the agreement subsists. Although, it may be possible for the employer to obtain an injunction to restrain such breach and/or damages, if a director threatened to join a competitor it should be noted that this will not be available in all circumstances. Garden leave clauses have the best chance of being upheld by the courts (i.e. by way of injunction) where: **11–101**

- the garden leave period is not too long (any period of longer than six months may be difficult to justify on the basis that it is too onerous for the director);
- the skill of the employee is not one which is likely to degenerate quickly while the director is on garden leave;
- the director has been exposed to/is in possession of valuable confidential information of their employer; and
- he/she is leaving to join a competitor where serious damage could be done to the company by way of their having access to that information.

Restrictive covenants

11–102 These clauses are designed to protect the company's business primarily by protecting the executive's ability to compete with the company following the termination of his/her employment. For the venture capitalist the restrictive covenants will be an important consideration in protecting his/her investment; for individuals, restrictive covenants can be an emotive area.

The covenants may also be included in the investment agreement, in which the venture capitalist is a party and is therefore the covenantee (as opposed to the company in the service agreement). Enforcement of the covenants by the venture capitalist directly may prove to be an easier route than via the company, which will require the co-operation of the directors' former colleagues, and in some instances it may be easier for a venture capitalist to prove loss rather than the company. In addition, it can be argued that the venture capitalist is interested in protecting the goodwill of the investment he/she has made and this may give him/her a stronger bargaining position than the company so enabling the court to enforce the covenants more readily.

11–103 The courts treat covenants in a service agreement and in an investment agreement very differently. When included in a service agreement, the covenants will be subject to the doctrine of restraint of trade. The effect of the doctrine is that a restriction will be unenforceable as being contrary to public interest (namely, an individual's right to work and earn a living) unless it:

- protects a legitimate proprietary interest of the employers. The types of interest capable of protection are goodwill, customer connections, confidential information, trade secrets and a stable workforce; and
- goes no further than is reasonably necessary to protect the interest in question.

The crucial factor in determining the enforceability of restrictive covenants is demonstrating that they have been tailored to the particular circumstances. This includes the particular business, the legitimate proprietary interests that it needs to protect and the skills and experience of the particular director. Therefore, specific and tailored definitions and covenants should be drafted to maximise the chance of enforceability.

11–104 The typical types of clause used to protect these business interests are non-competition, non-solicitation of customers, non-dealing with customers and clauses concerning staff poaching. A basic example of a non-compete and non-solicitation of customers covenant would be:

> The executive undertakes with the company that he/she will neither during the employment nor during the Restricted Period without the prior written consent of the company

(such consent not to be unreasonably withheld) whether by him/herself, through his/her employees or agents or otherwise howsoever and whether on his/her own behalf or on behalf of any other person, firm, company or other organisation, directly or indirectly:

(1) in competition with the company within the Restricted Area be employed or engaged or otherwise interested in the business of [developing, manufacturing, selling, supplying or otherwise dealing with] the Restricted [Goods/Services];

(2) in competition with the company, solicit business from or canvass any customer or prospective customer if such solicitation or canvassing is in respect of Restricted Goods or Restricted Services.

A non-competition clause as in (1) can be difficult to justify where its purpose is purely to protect goodwill as opposed to confidential information and trade secrets. Goodwill can often be adequately protected by a non-solicitation covenant as in (2) and if the court considers that it can, it will not uphold a non-competition clause (*Office Angels Ltd v Rainer-Thomas* [1991] IRLR 214). It is worth noting that a non-solicitation clause like (2) should be accompanied by a non-dealing clause as it can be difficult to prove which party first approached the other.

The reason that a non-competition covenant can be justified more readily **11–105** where the purpose is to protect confidential information or trade secrets is that it is often difficult to prove that such information has been used or disclosed to a third party.

However, a non-competition clause may also be justified if the nature of the business is such that there will be difficulties in monitoring or proving contact between customers and the executive. Additionally non-competition clauses may be enforced where the business relies on "passing trade" or whose client base is unknown.

Non-competition clauses will be deemed to have worldwide effect (and consequently will often be unenforceable) in the absence of a geographical restriction. The area in which the restriction is to operate should be defined with care. It may be a specific geographical area which can be defined where appropriate by a map marking out the relevant area. Alternatively, if the company has an expanding business which operates in different localities, the restricted area may be defined as the area lying within a specified radius of the sites where the company's operations are based. This can be drafted in such a way as to include sites not in existence at the time the contract is entered into.

The size of the area which can reasonably be protected would depend on the nature of the interest which needs protecting. Covenants restricting an employee from competing within a certain geographical area are usually framed to protect the employer's customer connections. Where confidential information is being protected, it will be easier to justify a wider area than if the purpose of the clause is to protect goodwill. In the former case, the area specified can be the area from which the company draws its market. With the inclusion of a clause intended to protect goodwill, then (assuming that a non-competition clause is justifiable at all) the area should be defined by reference to the area in which customers over whom the executive had an influence are based.

Practitioners have observed a recent "sea-change" in the willingness of the courts to uphold a well drafted and tailored non-competition clause on the basis of the protection of confidential information. The Court of Appeal confirmed this view in the case of *Thomas v Farr Plc* [2007] EWCA Civ 118 and upheld a 12-month non-competition clause against a specialist insurance broker. The general view is that the more senior an individual the more likely it is that a clause of this nature will be enforced (see also *TFS Derivatives v Morgan* [2005] IRLR 246). However, the courts will scrutinise covenants carefully and will be quick to strike down a covenant that is badly drafted or goes further than is needed to protect the business.

11-106 Another restrictive covenant that is likely to be required is a clause preventing the solicitation of employees. A basic example would be:

> (3) solicit or induce or endeavour to solicit or induce any person who on the termination date was a [director, manager, salesman or consultant] of the company with whom the executive had dealings during his/her employment to cease working for or providing services to the company, whether or not any such person would thereby commit a breach of contract.

In *Alliance Paper Group Plc v Prestwich* [1996] IRLR 25 and *Ingham v ABC Contract Services Ltd* FC2 93/6609 FCA, it was recognised that employers have an interest in protecting the "assets" of their staff in terms of the time and money they invest in their employees. In *Ingham*, it was stated that employers "have a legitimate interest in maintaining a stable, trained workforce in what is acknowledged to be a highly competitive business" (the business was a recruitment agency).

As noted above, the main consideration in drafting a restrictive covenant is to ensure that the clause protects a legitimate business interest. In the context of non-solicitation of staff, the clause should be restricted, for example to specific employees defined in terms of job description or salary, those in possession of confidential information, or should only relate to those individuals with whom the executive in question had dealings during his/her employment. Otherwise, the clause will cover all employees, including those who are not crucial to the business. As a result, it would be too wide and would be unenforceable.

11-107 Consideration also needs to be given to the duration of the covenants. Most employee covenants are for a short period of time. Whether a restraint is invalid for excessive duration depends upon the nature of the business to be protected. The general view is that it is not possible to justify a period of over 12 months; in many circumstances, the reasonable period may be considerably shorter. For example, in the field of technology or financial services where developments are rapid and confidential information quickly becomes out of date, it may be difficult to justify a period in excess of six or even three months. On the other hand, in the insurance industry, non-solicitation or non-dealing covenants are typically drafted for 12 months as business tends to be written on an annual basis. The key to enforcement is the "nexus" or connection between the period and the interest being protected.

Another consideration is the period previously spent on garden leave. Many covenants are drafted to reduce their currency by any such period (a so called "Credit-Suisse" clause—see discussion in *Credit-Suisse Asset Management v Armstrong* [1996] IRLR 450, CA) and this should be the usual approach. Otherwise, the total period of restraint is likely to be too long to be justifiable.

If the court considers a period of restraint to be too long (or any other aspect of it to be unreasonable) the covenant will be unenforceable. Unlike with garden leave clauses, the court has no power to re-write restrictive covenants in order to impose, for example, a shorter period of restraint.

Consideration should be given to whether it is reasonable to apply the same time limit for both the non-competition and the non-solicitation covenants. A reasonable period for the latter might equate to the length of time it would take the executive's replacement to build up a relationship with the company's customers and, therefore, it may not be possible to justify the same length of protection in relation to all covenants.

Chapter 12

Restructuring

This chapter will deal with the restructuring of a company on the brink of insolvency.   **12–01**

The chapter is divided, like Gaul, into three parts. The first part will describe what a restructuring is and introduce other important related concepts. The second part will go through a restructuring as it occurs and the last part will go into some ideas in greater detail. Cross-references will be provided.

12.1 The concepts

What is meant by "restructuring"?   **12–02**

What is "insolvency"?

Who are the players?

12.1.1 Restructuring

Restructuring follows a recognition that there is too much capital employed in the business.

Restructuring of a business is generally understood to mean the process which is   **12–03**
begun when it is recognised by the stakeholders that there is too much of their capital employed in the business; that the business will never be able to produce an economic return on the capital employed or/and to refund the principal invested—unless steps are taken to change what the business does and/or how it does it.

It follows that a failure to deal with this problem will lead to an insolvency if it hasn't already done so.

Restructuring

Restructuring leads to a downsizing

12–04 Restructuring invariably involves downsizing. The resultant entity is generally smaller.

Asset disposals   Restructuring involves an investigation to see whether there are divisible parts of the business. These might be separate businesses capable of being carried on alone. The business may be vertically divisible, such as the business of distributing the product made elsewhere in the enterprise as well as horizontally divisible, e.g. the provision of a different service. The divisible part may simply be unused land that could be sold for development.

Once divisible parts have been identified, the question will be whether it is better in the long term to keep them or to sell them and use the proceeds of sale to reduce the capital employed in the enterprise and/or fund the making of the retained part(s) more profitable.

12–05 *Shut-downs*   The investigation may however identify a divisible part of the business which is simply uneconomic whatever is done. The cheapest option will be to shut it down and take the cost of doing so on the chin as the price of avoiding larger continuing losses.

Cost savings   And there will be investigations into cost savings in men and material. There will be inevitable over-manning and over-indulgence if the process has not been conducted recently. There will again be closure costs but again they will be the price of avoiding larger continuing losses.

12–06 *Capitalising/writing-off debt*   After all the disposals, shut-downs and cost savings have been planned, it will be possible to see whether the capital supplied by the debt and equity providers (the banks, the bondholders and shareholders) can be supported (in the sense of receiving an economic return and their principal back at the end of the day) by the resulting enterprise.

To the extent that this is not possible, then some hard decisions will have to be made.

Dilution of equity   The debt providers will expect the equity providers to bear the brunt of the pain as the equity providers are at the bottom of the pile if, and when, the assets have to be sold and the proceeds divided out among the stakeholders. Please see the Armageddon calculation at 12.3.7 for an explanation of the order of application in these circumstances.

12–07 This will usually be achieved by the debt holders converting part of their debt—the part that now seems beyond recovery—into equity, perhaps in a class ahead of the existing equity (e.g. preference shares) and at least of the same class as the existing equity, diluting their interests.

The concepts

For the existing equity holders, having a smaller part of a cake is better than having a large part of no cake at all.

New money Of course if the existing equity holders take a less pessimistic view of the prospects than the debt holders, then they may be prepared to put in new equity and may be able to persuade the debt holders that this new money be afforded some priority as superior equity or even superior secured debt.

12–08 It may be that in any event, even after all the asset disposals, the shut-downs, the cost savings and the capitalisation/write-down of some of the debt has been accomplished, the company is still not thought to be viable without the addition of new money—and yet is thought to be capable of saving if new money were to be supplied. But it has to be said that the obtaining of new money from any stakeholders at this juncture is usually a forlorn hope. The adage of not throwing good money after bad is very strong. The other opportunities which seem to be available for the new money always seem safer and more lucrative. Equity stakeholders have a cast of mind which finds writing an investment off almost a virtue. Don't hang on to your dogs. Bondholders are not in the business of putting up new money. Commercial banks will find some new money at a pinch but only if they see it as the only alternative to a really appalling loss on their debt which will strike at the root of their own financial stability and that means a gross overexposure to the company on their part.

Restructuring rarely but possibly involves new developments/acquisitions

12–09 There are some well-known examples of good new businesses which have been grown in restructurings. There are examples of some brilliant results from acquiring other similar businesses to capture/consolidate existing market share. But in general these opportunities are few and require considerable courage on the part of the stakeholders.

Restructuring can happen well short of and out of sight of insolvency

12–10 It is in the nature of everything which has been said that a restructuring can be carried out well before insolvency is even a possibility. And that happens all the time wherever boards of directors are vigilant and energetic.

The bonus of doing the restructuring out of sight of insolvency is of course that the pressure is very much less and "normal" rules apply. The pain to be taken by the stakeholders will be very much less because the damage will have been stopped much earlier.

12.1.2 Insolvency

12–11 Insolvency is not easily defined and there is as a result much confusion about it. There is "the balance sheet test" and "the cash flow test". Which is relevant? When is it relevant anyway? What is it relevant to?

The starting point is to understand that:

- insolvency effectively occurs for most relevant purposes when to continue trading is reasonably likely to incur further losses; and
- to go on beyond that point can risk the directors being found personally liable to contribute to the company's losses.

12.1.3 The stakeholders

12–12 The players involved will obviously be the company itself and its board of directors.

In addition there will be the persons and entities with a stake in the company and its fortunes. In case this is not obvious these will comprise the shareholders and the creditors.

The creditors can be divided into:

- the financing creditors, i.e. the company's lending bankers, bondholders and other lenders;
- other major creditors, i.e. other creditors owed significant amounts, e.g. HMRC, suppliers and claimants for defective products or services or for breach of warranties in, or outstanding consideration for, capital transactions;
- other creditors for small amounts.

12–13 Holders of small amounts of shares and creditors for small amounts will not normally need special regard by the company because their interests are insufficient to cause them to go to much trouble to protect their interests. These are not therefore really stakeholders in the sense in which we will discuss them.

Other players will be the employees and retail customers. In past years of higher employment, employees generally used to be a serious factor to be taken into account and in certain industries still will be. Key employees will of course be very important to the value of the business.

The concepts

Retail customers have more recently become a very important consideration and it is sometimes difficult to reconcile what they are legally entitled to from the company with the political pressure that they can exert on or give rise to, for the insolvency officers, bank creditors and other stakeholders with a vulnerable public profile. Courts can be expected to give weight to their position in any dispute over their rights.

HMRC may also be an important consideration in circumstances where there are significant tax arrears of any kind. Likewise, a company pension scheme deficit may often prove to be a significant cash flow pressure on a company, and this deficit needs serious consideration.

12.1.4 Insolvency officers and proceedings

It might fairly be said by the uninitiated that insolvency law and consequently any discussion of it is unnecessarily complicated by a plethora of different proceedings and persons, some of which have unfortunately similar descriptions. Without making any admissions here is a short glossary. In this chapter the expressions "insolvency proceedings" and "insolvency officers" will be used to refer to all the proceedings and the people who run them. **12–14**

This chapter does not go into much detail as to their differences as most successful restructurings take place outside insolvency proceedings. Their main importance in a discussion on restructuring is so that directors and stakeholders appreciate what the alternative is and why compromise in a restructuring is only likely to be better.

These proceedings apply to companies and, with modifications, partnerships. (People, however, are made "bankrupt" although they can as an alternative enter into "individual voluntary arrangements".) **12–15**

Proceedings and their related officers:

- Receiverships:
  - Fixed charge or LPA receivership for particular assets, usually property: Receivers.
  - Administrative receiverships for all a company's assets: Administrative receivers.
- Administrations: Administrators.
- Voluntary arrangements: Supervisors.
- Liquidations: Liquidators.

Administrative receiverships are becoming less common following their abolition by the Enterprise Act 2002 in respect of security taken after September 15, 2003 (see 12.3.6).

12.2 Restructurings as they occur

12–16 One way of understanding restructurings is by dealing with examining events as they are likely to occur.

12.2.1 In the beginning

12–17 It is useful to start at the very beginning when the original investments are made and the borrowings are first taken as the tests which are applied then are in essence the same tests that a board of directors must apply later in the event of a restructuring although they may not of course perceive them in the same light as they will later on.

The board's original decision

12–18 When the directors of the company decide to take on borrowings they will at least implicitly be considering whether the company will be able to repay them—and pay interest on them in the meantime.

Their consideration is "implicit" because there will have been a bigger and earlier decision taken by the board to undertake the business for which the borrowings and perhaps the investment will have been planned. That decision will doubtless have been based upon studies which are the subject of much of the earlier chapters in this book and should in essence have concluded that it is at least reasonable to expect that all the things which are planned will be achieved and among those things will have been the necessary borrowings and their eventual repayment, perhaps through refinancings over time which themselves could be reasonably expected to be available.

It follows from all this that the board passed the wrongful trading test laid down in s.214 of the Insolvency Act 1986 that none of them "knew or ought to have concluded that there was no reasonable prospect that the company would avoid going into insolvent liquidation". Please see 12.3.8 for a detailed discussion of this issue.

Financial prospects supported by appropriate advice

12–19 However in some cases the highly leveraged nature of the borrowings would make the decision as to whether the plans would work more knife-edge. In those cases—as when a restructuring occurs—the board would be advised to take and rely upon external professional advice.

This would be particularly true in the case of the board of a minor subsidiary being asked to enter into the invariable cross-guarantee of the whole borrowing.

A constant theme for directors in restructurings should be to make sure that as far as possible their exposure is reduced by taking external advice wherever they can, wherever expert advice is available on the topic. Please see 12.3.1 for a detailed discussion on this issue.

12.2.2 Solvent restructurings

At some point in time it may be that the directors sense that the company's fortunes are not as rosy as they were in the beginning. **12–20**

It is likely that the problem is considered to be one of profitability. Insolvency will not be considered a problem—although it would be advisable to test that event informally. Please see 12.2.3 for a description of how that is done.

The board may decide of its own volition or perhaps at the prompting of an equity stakeholder to review all its operations and carry out the same sort of restructuring exercise as it would when it is closer to insolvency.

However that exercise is not within the remit of this chapter, which deals with restructurings conducted in the harsher environment of possible insolvency—even though the changes which will be examined will be very similar.

12.2.3 Taking the temperature

Innocent directors can be made personally liable for the debts of the company if they allow it to trade after a time when they "knew or ought to have concluded that there was no reasonable prospect that the company would avoid going into insolvent liquidation" (s.214, Insolvency Act 1986). See 12.3.8 and also 12.3.9. **12–21**

If a company is in restructuring, the board should review this question every so often. The frequency will depend upon intervening developments.

12.2.4 Trigger events

There are certain events which traditionally mark the beginning of a restructuring. They do so either because they cause the directors to take stock of the financial **12–22**

Restructuring

position or shareholders to consider taking action to improve the management or because they entitle a creditor to recover his/her debt earlier than expected.

A good board of directors will be on top of the problem as it arises but, struggle as it might, it may be that the position has to be disclosed to shareholders in annual or interim accounts or in more frequent management information already agreed to be made available to key investors or by reason of announcements required by the stock exchange or dealing facility in order to prevent a false market in the shares.

Major non-finance creditors may possibly have an entitlement to early warning of the company's failing financial performance. Major finance creditors almost certainly will.

As these events occur the company is forced to explain its financial position to its stakeholders and make proposals for solutions.

Bad claim

12–23   Disaster can overtake a business when there is a large litigation claim.

This can arise from major product or service failure; a claim that the product or service infringes someone else's intellectual property rights; a claim for substantial breach of warranty on the recent sale of a large asset; a claim for substantial further purchase monies for an asset recently purchased under some formulaic consideration. All these are well known examples. The "Acquisition Too Far" has almost become a campaign medal.

The board must—with the assistance of their lawyers—make an early assessment of the likely success of the claim and its likely cost. They must treat the result as a liability and assess the company's financial prospects accordingly.

Loss of key employees

12–24   In a people business the loss of a team or even an individual can prove a body blow.

Loss of key customer

12–25   Some businesses, despite every effort to achieve a different position, are inevitably beholden to a small number, sometimes a very small number, of key customers. The failed attempt by Gent to make Marks & Spencer somehow responsible outside the normal contractual position underlined the risks here.

About to break financial covenant(s)

Major non-finance creditors may possibly have an entitlement to end or accelerate rights in the event of the company's failing financial performance. Major finance creditors almost certainly will. **12–26**

A term loan from a bank will now invariably contain events of default in the event that the company fails to meet or even expects to fail to meet a variety of financial targets ranging from cash flow targets through profit ratios to asset value levels. All these are designed to give the bank early warning of trouble and enable the bank to see how the company plans to deal with the problem.

Always negotiate sufficient headroom in these financial covenants to avoid being caught out unnecessarily.

Profit drop

Of course, trading may simply be against the business. Despite the best efforts of the cleverest in the land we seem to be condemned to an endless cycle of boom and bust. **12–27**

Pension shortfalls

Following recent changes to the pensions' regulatory regime and the method by which an occupational pension's funding requirement is calculated, it is becoming increasingly common for trustees or the regulator to require employers to make very substantial contributions to funds. In many cases, these demands exceed the company's ability to pay and can trigger a restructuring or insolvency. **12–28**

12.2.5 The business plan

The board must assess the financial position and prospects of the company in the light of the event(s) which have just triggered and prepare a plan of action to deal with the position. **12–29**

Interim notification

This can never be done overnight and it may be that there are stakeholders who must be told about the problem in summary form and assured that a detailed assessment and plan is being prepared and will be available by a particular date. **12–30**

The failure to produce timely management information to key shareholders, the need to make public announcements in respect of publicly traded stock and to inform banks are likely to be the most pressing requirements.

Preparation

12–31   In disclosing the company's financial position and prospects it is vital for the board to understand the high level of scrutiny which this is likely to attract.

The board should also appreciate that any failure to describe the position correctly is likely to reduce their future credibility—which may already be in question as a result of the trigger event(s). This will not simply be a value judgement made by stakeholders it will be a judgement made if only because the judgement of those at the stakeholders' would be called into question if they relied any further on what the board may say. For this reason alone, the board would be advised to call on professional assistance to prepare the assessment.

There are many other reasons why professional assistance is strongly advisable. The professional stakeholders will expect to be able to see the answers to certain questions clearly. The very fact that the professional assistance—if appropriately well known—has been employed will lend enormous credibility to the result. Indeed commercial bankers are likely to insist upon it. See 12.3.1 and 12.3.8.

12–32   It is easy to write this advice but experience shows that it usually takes very valuable time to persuade a board of the need for professional advice at this juncture. Later they can see the wisdom of it as clear as day. But to begin with they understandably feel a certain usurpation of their role without appreciating that, with occurrence of the trigger events, a certain process well understood by financial stakeholders has begun.

It follows therefore that if the plan which the board puts forward requires financial commitment from a commercial bank it must have been prepared or commented upon by well-known professional advisors.

12–33   Commercial banks will be unwilling to make financial commitments to a business in trouble without a business plan which has not been prepared or commented upon by well-known professional advisors.

While professional equity stakeholders will not require that assistance, if they are to make a financial commitment they will need to make a level of due diligence which might not be feasible for them to undertake given their exposure to loss, and they may decline the commitment for that reason. With the assistance of a plan prepared or commented upon by well-known professional advisors, the chance of the commitment being made will be enhanced.

Finally for the same reason as it is important to get the facts right, it is almost as vital to deliver what is promised when it is promised. And while this comment applies importantly to the steps of the plan, it also applies to the timing of the initial delivery of the plan to the stakeholders. The board's credibility at this early stage very much hangs in the balance. **12–34**

The board should prepare an Armageddon calculation (see 12.3.7) and consider using it to persuade stakeholders to adopt the plan because the calculation will show, or should show, how much better off each of the stakeholders will be if insolvency can be avoided.

12.2.6 Negotiations with the stakeholders

Generally

The business plan must be taken to the stakeholders (see 12.1.3) to gain their approval to the part they are asked to play. **12–35**

First, the bank and any other severely pressing creditors will have to agree a breathing space to enable the plan to be agreed by all the stakeholders.

Next, if there is a requirement for new money, that needs to be taken with the relevant stakeholders first, as without it the plan will have to go back to the drawing board.

Secured creditors will need to agree any asset disposal and their share of the proceeds if less than 100 per cent.

Financing and possibly major non-financing creditors will need to agree any capitalising/writing-off debt. **12–36**

Shareholders will need to agree any dilution of their equity.

As this is necessarily a piecemeal process, the most powerful stakeholders should be consulted first and so on. Formal commitments cannot be expected initially. Minor and even major changes to the plan may have to be conceded.

Gradually the segments of the plan will be agreed and the plan—as amended during the process—will need to be reissued and final agreement obtained by the stakeholders before proceeding.

Unsecured creditors

12–37 One group of stakeholders where it is most difficult to achieve movement is the unsecured creditors. The smaller creditors will be uninterested. However any bondholders and other major non-finance creditors should have a sufficient interest to want the rescue to succeed.

They should be persuaded to drop that part of their debt claim which is unrecoverable and, say, convert it into equity so that if the business is saved they get it back. Arguments to be deployed would include the Armageddon calculation (see 12.3.7) to show the creditor that in an insolvency proceeding it could only expect to recover a percentage of its claim.

12–38 In the case of claims (e.g. for defective products and services or breach of warranty) the company should deploy its lawyers to demonstrate the weaknesses in the creditor's case; the time and money it will take to gain definitive resolution and the likelihood that the cupboard will be bare.

The company should position itself so as to be able to say—as surely will be the case—that a company's main creditors—usually its bankers—are already taking pain and are not prepared to do so unless other major creditors share the burden. If necessary the company should join the bankers to the negotiations.

12–39 These will be some of the more difficult negotiations of a restructuring and require considerable nerve as the company is taken to the very brink of insolvency proceedings in order to demonstrate to the creditors concerned that it means business.

Should the creditor actually issue a winding-up petition it is thought that the company should be able to persuade the Court to dismiss the petition. The arguments to be used are that:

> A process akin to the liquidation being sought is currently being carried out in the restructuring process: the Court can be shown that independent insolvency accountants (i.e. insolvency practitioners) have reviewed the company's financial position and established its assets and liabilities, just as a liquidator would do.

12–40 It can be demonstrated to the Court that it is not in the interests of creditors generally—as opposed to the selfish interest of the petitioning creditor—that the restructuring process should be halted by a liquidation. As many other creditors as possible should be encouraged to support that proposition in Court.

The Court can be shown that the petitioning creditor will hopefully receive in the restructuring proposals at least as much as it would get in a liquidation. A comparison of the restructuring proposal and the Armageddon calculation can be produced to demonstrate that.

There is no clearly established case law here but the threads can be drawn together from case law and a statutory provision granting similar relief in the case of the insolvency of individuals. The writer has deployed the argument with success in that petitions have not been issued. **12–41**

It may be that it is necessary to additionally secure part of the unsecured creditor's claim so as to enhance its value in compensation for the creditor dropping part. This can be done at no cost to the company but it is likely that the existing secured creditors (i.e. usually the bankers) will have to give the new security some priority or pari passu ranking if it is to have value.

Secured creditors

Secured creditors are usually experienced and professional in their approach to restructurings. As noted elsewhere in this chapter, banks—at least UK banks—have come under public and governmental pressure to try and save businesses and the London Approach developed in the 1970s has formed the basis of modern restructuring. Given a reasonable business plan supported by insolvency professionals of repute, UK banks can be expected to be supportive. **12–42**

However when dealing with a group of banks it is usually necessary to get the agreement of every bank and experience has all too often shown that foreign banks, whose exposure is usually less than UK banks in UK situations and often comparatively small, can be unresponsive to the proposals.

But English law, in the shape of s.896 of the CA 2006 could be brought to bear on the problem and the power of the majority used to bring the recalcitrant bank into line. **12–43**

Also s.91 of the Law of Property 1925 can be used to force banks to agree reasonable asset sale values.

12.3 Items of particular interest

12.3.1 Importance of professional insolvency advice

If a business in trouble is to achieve the support of its financial stakeholders it is most unlikely to do so without the assistance of professional insolvency advisors. **12–44**

Restructuring

These advisors will be solicitors and, in most cases, accountants. In larger and some medium-sized cases, investment bankers will be additionally appropriate. In some medium and large cases "company doctors" or "turnaround professionals"—who are usually one or a team of two or three experienced individuals are needful additions to a hard pressed or depleted management team and/or to carry out specific tasks outside the ordinary running of the business.

Importance to the company

12–45 The importance of professional insolvency advisors to the company arises because:

- the occurrence of the trigger event(s) (see 12.2.4) are likely to have shaken the main financial stakeholders who are likely to have lost some faith in the board's judgement;
- the preparation of, or (favourable) comment upon, any proposals by the company by the accountants/investment bankers will greatly add to the value of the proposals in the eyes of the financial stakeholders;
- professional insolvency advisors will know better than the board what the professional financial stakeholders will want in terms of information as to the position and prospects of the company, and what stakeholders are likely to find acceptable in terms of solutions (which they must be asked to approve or finance).

Professional insolvency advisors can provide the extra pairs of temporary hands often needed at this time.

Importance to the directors

12–46 Professional insolvency advisors are important to the directors because:

- for the executive directors who have not been here before they will map out the road ahead and the likely attitudes of the stakeholders. They will also highlight the risks to directors in trading a business in financial difficulties. See 12.3.9;
- for the non-executive directors the solicitors will show the limit of their responsibilities;
- for all the directors the solicitors will guide the board as a whole through the process and so protect the directors from personal liability.

Items of particular interest

Importance to the main creditors

For the financial stakeholders, the professional advisors of course bring the corresponding benefits which the company will enjoy. **12–47**

Where further financial commitment is required from professional equity stakeholders it is likely that the cost of the level of due diligence required may be prohibitive and that the use by the company of its own professional advisors will enhance the possibility of the commitment being received.

For financial creditors, the involvement of professional advisors by the company is likely to be a sine qua non of any consent let alone financial commitment required of the creditors.

12.3.2 Appropriate advice for the board

The conduct of directors of a company is subject to scrutiny by insolvency officers (receivers, administrators and liquidators) who must report upon it to the Secretary of State. The Secretary of State may take action to disqualify a director from subsequently acting as such in the case of other companies. A liquidator has power to take action against directors for misfeasance or other breach of duties. See e.g. 12.3.8 and 12.3.9. **12–48**

There are various particular duties which the possibility of insolvency will give rise to and as to which the directors can expect that the company's solicitors will draw their attention to.

However, central to everything that the directors will do will be the taking of decisions collectively as a board. For example: **12–49**

- Should this asset be sold?
- Should it be sold on particular terms?
- Should the company continue to trade? What are the implications for the directors?
- Is it likely that the bank will appoint a receiver or administrator?
- Will this major (but unsecured) creditor give the company time to provide a solution before seeking the appointment of a liquidator?
- Is it reasonable to expect that the board's rescue plan will be acceptable to the stakeholders?

12–50 A director is most unlikely to be criticised for taking a decision which seemed reasonable at the time even if it subsequently turns out to be wrong. In order for a decision to be a reasonable one it must be based on a reasonable enquiry into the facts and a reasonable examination of the options. A director is not expected to have or apply expertise which he/she doesn't possess but ought to appreciate the limits of his/her expertise and seek appropriate expert advice if that is available. If he/she takes appropriate expert advice then it would be reasonable for the director to follow it. Indeed it would be dangerous not to follow it without good reason.

Therefore a director can protect him/herself by taking appropriate professional advice and will be more exposed to criticism if he/she doesn't.

12.3.3 Restructuring as an opportunity

12–51 A company in trouble does of course present an opportunity to pick up businesses or assets cheaply.

The process of purchasing from a possibly insolvent company is apparently the same as when buying from a solvent entity in that (limited) due diligence may be carried out and contracts are negotiated and exchanged. However the following important differences eventually make themselves known:

- due diligence of a business in crisis can be somewhat fraught and unsatisfying;
- during the due diligence, it probably becomes clear that warranties, the usual alternative to good due diligence, are unlikely to be worth the paper they are written on—save to the extent of any retention of the consideration which can be negotiated. The buyer has to expect that the seller could well be in some formal insolvency process by the time a claim is made;
- creditor pressure on the seller may, the buyer thinks, help to keep the price down but it becomes pressure on the buyer to conclude the purchase more quickly than he/she would like and sometimes compels the buyer to assist the seller to keep the business alive by injecting some funding to ease creditor pressure.

12–52 As noted under 12.3.5, any person or entity dealing with a possibly insolvent company in the capacity of an existing or future equity or debt stakeholder, or in merely giving advice, needs to be wary of becoming a shadow or a de facto director and liable to contribute towards the company's debts. See also 12.3.8 and 12.3.9.

It is not immediately obvious why someone merely seeking to buy a possibly insolvent company or perhaps assets and some liabilities from it should run the risk of becoming a shadow or a de facto director. However the situation often arises because of the competing problems of carrying out due diligence on a company in crisis and the need for temporary funding to keep the business alive in the meantime. Quite apart from the somewhat hairy problem of taking adequate and valid security for the funding from a company in crisis, the very act of propping the business up has its own problems, as doing so probably enables the business to take on further credit which might not be repaid.

For the person or entity who is looking to buy the whole or part of the business from a company which may be insolvent, but is not in a formal insolvency process, this danger can seem to be a form of double jeopardy when it is likely that they do not wish to become liable for all of the debts or at least debts of which they are unaware. **12–53**

A prima facie conclusion often reached by buyers is to wait until the company goes into a formal insolvency process and buy from the insolvency officer without this danger. However, this is often not a choice as the business is often of a type, or carried on with benefit of contracts of a type, which simply fall away on a formal insolvency. The goodwill may simply evaporate.

A buyer needs to take expert insolvency advice as he/she proceeds through this minefield.

12.3.4 Pre-pack administrations

The potential damage to a business as a result of it entering into a formal insolvency process is one reason we now see more and more "pre-packaged" administration business sales ("pre-pack"). **12–54**

A pre-pack is where the directors of a distressed company, with significant help from an insolvency practitioner, effectively arrange a sale of the company's business and assets, prior to the company formally entering into administration, such that a deal to sell the business and assets of the insolvent company can be concluded (i.e. contracts agreed, etc) immediately on the company entering into administration.

One of the main benefits of a pre-pack is the apparently "seamless" transition of the insolvent business from one company to another, ensuring minimum interruption, and hopefully minimising the loss of confidence associated with a formal insolvency process.

12.3.5 Shadow and de facto directors

Section 250 of the Companies Act 2006 ("CA 2006") defines a director as "any person occupying the position of director, by whatever name called". This means **12–55** that one can become a director of a company without being formally appointed as such. A company or other entity can also be a director of another company. Entities can of course only act though persons who represent them and the representatives could equally become directors of the other company. A person or an entity or its representative who is formally appointed as a director by the shareholders or the board is called a de iure director. A person or an entity or its representative who is determined to be a director even though he/she or it has not been formally appointed is known as a de facto director.

In addition a person, an entity or its representative may be determined to be a shadow director, a new type of director introduced by s.251.

12–56 It is not an offence to be a de facto director or a shadow director—although it is in the nature of the beast that offences in relation to the reporting and listing of a de facto director as one of the company's directors will have been committed. Indeed the close attention to the business of the company which is usually part of being a shadow director is the perfectly legitimate protection of a stakeholder's interests. However it does have the consequence of making the stakeholder more responsible than it probably anticipated.

De facto and shadow directors will have all the responsibilities and liabilities of de iure directors, including most relevantly liability for wrongful trading.

12–57 Therefore persons and entities and their representatives involved with businesses which may be insolvent (e.g. "company doctors", shareholders and their representatives and major creditors such as banks) are naturally wary of becoming de facto or shadow directors because in doing so they may become responsible to make good the businesses' debts. See 12.3.8.

The Court of Appeal in *Kaytech International Plc, Re; Potier v Secretary of State for Trade and Industry* (1999) said that there is no single decisive test to determine whether someone is a de facto director but gave a number of examples of relevant factors: Was the person held out as a director? Did the person use the title of director? Did the person have proper information (such as management accounts) on which to base decisions? Did the person make major corporate decisions in a manner akin to a de iure director? Where there was doubt the Court said there should be a presumption that the person had not acted as a director.

12–58 A shadow director was first defined by CA 2006 s.251 as a person in accordance with whose directions or instructions the (other) directors of a company are accustomed to act.

The section excluded the giver of professional advice from being a shadow director. Subsequent cases have noted that this protection is only available for normal

Items of particular interest

professional advice and does not cloak the advisor for anything he/she may do beyond giving professional advice.

For some time it was thought that "accustomed to act" meant that the (other) directors had to have been generally ready to follow the shadow director's lead. However, the Court of Appeal's decision in *Secretary of State v Deverell* in 2001 clarified the position so that to be a shadow director, while his directions or instructions must carry real influence and will normally be followed, it is not essential that they be habitually followed.

Candidates for shadow director or de facto director can be from within or from outside the company. A de facto director is more likely to be a major shareholder or a representative of a major shareholder or part of the internal management. A shadow director could be an influential shareholder—including a holding company—or his/her representative or a creditor—including a bank. **12–59**

Commercial bankers are now well aware of this problem. This—sadly for the rescue culture—has led them to be more elliptical and less forthcoming when asked for views by the directors. Commercial bankers have been advised to stick to answering questions directly arising from their legal relationship with the company, such as whether they will waive events of default, whether they will allow assets subject to their security to be sold for such and such a price, whether they will grant loan facilities. They have been advised to avoid commenting upon a company's plans in relation to its business or changes in personnel. They look to applications for extensions of credit to be supported by business plans commented upon by professional advisors. Indeed they prefer to conduct discussions on the company's plans with the professional advisors.

This attitude dovetails with the commercial banker's general withdrawal from the field of corporate advice. **12–60**

Venture capitalists also have a special problem because of their natural desire to monitor their investment closely. This necessarily involves the timely and frequent receipt of management information and often attendance at board meetings. Attendance at board meetings is advisedly only with observer status but even that will not protect the venture capitalist entity or its representative if the line is actually crossed. It is vital that the observer should not participate in the board meetings but merely report to his/her employer.

Persons who represent venture capitalists in their relations with possibly insolvent investments may consider asking their employers for indemnities against personal liability. If the representatives are themselves directors of the (corporate) venture capitalist there are rules restricting the scope of such indemnities.

12.3.6 The Enterprise Act

12–61 The most recent insolvency legislation of relevance is Enterprise Act 2002 Pt 10 and this act (as well as the subordinate legislation issued under it) has been taken account of in this chapter.

Its principle effect on restructurings has been to increasingly limit the bank's options to the appointment of an administrator rather than an administrative receiver. "Increasingly", because for some time to come business failures are likely to involve security given before September 15, 2003, meaning the bank will still be able to appoint administrative receivers.

12–62 The principal difference for a bank in being able to appoint an administrator rather than an administrative receiver is that an administrator owes his/her principal duties to all the creditors and has a statutory duty to attempt to preserve all or part of the company's business as a going concern, while an administrative receiver only owes duties primarily to the bank which appoints him/her. A receiver or administrative receiver is therefore able to look after the interests of the bank before worrying about other creditors. Therefore, if the factory can be sold for a price which will repay or substantially repay the bank, it matters little that the business carried on at the factory may, as a result, die. An administrator must look to the interests of all creditors and might well wait on selling the factory until he/she had decided whether the business could be sold as a going concern and then try to sell the two together. By that time the property market might have dipped—as it has a habit of doing in a recession—and, although the business was sold for something, the result to the bank might be worse even though the result for creditors and employees overall might be better.

12.3.7 The Armageddon calculation

12–63 This is the calculation done to work out how much a stakeholder would recover if the company was put into an insolvency proceeding (receivership, administration or liquidation) and all the assets were sold off, essentially at "fire sale" values.

Fire sale values don't allow for much hanging about trying to keep the business going while a purchaser is found to take it over as a going concern.

This is the worst-case scenario.

12–64 The calculation requires some knowledge of the respective rights of the stakeholders and of the law relating to the application of assets upon an insolvency.

Items of particular interest

An amount must be included for the costs of the wind-down and sales and payment of creditors and also for the statutory reporting processes incumbent upon the insolvency office holders.

The result shows each stakeholder where his/her bottom line is and—and this is the real importance of the exercise—how much better for him/her the board's plan is.

The exercise will certainly be done by the commercial banks and it should be done by the company to see what use it can be in persuading stakeholders to agree the board's plan. **12–65**

The order of application of assets on an insolvency of a limited company is broadly as follows:

- secured creditors for assets subject to fixed security in order of priority among themselves;
- expenses of insolvency;
- employees' wages and other compensation up to limits;
- a proportion of the balance up to £600,000 for unsecured creditors if floating charge executed after September 14, 2003 (known as "the prescribed part");
- secured creditors for assets subject to floating charge security in order of priority among themselves;
- unsecured creditors of all types including secured creditors for amounts not secured—pro rata among themselves;
- subordinated creditors;
- preferential shareholders;
- ordinary shareholders;
- deferred shareholders.

One of the unfortunate results of a calculation which shows a secured creditor, for example, that it may be able to recover all or most of its money in a worst case scenario is the temptation for it not to agree any form of restructuring which might put that position at risk. The temptation is to wait until the worse case becomes the only case. **12–66**

Conversely where security has not yet "purified", the holder of the security can be expected to be wary of enforcing it until it has. Security is said to purify when the time periods during which it is capable of being set aside have all expired.

This is a complex matter and depends on the type of security and the circumstances under which it was taken including the relationship of the creditor to the company. See Insolvency Act 1986 ss.238–245. Suffice it to say the company should take advice as to whether the security has purified if the security was taken within the previous five years, although in general security given within two years is more likely to be at risk.

12.3.8 Wrongful trading

12–67 This is the most important idea for directors of a company being restructured to understand. Those who perennially advise in the area often wonder why the idea is not more widely understood than it is. The answer is probably simple; no-one expects to get into a position where they need to know. Yet with our seemingly unshakeable cycles of boom and bust, that is not a realistic expectation.

Innocent directors can be made liable for the debts of the company if they allow it to trade after a time when they "knew or ought to have concluded that there was no reasonable prospect that the company would avoid going into insolvent liquidation" (Insolvency Act 1986 s.214).

Innocent directors can include shadow directors. There is nothing wrong in being a shadow director (see 12.3.5) but one of the important adverse consequences is that the shadow director might be made liable for wrongful trading.

12–68 Innocent directors can also include de facto directors, persons who are not formally, not legally, directors but who are treated as directors (see 12.3.5).

The first occasion when this might need to be thought of in a venture capital context is if the business is highly geared (see para.12–18).

However the point would only be relevant again if there is a downturn in the company's fortunes.

12–69 In order to trade a business needs to engage people to work for it, order supplies and use services which it will, in the ordinary course, not have to pay for until later. Even switching on the light is taking credit in this way. The law obviously makes it wrong to take this credit knowing that it cannot be paid for—or even recklessly as to whether it can be paid for. See e.g. 12.3.9. The law also draws a line if directors of a company do so when they "knew or ought to have concluded that there was no reasonable prospect that the company would avoid going into insolvent liquidation".

If directors allow the company to carry on after that time a court can order that they be made jointly and severally liable to contribute towards the losses of the insolvent company.

Items of particular interest

12–70 One of the duties of a liquidator of a company (and indeed of administrative receivers and administrators—other insolvency officers who may be appointed) is to examine this question and make a report on it to the Secretary of State who may, as a result, institute proceedings. If there is an adverse finding the directors may also be disqualified from acting as such in the future. It is therefore not to be taken lightly.

It is often said that these things are not often pursued; that neither the State nor the private liquidator has the funds do so and the creditors are usually sufficiently disparate and/or disinterested to provide the funds and waste good money after bad. Yet the case reports are growing. Moreover there are now in existence insurance providers and expert businesses with funds at their disposal to arm liquidators to take action against directors.

12–71 However as a matter of general reassurance, directors who behave properly and ensure that their proper actions are recorded for posterity should come to no harm.

Should any director (and this is not a matter for majority decisions) be unable to conclude "that there was no reasonable prospect that the company would avoid going into insolvent liquidation", then he/she should try and persuade fellow directors to put the company into an insolvency proceeding (receivership, administration, liquidation or, perhaps, a company voluntary arrangement) or, if that fails, resign. Thankfully he/she has no duty to specify why he/she has resigned, although the mere fact of this resignation will often be very damaging to the future prospects of the company. In order to avert that damage the director may be asked to agree to some reassuring statement.

12–72 However, so long as the directors examine the question of wrongful trading regularly, arrive at their decisions reasonably, and minute their investigation and findings properly, they should come to no harm. This process has become known as "taking the temperature".

Banks and other financial lenders who usually have an interest in seeing the business continue (see 12.3.10) are now much more aware of the directors' difficulties in this area and are much more inclined to be sympathetic to the directors, without whom the business cannot continue and their losses are likely to be greater.

In order to take the temperature the directors need to meet with each other regularly, although if they will not meet then each director must try and work this out himself. He/she is not absolved because colleagues will not assist, although in the case of a non-executive director without direct access to the latest information, the task becomes so difficult that the director will surely resign.

12–73 As a starting point, there is the question of the current prospects for trading profitability.

Then there is the question of whether the creditors are likely to be paid when they are due to be paid or, if not, within whatever further time they are likely to allow before seeking to wind up the company (present a winding-up petition which if accepted by the court will result in a liquidator being appointed) or (in the case of a secured creditor) appointing an administrative receiver or an administrator.

Creditors can be surprisingly patient so it is not unreasonable for directors to conclude that they will wait.

12–74 There are likely to be some creditors whose debts are not clearly established. These will include claims for defective supplies by the company, perhaps large litigation claims. These will require the directors to try and assess the real value of these claims as well as the strength of creditor pressure.

There may be, and, as time goes by, there will be, proposals for rescuing the business which will require the directors to assess the commitment of the rescuers to bring them to fruition and, in some cases, the very ability of the rescuers, even the very profitability of the rescuers necessary, to carry through the rescue proposals.

12–75 Any rescue proposals will usually require some restructuring of the business. The board may have, ought to have (see 12.2.5), their own restructuring proposals. These will of course have required at their inception an assessment of the chance of their success. Will it be possible to sell this asset for that price? Can a particular part of the business still be profitably carried on if these savings are made? Will these creditors and/or those equity holders agree to reducing or changing their rights? All these points will need to be reviewed when taking the temperature.

All this should be minuted carefully. The court will take great cognisance of a contemporary note and only a limited view of a distant recollection. As one QC remarked, "Five pages of minutes are worth five hours swearing in a court five years later".

12–76 How often should the temperature be taken? Obviously the first time it is done it is quite an undertaking even though it should be much less onerous than the time they first considered the venture capital project. Nevertheless if it is carefully minuted by way of reference to a rolling memorandum then that can be fairly easily updated on each subsequent occasion.

So, how often? Certainly at every regular board meeting. Board meetings are likely to be, ought to be, held much more regularly in this crisis time. Even so board meetings should be called especially if there should occur some major change in one of the key facts the board would consider in taking the temperature. After all in a trading business credit is being incurred all the time. Lights are being turned on at least daily.

But directors should not carry the entire burden. They should not try and assess matters where experts can be called on to advise (see 12.3.1). There are experts of every hue. There are not only experts as to how much assets are likely to be sold for, there are also experts in insolvency, experts capable of advising as to the criteria to be applied in assessing whether the bank will wait and for how long, whether this creditor is likely to accept that proposal and whether the directors' proposed view is likely to be regarded by the court as being reasonable and therefore not blame worthy. These experts are usually lawyers or accountants although there are increasing numbers of other professionals, businessmen and bankers, who have had direct experience of the process and hire themselves out to assist others. **12–77**

All this should be fully minuted. Some board minutes tend to be sparse and almost wholly uninformative. Some are almost merely an embellishment of the agenda. Others are only apparently informative indicating that a matter was discussed and a certain decision was made but not explaining what was said, what points were weighed up. There is no material in such a minute giving a court purchase to come to a conclusion that the directors arrived at the decision reasonably. **12–78**

The directors must look forward and imagine that, with the benefit of hindsight, it is clear that the decision which they are about to make is found to be wrong. The directors need to ensure that what they knew and what they took into account is minuted so that posterity can see that they did the best they could. Indeed the very exercise will invariably ensure that the proper decision is taken.

There is a need to strain the intellectual muscles to justify the continuance of trading, and avoid following the emotional highs and lows which the stress of the process generates. **12–79**

It was mentioned earlier in this chapter that, if any director is unable to conclude "that there was no reasonable prospect that the company would avoid going into insolvent liquidation", then he should try and persuade his fellow directors to put the company into an insolvency proceeding or, if that fails, resign. However subs.(3) of s.214 of the Insolvency Act 1986 does relieve a director if "[he] took every step with a view to minimising the potential loss to the company's creditors as (assuming him to have known that there was no reasonable prospect that the company would avoid going into insolvent liquidation) he ought to have taken." This means that the directors can continue the business perhaps with a view to a better realisation of assets outside an insolvency proceeding so long as the position of creditors is not worsened. But this is a tricky road requiring even greater vigilance and advice.

12.3.9 Fraudulent trading

It was mentioned in the discussion of wrongful trading (see 12.3.8) that the law obviously makes it wrong to take credit knowing that it cannot be paid for—or **12–80** even recklessly as to whether it can be paid for. That is after all quite simply common law fraud. However the Insolvency Act 1986 s.213 also makes those "who were knowingly parties to the carrying on of the business ['with intent to defraud creditors of the company or creditors of any other person, or for any fraudulent purpose'] . . . liable to make . . . contributions . . . to the company's assets . . ." These persons are likely to be the directors (including, therefore, shadow and de facto directors, see 12.3.5) but can include others, such as a holding company or major creditor, such as a bank.

The test of "knowingly . . . carrying on . . . the business ['with intent to defraud creditors . . .'] . . ." is a high one and should not concern the innocent. The lower test of being reckless is more worrying but there has always been a reluctance to pursue fraud unless it has been heinous.

CA 2006 s.993 also provides that fraudulent trading is a criminal offence.

12.3.10 The classic restructuring solution

12–81 Whatever particular remedies the board settles upon in its plan for the restructuring of a potentially insolvent company (asset disposals, shut-downs, cost savings, writing-off debt, etc), the board will need time to achieve agreement to them from the stakeholders and then time to implement them.

On the other hand any creditor with a clear claim can force the company into an insolvency proceeding by petitioning to wind it up.

12–82 While it should be generally possible for any (viable) restructuring plan to be carried out from within an insolvency proceeding, particularly an administration, all forms of insolvency proceeding tend to greatly reduce the chances of a successful restructuring and to limit what can be achieved in any restructuring, even though the creditor pressure is eliminated.

- Goodwill disappears entirely or at least ebbs away:
  — Businesses find it much harder to trade on in an insolvency proceeding. There is the initial publicity and, in the case of businesses other than retail businesses—where the public's perception that it is in an insolvency proceeding can die away—there is usually the constant reminder to the counter-party that he/she is dealing with something that is broken.
  — In some businesses the key contracts necessary to continue trading simply fall away and have to be renegotiated.
- Lower recoveries on disposals mean less money to fuel the recovery: it is invariably the case that assets will be sold for less once the company is in

Items of particular interest

an insolvency proceeding. This is because buyers expect to pay less in an insolvency proceeding and no-one will expect the insolvency officers to take too long about selling assets. Paradoxically the recent Enterprise Act's severe limitation on the period for which administrations are supposed to run will effectively rule out any long or even medium-term recovery strategy in insolvency proceedings.

- Finance is very hard and expensive to come by.
- The fees of the insolvency officers and their staff are a necessary additional burden.

12–83 The Insolvency Act 1986 did introduce the concept of the voluntary arrangement and the Act of the same name in 2000 did give it some additional protection. However, as a process it has never really had the confidence of the finance community and has largely only been used for very small companies—apart from its technical use as an exit strategy from administrations after the restructuring has been tried. A voluntary arrangement is the true "debtor in possession" insolvency proceeding. The directors are left to run the business without any real monitoring by the creditors. The insolvency officer has a limited and somewhat hairy supervisory role and there have been some unfortunate results. As voluntary arrangements in any event require agreement from the majority of the creditors (half in number and three-quarters by value) the trouble needed to be taken is the same as in a work-out.

The better alternative is a work-out, a restructuring outside an insolvency proceeding. And if the company's bank will agree, this is very possible.

12–84 The bank will be motivated to assist for the following reasons.

- Banks received a great deal of public and governmental opprobrium for their perceived role in the 1990s and earlier recessions in putting businesses under when they could have been saved. The governmental opprobrium was reflected in windfall taxes and threats of windfall taxes and, most recently in the Enterprise Act 2002, in the reduction of their perceived protections in the use of administrative receivership.

- Banks usually have security, and restructuring plans usually involve substantial asset disposals and bankers invariably expect the lion's share of the disposal proceeds in reduction of their debt. Bankers are as aware as the next person that asset disposals are likely to yield more if they can take place outside an insolvency proceeding and could well be postponed in an administration both in timing and in priority to the needs of preserving businesses in which the bank may have a lesser security interest.

If banks are seen to be supportive, other creditors will generally be much more relaxed, although bondholders of larger companies—a significant part of whose bonds will by this stage in the crisis have passed into the ownership of aggressive US vulture funds—can make an unhelpful amount of trouble as they seek to upgrade their position.

12–85 If banks can be persuaded to support a restructuring outside an insolvency proceeding, there is one other ingredient which is often more troublesome and certainly more time consuming: the company's senior management.

Unless the restructuring is taking place commendably early—a state of grace more devoutly to be wished than usually occurring—the company's senior management is likely to have already been toiling manfully to avert the problem working long hours in extremely stressful conditions. If the management were once the brightest and best for the future of the company it is likely that they now need a rest.

12–86 The employees and the customers and the public perception of the business would in any event receive a great boost if new senior management of ability and reputation were to take over.

But for perfectly human reasons it is difficult to achieve this. It is hard enough to engineer a smooth succession in management in the best of houses. To do so in a company in crisis is more difficult. And the incumbents naturally feel that they deserve better. The inevitable appellation of failure seems so unfair. And they may be significant owners of the business as well thereby feeling an additional entitlement to stay as well as possessing some of the legal roadblocks making their involuntary departure difficult.

This is an area where there are no prizes for second place and that needs to be borne in mind by all parties when negotiating.

Chapter 13

Key Issues for Management

A private equity transaction generates a vast volume of documentation, produces 13–01
lots of meetings, an unearthing of lots of historic information and the drawing up
of plans and forecasts for the future of business. However as in any transaction
or project there are a number of key issues that are more important than others,
the 80:20 rule. The purpose of this chapter is to provide a guide to those key
issues that should consume more of the attention of the managers and their
lawyers alike.

13.1 Management duties

The fiduciary duties which a director owes to his company are founded on the 13–02
simple concept that a director must act not only honestly, but in the interests of
his company and not in his own interest. Such duties derive from the decisions of
the Courts of Chancery in the eighteenth and nineteenth centuries, intended to
ensure that persons/trustees who held assets or provided services for the benefits
of others did so in good faith and for the benefit of those they represented. It
was in the nineteenth century that fiduciary duties were extended to company
directors. Sir George Jessel M.R. in *Forest of Dean Coal Mining Co, Re* (1878)
10 CH D 450 said:

> "Directors have sometimes been called trustees, or commercial trustees, sometimes they
> have been called managing partners; it does not matter much what you call them as long
> as you understand what their true position is, which is really that they are commercial men
> managing a trade concern for the benefit of themselves and all the other shareholders . . .
> they are bound to use fair and reasonable diligence in the management of the company's
> affairs and to act honestly".

As a consequence, fiduciary duties continue to apply to the directors of a company and to "shadow directors" (persons whose instructions or directions often determine the decisions of the board of directors). It is unlikely that employees (who are not shadow directors) owe such a high level of duty to the company, though they are still subject to a lower degree of good faith and confidentiality.

Key Issues for Management

13–03 One of a director's fiduciary duties of particular relevance in management buy-outs is that he must not put himself in a position where his duty to the company may conflict with his personal interest. The duty arises from the real concern that the management may benefit from an opportunity which properly belongs to the company and its shareholders. Lord Herschell, in *Bray v Ford* (1896) AC 44 (p.51) said:

> "A person in a fiduciary position ... is not ... entitled to make a profit; he is not allowed to put himself in a position where his interest and duty conflict".

The breach of duty consists in not of allowing the conflict of interest to arise because that is often outside the control of the director, but of the director's preferring his own personal interest to those of persons for whom he acts as fiduciary, or of taking advantage of such a position. For example, the director must take care not to withhold from the company's shareholders information that would, if provided to them, enable them to negotiate a fairer price for the company. It is not unusual to see management prepare one business plan and profit projection for the benefit of the company's owners and to be used by them in determining the price at which they will be prepared to sell, and another more optimistic plan and projection for themselves.

13–04 The issues for directors have been codified over recent years and are as follows:

- general duties owed to the company of which they are a director (ss.171–177 of the CA 2006);
- disclosure obligations under ss.177 and 182 of the CA 2006;
- possible need for shareholder approval of the transaction under s.190 of the CA 2006;
- any provisions in the employment contract of management and any duties of confidentiality.

The CA 2006 codifies the general duties which directors owe to the company as follows:

- a duty to act within the powers of the company's constitution (s.171);
- he must act in ways that will promote the success for the benefit of its members as a whole (s.172);
- he must exercise independent judgement (s.173);
- he must exercise reasonable care, skill and diligence (s.174);
- he must avoid conflicts of interest (s.175);
- he must not accept benefits from third parties (s.176); and

Management duties

- he must declare any interest in proposed transactions or arrangements with the company (s.177).

A management buy-out will always raise issues of conflict for the various directors. They have a duty to manage the target business having regard to the interests of the owners of the target. However, they will become distracted from this task as they seek to put together the transaction. In addition, while on the one hand they have a duty to disclose price sensitive information to the owners of the target to enable them to set a fair price for the business, on the other hand they will want to maintain the price as low as possible. By way of expansion all relevant information in the possession of the target directors must be disclosed to the seller so they can evaluate the sale, the issues and the risks and the impact on price. If they fail to do so and if they do not, they could face a claim for breach of duty including secret profit. **13–05**

In some cases, and where the seller can operate for a period without senior management, management are put on garden leave for the duration of the transaction. However in many cases the management are left in situ but an independent committee of the board is formed to negotiate the sale to the management team, and at the same time taking independent advice.

To avoid any breach of their duties, and to formalise matters for their own protection, management should disclose the potential conflict and obtain approval from the owners of the target business before commencing the buy-out. Without doing so the owners may have a claim for breach of duty, breach of confidentiality and breach of terms of the service contract against the director. However the reality is this will only happen if the buy-out does not succeed and the parties fall out.

There are a few very specific provisions that need to be addressed. **13–06**

- A director must disclose to the meeting of the directors of a company any interest he has in a contract or proposed transaction or arrangement with the company (ss.177 and 182). This should be done by notice in writing (s.184) or at the first board meeting at which the possible sale is discussed (assuming the director has started to pull together the bid).

- Directors are required to obtain shareholder approval for any substantial property transaction (s.190). This is not usually an issue in most buy-outs; however care should be taken where the buy-out involves a purchase of assets. It is important that the details are considered on every transaction.

Finally, it is important that a directors' employment contract is reviewed to ensure that there are no contractual provisions that either prevent the manager from being involved in the buy-out or need to be addressed, such as restrictive covenants or notice periods. At the same time there are likely to be confidentiality clauses included and even if not there are common law issues of confidentiality to adhere to.

13.2 Business focus

13–07 Completing a management buy-out is one of the most complicated transactions a corporate lawyer will be involved in because of the many different aspects and the sheer volume of documentation involved. However a lawyer should always remember that he is in reality a very small part of the whole process and probably a very insignificant part at that. By the time it has reached the lawyers, it is quite likely that both the management and the funders have moved on and are beginning to plan the integration stages and the 100 day plans. The managers will be at the centre of most things, all types of due diligence, funding, the acquisition, planning integration and all major issues are likely to find their way back to them. At the same time they have to do the most important thing, and that is to keep their focus on the business. This often gets forgotten and is one of the major reasons why the price is re-negotiated at the last minute, because the management accounts delivered before the transaction was due to complete showed a downturn in the business.

The lawyer can play his part by establishing an efficient process at the outset that takes account of both an efficient use of meetings, document production and the availability of key management resource. A good lead lawyer that has the ability to both lead the deal and also project manage is a valuable but, it has to be said, a rare resource.

13.3 Management of the company

13–08 From the first day after the buy-out there will be a new structure in place that will involve the interests of new funders, both debt and equity. There will be an excitement about the future that the managers will hope to spread to all of the company's employees. Prior to that the managers and funders will have entered into a subscription or investment agreement that amongst other things will have set out the governance of the company, the role of the chairman and non-executive directors, the number of board meetings and information required. More often than not this is determined from a precedent document produced by the lawyer and usually very little is changed that reflects on how the company is run going forward. The investor may have certain requirements and preferences but he doesn't have all the answers. A good lead manager will have his own ideas. He is likely to have much more experience than the investor director in running businesses. A good lawyer will draw them out and try to reflect them in the agreement. This is an opportunity for the CEO to impress his leadership and embed his culture on the business. For such an important part of the business it can't be correct that buy-out teams should adhere to precedent drafting. Is it correct to have a board meeting once a month? How does the investor and CEO ensure that these are collaborative board meetings and not just reporting requirements? (Often management teams have pre meetings to prepare for the board meeting. That must be wrong and is a symptom of the investor approach.) Is there time set aside for strategy meetings, usually offsite? Are the CEO and the investor scheduling quality time together? What happens if the CEO and the chairman do not work well together or if the CEO and the investor director do not get on?

But more importantly than anything, and despite all the documentation and processes, at the end of the day a successful private transaction, like so many other things, is about the success of key relationships, the management and the employees, the CEO and the chairman, the management team with each other and the management team and the investor director. A good lead lawyer will remind his management team to maintain those relationships throughout the process.

13.4 Warranties

Warranties have been discussed elsewhere in this book. The purpose of raising them again in this chapter is because of their importance to management. The level and the nature of the warranties that the managers are asked to provide can often spook them. Their lawyer can play a pivotal role in not only negotiating maximum protection in making the warranties as specific as possible, ensuring that proper limitations are in place and in conducting a full due diligence and disclosure exercise but also in giving comfort to the managers of the reality of warranty claims. **13–09**

Warranties will be requested from the managers in the Investment or Shareholders Agreement. If the investors obtain a strong set of warranties from the vendor, then they are likely to seek less from management. However the vendors are likely to resist giving extensive warranties since it is the managers, not they, who have been involved in the day-to-day running of the company. At its extreme, they may even be reluctant to warrant the audited accounts on the basis that the auditors could certify them only following representations from management.

It is normal in a sale and purchase agreement to exclude liability for representations made in pre-contractual negotiations, but this is unlikely to be acceptable in the investment agreement as investors will have relied heavily on input from management before agreeing to proceed. Where a director or employee makes fraudulent or recklessly misleading statements during a management buy-out, there are a number of potential actions that he exposes himself to, which include both criminal and civil claims. Where the director or employee makes a deception and there is either an actual injury or a possible injury, the director or employee will be **13–10** liable under the common law for fraud. "Injury" can mean financial loss suffered by a vendor. In addition the Theft Act sets out a number of offences that are connected with obtaining benefits by deception. Section 15(1), for instance, provides that where a person dishonestly obtains property, including money belonging to another, by deception, with the intention to permanently deprive the other of it, he will be liable on conviction on indictment to imprisonment for a term not exceeding five years and an unlimited fine. More specifically it is also a criminal offence under s.47(1) Financial Services Act 1986 to induce a person to buy or sell shares by a fraudulent statement or the concealment of material facts.

Clearly the repercussions for a fraudulent management team can be extreme but it is very rare that a management team will fall into this category.

13–11 The equity investors will always seek certain specific warranties directly from the managers to themselves. These will include warranties in respect of Newco, usually a new "off the shelf" company administered by management's lawyers and in respect of information about themselves given in a management questionnaire. They will also seek warranties in respect of the business plan, future financial forecasts and with regard to the due diligence reports. The wording is usually sufficiently anodyne for these not to be a problem. The investors do not perceive the warranties as providing them with a course of action, but as a way for management to confirm the business plan and the facts of the various reports, and provide as much information as possible about the business to be acquired. This can be achieved without management feeling pressured into providing onerous guarantees, and without damaging the relationship between the management and the investors. For example, the investors may accept that the managers may be severally liable for the warranties, that the warranties may be restricted to their actual knowledge, that the maximum claim brought against a manager for a breach may be limited to one or two times salary (enough to concentrate their minds), that a high de minimis be accepted and that the time period for warranty claims may be limited to twelve months after closing. In short it is almost unheard of and probably not worth the while of an investor to bring a warranty claim against a manager under these warranties. As much as anything an investor will not wish to bring claims against his own management teams. However, where there is fraud of some description, as described in para.13–10, and the limitations fall away, then he will or is likely to bring a claim.

13–12 Where warranties against a manager are much more likely to bite is if the manager is also one of the vendors and is providing warranties to Newco. In that case the warranties will be perceived much more as a mechanism to achieve the price, the limitations will be less generous and a claim will be seen as justifiable to correct the price. This is where the lawyer advising management should focus his greatest efforts, taking care to ensure that the warranties are specific and that the limitations and the disclosure exercise provide the management with the maximum comfort.

Warranties

Warranties on exit

The position of the equity investor in relation to warranties on an exit is often the focus of negotiations on every trade sale. The investor will wish to realise his investment without having to give any warranties that could impact the return to his investors. However the management are not so lucky and will be expected to provide a full set of warranties. In fact a clause to this effect will have been included in the investment agreement at the beginning of the investment. Their real value will however be limited, usually to the amounts received by them which will fall well short of the consideration being paid. In addition the buyer may wish to involve the managers in the business going forward and so will be reluctant to pursue them for warranty claims.

A number of solutions have developed, very rarely satisfactorily and each party will have to compromise in some way. **13–13**

- The managers provide warranty cover in excess of their proceeds and the investor provides a contribution through a deed of contribution. The investor retains its no warranty position but will have to retain some of the proceeds in the event of a claim and so can't distribute to its funders.

- The management team give warranties with claims being made only against a ring-fenced escrow fund or retention account to which all the sellers have contributed a proportion of the proceeds

- The management give warranties but they are insured with warranty and indemnity insurance. Details of this are discussed earlier in the book. Many insured deals are negotiated on a slow recourse basis in which the buyer's recourse for breaches of the warranties is solely against the insurer after an initial threshold has been breached. The threshold may be payable wholly or in part by the warrantors.

There are signs that the traditional refusal of investors to give warranties may be changing. In particular this is following the American experience whose investors aren't so intransigent.

13.5 Good and bad leaver provisions

Provisions will be included in the articles that provide for the situation where a manager leaves the business and the effect on his shares. The key to the success of the investment made by the investor is likely to be a combination of the price he pays as well as the leadership qualities of his management team. He will expect the management team to stay for the duration unless he chooses to get rid of them and he will believe that they are being offered a very significant opportunity. **13–14**

However nothing is black and white and he will consider the various scenarios that may arise.

- A manager simply wants to leave. He has become bored or has decided it's not for him.
- A manager has become ill, or a close member of his family has.
- A manager is guilty of gross misconduct.
- A manager is underperforming.

What is certain is that the investor will wish to see the managers shares transferred. The only question that remains is the price at which they transfer. This is where the distinction between good and bad leavers arises. It will be argued that bad leavers should either get nothing from the sale of their shares or a limited amount as a result of some form of vesting provisions but not the full value. The definition of a bad or good leaver will vary according to each case but usually it is accepted that managers who walk away from their commitment are bad leavers, in the same way that managers who are dismissed for gross misconduct are. Sometimes it will also include managers who are dismissed for under performance, but there is often an opportunity to negotiate a form of vesting which allows for a manager to at least get a percentage of full value depending how long after the buy-out the dismissal occurs. Good leavers should however be allowed to realise the full value of their shares on leaving. They are often defined to include managers who retire on health grounds, the personal representatives of managers of who die and managers who are dismissed but who have not underperformed or are not guilty of any breach of any employment contract.

When negotiating these clauses the lawyer should ensure that they are not negotiated in isolation from the proposed service agreement of the manager. Clauses in the service agreement and in particular in the termination clauses will have an effect on the nature of the departure of the manager and so should be considered when negotiating the good and bad leaver provisions.

13.6 The purchase of shares of a departing manager

13–15 One of the knock on effects of good and bad leaver provisions which is often not considered properly is the ability to find a ready purchaser for the shares of an outgoing manager. First and foremost the managers must agree with the investor who is allowed to purchase the shares. The managers may wish to share those shares amongst themselves; the investor may want to make them available to a replacement. Even if allowed to buy the shares they may not be able to afford to do so.

The purchase of shares of a departing manager

There is no easy solution. The articles may allow for the shares to be purchased by the company but the company may not have sufficient distributable profits to do so. Many employee share ownership schemes will involve a trust which is used to hold shares on a temporary basis and ultimately make them available to employees. Such trusts can be convenient vehicles to hold shares of outgoing managers until such time as an incoming manager can be found or can raise the funds to purchase the shares. Even if an incoming manager is found it is likely that shares will only be transferred to him after a sufficient period of time has elapsed that allows him or her to prove him or herself.

13.7 Ratchets

Ratchets are found in many buy-outs or private equity transactions. There are a number of reasons given. **13–16**

- They provide an incentive to management. By gaining an increased share of the equity management will become more incentivised over the life of the buy-out.
- It will encourage an exit. By gearing the ratchet towards the exit timescale preferred by the investor, he will be able to achieve his desired return.
- It can be seen as a selling point for a private equity house when competing against other houses for the buy-out.
- It skews the buy-out towards a capital return, ensuring that the management focus on the exit and not on returns during the life of the investment.
- It can provide the investor with the insurance of getting the price right. Management get a disproportionately high share of the equity. If there is a disagreement about how much they should get it can often be bridged by the use of a ratchet.

Ratchets have been discussed at length earlier in the book. The main point to note here is just how important they are to management. Lawyers often believe that this is the realm of the corporate financier, usually because it is mathematical and he or she doesn't understand it. Any lawyer that takes the time and effort to understand the ratchet, to simplify and clarify it and understand the implications of it, will set himself apart from other management lawyers.

13.8 Service agreements

Too often corporate lawyers allow their employment counterparts to negotiate the service agreements. This is generally a mistake. Of course it is right to ensure that **13–17** the service agreement is technically correct but it is part of the overall package negotiated with the investors on behalf of management. The lead corporate lawyer is closest to the managers and to understanding their requirements and should see it as part of his role to negotiate such a key document. It will be one of the key issues that management have to ensure that this document is to their liking. It's often the only document they read from cover to cover.

13.9 Heads of terms

13–18 Sometimes lawyers are brought in to a transaction after the heads of agreement have been negotiated. This is a mistake. The lead lawyer should insist that he is brought in at an early stage. Too often heads are drawn up with the aim of agreeing certain key terms down the line. Not only will this mean that the transaction will be more acrimonious than is necessary, but it will also lead to a very inefficient process. It is much easier to agree principles that are reflected in a five or six page document than in several documents of hundreds of pages. If the process is slowed at the outset and care taken on the key issues such as set out in this book it is a lot less likely that the parties will fall out and more likely that the parties will move to closing efficiently.

Appendix 1

Glossary

Accountants report: An independent report produced by accountants into the affairs of the Target and its group with special emphasis on its accounts, financial records, budget and business plan. Often a key document in the decision to fund a deal.

Acquisition funding: Normally takes the form of a reducing term loan. The bank funds the loan through borrowing from the money market, with interest on the loan consequently being linked to LIBOR.

Acting in concert: A Blue Book term which defines a group of shareholders ("concert parties"). Many rules in the Blue Book regulate what concert parties may do in relation to a Plc.

Advance corporation tax: Advance Corporation Tax has been abolished previously. UK companies, when paying a dividend or distribution, were required at the same time to make a payment to HMRC of Advance Corporation Tax ("ACT"). This ACT could then be offset as a down payment against the company's corporation tax liabilities (mainstream corporation tax). The shareholder receiving the dividend obtained a tax credit of an equal amount. Special rules applied for dividends in a tax group.

Allotment: The right to subscribe for new shares in a company, usually based on a board decision. Allotment technically occurs when the right becomes unconditional.

Allotment letter: A document issued by a company and setting out the terms of an allotment. See also PAL.

Arbitration: The legally effective adjudication of disputes otherwise than by the ordinary procedure of the courts.

Arrangement fee: A fee payable on a transaction, usually to a person putting in debt or equity finance, and calculated as a percentage of the money introduced.

Glossary

Articles of association: One of the constitutional documents of a company setting out the internal rules for its operation and the rights attached to different classes of shares. Usually adopts Table A with modifications.

Assignment of contracts: The transfer of contractual rights so that the assignee may sue the debtor or other party.

Associate: In general, will include a close relative (such as a spouse, parents, children, brother or sister) or partner or any connected company. The true definition may vary according to the circumstances in which it is used.

Attorney: An agent formally appointed by deed to act on behalf of another (the principal). An attorney has more authority than a mere agent and special rules protect a third party dealing with an attorney.

Bad leaver: A person who ceases to be a director or employee of a venture capital backed company (or group) and who must offer up his shares, usually at a price below market value. Often based on the circumstances of departure—a manager dismissed for gross misconduct will often be a bad leaver. The term is generally only used in articles of association. Contrast to good leaver and early leaver.

Beneficial ownership: The economic and real ownership of a right or asset entitling the owner to the full benefit of it, even though the asset may for example be legally owned by or registered in the name of a Nominee on behalf of the beneficial owner.

BIMBO: A "Buy-In Management Buy-Out"—a transaction where the management team backed to buy the Target includes both existing managers and managers new to the business. New managers are usually in more senior positions.

Blue Book: The City Code of Takeovers and Mergers—a non-statutory code which regulates, among other things, the acquisition of control of an English Plc (whether or not listed). So-called because it is a loose-leafed book in a blue file.

Bond: A document, usually transferable, which reflects a debt owed by a company.

Bonus issue: An allotment of shares in a company to existing shareholders paid for by the company—for example, out of share premium account.

Bought deal: Sometimes, in order that the parties can move quickly, the provider of finance will facilitate the purchase of a target company ("buy

Appendix 1

the deal") and hold it until such time as it is able to restructure and syndicate the finance.

Bridge financing: Finance (usually debt) borrowed for a temporary purpose in the expectation that it will be repaid either from term facilities or, for example, proceeds of a rights issue.

Business angel: A wealthy individual who invests for shares or loans in a private company. Business angels are often used when the total amount required is below the level of interest to a venture capitalist. Business angels often invest together in informal clubs or syndicates.

Business Expansion Scheme ("BES"): A former tax regime existing 1988–1993 which gave favourable income tax and capital gains tax treatment to investors in private companies. The rules became increasingly strict over time to deny BES for lower risk activities (e.g. property investment). Replaced by EIS and in part by the VCT regime.

Business plan: A document which contains full details of the management team's plans for the future, with financial forecasts. Produced by the management, sometimes with the financial advisers, at an early stage and is essential in persuading financiers to back the management buy-out.

BVCA: British Venture Capitalists Association—an association of leading providers of private equity finance in the United Kingdom.

Call option: An arrangement whereby someone who is the owner of an asset agrees to sell the asset if the potential buyer exercises the right to call for the asset. In a call option, the owner is the grantor of the option and the potential buyer is the grantee.

Caps, collars and floors: Terms applicable to interest rates on a loan: a cap indicates a maximum rate above which the interest rate cannot rise; a floor is a minimum rate below which the interest rate cannot drop; and a collar is a combination of the two, i.e. the rate will move up or down below a cap and above a floor.

Capital losses: Vendors should ensure that any available capital losses may be set against a gain arising on the sale of target. If the vendor is a member of a group, there may be a "capital loss" company to which target should be transferred prior to sale.

Capital redemption reserve: A balance sheet entry arising on certain transactions in the Companies Act (for example, redemption of shares out of distributable reserves). Effectively, it is used to re-balance the balance sheet. It is not distributable by way of dividend but may be used, for example, to pay for a bonus issue.

Glossary

Capitalisation issue: See bonus issue.

Captive funds: Venture capital funds whose manager is owned by, for example, a bank and who invest only monies provided by such bank.

Carried interest: An arrangement whereby certain individuals who are managers of a venture capital fund invest alongside that fund on its investment when it makes an investment. Generally, carried interest is only in the riskiest element of the investment (usually equity shares). Accordingly, the individuals in the venture capital organisation have a direct personal interest in the success of the investment.

Cash flow: A term to describe the cash generated over a period by a business. Used in the context of financial covenants, or for a cash sweep (see below). Financial covenants in a loan agreement will invariably require cash generated by a business over a period of time to be at least equal to the interest payments, loan repayments and dividends which the company wishes to pay.

Cash sweep: A requirement to apply a mandatory prepayment of a loan an amount of the cash generated by the company each financial year from its ordinary trading activities. These are usually strongly negotiated, and, for example, may require that excess cash flow over a threshold need only be prepaid, and/or that a proportion only of the company's excess cash flow be applied in mandatory prepayment.

Certificate of title: Certificate, usually issued by a solicitor, which deals with the title of an owner to land. It would cover, for example, whether the owner has good and marketable title and details of restrictive covenants, etc. It would not relate to the condition or repair of the premises or give an opinion on valuation. When someone wishes to invest in a company, the investor will often take a mortgage over land. Sometimes the lender's own lawyers will investigate title. In other situations they will rely on a certificate of title issued by the company's solicitors.

Change of control: Generally, where the ownership of a company or group of companies passes from one shareholder or group of shareholders to another. The precise definition varies but usually a change in ownership or control of a majority of the voting shares is sufficient. Funders often require loans and preference shares to be repaid on a change of control. Sometimes there are restrictions on a change of control—see for example tag along and drag along.

City Code on Takeovers and Mergers: See Blue Book.

Class rights: Legal right attached to a class of shares—usually, two or more classes of shares will have different rights (for example, on dividend, return

Appendix 1

of capital voting, etc). These are class rights. It is difficult to change class rights, even if the class is only a small percentage of the total company. Often a way to entrench rights for minorities.

Convertible loan stock: Loan stock where the creditor has the right in certain circumstances to convert the whole or part of the debt into shares in the company. The conversion right is often a remedy available if the loan has not been repaid on time. The creation of convertible loan stock often gives rise to rights of pre-emption for existing shareholders.

Convertible preference share: Preference shares which, in certain circumstances are convertible into shares of one or more other classes—usually a mix of equity shares and deferred shares. Sometimes the right exists throughout the life of the preference share, enabling the holder to change the nature of his investment into equity. In other situations, the right to convert to equity is a remedy, available if the preference shares are not redeemed on time.

Coupon: The amount payable on a preference share or loan stock, usually on fixed dates and of a fixed amount. The phrase originates from the practice of having detachable coupons on the certificate which were presented by the holder to the company to claim the payment. Such detachable coupons are rarely seen now.

Cum dividend: A transfer of shares where the transferee acquires the right also to receive a dividend declared but not paid on the shares. See also ex-dividend.

Cumulative preference share: A preference share which has a dividend (usually of a fixed amount) which is cumulative in nature—i.e. if not paid in a particular year, it carries forward and is payable in a later year in addition to the normal dividend in that year.

Damages: Monetary compensation for the infringement of a right. In tort their basic purpose is to put the injured party in the same position as if the tort had not been committed, whilst in contract it is to place him in the same position as if the contract had been performed.

Debenture: Technically, any document evidencing debt by a company. Nowadays is used to refer to a charge created by a company in favour of a lender, usually containing both fixed and floating charges over its assets.

Debt: Unlike holders of equity who are "members of the company", the provider of debt finance is a creditor of the business just as is a supplier of raw materials. Debt providers are repaid over a long period and take security for their lending.

Glossary

Deferred share: A share which ranks behind an equity share and often only entitles the holder to a fixed amount once a large return has been paid on the equity shares. Deferred shares are usually practically worthless and can result from some re-organisation of the share capital (for example, following conversion of convertible preference shares) or sometimes from a ratchet.

Development capital: Finance raised from venture capitalist to assist the evolution, expansion or rescue of an existing company. Generally, the venture capitalist will end up with a minority stake in the business and the existing shareholders will remain in control. Sometimes used to enable existing shareholders to buy out, for example, a departing manager or family member who, for whatever reason, is no longer to remain a shareholder.

Director: A person who carries out the office of director of a company. The title given is not conclusive (for example, the term "governor" may be used if the company is in fact a school).

Directors' questionnaire: A questionnaire completed by a potential director of a company setting out personal details, including personal business history. Often modelled on the questionnaire used for prospective directors of listed companies. This is often an important document to gain background information for funders, especially if they wish to take up personal references on the directors. The inclusion of a question on net worth can prove controversial.

Disclosure letter: A letter written by or on behalf of someone giving warranties and setting out details where the warranties would otherwise be incorrect. A disclosure letter is given to the person receiving the warranties at the same time as the warranties themselves and usually no claim may be brought under the warranties for what is mentioned in the disclosure letter. Most commonly seen in the context of warranties given regarding a subscription for shares. Less frequently seen in the context of warranties in a bank loan agreement, as those warranties serve a different purpose.

Discounted cash flow: A commonly used formula for the valuation of a business based on the principle that value today will always equal future cash flow discounted at the opportunity cost of capital (where it may otherwise be invested).

Distributable profits: English law generally prohibits a company returning capital to its members and allows a dividend only out of profits made in the company and evidenced by accounts (sometimes, but not always, audited accounts). Generally, only realised profits are available for distribution.

Distribution in specie: A dividend paid by a company to its members otherwise than in cash—for example, by transferring to the member land owned by the company or shares in a subsidiary. Special accounting and tax rules apply.

Dividend cover: The number of times that the net dividend is covered by the net earnings attributable to the equity holders.

Dividend policy: Terms agreed between the shareholders as to when a dividend will be paid by the company and its amount. Most venture capitalists would prefer a hard right to a definite dividend under the articles of association.

Dividend yield: The amount of dividend payable on a share compared to the amount paid to the company for the share—see also coupon.

Drag along: Usually, a buyer will want to acquire 100 per cent of the shares. A drag along is a mechanism whereby certain shareholders (usually a weighted majority or perhaps the holders of a particular class, e.g. the investors) can compel all shareholders to join in the sale and therefore receive a price reflecting 100 per cent of the equity. Drag along is often difficult to negotiate and hard to achieve in practice.

Due diligence: The investigation undertaken by the investors and the bankers, along with their advisers, before determining whether to back the buy-out. The results of the exercise take the form of a report, usually prepared by the accountants.

Earnings valuation model: A formula used to value a private company based on the premise that the company's value is the sum of its discounted future earnings stream. A discount factor is applied to future earnings, the uncertainty of which leads to setting a multiple of current or future earnings.

Early leaver: A term used in articles of association of a venture capital backed company, usually suggesting that a manager who ceases to be a director or an employee in the group before a particular date will be required to offer back his shares at a discount to market value. Often, the date is the only factor and the other circumstances surrounding the departure are not taken into account. See also Good Leaver and Bad Leaver.

Earn-out: An arrangement whereby the seller of an asset receives the whole or part of the price by reference to the performance of that asset after sale—for example, a seller of a company may receive a price dependent upon the future turnover or profitability of the business for a given period after the sale. Often used where a service business is being sold or where the continued involvement of the vendors in the business after the sale is a relevant factor for the purchaser.

Glossary

EMI Options: Options granted under the Enterprise Management Incentives Scheme. These are tax advantaged options granted to employees/directors. Tax advantages require a number of conditions to be satisfied before EMI Options can be granted.

Employee buy-out: A buy-out where managers and the more general workforce become shareholders following the buy-out. Generally tends to be seen on privatisations or other transactions with a former public sector involvement. Although general employees are included, their individual stakes are usually much smaller than managers' and often on different terms.

Enhanced voting rights: Mechanism, usually found in articles of association, designed to increase votes attached to particular class of shares or particular shareholder. Sometimes, the enhancement is to multiply the number of votes, other occasions to bring the total for the class up to a particular percentage of the Company (for example 75 per cent). Triggered by some event of default such as late payment of dividends.

Enterprise Investment Scheme ("EIS"): A tax regime (partly replacing the old BES) designed to give Income and Capital Gains Tax breaks to individuals who take minority stakes in unlisted UK companies. The conditions for relief are strict including restrictions on the trades that the group may operate.

Equity: Another way of describing ordinary shares—the voting share capital of the company.

Equity kicker: Rights, warrants or options to take a proportion of the equity granted to a lender. They are frequently used in connection with the lower-level debt, such as mezzanine finance.

Equity share capital: Defined in the Companies Act as any shares other than ones that have a fixed right to both income and capital. In practice, the term is often synonymous with ordinary shares. They often represent the most valuable and riskiest type of shares in a company when compared to a prior ranking preference share which has only a fixed up side.

Equity shares: Shares which are neither preference shares or deferred shares.

Event of default: An event or occurrence which entitles a person to exercise a remedy which, for example, causes term debt to become immediately payable. Sometimes an event of default is automatic, but more usually the relevant party (e.g. lender) must actually make demand for repayment following the occurrence of the event of default.

Appendix 1

Ex-dividend: With extra transfer of shares where the transferor retains the right to receive a particular dividend. In listed companies, share prices are often quoted ex-dividend in relation to dealings after the record date before the dividend is actually paid.

Executive director: A director in the employ of the company who generally has operational responsibilities.

Exit: Investors "exit" when they realise their investment, either in cash or marketable securities. They generally do so by way of a stock market flotation, a trade sale or a buy-back of shares.

Exit capitalisation ratchet: See ratchet.

Facility agreement: The principal document or series of documents regulating the terms upon which debt (usually secured) is to be advanced to a company by a bank or similar institution.

Factoring/invoice discounting: Similar to invoice finance or invoice discounting, this is a means of easing the cash flow of a business. It involves the company transferring its debtors to a third party, which in return pays an agreed percentage of the money due on the debts. The person who has bought the debt then collects the debts.

Financial assistance: A rule in the Companies Act designed to protect the creditors of a company from the use of its assets and credit to assist in the acquisition of the shares in that company or a holding company. It is a criminal offence to contravene the rules. Not all financial assistance is unlawful, however, and certain acts which would otherwise be unlawful financial assistance can be made lawful by the whitewash procedure.

Financial projections: Projections for the next three to five years covering both profit projections and forecast working capital requirements.

Financial Services Authority ("FSA"): The principal public body charged under the FSMA to regulate investments and investment advisers in the United Kingdom.

Fixed charge: Security (such as a mortgage) on assets, such as land and buildings, provided to a lender which is fixed in nature. This usually means that the consent of the lender will be required for any dealing with the charged asset.

Flotation: When the company is first quoted on the Official List maintained by UKLA, it is said to be "floated". Synonymous with listing and listed.

Floating charge: A charge over all of the assets of the business provided to a lender. The company is usually allowed to deal with assets subject to a floating charge only without restriction. The floating charge will crystallise into a fixed charge on the occurrence of certain events.

Forced sale: A sale under a provision in the articles of association forcing a minority shareholder to sell his shares if a bid for the major equity investor's shareholding has been made and accepted. Synonymous with Drag Along.

Foreign currency exposure management: Foreign currency issues can arise in the context of a MBO, for example where the vendor has had a policy of not hedging foreign currency receipts from overseas sales. The new management may prefer to manage this risk, for example by forward exchange contracts.

Fraudulent trading: A statutory term under the Insolvency Act which enables the Court to penalise directors who have normally conducted the affairs of the company with a view to defrauding creditors.

Full title guarantee: A full statutory phrase under the Law of Property (Miscellaneous Provisions) Act—the highest quality of title usually available in English law. It is representation by the owner that he owns the asset and is free to deal with the same free from any charge or encumbrance, etc.

Fully diluted: After taking into account all allotments of shares during the exercise of any subscription rights or conversion rights. The term is often used for defining a particular percentage of a company which shareholder (or option holder) is to receive (e.g. five per cent fully diluted means that proportion of shares which are to take into account of all other options and conversion rights will result in a holder having five per cent of the company).

Furniss v Dawson: A leading tax case under which English courts developed a doctrine to attack artificial steps inserted into a transaction or series of transactions for no commercial purpose (other than to avoid or reduce tax exposure). When applicable, it enables the court to cut out the offending step or steps and permit the underlying taxation to be assessed on the adjusted arrangement.

Gearing or leverage: The ratio of debt to equity, or the relationship of the total debt of the company (including all bank overdrafts and loan stock) to the company's paid-up share capital.

Golden handshake: An initial payment made for example, on recruitment of a new director. Golden handshake is designed to attract the director and is often designed to compensate the director for some loss which he may suffer as a result of moving straight across to the second company (for example, the loss of options or bonus entitlement in previous employment).

Appendix 1

Golden hello: See Golden handshake.

Golden parachute: An arrangement designed to give a "soft landing" to executives for example, on loss of employment. An example would be a bonus payable on change of control or particularly a generous termination entitlement under the contract.

Good leaver: See Bad leaver.

Guarantee: A form of personal security under which a guarantor or surety undertaken by contract to a creditor to answer for the debt, or default of another, the debtor, if the debtor does not fulfil his obligations.

Hands-on/hands-off: Often used to describe the venture capitalist or bank taking a more active role in the management of an investment rather than simply receiving information, etc. A venture capitalist who takes an active role in the budget and strategy planning of the business is said to be hands on.

Hive-down: A transfer of the whole or part of the business of a company to one or more of its subsidiaries—often with a view sooner or later to selling the shares in the subsidiary to a third party. This mechanism is often used in receiverships.

Hive-up: A transfer by a company of the whole or part of its trade to a holding company. This is often done to reduce the number of operating companies in a group or, perhaps, to take out of the subsidiary a business which it wishes to retain as a preliminary step to selling the subsidiary with the rest of its trade to a third party. In that event, watch out for financial assistance, especially if the holding company does not pay at the time of the hive-up.

Inability to pay debts: The inability to pay debts is one of the statutory definitions of insolvency under s.123 Insolvency Act 1986. Serious consequences follow under the insolvency regime if a company is unable to pay its debts.

Indemnity: A contractual arrangement whereby a person (A) has a liability to (B) and a third person (C) promises to A to fund its liability to B. Most insurance is an indemnity.

Insolvent: Strictly, a statutory term under the Insolvency Act 1986 s.123. It includes the inability of a company to pay its debts, failure by a company to respond to certain statutory demands and ballot sheet insolvency where the liabilities on the balance sheet exceed the assets.

Internal rate of return: The average annual rate of return which a venture capital institution will seek to achieve, comprising the running yield and the proceeds of realisations or redemptions. Often known as IRR.

Glossary

Interest cover: Like dividend cover, interest cover is a measure of the ratio between loan interest to be paid by a company and its gross earnings. It is an indicator of the business's ability to meet its interest debt; if cover is low, there is a danger that the company will not be able to pay interest when it falls due.

Interest rate exposure management: High levels of gearing are common in MBOs. Although this means that the return of the investors will be enhanced, the financial results of the business will be sensitive to interest rate movements. It is therefore prudent for the business to hedge against increases in interest rates.

Investment agreement: An agreement between managers, venture capitalists and, usually, the company itself. The Investment Agreement sets out the terms that venture capitalists will subscribe for shares in the company and regulates the ongoing management of the investment (for example, giving rights for the investors to receive management accounts, etc.). Usually, it contains restrictions and vetoes on the conduct of the company whereby certain matters can only be transacted with the consent of the investor (or sometimes the investor director).

Investor consents: Consents sought or acquired from investor and/or the articles of association. Often, a particular percentage of investors is sufficient (usually either 51 per cent or 75 per cent by value of investment).

Investor Director: A director appointed to the board of a company by the investors under rights conferred on them in the articles of association or, occasionally, the articles. Not all investors will seek the right to appoint an investor director and, even where the right exists, it is not always the case that the investor director will be in office. Often seen as "spy in the camp" the investor director is nevertheless also a full director of the company and owes fiduciary duties to which and its shareholders and creditors as a whole.

Invoice discounting: See factoring.

IPO: **Initial Public Offering**—equivalent to flotation issue. In the context of shares, new shares are only issued when the allottee has been entered in the register of members as their holder. It is at that moment that the allottee becomes a member of the company.

Joint and several: A basis upon which two or more persons may share an obligation for liability of the English law. Where an obligation is joint and several, the creditor may proceed against any or all of the obligors and the death or release of one obligor will not reduce or discharge any other obligor. A common status upon which liability in this nature are shared.

Appendix 1

Junk bonds: High-yielding, high-risk unsecured financing originally used in the United States in highly leveraged buy-outs. They were developed for companies with relatively low credit ratings or for companies which are not formally credit rated.

Junior debt: Financing which ranks for repayment behind other borrowings; also commonly known as subordinated debt, but see the term subordinated debt.

Jurisdiction: The authority attaching to a court or other similar authority. This may be defined by a territory of by an area of authority.

Usually used in the context of a contract whereby the parties agree that any dispute will be dealt with by a particular court or legal system. Freedom for parties to choose the jurisdiction is often restricted either under the relevant national law or as a result of international treaties and conventions.

Keyman insurance: Insurance on the health and lives of personnel essential in the business; often insisted upon by investors (and banks) to provide some compensation in the event of death or inability to run the business. The policy generally pays out to the company to cover the dislocation costs and recruitment costs following, say, the death of the CEO. Usually, policies are also obtained which are assigned in favour of the bank by way of security. Often an area of discussion with the bank on structured deals is whether the proceeds may be used for this purpose or must be used to repay term debt.

Lead bank: Where two or more banks are lending in a syndicate, the principal bank driving the transaction is known as the lead bank.

Lead investor: Where two or more venture capitalists are investing in a syndicate, the principal investor driving the investment is known as the lead investor.

Leveraged buy-out: A buy-out geared or financed by borrowings, often to a level beyond that generally found in normal trading companies in the sector.

LIBOR: The London Inter Bank Offered Rate: it denotes the interest rates payable in the financial markets for monies lent by institution to one another. It usually determines the interest rate applicable to a loan, together with the margin, and reflects the cost to the lender of obtaining funds in the financial markets which then lends to the borrower.

Liquidation preference: The priority in which the assets of the company will be divided on a winding up. If the company is solvent, the liquidation preference determines the priority in which the surplus assets (after paying off creditors) will be divided between the different classes of shares. Often, preference shares will rank ahead of equity shares. Similarly, the equity shares held by institutions will usually rank ahead of equity shares held by management.

Liquidity ratio: Cash flow now commonly used instead.

Loan arrangements: For large MBOs the documents involved in the banking side might include a senior loan agreement, a mezzanine loan agreement, an inter-creditor agreement (recording the relationship between the senior and mezzanine debt) and the security documents which will be entered into by Newco and all members of the target group in order to secure both senior and mezzanine facilities.

Loan note: A document evidencing a loan made to a company. Loan notes are often in registered form and are transferable, providing an effective way for transferring the benefit of the debt. Loan notes were a common feature of sales in the UK, enabling the seller to postpone CGT till the notes themselves were cashed in. Taper relief makes this a less likely feature now. Loan notes are still used as the mechanism for the bulk of the investors' investment in private equity transactions.

Loan note instrument: Document creating loan notes.

Lock-out agreement: A contract between a potential seller and buyer designed to give exclusivity to potential seller, usually for a fixed period of time. This enables the potential buyer to incur costs, etc, on due diligence with some comfort that he will not be gazumped. Sometimes combined with a cost underwrite.

Management buy-in ("MBI"): The purchase of a company in such a way that outside or new management will have a significant share of the equity and future direction.

Management buy-out ("MBO"): The purchase of a company in such a way that its existing management will have a significant share of the equity and future direction.

MWO: Management Walk Out.

Mandatory transfer: Or compulsory transfer or clawback—a mechanism whereby in certain situations a shareholder is required to offer his shares to other shareholders or to the company. In venture capital transactions, this often occurs if a manager ceases to be employed in the group. A principal issue is the price at which the shares are to be offered. See also good leaver and bad leaver.

Appendix 1

Memorandum of association: One of the two constitutional documents of a UK company. It sets out the name, jurisdiction (i.e. English or Scottish), its objects and provides whether the company is limited or unlimited. Usually, it states that the liability of the members is limited by shares and the authorised share capital. In the case of a Plc, it must also state that the company is to be a public company.

Mezzanine finance: A form of funding somewhere between debt and equity. It is often unsecured (or, if secured, second ranking behind the senior bank, with a greater risk that the security will not cover the exposure) and therefore involves a relatively higher degree of risk for the lender. To compensate for the risk, it usually carries rights to a higher interest rate and to equity participation with a warrant.

Monitoring fee: A fee payable to a lender or investor whilst a loan or investment is in place. Designed to reflect the expense incurred in monitoring the investment. In practice, it is often a way for the fund manager to receive income.

Mortgage (or charge): A form of real security where the borrower (mortgager or charger) normally retains possession of the property mortgaged but grants a proprietary interest to the lender (mortgagee or chargee).

Negligence: In tort negligence may indicate the commission of some tort through lack of due care. The requisites of tort are a legal duty of care between the parties and breach of that duty by a failure to attain the proper standard of care.

Net asset value: The value of a company (or sometimes of a particular business) as evidenced by reference to its accounts. It does not always reflect the full value of the company to a potential purchaser—e.g. goodwill is generally not recorded as an asset.

Newco: A company set up for a particular purpose, for example, to be the company that acquires the target in a management buy-out. It is very similar to an SPV (or special purpose vehicle) used in a joint venture or a property development project.

New issue: In the context of an IPO, this means the original allotment of shares to the public on listing.

Nil paid: A description of shares: meaning the member has not paid to the company any part of the amount payable for the new share. Subscriber shares are issued nil paid. Articles of association usually require board approval of the transfer of a nil paid share or other share that is not fully paid.

Glossary

Nominal value: All UK company shares have a monetary amount in the name (for example, ordinary share of £1, preference share of 50p). This monetary amount is the nominal value. Unless the company is a Plc there is no requirement that the monetary value be in Sterling—any currency or combination will suffice. The nominal value of a share is the lowest price the company may agree for the issue of the share. If issued at a price above nominal value, the excess is said to be a premium and separately recorded on the balance sheet. Many shares are worth more than nominal value and the expression can sometimes be misleading if its technical meaning is not clearly understood.

Non-cumulative preference share: Preference shares which have a fixed dividend e.g. five per cent per annum but if in a particular year there are insufficient profits to pay the dividend in full, the unpaid amount does not carry forward but is lost. Such shares are rarely seen.

Non-distributable reserves: Those reserves which a company is not able in law to pay out by way of dividend. These include capital redemption reserve and revaluation reserve and, in effect, share capital and share premium account. Whilst reserves can be used for some purposes (for example, share premium account may be used to pay to fund a bonus issue or to write off certain expenses).

Non-executive director: A director who is not employed by the company in an executive capacity, but nevertheless has the same responsibilities as any other director.

Non-recourse finance: A term used to denote that the lender or provider of the finance does not have recourse other than to either certain assets or to certain companies. For example a lender may provide a loan to buy a property. The loan may be secured only against that property, and would be described as a limited recourse loan.

Novation: The replacement of one contract by another, often, but not necessarily with some change of parties.

Observer: Many investment agreements entitle an investor to appoint an observer to attend at board meetings. The observer is not a director and is not entitled to vote at meetings. Sometimes, the right to observer exists instead of an investor director. Sometimes, it arises only if there is at the time being no investor director in office. Sometimes both occur at the same time.

Option: A right granted by a person to acquire an asset. In the case of the company, subscription options are often granted to employees or warrant holders which from time to time entitle them to subscribe for shares in the company.

Appendix 1

Overdraft: A form of loan provided by a bank or other institution whereby the balance changes day to day as debts and credits are processed through the account. Overdrafts are usually repayable on demand without any default or notice period required.

Par value: Equivalent to a nominal value.

Partly paid share: A share where the member holding it has paid some, but not all of the amount. Under Table A, partly paid shares are not really transferable.

Performance ratchet: See ratchet.

Permitted transfer: A mechanism under articles of association whereby a shareholder may transfer shares to some other person without giving rise to any pre-emption rights in favour of existing shareholders—examples include a transfer between members group of companies and a transfer by an individual to his spouse, family trust, etc.

Personal guarantee: A guarantee given by a director or shareholder to a bank or similar institution in respect of the borrowings of the company, a hp agreement or similar. As a result of personal guarantee, the guarantor is liable to pay if the company defaults on the obligations.

P/E ratio: Often used as a guide in determining the current multiple to apply in valuing a company by obtaining relevant comparison companies' price/earning ratios. The P/E ratio of a quoted company will probably need to be adjusted downward for a private company to reflect illiquidity; on the other hand a premium will be required to obtain control.

Phoenix company: A company which arises from the ashes—for example, where a business has gone into insolvency and a new company is set up by some or all of the previous directors or shareholders carrying on a similar trade. Special rules apply under the Insolvency Act in the case of phoenix companies.

Plc: A public company (or a Plc) under the Companies Act. Many rules in the Companies Act apply differently to public companies and private companies. A public company may offer its shares to the public (under strict rules) but most do not. It is questionable if the extra restrictions applicable to a Plc make it a best choice for business medium if there is no intention to offer shares to the public.

Poison pill: Something designed or likely to make a takeover, etc. impossible or less attractive—e.g. the fact that someone is entitled to a generous severance package or that some key IP or property licence may be

Glossary

lost on a change of control. Special rules apply under the Takeover Code to regulate such matters.

Power of attorney: A document executed as a deed whereby one person is appointed the attorney of the other. It is a form of agency. Special rules apply to protect third parties when dealing with an attorney. It is possible to be appointed irrevocably in certain cases—i.e. so that the appointer cannot cancel the agency. This is a common feature of mortgages, charges and options for this reason.

Pre-emption rights: The right to be offered something before someone else. Under the Companies Act existing equity shareholders have limited rights to be offered new equity shares before they are allotted for cash to others.

Pre-sale dividend: The vendor might contemplate extracting a pre-sale dividend as a method of reducing the capital gain that it might make on the sale of shares in the MBO.

Preference shares: Shares which carry the right to be paid the dividend (usually fixed) in priority to the ordinary shareholders. Preference shareholders usually also rank in front of ordinary shareholders on a winding-up of the company, but behind debenture and loan stockholders. Generally their rights are fixed and so extra profit does not belong to this class.

Preferred ordinary shares: A share which has some better rights than an ordinary share but then ranks alongside the ordinary share. Contrast to a preference share which has priority over an ordinary share but is usually fixed and does not rank along the ordinary share beyond the priority.

Premium: In the case of shares, the difference (if any) between the price or value for which the shares are allotted and their nominal value. Generally, this difference is credited to share premium account.

Private equity: External equity funding (with or without debt) available to businesses and not accessed via public markets (e.g. not obtained by a listing or public rights issue by a listed Plc). It is usually advanced by specialist professional investors who either invest their own money (or that of a parent bank, etc) or who raise money from institutions (such as pension funds) or from the public (as an Investment Trust or Venture Capital Trust).

Privileged relation: One of the permitted transferees to whom shares may be transferred without pre-emption in favour of other shareholders. Often found in the articles of private equity backed companies to assist tax

Appendix 1

planning, though whether this is as "necessary" in the age of taper relief is a moot question. Issues may arise as to who should be in the class, especially as many shareholders have personal circumstances and loved ones not based on marriage. Related issues involve clawing back shares if the original transferor ceases to be employed, etc, and what happens if the relationship between the permitted transferee and the transferor ends. Be careful before allowing transfers to persons aged under 18—it can make a sale difficult if the transferee is still under 18 at the time. If it is necessary to transfer to the beneficial ownership minors, use a trust.

Proceeds ratchet: A form of ratchet where value is transferred not by changing the number of shares in issue or the ratio between the classes but by changing the entitlement of one class at the expense of another. This creates a different price per share. This is not the easiest form of ratchet mechanism if a flotation is envisaged as a possible exit.

Prospectus: A public document setting out prescribed information required to be issued by a Plc before certain share issues. The directors of the company and certain others can face personal liability in respect of a prospectus.

Proxy: A person appointed to act as the agent of another at a meeting. Under the Companies Act, in a company with a share capital a proxy need not be a member of the company and the notice of meeting must state this fact.

Proxy card: The document evidencing the appointment of a proxy. The articles often contain rules about the latest time for lodging a proxy—though the Companies Act also regulates this area. A listed company is required to send out a proxy card for any meeting at which a voting decision is required.

Public to Private (PTP): A public to private is a takeover offer which is in effect a MBO of a listed company, so named because, if the takeover is successful, the company will come off the Stock Exchange and become private. Special rules and considerations apply as the target is listed and the Takeover Code applies in a special way due to the insider nature of the directors, etc, who are participating in the MBO. Financial assistance whitewash timing can also be tricky as the target is a Plc and the use of the s.428 statutory drag to sweep non-accepting minorities can also be more complicated by the particular structure of the deal.

Pure equity: Equity is usually permanent. It is the highest risk finance. The equity shareholder has a right to income only after all the other providers of finance have taken their return, and similarly only a right to whatever assets of the business are not required to repay other providers of finance. The amount of pure equity may be insignificant in the context of the overall

Glossary

financing. Its small size is a function of the desirability of allowing the management team to hold considerable voting power and ensuring they have a significant financial stake in the ultimate success of the business.

Purple Book: The listing rules published by the UKLA which set out special rules for listed companies and those seeking listing.

Put option: An arrangement whereby someone who is not the owner of an asset agrees to buy the asset if the owner exercises the right to put the asset on him. In a put option, the potential buyer is the grantor of the option and the owner is the grantee.

Quasi equity: Since the amount of "pure equity" is insufficient to support the level of borrowings required, "quasi equity" must be contributed from sources other than the management team, typically by a private equity fund or similar entity. One suitable form is redeemable preference shares which can be converted into ordinary shares. From the point of view of the financiers, the desirable features of quasi equity are that it should yield income when there may be no dividend on the ordinary shares, that it should represent a reasonable level of potential equity interest if things go wrong and that it should have a built-in incentive for the management team.

Ratchet: A mechanism whereby the management team is rewarded according to results, by adjusting the percentage of equity or share of proceeds the managers will receive on a sale or listing in line with a pre-determined scale of performance. It is often linked to the IRR achieved by the investors on their investments and usually allocates to the managers a greater share of the value achieved over the level at which an IRR hurdle is met.

Redeemable shares: Shares which can be redeemed by the company on terms specified in the articles of association.

Redemption date: The date fixed for redemption.

Related party transaction: A regime applicable to listed companies under Ch.9 of the Purple Book. It is similar to but not the same as the requirement of the Companies Act, s.320 (which may also apply depending upon the precise facts). Chapter 9 requires shareholder approval of most capital transactions entered into between a listed company or one of its subsidiaries on the one hand and related parties on the other. The definition of related parties is broad and includes directors of any group company, certain substantial shareholders and certain companies or trusts, etc, in which such persons have a material interest. The definition extends to anyone who was in that capacity in the previous 12 months. Special disclosure rules apply and, generally, the related parties, etc, cannot vote on the resolution.

Appendix 1

Relevant securities: A term used in the CA 2006 which makes it a criminal offence for the directors to allot relevant securities without prior shareholder consent (though the validity of the allotment is not affect by its transgression). The term has a precise technical meaning but, as a rule of thumb, relevant securities include shares and also the grant of rights to subscribe for or convert into shares (otherwise than under an employee share scheme).

Remuneration committee: A committee of the board body charged with determining the remuneration and other benefits of managers in a private equity investment. The composition of the committee is often a heated matter, though a usual balance is the Investor Director, the CEO and the Chairman. This makes the ability to choose the Chairman of particular importance. The precise ambit of the committee's powers vary and can sometimes include disciplinary and dismissal matters.

Repayment: The combination of the amount of the loan, cash flow and the term will dictate the ability of the business to cover operating expenses, interest and capital repayments.

Restrictive covenant: A promise not to compete, or to solicit customers, employees, etc, often found in sale agreement service agreements and increasingly in investment agreements. The precise scope of the covenant is often hotly debated. As a general rule under English law a restrictive covenant is void in restraint of trade unless the person seeking to rely on it has an interest meriting protection and can show that the covenant is no more onerous than is necessary to protect that interest and is not unreasonable as between the parties or the public interest. If the test is not met, and the court does not or cannot cut out wording to leave the balance enforceable, then the covenant will be void. Asking for too much risks losing all. Even if a covenant is not void for this reason, it may not be enforceable on its facts for other contravention of competition and monopoly laws.

Return on capital: The amount received back for an investment, often expressed as a percentage.

Reverse takeover: A takeover by a listed company whereby the Plc takes over another company in exchange for the issue of Plc shares. Originally, it was only a reverse if the sellers receive so many shares in the Plc that they in fact gain control of it. Under the Purple Book, the special rules applicable to a reverse can arise on transactions which strictly do not meet that precise threshold.

Rights issue: An offer to existing shareholders by or on behalf of a company of new shares for cash. Section 89(1) gives limited pre-emption rights entitling shareholders to such an offer. The Purple Book and market practice modifies this for a listed company and makes special distinctions, e.g. if the shareholder is subject to foreign laws or when fractions arise.

Scrip issue: An allotment of bonus shares.

Secondary buy-out: A MBO of a business which has already been the subject of a MBO and accordingly includes venture capitalists among its sellers. Effectively one venture capitalist backs a team to buy out an earlier venture capitalist. It is therefore one kind of exit. Existing managers who had equity on the first MBO sometimes exit in full or in part and often second tier managers join the equity participation in the new MBO vehicle. Some tertiary buy-outs are now also seen.

Senior debt: Debt provided by the financial backers of the buy-out which is secured, and ranks ahead of junior and mezzanine debt.

Service agreement: An employment contract between the company and the manager setting out the rights and obligations of the parties and the salary and other benefits. The notice period and circumstances entitling dismissal can often be hotly debated.

Shareholders' agreement: See investment agreement.

Shareholders' funds: That part of the balance sheet that is not needed to pay creditors, etc. As a rule of thumb, it is the amount which balances on the balance sheet. It usually comprises share capital, share premium account and other reserves (distributable and non-distributable). In theory it is the amount that would go to shareholders in a winding-up; although in practice there would be taxes and costs to meet and so the whole value is unlikely to go to shareholders.

Share premium account: The difference between the price or value for which a new share is allotted and its nominal value is credited to the share premium account. The share premium account cannot be used to pay a dividend but can be used to finance a bonus issue and to write off certain costs that would otherwise have to go through P&L.

Specialist finance: Specialist finance such as factoring, invoice discounting, leasing and hire purchase. These methods may offer lower costs and higher percentage advances than a bank may be willing to provide. They are usually based upon the lender financing specific assets or classes of assets, often with the lender having legal ownership of the assets.

Spin-off: The retention by a vendor of an interest in the company it has sold, often in the form of an equity stake, and, possibly, a continuing trading relationship.

Appendix 1

Springloaded share: A share, the issue of which automatically changes the rights of another share (usually with the consequence that value is vested in the springloaded shares).

Stamp duty: A tax payable on certain documents (including transfers of land and transfers of shares). When the duty is paid, a stamp is formally impressed into the document to record the date of payment and amount paid. A court will not admit in evidence a document which is stampable and not correctly stamped. It is also an offence to register such a document.

Its imposition in the American Colonies was part of the background to the American Declaration of Independence. This has not affected the willingness of the Exchequer to use it in the UK and it is now a material cost in larger land transactions.

Stamp duty reserve tax: A tax which taxes certain transactions at the share stamp duty rate (currently 0.5 per cent). The charge arises automatically upon the contract becoming unconditional. It will be cancelled however, where a duly stamped conveyance comes into existence within six years of the contract date. It enables the Exchequer to "stamp" paperless transactions which otherwise would have escaped stamp duty when Stock Market dealing rules were changed in the 1980s.

Stock exchange: A market for the public offering and trading of shares, stocks or other securities.

Subdivision: The division of a share into two or more shares of smaller nominal value (e.g. to subdivide an ordinary share of £1 into 10 ordinary shares of 10p each). The key thing is that the total nominal value is not changed. Also if the shares are partly paid, this must also be spread evenly over the shares resulting from subdivision.

Subdivision is often done if the shares have become too valuable in market terms—splitting them up so as to facilitate trading in the smaller shares e.g. it is often done in association with a bonus issue as a preliminary step on flotation.

Ironically, it is also seen if the shares have become worth less than the nominal value—e.g. if a share has a nominal value of say 25p but is trading at 15p then it is difficult for the company to offer new shares to the public at a nominal (and therefore minimum) value of 25p as no one would buy them. Accordingly the old shares are divided (say into one ordinary share of 5p and four deferred shares of 5p). The deferred shares have class rights which render them worthless and so all the 15p value is now in the 5p ordinaries. The company can now offer new 5p ordinary shares at say 14p to encourage subscription.

Glossary

Subordination: The ranking of debt so that it ranks behind and is subordinated to other debt. For example, mezzanine debt is generally subordinated to senior debt by an intercreditor arrangement. If the assets of the creditor are insufficient, the order determines how the assets are applied and a subordinated creditor is therefore less likely to be paid out in full.

Subordinated debt: In strict legal terms, subordinated debt is debt that ranks, on its terms, behind all other debt obligations of a company, and behind the claims of all unsecured creditors against that company. This means the subordinated debt would be paid on a winding-up ahead only of any return to shareholders. The term is also often used to denote a class of debt that ranks behind another class of debt.

Subscription agreement: See investment agreement.

Swamping rights: The power of a shareholder (usually an investor) to exercise greater voting rights in a default position so as to swamp a shareholders' meeting and pass resolutions. Classically this was done by having preference shares that are entitled to vote only in certain default positions but, if that occurred, their number ensured control. For tax reasons this structure is still seen in certain deals. Nowadays swamping is usually done by increasing the votes per share on the investors' equity shares.

Sweet equity: A term applied to managers' equity. It reflects the fact that this equity was available at a lower overall risk. Investors generally pay the same price as managers for their shares but unlike managers usually have to invest extra money as well, e.g. for preference shares or more usually loan notes. Accordingly it is not unusual for an investor to have to invest in total many times as much in the company for each per cent of equity as the manager—whose equity is seen as sweet by comparison. The manager may prefer to describe this as the sweat/envy ratio and as a reward for the work he will have to do to grow and exit the investment.

Syndication: The sharing of a risk among several providers of finance, where the risk is too great to be comfortably carried by a single investor or where tax or accounting reasons make a single investor reluctant to carry the full investment (e.g. if it would require the investor to consolidate the investment in its own group balance sheet).

Tag along: An arrangement, often deriving from a clause in the articles, whereby a purchaser offering to buy a minority shareholder's stake in the management buy-out company must extend that offer to all shareholders. Sometimes known as a "piggy back" or "sell alongside".

Takeover Code: The City Code on Takeovers and Mergers, administered by the Panel on Takeovers and Mergers; it lays down a set of rules and general

Appendix 1

principles which govern the conduct of public company takeovers and mergers.

Taper relief: A CGT provision which when available can lower the effective rate of CGT paid by an individual from 40 per cent to 10 per cent on certain investments. Other conditions and restrictions apply but it is an attractive regime which discourages much of the tax planning that would otherwise have been a feature.

Its attraction when compared to 40 per cent higher rate income tax (and usually NI for the company) makes a capital gains treatment highly desirable for managers. HMRC rules can however sometimes produce the less desired result and advice must always be taken—especially if any change is being made—e.g. inserting a new incentive on a rescue or if a ratchet is bust.

Tort: A civil wrong which may arise independently of any contract between the parties, always remediable by an action for unliquidated damages and sometimes by an injunction.

Trade sale: A common exit route, where the company which made the management buy-out is sold to a trading company. Often preferable to a flotation as it can allow 100 per cent exit both for managers and investors.

Vendor finance: Generally an aspect of deal structure in which the vendor, in part, finances the cost by agreeing to defer part of the consideration. In practice, this is often done by taking part of the sale consideration in the form of loan notes (usually unsecured and rarely bank guaranteed) issued by the purchaser and subordinated to the senior lender (and any other senior creditor). Occasionally the vendor will receive equity in the purchaser in addition to or instead of loan notes. Clearly the terms upon which the vendor will be paid and the vendor's rights in default can be difficult questions. The issue of set-off or similar against the deferred element in the event of sale agreement warranty claims, etc, can sometimes be difficult.

Vendor placing: An arrangement whereby when a listed company purchasing a target in exchange for Plc shares, those shares are sold via a simultaneous placing or underwriting arrangement so as to generate a pre-determined cash sum for the vendor. The purchaser gets the advantages of buying for paper and the vendor ends up with cash.

Classically, the transaction was done by the consideration shares allotted to the vendor being renounced by the vendor in favour of the placees for a cash payment by them to the vendor. Now, partly to mitigate stamp duty/SDRT, it is usual for the vendors to sell the target to the Plc in consideration of its allotment to the placees of Plc shares credited as fully paid in consideration of the placees making the cash payment to the vendor.

Glossary

Venture capitalist: A person (usually either a company or a limited partnership) which provides equity and sometimes debt finance as well to companies and receives as its return or as part of its return a share of ownership (usually in the form of equity shares) which is valued according to the enterprise value of the business and not (for example) according to the duration of the investment or the cost of money.

Venture Capital Trust ("VCT"): A special form of listed Plc, similar to an Investment Trust, whose shareholders benefit from a beneficial tax regime which in turn fetters the nature and size of investment which the VCT can make. It is one type of venture capitalist in the UK.

Voting rights: The right (usually attached to a share) to vote on a show of hands or on a poll.

Warrant: A subscription option to subscribe (usually at par for cash) for shares in a company. Warrants are a common feature of mezzanine finance. The holder usually waits until just before the exit before subscribing for the shares (and sharing in the exit proceeds as a shareholder accordingly, thus improving the overall return on the investment). It is not a form of security (since if the company is in serious difficulty the warrant is usually worthless) and is not cancelled by repaying the debt to which it was originally linked. The rights of a warrant holder if there is a further equity funding round before the exit should be carefully considered.

Warranty and indemnity insurance: A policy (taken out by the vendor or the purchaser) to provide insurance cover against some of the risks associated with the warranties and indemnities given by the vendors (or some of them) to the purchaser in a share sale. The precise terms and cost of cover vary from deal to deal and not all risks are insurable in the market. It can provide a degree of comfort to a purchaser (and to its funders) in deals especially if some of the sellers (such as venture capitalist) are not prepared to give warranties or to put that part of the price received by them at risk of return.

Warranty: A contractual promise (usually but not necessarily in writing) which, if untrue, can entitle any person to whom it was made and who can show a loss to compensation by way of damages and even in some cases may entitle the contract itself to be rescinded. In a share sale or share subscription, the warranties will usually be keenly negotiated together with limitations or other contractual provisions that affect the nature and extent of the liability of the warrantor for breach.

Classically warranties also serve the purpose of forcing the warrantor to make disclosure of matters known and which would otherwise be a breach of the warranties. This disclosure will often affect the deal in different ways; for example it may result in a price change or some other special arrangement to address the concerns raised by the disclosure.

Appendix 1

Whitewash: In acquisitions and banking, a whitewash is the procedure under the CA 2006 which permits a private company to give what would otherwise be unlawful financial assistance. It involves a declaration of solvency by the directors of the target company (and of any subsidiaries involved in the assistance) that the company is solvent and will remain so for 12 months afterwards. The declaration is accompanied by an audit report and often a shareholder resolution.

Withholding tax: Sometimes persons making payments (e.g. interest) to another are required to withhold tax from the payment and to account for it to the tax authorities.

Working capital facilities: These are the banking facilities which any business needs to support its normal activities; they include overdrafts, revolving money, market loans, acceptances, documentary credits, bonds and guarantees, negotiation and foreign exchange dealing lines. The MBO provides an opportunity to review both existing and future requirements of the business.

Wrongful trading: An insolvency concept (s.214 Insolvency Act 1986) which can result in a court ordering a director or shadow director to make a contribution to its assets on insolvency. This is discretionary, and the jurisdiction arises if the director knew or ought reasonably to have known that an insolvency was likely unless the director can show that (s)he took all such action as (s)he ought reasonably to have taken to protect the interests of creditors.

Wrongful dismissal: A termination of a service contract in circumstances which amount to a contractual breach by the employer of its terms (express or implied).

Yellow Book: An archaic version of (and now replaced by) the Purple Book, containing listing rules issued by the London Stock Exchange. Named after the yellow ring binder in which it was stored.

Zero company bond: A loan note issued by a company which has no interest yield during its life but is redeemed on maturity at a price greater than its original issue price.

Appendix 2

MBO Model
Acquisition of Share Capital

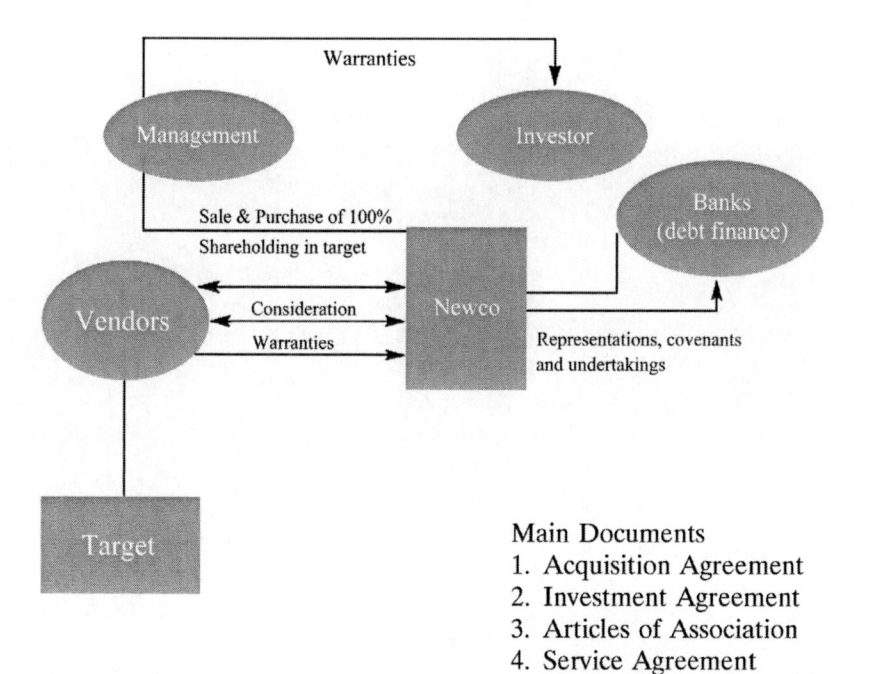

Warranties

Management   Investor

Banks (debt finance)

Sale & Purchase of 100% Shareholding in target

Vendors — Consideration — Newco
Warranties →

Representations, covenants and undertakings

Target

Main Documents
1. Acquisition Agreement
2. Investment Agreement
3. Articles of Association
4. Service Agreement
5. Debt Finance Documents
6. Disclosure Letters

Appendix 3

Legal Agreements

Summary of the legal agreements

This Appendix is a short summary of the main legal agreements used in private equity transactions and some of the issues that these documents will raise. This section does not cover sale and purchase agreements.

Investment Agreement

Articles of Association

Bank Facilities Agreement

Inter-Creditor Agreement

Management Disclosure Letter

Due Diligence Reports:

- Accounting
- Property
- Environmental
- IPR
- Employment
- Pensions
- Tax
- Contracts

Management Service Contracts

Financial Assistance Documents

Management Declarations

Board Minutes

Key areas of negotiation between management and the private equity house

(excluding financial terms)

Directors' packages (contained in Service Contracts)

Warranties (contained in Investment Agreement)

Share Transfers (contained in Articles of Association)

Consents (contained in Investment Agreement)

Dividend Rights (contained in Articles of Association)

Investment agreement

Purpose

This document regulates the basis on which the cash of the Private Equity House is introduced to the buy-out vehicle and the relationship between management and the investors. In particular it contains warranties—confirmations from management that particular facts are true and that opinions are believed to be true.

Title heading of contents:

1. Definitions
2. Completion
3. Purpose of Investment
4. Business Conduct
5. Information Requirements
6. Board Composition
7. Consent Procedures
8. Obligations of Promoters
9. Warranties
10. Cost and Expenses
11. Listing and Sale
12. Publicity/Disclosure of Information/Confidentiality
13. Schedules, inter alia

Appendix 3

Consents

Establish Option Scheme/Employee Share Scheme Changes to:

    Accounting Period

    Bankers/Auditors

    Nature of Trade

Material changes to Annual Business Plan

Level of Borrowing

Re-Financing

Capital expenditure over agreed limit

Grant of Options

Capitalisation of reserves

Expenditure outside Annual Business Plan

Acquisition/Disposal Fixed Assets

Acquisition/Disposal IPR

Entering into contracts (% of turnover)

Sale of Shares

Acquire/Disposal of subsidiary

New Joint Ventures

Entering into Service Contracts

Undertake acquisitions or diversification of the business

Appointment of overseas agents

Changes to accounting policies

Making of Loans

Contracts not on arm's length basis

Changes to insurance cover

Political contributions

Changes to professional advisers (excluding auditors)

Exception of Service Contracts or employees

Commencement of litigation

Legal Agreements

Warranties

Warranties are always an area of considerable tension and as a result require careful negotiation. Below are the issues that will require most focus.

Typical limitations on warranties

Financial limit:	3 × salary
Minimum claim:	£25,000
The limit:	3 months after receipt by VC of two subsequent audited accounts.

Typical warranties from management to VC

Individuals

- No interest in competing business
- No current/pending litigation
- Financial background of individuals
- Entering into agreement does not breach existing service contract
- Other share interests
- No criminal records

The Company

- Accuracy of Information including factual content of third-party report, business plan, accountant's report.
- Audited accounts
- Management accounts
- Bad and doubtful debts
- Accounting records
- Trading/Actions since last audited accounts
- Shares
- Financial and Capital Commitments
- Subsidiary
- Contracts

- Trading and Trading Practices
- Ownership and Condition of Assets
- Employment
- Intellectual property
- Licences
- Litigation and disputes
- Insolvency
- Insurance
- Property
- Taxation
- Pensions

N.B. The extent of the warranties is governed in part by the degree of comfort available from the vendor in the acquisition agreement and from third parties in specific reports.

Information requirements

The Private Equity House (and other funder) will always require a certain level of information from the Company. These include:

Management Accounts—monthly

Audited Accounts

Budgets

VC and management will together with the bank agree appropriate timescales and the contents of this information.

Management declarations

List of questions to give a VC appropriate knowledge about the management team background. Focus on:

- Other business activities
    — are they in competition?
- Criminal record
    — hopefully none.
- Health.

Articles of association

Purpose

The memorandum establishes the Company's power to operate in its external relations. The Articles establish the internal regulations of the Company (i.e. what the directors and shareholders can do) and sets out the relations between the members of the Company.

Title heading of contents:

- Share capital
- Dividends:
  — priority
  — management dividends
- Capital
- Redemption of preference shares
- Ratchet mechanism/Class rights
- Use of trusts by Management
- Shares for employees—warehouse mechanism
- Dividend policy—management dividends
- Management shares—what happens if someone leaves? "deemed transfer"
- Ratchet mechanism
- Sale of business—come along option
- Limitation on Transfer of Control
- General meetings and resolutions
- Voting
- Directors
- Board meetings
- Borrowing powers
- Powers, duties, proceedings of Directors
- Transfer of Shares:
  — family trusts
  — Pre-emption rights/deemed transfer

Appendix 3

Come along option—What is it?

- Mechanism which prevents minority shareholders from blocking the sale of the business
- Does not allow VC to sell the company.
- Based on majority of ordinary shareholders wanting to sell.

Management shares—what happens if someone leaves? "Deemed transfer".

Some typical issues:

- For all transfer of shares there should be a mechanism that allows free shares to be offered to "board invitees", i.e. incoming senior employees.
- This will hold for six months and then normal pre-emption rights.
- Why important?
  — If need new equivalent management then must ensure shares are available.
- Par value for shares for two years after completion.
- Thereafter good leaver/bad leaver.
- Good leaver will get fair value.
- Bad leaver will get lower of fair value or par.
- Bad leaver tightly defined to events which VC and Management agree are "bad":
  — e.g. Fraud on the company, etc.

Service contracts

Title heading of contents:

- Remuneration
- Term
- Car
- Expenses
- Pension Scheme
- Health Insurance
- Life Assurance

Legal Agreements

- Holiday
- Incorporate:
  — Restrictions during employment
  — Non-competition
  — Termination
  — Intellectual Property

Key issues to discuss

Remuneration package/Bonus scheme.
Length of contract/Notice period.
What happens if someone leaves?

Remuneration package

Consistent with current practice.
No incremental costs to the business.
Increases once performance is secured.

Length of contract

A 12-month contract in length.
A 6-month notice.

When management leave

Restrictions on any direct competition.
Payment of salary in lieu of notice is acceptable where relationship has come to an end.

Appendix 4

Manager's Personal Status Questionnaire

DATED _____ 200◆

LIMITED

MANAGER'S PERSONAL

STATUS QUESTIONNAIRE

Manager's Personal Status Questionnaire

QUESTION		ANSWER
1.	**PERSONAL DETAILS**	
1.1	Present surname and any former surname(s):	
1.2	Present forename(s) and any former forename(s):	
1.3	Do you use or are you known by any other name?	
1.4	Date of birth:	
1.5	Nationality and former nationality (if any):	
1.6	Do you have dual nationality status?	
1.7	Residential address:	
Postcode:		
1.8	Telephone numbers:	Home:
		Work:
		Mobile:
1.9	Email address:	
1.10	Professional qualifications (if any):	
2.	**DIRECTORSHIPS**	
2.1	Are you, or have you ever been, a director (whether executive or non-executive) or shadow director of any company [(other than the Company)]?	
	If so, please state in respect of each such company:	
2.1.1	Name of company:	
2.1.2	nature of business of company:	

Appendix 4

QUESTION	*ANSWER*
2.1.3 dates of appointment and resignation as a director:	
2.1.4 whether quoted and, if so, where:	
2.1.5 [whether such a company is a supplier/customer of or in competition with the Company or any of its subsidiary undertakings:]	
2.2 If you are a director of, involved in the management of, or provide services to another company or business, please indicate your position and approximately how many hours a week/month this position requires of you:	
3. **PARTNERSHIPS**	
Are you or have you at any time been a partner in any partnership?	
If so, please state in respect of each partnership:	
3.1 name of firm:	
3.2 nature of business of firm:	
3.3 principal business address:	
3.4 date of admission/cessation as a partner:	
4. **SHAREHOLDINGS**	
Do you hold or have you ever held or does anyone hold or has anyone ever held on your behalf shares, options, warrants or other securities in any company [(other than the Company)]?	

Manager's Personal Status Questionnaire

QUESTION		ANSWER
	[Have you or has anyone on your behalf disposed of shares in the last two years in any public company or in any company which is a customer/ supplier of the Company (or any of its subsidiary undertakings) or the business of which is similar to or in competition with the business of the Company (or any of its subsidiary undertakings)?]	
	If so, please state:	
4.1	name of company:	
4.2	nature of business of company:	
4.3	number of shares held:	
4.4	percentage of issued share capital:	
4.5	[date of disposal (if relevant):]	
5. OTHER BUSINESS INTERESTS		
	Are you or have you at any time been engaged or interested (other than as an employee) in any other business not listed at questions 2, 3 or 4 above?	
6.	**EMPLOYMENT**	
6.1	Please give details of your employment in the last 10 years:	

Name of employer	Position held	Period of employment	Reason for leaving

Appendix 4

QUESTION		ANSWER
6.2	Have you ever been dismissed or suspended from or asked to leave any office, position of trust or employment?	
6.3	Are you subject to any restrictive covenants or other obligations in connection with any existing or previous employment?	
6.4	Have you held any fiduciary office or position of trust in the last 10 years [other than in respect of your family's estate(s),] whether or not remunerated? If so, please give details and, if you no longer hold such position, state the circumstances in which you vacated the same:	
7.	**CONVICTIONS, DISQUALIFICATIONS, ETC**	
7.1	Have you ever been disqualified by a court from acting as a director of any company, or from acting in the management or conduct of affairs of any company or been subject to a disqualification undertaking?	
7.2	Have you or any of your employers in the last 10 years been censured or disciplined by any organisation, body or authority in relation to your business or professional activities?	
7.3	Are you currently the subject of any investigation or disciplinary procedure on the part of any professional or trade society, institution or association or other business organisation?	

Manager's Personal Status Questionnaire

QUESTION	ANSWER
7.4 Have you, in the United Kingdom or elsewhere, been concerned with the management or conduct of affairs of any company or partnership which has been:	
7.4.1 investigated by an inspector under companies, taxation or insolvency legislation or other securities enactments or by any other regulatory body; or	
7.4.2 required to produce books and papers to the Secretary of State for Trade and Industry or HM Revenue and Customs (or its predecessors) in relation to any matter arising at a time during which you were concerned in that company or partnership?	
7.5 Have you, in connection with the formation or management of any company, partnership or unincorporated association been adjudged by a court in the United Kingdom or elsewhere civilly liable for any fraud, misfeasance or other misconduct by you towards it or towards any of its members?	
7.6 Are you or have you ever been the subject of any investigation by the Police, HM Revenue and Customs (or its predecessors), the Department of Social Security, the SFO, the Office of Fair Trading, the EC Commission or any other national or supranational government body?	
7.7 Have you as an individual at any time or has a company of which	

Appendix 4

QUESTION	ANSWER
you were a director or shadow director at the time of the offence been convicted in the United Kingdom or elsewhere of any (a) criminal offence (other than a minor road traffic offence) or (b) offence under legislation (whether or not in the United Kingdom) relating to companies (including insider dealing and market abuse), building societies, industrial and provident societies, credit unions, friendly societies, insurance, banking or other financial services, securities, insolvency, competition law, consumer credit or consumer protection? If so, please give full details of all such offences, including:	
7.7.1 the court by which you were or the company was convicted:	
7.7.2 the date of conviction:	
7.7.3 full particulars of the offence:	
7.7.4 the penalty imposed:	
(Details must be disclosed of all convictions of the kind described above even though they may be "spent" convictions within the meaning of the expression contained in the Rehabilitation of Offenders Act 1974.)	
7.8 Have you at any time been prosecuted (whether or not successfully) or threatened with prosecution for any criminal offence (other than a minor road traffic offence)? If so, please give details.	

Manager's Personal Status Questionnaire

QUESTION		ANSWER
7.9	Have you ever been the subject of a civil claim involving allegations of fraud or dishonesty?	
7.10	Have you, in the United Kingdom or elsewhere, been refused admission to or renewal of membership of any professional body, trade society, institution or association or investment exchange or been censured or disciplined or had membership withdrawn by any such body to which you belong or belonged or have you held a practising certificate or membership subject to conditions?	
8.	**BANKRUPTCY, COURT JUDGMENTS ETC**	
8.1	Have you at any time been adjudged bankrupt or sequestrated either in the United Kingdom or elsewhere? If so, please state the court by which you were adjudged bankrupt and, if discharged, the date and conditions on which you were granted your discharge. Please also provide details of any bankruptcy petitions received at any time by you.	
8.2	Has anyone claimed against you an amount which remains unpaid?	
8.3	Have you at any time been a party to a deed of arrangement or any form of voluntary arrangement (as defined in part VIII of the Insolvency Act 1986)?	

Appendix 4

QUESTION		ANSWER
8.4	Has any company been put into compulsory liquidation or had an administrator or an administrative or other receiver appointed during the period when you were (or within the preceding 12 months had been) one of its directors or shadow directors or within a period of 12 months after you ceased to be a director?	
	If so, please state:	
8.4.1	name of company:	
8.4.2	nature of business of company:	
8.4.3	the date of commencement of winding-up, administration or receivership:	
8.4.4	the amount involved by which the company's liabilities exceeded its assets and an indication of the outcome or of the current position:	
8.5	Has any partnership been put into compulsory liquidation or been sequestrated or have any of the partners been declared bankrupt during the period when you were (or within the preceding 12 months had been) one of its partners or within a period of 12 months after you ceased to be a partner?	
	If so, please state:	
8.5.1	name of firm:	
8.5.2	nature of business of firm:	
8.5.3	the date of commencement of winding-up or sequestration:	

Manager's Personal Status Questionnaire

QUESTION		ANSWER
8.5.4	the amount involved and an indication of the outcome or current position:	
8.6	Have you ever been the subject of any civil action (whether in the United Kingdom or elsewhere) which has resulted in a finding against you by a court involving any liability or been subject to any adverse arbitral awards or otherwise had any sums awarded against you following any other dispute resolution process?	
8.7	Are there any unsatisfied judgments, arbitral awards or other sums awarded following any other dispute resolution process outstanding against you or any firm or company in which you are a partner, shareholder, director or proprietor (other than a listed company in which you hold not more than one per cent of the equity share capital) or other actions pending or threatened by or against you or such firm or company or any circumstances which you know or ought reasonably to know are likely to give rise to such action(s)?	
8.8	Are there any professional or trade societies, institutions or associations relevant to you [or to the Company (or its subsidiary undertakings)] for which you have [or the Company or its subsidiary undertakings (as the case may be) has] not applied for membership?	

Appendix 4

9.	**BUSINESS DEALINGS**	
9.1	Have you ever given evidence in any trial involving fraud or similar misconduct otherwise than as an expert witness?	
9.2	Have you, or any other persons who were acting in concert with you (as that term is defined in the City Code on Takeovers and Mergers) made an offer for a public company or been the subject of or witnesses at any investigation by the Panel on Takeovers and Mergers or any committee of it?	
9.3	Have you at any time or has any company or firm of which you have at any time been a director, shareholder, partner or proprietor or with which you have otherwise been connected at any time during the period of your involvement with it been the subject of adverse national, local or trade press comment?	
9.4	Have you, to your knowledge, ever been "blacklisted" by any stockbroker or by the London Stock Exchange Plc?	
9.5	[Have you had any interest, direct or indirect, in the promotion of or in any assets which have within the past two years been acquired or disposed of by or leased to the Company or any of its subsidiary undertakings or are proposed to be acquired, disposed of by or leased to the Company or any of its subsidiary undertakings?]	

Manager's Personal Status Questionnaire

QUESTION	ANSWER
9.6 [Are there any contracts or arrangements between you and the Company or any of its subsidiary undertakings?]	
9.7 [Has any cash or securities been paid or benefit given to you by the Company or any of its subsidiary undertakings in the past two years?]	
9.8 Does any agreement or understanding exist under which you (or any person connected with you) are entitled to receive, or have received, from any person, any finder's or other fee, brokerage or commission in connection with the proposed investment, or are you aware of any person entitled to receive such a fee?	
10. **HEALTH**	
10.1 Do you suffer or have you ever suffered from any serious disease or physical or mental illness, disorder or disability?	
10.2 Please give details of any medical condition which you have or in connection with which you are currently receiving medical advice or medication:	
[Details given in response to questions 10.1 and 10.2 will be kept confidential and may, if preferred, be given directly to our doctor.]	
10.3 Have you ever been refused life assurance, private healthcare insurance or permanent health insurance or been offered it on limited or less favourable than normal terms?	

Appendix 4

QUESTION	ANSWER
10.4 Have you ever been off work sick for either a continuous period of two weeks or more or, in aggregate, in excess of four weeks in any year? If so, please give details:	
11. **GENERAL**	
11.1 Are you satisfied that you have the financial resources to meet your existing and anticipated financial liabilities?	
11.2 Are there any other facts or circumstances relating to you or your business career which you are aware may be relevant to a prospective subscriber for or holder of shares in the Company?	
11.3 Do you or have you at any time during the previous five years, used or taken any illegal substance?	
11.4 Is there any other information material to your directorship of the Company, the omission of which might affect the import of the information contained in your responses to this questionnaire?	
11.5 Please confirm that if all the questions set out above were extended to your spouse and children, none of the answers would reveal any facts or circumstances which might be relevant to a prospective subscriber for or holder of shares in the Company or which might be material in the context of the proposed investment:	

Manager's Personal Status Questionnaire

QUESTION	ANSWER
11.6 Do you have any hobbies, pursuits or interests (commercial, financial or otherwise) which will or might detract from your ability to devote substantially all of your time and attention to the business of the Company?	
12. **PERSONAL NET WORTH**	
Please provide a statement of your net assets showing all your material assets, with your best estimate of their current value, together with details of all your material liabilities, mortgages or other charges and any other significant financial commitments.	

To: [Name and address of institutional investor]

I declare that the answers to all the above questions [including those contained on the attached sheets] are true and complete in all respects and that I have not omitted any information which might render the same misleading.

Signature .... Date ....

Appendix 5

Common Limitations to Management Warranties

The liability of the Managers in relation to the Warranties shall be limited as follows:

1. No liability shall arise unless the aggregate amount of all claims in respect of the Warranties exceeds £◆ but once the aggregate of all such claims exceeds this amount, the whole amount of such claims shall be recoverable.

2. For the purposes of clause ◆ .1 claims in respect of the Warranties of ◆£ or less will not count towards such aggregate amount.

3. [The Warranties are given severally by each of the Managers, and][1] the aggregate liability of each of the Managers in respect of the Warranties shall not exceed the amount set opposite his name in column ◆ of schedule ◆ .

4. Subject to clause ◆.3, the liability of each Manager in respect of each claim under the Warranties shall not exceed [an amount equal to ◆ per cent of the total value of the claim]/[that proportion of the total value of the claim set opposite their respective names in column ◆ of schedule ◆].

5. No liability shall arise unless notice [in writing] giving reasonable details of the breach alleged and, if possible, a pre-estimate of the amount of the claim, has been given to the Managers not later than the [second] anniversary of the date of this agreement and proceedings in relation thereto are not served within six months of the date of notification.

6. Where a claim arises under the Warranties and the subject matter of such claim also gives rise to a claim pursuant to the Acquisition

---

[1] This may be included in the operative warranty provisions, and therefore unnecessary here.

Common Limitations to Management Warranties

Agreement then no such claim shall be pursued under this agreement until all relevant remedies pursuant to the Acquisition Agreement have been exhausted and then only to the extent of any unremedied loss.

7   The liability of any of the Managers in respect of any of the Warranties shall be extinguished if and to the extent that the subject matter of the claim has been made good or is otherwise compensated for. The Investor agrees that it will not knowingly use its powers as a shareholder of the Company to prevent the Company from taking all reasonable steps to mitigate any loss or damage which would otherwise give rise to a claim under the Warranties including without limitation taking action against any other person in relation to such loss or damage or making any claim in relation thereto under any policy of insurance.

8   If the Managers (or any of them) pay to the Investor or the Company an amount in respect of the Warranties and the Company or the Investor subsequently recovers from a third party a sum which is referable thereto the Investor or the Company shall, as appropriate, as soon as reasonably practicable repay to the Managers a sum equal to the lower of the amount paid to the Investor and the Company, as appropriate, and the sum so received, in each case less the reasonable costs of recovery.

9   No claim shall be made and the Managers shall not be liable under any of the Warranties or any other provision of this agreement in respect of any matter arising or increased as a result of any change in the law or of any change in the rates or principles of taxation whether or not such change purports to be retrospectively effective in whole or in part.

10 The Managers shall not be liable under any of the Warranties to the extent that provision, reserve or allowance has been made in the Accounts in respect of the liability in question or to the extent that payment or discharge thereof has been taken into account in the Accounts.

11 The Managers shall not be liable under any of the Warranties to the extent that such liability arises or is increased as a result of any voluntary act, transaction or omission of the Company after the date of this agreement in the ordinary course of business of the Company or otherwise with the consent of or at the direction of the Investor Director(s).

12 The Managers shall not be liable under any of the Warranties to the extent the Investor had actual knowledge of the facts, matter or circumstance which may give rise to a claim under the Warranties and it was reasonable for the Investor to appreciate that such facts

Appendix 5

matter or circumstance may give rise to a liability on the part of the Managers should the Investor choose to bring a claim under the warranties.

Over-provisions and corresponding benefit

13   If:

13.1   any provision for tax in the Accounts proves to be an over provision;

13.2   the amount by which any right to repayment of tax which has been treated as an asset in the Accounts proves to have been under-stated; or

13.3   a payment by the Managers in respect of any liability under the tax Warranties or the matter giving rise to the liability in question results in the Company receiving or becoming entitled to any relief, allowance, credit, deduction or set off in each case in respect of Taxation or a right to repayment of Taxation which it utilises (including by way of repayment of tax) ("**Corresponding Relief**")

then an amount equal to such over-provision, under-stated right to repayment of tax or the tax saved by the corresponding relief at the date such corresponding relief is utilised ("**Relevant Amount**") shall be dealt with in accordance with clause ◆ below.

14.   The Relevant Amount:

14.1   shall first be set off against any payment then due from the Managers under the warranties;

14.2   then, to the extent there is an excess of the Relevant Amount, a refund shall be made to the Managers of any previous payment or payments made by the Managers in respect of any claim under this agreement and not previously refunded under this clause up to the amount of such excess; and

14.3   to the extent that the excess referred to in clause ◆ .12.2 is not exhausted under that sub-clause, the remainder of that excess shall be carried forward and set off against any future payment or payments which become due from the Managers under any claim under this agreement.

Appendix 6

British Venture Capital Association Membership Listing

PE/VC firms
3i
AAC Capital Partners
Abingworth LLP
Accel Partners
Acorn Capital Partners
ACT Venture Capital Ltd
Active Private Equity Advisory LLP
Adamant Partners Ltd
Advent International
Advent Venture Partners LLP
AGC Equity Partners
Albion Ventures
Alchemy Partners LLP
Alliance Fund Managers Limited
Altitude Partners
Amadeus Capital Partners Limited
AnaCap Financial Partners LLP
Andromeda Capital Ltd
Antrak Capital LLP
Apax Partners LLP
Aquarius Equity Partners
Asclepios Bioresearch

Aspiration Capital Management LLP
August Equity LLP
Azini Capital Partners LLP
B.P. Marsh & Partners Plc
Bain Capital Ltd
Baird Capital Partners Europe
Balderton Capital Management
Barclays Natural Resources
Barclays Private Equity Limited
Barclays Ventures
BC Partners Limited
Beringea LLP
Bestport Ventures LLP
Betfair
Blackstone Group International Ltd
Bowmark Capital LLP
Braveheart Ventures
Bregal Capital LLP
Bridgepoint
Bridges Community Ventures Limited
BVIG Capital
Cabot Square Capital LLP
Caird Capital

British Venture Capital Association Membership Listing

Calculus Capital Ltd
Carbon Trust Investments
Catapult Venture Managers Ltd
CBPE Capital
CCMP Capital Advisors LLP
Chamonix Private Equity
Charterhouse Capital Partners LLP
Cinven
Clarendon Fund Managers Limited
Clayton Dubilier & Rice (CD&R) LLP
Cognetas LLP
Company Guides Venture Partners Ltd
Connection Capital
Core Capital LLP
CVC Capital Partners Limited
Darwin Private Equity LLP
Derbyshire First Investments Ltd
DFJ Espirit LLP
Doughty Hanson & Co Ltd
Duke Street
Dunedin Capital Partners Limited
ECI Partners LLP
Eden Ventures UK Limited
Elderstreet Investments Limited
Electra Partners LLP
Endless LLP
Enterprise Equity Fund Management (NI) Limited
Envestors LLP
Environmental Technologies Fund
EPIC Private Equity
Epi-V LLP
Equity Ventures Ltd
E-Synergy Ltd
European Capital Financial Services Ltd
EV Limited
Exponent Private Equity LLP
Ferranti Limited
FF&P Private Equity Limited
Fidelity Growth Partners
Finance Cornwall Limited
Finance South East Limited
Finance Wales Investments Limited
Frontiers Capital Limited
Fung Capital Europe
GCP Capital Partners LLP
Generation Investment Management
Global Infrastructure Partners
Goldman Sachs Capital Partners
Graphite Capital Management LLP
Gresham LLP
Growth Capital Partners LLP
H.I.G. Capital
HBG Holdings UK LLP
Helios Investment Partners LLP
Herald Investment Management Limited
HgCapital
Hotbed Limited
HSBC Private Equity (UK)
Iceni Capital
IK Investment Partners
Impax Asset Management Ltd
Imperial Innovations Limited
Index Ventures
Infinity asset Management LLP
Inflexion Private Equity
Ingenious Ventures Limited
Innvotec Limited

Appendix 6

Invest Northern Ireland	Oakley Capital Limited
ISIS EP LLP	Octopus Investments Ltd
Javelin Ventures Ltd	Oxford Capital Partners
Kelso Place Asset Management LLP	Oxford Spin-Out Equity Management
Key Capital Partners LLP	Palamon Capital Partners LP
Kings Park Capital	Palatine Private Equity LLP
Kohlberg Kravis Roberts & Co Ltd	Par Equity
Langholm Capital LLP	Penta Capital Partners LLP
LDC	Pentech Ventures
LGV Capital	Permira Advisers LLP
Lion Capital	Phoenix Equity Partners
Loudwater Investment Partners Ltd	Pi Capital
Lyceum Capital Partners LLP	Piper Private Equity LLP
Matrix Private Equity Partners LLP	Platina Partners LLP
Maven Capital Partners UK LLP	Pond Venture Partners Ltd
Midven Limited	Primary Capital Ltd
Milestone Capital Partners LLP	Privet Capital LLP
Mitsui & Co Europe Plc	Providence Equity LLP
MMC Ventures Ltd	Quilvest
Mobius Technology Ventures	RCapital
Montagu Private Equity LLP	Risk Capital Partners
Moorfield Investment Management Ltd	Riverstone
Morgan Stanley Private Equity	RJD Partners Limited
Mosaic Private Equity	Royal Bank of Scotland Equity Finance
MTI	Royal Society Enterprise Fund
NBGI Private Equity	Rutland Partners LLP
NEL Fund Managers Limited	Scottish Equity Partners
NESTA Investments	Seraphim Capital (General Partner) LLP
Next Wave Ventures	Shackleton Ventures Ltd
Nomura Cleantech VC fund	Silver Lake
NorthStar Equity Investors Ltd	Silverfleet Capital Partners LLP
Notion Capital	SL Capital Partners LLP
novusmodus LLP	Smedvig Capital Limited
NVM Private Equity Limited	Solar Energy Partners

British Venture Capital Association Membership Listing

Sovereign Capital Partners
SPARK Ventures plc
Spirit Capital Partners LLP
STAR Capital Partners
Sun European Partners LLP
Sussex Place Ventures
SV Life sciences Advisers LLP
Synova Capital LLP
TDR Capital LLP
Terra Firma Capital Partners Limited
The Carlyle Group
The Summit Group Ltd
Top Technology Ventures Limited
TowerBrook Capital Partners (UK) LLP

TPG Capital LLP
TTP Venture Management Ltd
UK Steel Enterprise Ltd
Unilever Ventures Ltd
Veronis Suhler Stevenson International Ltd
Vespa Capital
Vision Capital LLP
Vitruvian Partners LLP
Warburg Pincus International LLC
West Bridge Fund Managers Limited
WHEB Partners LLP
WM Enterprise
Wyvern Seed Fund
Xpedite Ventures
YFM Private Equity Limited

Appendix 7

Heads of Terms

The heads of terms should contain the principal commercial terms of the deal. They are not intended to be definitive, but should be as specific as possible, particularly in relation to the consideration, and warranty and indemnity protection. The clearer they are the smoother the transaction will progress. Advisors should not start drafting documents until all the major issues have been agreed.

The heads of terms are usually expressed not to be legally binding, except for the provisions relating to exclusivity, confidentiality and costs. However parties will take them as establishing the deal and will be reluctant to vary them.

PRIVATE & CONFIDENTIAL

To: [The Directors] *[Seller's name and address]* (the **"Seller"**)

Dear Sir,

RE: Proposed acquisition of [the entire issued share capital of [insert name of Target] Limited and its subsidiaries (the "Target Group")/[the business and assets of [insert name of Target] (the "Target Business")]

Further to our previous meetings and correspondence, we set out below the basis upon which [, subject to approval by the Board of this Company,] this Company or one of its wholly owned subsidiaries (the **"Buyer"**), would be prepared (subject to contract) to purchase with full title guarantee [the whole of the issued share capital of the [Target Group]/[Target Business] free from any liens, charges or encumbrances and free from indebtedness [other than []] (the **"Acquisition"**) [and all dividends and distributions declared after [insert date]]. For the avoidance of doubt this letter is not exhaustive and is not intended to create legal relations between the parties save that paragraphs 11, 12, 13, 14 and 15 shall be legally binding on the parties and enforceable in the courts of England in accordance with paragraph 18.2.

Heads of Terms

[If a business sale: The Buyer will acquire the benefit of customer and supplier contracts, books and records, fixed assets, real property, intellectual property, book debts, prepayments [and cash] [others?] of the Target Business. The liabilities of the Target Business to be acquired are limited to those to the extent that they relate to the period following completion of the Acquisition (**"Completion"**). The Buyer will require the Seller to indemnify the Buyer in respect of liabilities of the Target Business to the extent that they relate to the period prior to Completion.]

1. CONDITIONS

The acquisition of the [Target Group]/[Target Business] will be conditional upon:

1.1 [OFT [and] EU [and other regulatory] clearances];

1.2 the approval of the Acquisition at an Extraordinary General Meeting of shareholders of [];

1.3 [tax clearances of [].] [The Buyer] [The Seller] will use reasonable endeavours to procure the satisfaction of the Conditions by [insert date].

1.4 [the Buyer conducting, and being satisfied with the results of, financial, legal taxation and commercial investigations into the [Target Business]/[Target Group](the **"Due Diligence Investigation"**) on the [Target Business]/[Target Group] being carried out on the basis described in clause 11 below and the Buyer not discovering anything which would [materially and adversely] affect its valuation of the [Target Business]/[Target Group] as set out in clause 2;]

1.5 [confirmation by the board of directors of the Buyer that nothing material has arisen from the Due Diligence Investigation that would affect their previous decision to approve the Acquisition;] [and]

1.6 [there being no material breach of the warranties and indemnities (as referred to in clause 4) [or the undertakings to be given by the Seller] on or before Completion.

1.7 there being no material adverse change in the business, operations, assets, position, profits or prospects of the [Target Business]/[Target Group] between the signing of these Heads and Completion.

2. CONSIDERATION

The consideration for the purchase of the [Target Group]/[Target Business] shall be £[AMOUNT] [as adjusted by completion accounts prepared as at the date of Completion]. The Consideration is to be satisfied as follows:

Appendix 7

2.1 Completion:

At Completion, the sum of £[AMOUNT] shall be paid to the Seller.

2.2 Following Completion:

Within [30] days of completion, [the Buyer]/[Target] Limited shall prepare draft Completion Accounts as at the date of Completion to determine the **[net asset value, working capital, fixed assets etc]**. The Seller shall be entitled to review these accounts. In the event that the Buyer and the Seller dispute the **[net asset value, working capital etc]** as set out in the draft Completion Accounts, the matter shall be referred to an independent expert to determine.

Any payment required to be made following the determination of the Completion Accounts shall be paid in cash.

3. POSITION BETWEEN EXCHANGE AND COMPLETION

The business and activities of the [Target Group]/[Target Business] shall be carried out in its ordinary course with a view to preserving the goodwill of the [Target Group]/[Target Business] [and in particular the Seller will give the Buyer such undertakings as to the operation of the business and activities of the [Target Group]/[Target Business] as the Buyer shall require].

4. WARRANTIES AND INDEMNITIES

The Seller will give warranties and indemnities in terms to be agreed in relation to the following matters: [list subject headings] [On a sale of shares: A full indemnity in respect of tax liabilities of the Target Group will be given by the Seller.] The Seller will require appropriate caps, as to liability, time limitations, carve-outs and exceptions to the warranties in a form to be agreed. If, during the course of the due diligence exercise, the Buyer identifies liabilities in the [Target Business]/[Target Group] the Seller agrees to consider providing the Buyer with suitable additional indemnity cover.

5. DIRECTORS AND EMPLOYEES

As soon as reasonably practicable following the Seller's agreement to the terms of this letter, the Seller will provide the Buyer with a schedule of the employees of the [Target Group]/[Target Business] and will keep the Buyer informed of any consultations with the employees of the [Target Business]/[Target Group].

6. PENSIONS

The Seller acknowledges that the Buyer will require to be satisfied (and to obtain appropriate warranty and indemnity protection) that the pension liabilities of the Target Group relating to the employees of the Target Business have been provided for on reasonable actuarial assumptions.

7. PROPERTY

[The Seller will give warranties in the form to be agreed in respect of the properties of the [Target Group]/[Target Business] and will provide the Buyer with full access to books and other records of the Seller so that the Buyer may investigate title to those properties.] [The Seller will provide to the Buyer certificates of title in the form to be agreed in respect of the properties.]

8. ONGOING SERVICES

The Seller and Buyer will agree a mutually acceptable way of dealing with any ongoing arrangements (i.e. shared properties/intellectual property etc) between the Target Group and the Seller [in particular in relation to product warranty claims]. The Seller shall procure that all inter-company debt is repaid to the Target Group at completion.

8. CONTRACTS

The Seller shall use its best endeavours to procure that all contracts of the Target Business are novated in favour of the Buyer and in the event that any of those contracts have not been or cannot be novated upon Completion, then the Seller will hold the benefit of any such contracts on trust for the Buyer and take such action as the Buyer shall reasonably require in relation thereto. *[Use where there is a business sale and renumber accordingly.]*

9. [ACCESS AND DUE DILIGENCE]

Prior to any agreement being signed, the Buyer will need to be satisfied as to the following:

[specifics]

The Seller grants to the Buyer access for a period of [ ] months to the properties, senior management, records, documents and papers of the [Target Group]/[Target Business] to enable the Buyer to carry out a proper due diligence exercise.

10. NON-COMPETITION

The Seller (for itself and on behalf of its subsidiaries) will enter into appropriate arrangements in respect of non-competition in relation to the current business of the [Target Group]/[Target Business] and the enticement of employees, suppliers and customers in a mutually acceptable form. This period of restriction will not exceed five years.

11. EXCLUSIVITY

The Buyer intends to proceed as quickly as possible with the proposed purchase. The Buyer and the Seller will negotiate in good faith with a view to exchanging the [Share Purchase Agreement] on or before [date] In consideration of the Buyer incurring costs of professional advisers and other expenses and expending further management time in considering the proposal to acquire the [Target Group]/[Target Business], the Seller agrees with the Buyer that during the period from the date of acceptance by the Seller to the terms of this letter until the earlier of [ ], completion of the Acquisition and the date on which discussions regarding the Acquisition are terminated by mutual agreement, the Seller will not make any initial or further approach to or enter into or continue any discussions with any third party with a view to disposal of the [Target Group]/[Target Business] or any part thereof to any person other than the Buyer or any of its subsidiaries and that the Seller will cooperate with the Buyer and its advisers in providing information about the [Target Group]/[Target Business] which is reasonably necessary for appropriate due diligence to be completed in a timely fashion.

12. CONFIDENTIALITY

The matters contemplated by this letter are to be treated in the strictest confidence and should not be disclosed to any person whatsoever (save to the extent required by law or the regulations of the London Stock Exchange Plc or the Listing Rules of the UK Listing Authority or by the rules and requirements of any other regulatory body) without the prior written consent of the other party hereto. In the event that the Acquisition is not completed, the Buyer undertakes that it will not disclose or make use of, for its own benefit, any of the information of a confidential nature relating to the [Target Group]/[Target Business] or the Seller which has been disclosed to the Buyer. The provisions of this paragraph 12 do not apply to any information which is publicly available at the time of disclosure unless disclosed through breach of this undertaking nor does it apply to any information disclosed by the parties to the extent that disclosure is required by law or any regulation.

13. COSTS

Save as expressly set out in this letter, both the Seller and the Buyer agree to bear their own legal, accountancy and other costs and expenses incurred in connection with the negotiation, preparation and implementation of this letter and the Acquisition.

14. CONSEQUENCES OF BREACH OF PARAGRAPHS 11–12 OF THIS LETTER

In the event that the Seller shall be in breach of the terms of the undertakings contained in paragraph 11 or shall during the exclusivity period withdraw from or cease to have any negotiations or discussions in respect of the Acquisition for any reason whatsoever other than breach by the Buyer of paragraph 12 of this letter, the Seller agrees to pay the reasonable legal, accountancy and other third party professional costs and expenses incurred by the Buyer in connection with the negotiation, preparation and implementation of this letter and the Acquisition.

If the Buyer shall be in breach of the terms of the undertakings contained in paragraph 12 the Buyer agrees to pay the reasonable legal, accountancy and other third party professional costs and expenses incurred by the Seller in connection with the negotiation, preparation and implementation of this letter and the Acquisition.

15. FURTHER ASSURANCE

Following Completion the Seller shall, forthwith upon request from the Buyer and at the Seller's own expense, do or procure the doing of all such acts and/or execute or procure the execution of all such documents in a form reasonably satisfactory to the Buyer for the purpose of vesting in the Buyer the full legal and beneficial title of the [Target Business]/[Target Group] or otherwise giving the Buyer the full benefit of the Acquisition.

16. [GOVERNING LAW AND JURISDICTION]

16.1 This letter (and any dispute, controversy, proceedings or claim of whatever nature arising out of or in any way relating to this letter or its formation) shall be governed by and construed in accordance with the law of England and Wales.

16.2 Each of the parties to this letter irrevocably agrees that the courts of England shall have exclusive jurisdiction to hear and decide any suit,

Appendix 7

action or proceedings, and/or to settle any disputes, which may arise out of or in connection with this letter (respectively, **"Proceedings"** and **"Disputes"**) and, for these purposes, each party irrevocably submits to the jurisdiction of the courts of England and Wales.

PLEASE SIGN AND RETURN A COPY OF THESE HEADS OF TERMS AS SOON AS POSSIBLE TO CONFIRM YOUR AGREEMENT TO THE ABOVE.

Yours faithfully,

. . . . on behalf of [the Buyer]

[On copy]

We confirm our acceptance to the terms of this letter by signing a copy of this letter.

. . . . on behalf of [the Seller]

Index

Accountants
  due diligence
    liabilities, 8–16—8–17
    management representations, 8–15
    objectives, 8–14
    reports, 8–13, 8–15
    terms of reference, 8–14
  reports, 8–13, 8–15
  role, 2–66, 2–67
  sensitivity analysis, 2–67

Acquisitions
  due diligence, 8–03
  funding, 1–27
  reasonableness of acquisition price, 3–65
  warranties, 9–10—9–13

Administrators
  restructuring, 12–61, 12–62

Agenda
  board meetings, 11–82
  transaction management, 6–29

Allotment of securities
  directors, 11–52

Alternate directors
  appointment, 10–60
  directors, 10–60, 11–06, 11–07, 11–85

Alternative Investment Market
  benefits, 9–109, 9–115, 9–117

Articles of association
  see also **Investment agreement; Minority shareholders; Ratchets; Share transfers**
  aim, 10–01
  amendments, 10–02, 10–07
  appointment of alternate directors, 10 60
  board meetings, 10–60, 10–61
  checklist, 10–62
  class rights, 10–07, 10–08, 10–09, 10–10
  complexity, 10–02
  directors' liabilities, 11–71
  generally, 1–33, 1–34, 10–01
  investor directors
    appointment and removal, 10–35
    fees, 10–36
    fiduciary duty, 10–37
    rights, 10–36
  negotiations, 9–87
  quorum, 10–61
  registration, 10–02
  rotation of directors, 10–60
  Russell v Northern Bank Development Corp Ltd, 10–03—10–06
  share transfers
    compulsory transfer notices, 10–18, 10–19—10–22
    controlling interest, 10–29—10–31
    employee benefit trusts, 10–24, 10–25, 10–27, 10–28
    forced sale provisions, 10–32—10–34
    generally, 10–14, 10–15, 10–16
    "good and bad leaver" provisions, 10–19, 10–20, 10–22, 13–14
    market value, 10–17
    pre-emption rights, 10–14, 10–15, 10–16, 10–17, 10–29, 10–33
    restriction clause for managers, 10–19
    termination of employment at crucial times, 10–23
    warehousing, 10–26
    wrongful dismissal, 10–21
  shareholder controls, 10–03—10–06
  standard format, 10–02, 10–60
  syndicates, 10–14, 10–15

Asset based debt capacity
  deal structuring, 3–67

Asset based finance
  debt finance, 3–22, 3–24, 3–27, 3–28, 3–31

Asset based valuations
  corporate valuation, 3–17

Assets
  order of application of assets on insolvency, 12–65
  warranties, 9–46

Auctions
  due diligence, 8–03, 8–06

Audit committees
  corporate governance, 9–92, 9–94

Index

Balanced portfolios
 industry sectors, 2–29
Bankruptcy
 legal due diligence, 8–27
Barriers to entry
 investment criterion, 2–16, 2–17
Board meetings
 agenda, 11–82
 articles of association, 10–60
 chairman
  election, 11–84
 corporate governance, 9–91, 9–103
 minutes, 11–87
 notice, 11–82
 procedure, 11–81, 11–84
 quorum, 10–61, 11–83
Bought deals
 management buy-outs, 1–22
British Venture Capital Association (BVCA)
 directory of members, 2–24
 fund preferences, 2–30
Business angels
 generally, 1–17, 1–28
 role, 1–28
 trade association, 1–28
Business asset taper relief
 abolition, 4–02
Business plans
 business detail, 2–50
 content, 2–43, 2–44, 2–48—2–54, 2–54, 2–74
 evidence file, 2–45
 example, 2–49
 executive summary, 2–49
 financial assumptions file, 2–46
 financial model, 2–47
 financial summary, 2–53, 2–54
 management, 2–52
 nature of business, 2–49
 objectivity, 2–51
 production, 2–45—2–54
 purpose, 2–44
 quality, 2–43, 2–44, 2–48—2–54, 2–54, 2–74
 required finance, 2–54
 restructuring
  approval, 12–36—12–43
  "Armageddon calculation", 12–37
  delivery of promises, 12–37
  disclosure, 12–31
  generally, 12–29
  negotiations, 12–35—12–43
  preparation, 12–31
  professional assistance, 12–32, 12–33, 12–34
  unsecured creditors, 12–37—12–41
 SWOT analysis, 2–54
Business property relief
 inheritance tax, 4–30—4–33
Buy-in/management buy-outs (BIMBOs)
 generally, 1–08, 1–23

Buy-outs without private equity
 drag along rights, 9–136
 exits, 9–136
 issues to consider, 9–131—9–134
 pre-emption rights, 9–136
 restricted matters, 9–135, 9–136
Capital losses
 tax relief, 4–25—4–29
Captives
 private equity firms, 1–03
Cash flow debt capacity
 deal structuring, 3–66
Cash flow lending
 debt finance, 3–22, 3–23, 3–26
Caveat emptor
 principle, 8–01
Ceasing to hold office
 directors, 11–89
Chairman
 due diligence, 7–19
 election, 11–84
 generally, 11–06
 negotiations over appointment, 9–84
 role, 11–06
Class rights
 articles of association, 10–07, 10–08, 10–09, 10–10
 management, 10–11—10–13
 shares, 5–37
Close companies
 tax relief
  interest paid on investment borrowing, 4–26, 4–27, 4–37
Compensation for loss of office
 directors, 11–43—11–44
Completion phase
 conditions precedent, 2–65
 due diligence, 2–66
 phase of investment, 2–65, 6–44
Confidentiality
 agreements, 8–21
 due diligence, 8–21, 8–57, 8–58, 8–61, 8–62, 8–63
 legal due diligence, 8–21
 prospective investors, 6–04
 sellers, 8–58, 8–61, 8–62, 8–63
 trade sales, 9–127
Conflict of interest
 directors, 11–19, 11–20, 11–21—11–41
 directors' powers and duties, 11–19, 11–20, 11–21—11–41
 management buy-outs, 11–20
 non-executive directors, 11–08
 service agreements, 11–29—11–31
 substantial property transactions, 11–32—11–34
Consideration
 contingent consideration, 10–57
 deferred consideration, 10–57
 ratchets, 10–57

446

Index

share issues, 5–06—5–08
vendor finance, 1–30, 1–31
Contingent consideration
ratchets, 10–57
Corporate governance
audit committees, 9–92, 9–94
board meetings, 9–91, 9–103
financial information, 9–91—9–92
provision of information, 9–90
remuneration committees, 9–92, 9–93
Corporate valuation
see also **Internal rate of return**
asset based valuations, 3–17
discounted cash flow
discount rate, 3–07
expected future cash flows, 3–05, 3–06
method of valuation, 3–04
earnings based valuations
enterprise valuation, 3–16
future maintainable profits, 3–09—3–11
method of valuation, 3–08, 3–16
profit multiples, 3–12—3–15
example data, 3–03
importance, 3–02
methods, 3–02
valuation methods, 3–02, 3–73
Corporate Venturing Scheme
venture capital trusts, 4–04
Covert surveillance
management due diligence, 7–09
Credibility
flotations, 9–111
Creditworthiness
legal due diligence, 8–26
Data protection
due diligence, 8–31, 8–32
Data rooms
due diligence, 8–06, 8–65
De facto directors
directors, 12–55, 12–56, 12–57, 12–59, 12–60
Deal structuring
asset based debt capacity, 3–67
cash generation capability, 3–71
cash flow debt capacity, 3–66
internal rate of return, 3–70
mezzanine finance, 3–68
principles, 3–64—3–71
process, 3–01, 3–64, 3–75
reasonableness of acquisition price, 3–65
total equity funding required, 3–69
Debt finance
asset based finance, 3–22, 3–24, 3–27, 3–28, 3–31
cash flow lending, 3–22, 3–23, 3–26
financial covenants, 3–25—3–27
generally, 3–74
interest rates, 3–30
limitations, 1–25, 1–38
repayment profiles, 3–29

security, 3–21
support for private equity market, 3–21, 3–22
Deceit
directors, 11–62
Deferred consideration
ratchets, 10–57
Deferred shares
ratchets, 5–66
Delegation
directors' powers and duties, 11–47
Directors
see also **Board meetings; Chairman; Directors' liabilities; Directors' powers and duties; Non-executive directors; Restructuring; Service agreements**
agents, comparison with, 11–05
allotment of securities, 11–52
alternate directors, 10–60, 11–06, 11–07, 11–07, 11–85
ceasing to hold office, 11–89
compensation for loss of office, 11–43—11–44
criminal offences, 11–53
de facto directors, 12–50, 12–55, 12–57, 12–58
de iure directors, 12–55, 12–56
definition, 11–04
disclosure, 11–74
disqualification orders, 11–88
employees, 11–05
Enterprise Investment Scheme, 4–13
executive directors, 11–06, 11–07
failure to file annual return, 11–53
fiduciary duties, 10–37, 11–09, 11–15, 11–16, 13–02
fraudulent trading, 11–49, 12–80
garden leave, 11–100, 11–101
generally, 11–03
individuals prevented from acting as, 11–90
insurance, 9–04, 11–91, 11–92
interests in transactions
disclosure, 11–80
key points, 11–93
managing directors, 11–06
meaning, 11–04, 12–55
misfeasance, 11–49, 11–51
misleading, false or deceptive statements, 11–53
names
business communications, 11–77
outside interests, 11–42
register of directors, 11–75
remuneration
disclosure, 11–79
resignation, 11–89
responsibility for the accounts, 11–54—11–59
role, 11–05
rotation of, 10–60

447

Index

shadow directors, 11–04, 11–06, 12–55, 12–56, 12–57, 12–58, 12–59
types, 11–06
warranties, 9–34
written resolutions, 11–86
wrongful trading, 11–49, 11–50, 11–51, 12–67—12–79

Directors' liabilities
see also **Directors; Directors' powers and duties**
articles of association, 11–71
contracts, 11–64, 11–65, 11–66, 11–67
deceit, 11–62
limited liability, 11–63
third parties, 11–63, 11–64, 11–65, 11–66, 11–67
torts, 11–68

Directors' powers and duties
see also **Directors; Directors' liabilities**
breach of duty, 11–11, 11–12, 11–69
  fiduciary duty, 13–03
  indemnity included in articles of association, 11–71
  limitation period, 11–73
  ratification, 11–70
  relief by the court, 11–72
care and skill, 11–09, 11–45, 11–46, 11–48, 11–60, 11–61
codification, 11–10, 13–04
conflict of interest, 11–19, 11–20, 11–21—11–41
delegation, 11–47
disclosure, 13–06
exceeding powers, 11–18
extent, 11–10
fiduciary duty, 10–37, 11–09, 11–15, 11–16, 13–02, 13–03
generally, 5–29, 5–30, 11–01, 11–49
interests in contracts, 11–24—11–28
interests in shares, 11–78
intermittent nature, 11–46
legislation, 11–01
loans and credit transactions, 11–35—11–41
management buy-outs
  business focus, 13–07
  departing manager's shares, purchase of, 13–15
  generally, 13–05
  good and bad leaver provisions, 13–14
  heads of terms, 13–18
  management of the company, 13–08
  ratchets, 13–16
  service agreements, 13–17
  warranties, 13–09—13–13
negligence, 11–60
owed to the company, 11–11, 11–46
personal profit, 11–21—11–23
promoting success of the company, 11–14
proper use of powers, 11–17
ratchets, 13–16

relief from liability, 11–69—11–73
responsibilities, 11–12, 11–13, 11–15
service agreements, 11–29—11–31, 13–17
substantial property transactions, 11–32—11–34
warranties, 13–09—13–13

Disclosure
see also **Due diligence; Warranties**
directors' powers and duties, 13–06
generally, 8–02
investment agreement, 9–51—9–52, 9–53
legal professional privilege, 9–65
trigger events, 12–22

Discounted cash flow
discount rate, 3–07
example, 3–06
expected future cash flows, 3–05, 3–06
method of valuation, 3–04, 3–52

Disqualification orders
directors, 11–88

Dividends
maintenance of share capital, 5–11—5–18
ordinary shares, 3–39, 3–40
preference shares, 3–46, 3–48, 5–44, 5–46, 5–50
preferred ordinary shares, 5–41—5–43
requirements, 1–32

Drag along rights
buy-outs without private equity, 9–136

Due diligence
accountants
  liabilities, 8–16—8–17
  management representations, 8–15
  objectives, 8–14
  reports, 8–13, 8–15
  terms of reference, 8–14
acquisitions, 8–03
auctions, 8–03, 8–06
completion stage, 2–66
confidentiality, 8–57
cross-border aspects, 8–09
data protection, 8–31, 8–32
data rooms, 8–06
employees, 8–30
environment
  compliance programme, 8–56
  documents, 8–51
  exits, 8–56
  generally, 8–46, 8–73
  indemnities, 8–48
  insurance, 8–56
  investigations, 8–50
  liabilities, 8–46, 8–47, 8–54, 8–55, 8–56
  process, 8–49, 8–50, 8–51, 8–52
  regulatory bodies, 8–52
  shortcomings of warranties and indemnities, 8–48, 8–53
  specialists, 8–53
  warranties, 8–48
exits, 8–04—8–07

448

Index

generally, 2–62, 2–63
investments, 8–03
lawyers, 8–09
legal
  bankruptcy, 8–27
  business documents, 8–25
  confidentiality agreements, 8–21
  costs, 8–20
  creditworthiness, 8–26
  information required, 8–21, 8–22
  opinions, 8–28
  purpose, 8–18
  review of materials, 8–29
  scoping the report, 8–19, 8–20
  searches, 8–24
  sources of information, 8–23—8–28
  statutory books, 8–25
management
  approach, 7–01
  best practice, 7–07
  chairman, 7–19
  communication, 7–01, 7–05
  covert surveillance, 7–09
  generally, 2–62, 7–01, 7–08, 7–20
  interviews, 7–16, 7–17
  legal, financial and professional checks, 7–10
  motivational factors, 7–08
  problems, 7–06
  profiling, 7–16, 7–17
  references, 2–62, 7–11—7–15
  reports, 7–18
  responses of management, 7–06, 7–20
pension schemes, 8–33
post completion audit, 8–75
process, 8–10
property
  generally, 8–34
  leaseholds, 8–39, 8–41—8–45
  liabilities, 8–34
  searches, 8–39, 8–40
  title to land, 8–35—8–37, 8–39
  warranties, 8–38
purpose, 8–01, 8–02
reporting lines, 8–09
reports, 8–13, 8–15, 8–74
sellers
  accounts, 8–71
  balance sheet, 8–71
  collection of information, 8–60
  confidentiality, 8–58, 8–61, 8–62, 8–63
  data rooms, 8–65
  disclosure of information, 8–58, 8–61, 8–62, 8–63, 8–66, 8–69
  information memorandum, 8–64
  insider dealing, 8–58
  investigation of problems, 8–67
  litigation, 8–68
  preparations, 8–59, 8–60
  properties, 8–73

records, 8–69
requests for information, 8–66
tax disputes, 8–68
tax mitigation, 8–72
third party consents, 8–70
team members, 8–08
types, 8–08
warranties, 8–11—8–12

Earn-outs
trade sales, 9–120

Earnings based valuations
future maintainable profits, 3–09—3–11
method of valuation, 3–08, 3–16
profit multiples, 3–12—3–15

Employee benefit trusts
share transfers, 10–24, 10–25, 10–27, 10–28

Employee share schemes
See also **Approved share schemes**
employee benefit trusts, 10–24, 10–25, 10–27, 10–28
enterprise management incentives qualifying options, 4–35
financial assistance, 5–68
generally, 5–68, 5–69
meaning, 5–67
purpose, 11–02

Employees
See also **Employee share schemes**
due diligence, 8–30
investor controls, 9–72, 9–73
loss of key employees, 12–24
shares, 5–67
warranties, 9–43

Enterprise Investment Scheme
aim of scheme, 4–10, 4–11
deferral relief, 4–15—4–17
directors, 4–13
qualifying companies, 4–05—4–09
qualifying investments, 4–03, 4–04
rates of tax, 4–10
redeemable component, 4–12
repayments of share capital, 4–12
shares, 4–11
tax relief, 4–03, 4–04, 4–10, 4–14

Enterprise management incentives
qualifying options, 4–35

Entrepreneurs relief
tax relief, 4–02

Environmental due diligence
See also **Due diligence**
compliance programme, 8–56
documents, 8–51
exits, 8–56
generally, 8–46, 8–73
insurance, 8–56
investigations, 8–50
liabilities, 8–46, 8–47, 8–54, 8–55, 8–56
process, 8–49, 8–50, 8–51, 8–52
regulatory bodies, 8–52

449

Index

shortcomings of warranties and indemnities, 8–48, 8–53
specialists, 8–53
Equity
expensive debt, 3–36, 3–37
generally, 3–35
rights, 3–38
Equity gap
private equity, 1–15, 1–16
Equity "give-away" factor
generally, 1–32, 1–38
Executive directors
role, 11–06, 11–07
Exit prospects
investment criterion, 2–18—2–23
Exits
See also **Internal rate of return; Ratchets**
buy-outs without private equity, 9–136
flotations
benefits of, 9–109
credibility, 9–111
employee incentives, 9–114
exit ratchets, 10–53, 10–54, 10–55
exit route, 2–19
flexibility for future, 9–112
partial sales, 9–113
process, 9–116
publicity, 9–110
regulations, 9–117
size of company, 9–115
generally, 9–108
negotiations, 9–85
secondary purchases, 2–23, 9–129—9–130
share buy-backs, 2–21—2–22
trade sales
all shareholders, 9–122
benefits of, 9–118
confidentiality, 9–127
earn-outs, 9–120
exit ratchets, 10–52
exit route, 2–20
flexibility, 9–124
loss of independence, 9–126
price, 9–119
size, 9–121
tax, 9–123
vendor control, 9–125
warranties, 9–128
Expansion capital
funding, 1–12
Fiduciary duties
breach of duty, 13–03
directors, 10–37, 11–09, 11–15, 11–16, 13–02
management, 13–02, 13–03
Financial advisers
role, 2–37—2–38, 2–74
Financial assistance
employee share schemes, 5–68
maintenance of share capital, 5–19—5–24

Financial covenants
debt finance, 3–25—3–27
failure, 12–26
Flotations
benefits, 9–109
credibility, 9–111
employee incentives, 9–114
exit ratchets, 10–53, 10–54, 10–55
exit route, 2–19
flexibility for future, 9–112
partial sales, 9–113
process, 9–116
publicity, 9–110
regulations, 9–117
size of company, 9–115
Forced sale provisions
share transfers, 10–32—10–34
Fraudulent trading
directors, 11–49, 12–80
Freeholds
warranties, 9–45
Funding
acquisitions, 1–27
deal structuring, 3–69
early stage of development, 1–13, 2–10, 2–31
industry partnerships, 1–29
investment agreement, 9–06, 9–07
key changes, 1–26, 1–27, 1–37, 1–38
organic growth, 1–26, 1–27
start-ups, 1–13, 2–10
technology companies, 1–19
Future maintainable profits
earnings based valuations, 3–09—3–11
Future profit prospects
investment criterion
barriers to entry, 2–16, 2–17
generally, 2–11, 2–12, 2–13, 2–17
industry prospects, 2–14
technology changes, 2–15
Garden leave
directors, 11–100, 11–101
Gearing
management buy-outs, 1–24
Generalists
private equity firms, 1–04
High technology companies
start-ups and early stage investments, 2–31
Independents
private equity firms, 1–02
Industry partnerships
funding, 1–29
Industry prospects
investment criterion, 2–14
Industry sectors
balanced portfolios, 2–29
preferences, 2–29, 2–30, 2–31
Inheritance tax
business property relief, 4–30—4–33
Initial market phase
fundraising, 2–59—2–61

Index

Insolvency
See also **Restructuring**
definition, 12–11
Enterprise Act 2002, Pt 10, 12–61, 12–62
gifts or contributions to shareholders, 5–25
meaning, 12–11
officers, 12–14, 12–15
order of application of assets, 12–65
proceedings, 12–14, 12–15
voluntary arrangements, 12–83
Insurance
directors and officers, 9–04, 11–91, 11–92
environmental due diligence, 8–56
keyman, 9–04
warranties, 9–20, 9–28, 9–29, 9–30, 9–31, 9–40
Intellectual property
warranties, 9–47
Interest rates
debt finance, 3–30
Internal rate of return
calculation, 3–53—3–63, 10–44, 10–45, 10–47
deal structuring, 3–70
example investments, 3–18—3–19, 10–49, 10–50
exit valuations, 3–57, 3–58, 10–50
limitations, 10–50
net present value, 10–45, 10–48
portfolio view, 3–60
structure of investment, 10–48
Interviews
management due diligence, 7–16, 7–17
Investment agreement
checklist, 9–137
conditions, 9–03—9–05
contents, 9–02
definitions, 9–05
disclosure letters, 9–51—9–52, 9–53
funding arrangements, 9–06, 9–07
generally, 9–01
interpretation, 9–05
keyman insurance, 9–04
mechanics of investment, 9–06, 9–07
negotiations
chairman, appointment of, 9–84
exits, 9–85
generally, 9–02, 9–80
investor directors, 9–84
obligations of Newco, 9–86
remuneration committees, 9–84
service contracts, links to, 9–83
precedents, 9–02
preparation, 9–02
purpose, 9–02
restrictive covenants, 9–82, 9–103
size, 9–01
standard form agreements, 9–02
warranties, 9–08, 9–09, 9–14—9–15, 9–81, 9–137

Investment agreement *See also* Articles of association; Investor controls; Minority shareholders; Warranties
Investment costs
warranties, 9–47
Investment criterion
exit prospects, 2–18—2–23
future prospects
barriers to entry, 2–16, 2–17
generally, 2–11, 2–12, 2–13, 2–17
industry prospects, 2–14
technology changes, 2–15
generally, 2–02, 2–72
management
age range, 2–04
capability and balance of team, 2–04, 2–05, 2–06
generally, 2–03
non-executive directors, appointment of, 2–06
"one-man band" entrepreneurs, 2–03
past performance
early stage investments, 2–10
generally, 2–07
improvements on, 2–07—2–09
start-ups, 2–10
Investment offers
choice
access to further funds, 2–71
deliverability, 2–69
offer terms and conditions, 2–68—2–69
relationships, 2–70—2–71
Investor controls
benefits to management, 9–67
categories of, 9–68
corporate governance
audit committees, 9–92, 9–94
board meetings, 9–91, 9–103
financial information, 9–91—9–92
provision of information, 9–90
remuneration committees, 9–92, 9–93
employment, 9–72, 9–73
exercise of rights, 9–76, 9–77
extent of, 9–68
financial, 9–71
future management of the business, 9–66
generally, 9–75, 10–03
management, 9–69—9–70
minority protection, 9–97
need for, 9–66
relationship between the investors, 9–78, 9–79
remedies for breach of, 9–95, 9–96
shareholdings, 9–74—9–75
voting rights, 9–76, 9–97, 9–98, 9–103
Joint liability
warranties, 9–23, 9–25
Joint and several liability
warranties, 9–21, 9–24, 9–25

451

Index

Keyman insurance
  investment agreement, 9–04
Lead partners
  transaction management
    leadership skills, 6–14
    responsibilities, 6–13
    support of manager, 6–13
Leaseholds
  assignment, 8–42, 8–43
  due diligence, 8–39, 8–41—8–45
  rent reviews, 8–44
  warranties, 9–45
Legal due diligence
  bankruptcy, 8–27
  business documents, 8–25
  confidentiality agreements, 8–21
  costs, 8–20
  creditworthiness, 8–26
  information required, 8–21, 8–22
  opinions, 8–28
  purpose, 8–18
  review of materials, 8–29
  scoping the report, 8–19, 8–20
  searches, 8–24
  sources of information, 8–23—8–28
  statutory books, 8–25
Legal professional privilege
  disclosure, 9–65
Limitation periods
  tax, 9–16
  warranties, 9–16
List of documents
  transaction management, 6–35, 6–47
Litigation
  warranties, 9–42
Loan stock
  interest, 1–32, 3–46
  ranking, 3–45
  redemption, 1–32, 3–47, 3–48
Management
  See also **Directors' powers and duties; Minority shareholders; Ratchets; Service agreements; Transaction management**
  business plans, 2–52
  class rights, 10–11—10–13
  duties
    breach of duty, 13–03
    fiduciary duties, 13–02, 13–03
    generally, 13–01
  investment criterion
    age range, 2–04
    capability and balance of team, 2–04, 2–05, 2–06
    generally, 2–03
    non-executive directors, appointment of, 2–06
    "one-man band" entrepreneurs, 2–03
  investor controls, 9–69—9–70
  restructuring, 12–85, 12–86
  shares
    tax relief, 4–34, 4–35
    warranties, 13–09—13–13
Management buy-ins
  BIMBOs, 1–08, 1–23
  extent of, 1–20
  generally, 1–08
  large MBIs, 1–21
  warranties, 9–11, 9–12, 9–13, 9–36
Management buy-outs
  BIMBOs, 1–08, 1–23
  bought deals, 1–22
  conflict of interest, 11–20
  directors' powers and duties, 13–05
    business focus, 13–07
    departing manager's shares, purchase of, 13–15
    generally, 13–05
    good and bad leaver provisions, 13–14
    heads of terms, 13–18
    management of the company, 13–08
    ratchets, 13–16
    service agreements, 13–17
    warranties, 13–09—13–13
  extent, 1–20
  gearing, 1–24
  generally, 1–07
  large MBOs, 1–08, 1–21
  management stakes in, 3–43, 3–44
  mezzanine finance, 1–24
  warranties, 9–12, 9–13, 9–36, 13–09—13–13
Management due diligence
  See also **Due diligence**
  approach, 7–04
  best practice, 7–07
  chairman, 7–19
  communication, 7–03, 7–06
  covert surveillance, 7–09
  economic recession, impact of, 7–02, 7–03
  generally, 2–62, 7–01, 7–01—7–03, 7–08, 7–20
  interviews, 7–16, 7–17
  legal, financial and professional checks, 7–10
  motivational factors, 7–08
  problems, 7–06
  profiling, 7–16, 7–17
  references, 2–62, 7–11—7–15
  reports, 7–18
  responses of management, 7–06, 7–20
Management representations
  accountant's report, 8–15
Managing directors
  directors, 11–06
Matching funds to propositions
  criterion
    degree of involvement, 2–33—2–35
    generally, 2–73
    geographical preferences, 2–32
    industry preferences, 2–29, 2–30, 2–31
    length of investment, 2–36

Index

size of investment, 2–25—2–27
stage of investment, 2–28
directory of BVCA members, 2–24
Mezzanine finance
deal structuring, 3–68
generally, 1–24, 3–32—3–34
management buy-outs, 1–24
Minority shareholders
generally, 9–99
investor controls, 9–97
investors, 9–103
management, 9–100—9–102, 10–11, 10–13
Minutes
board meetings, 11–87
Misfeasance
directors, 11–49, 11–51
Negligence
directors' powers and duties, 11–60
Offer phase
offer letter, 2–63, 2–64, 6–05
phase of investment, 6–03—6–05
Optimum funding solution
mixture debt and equity, 3–20
Ordinary shares
classification, 3–39, 5–38
dividends, 3–39, 3–40
management, 3–42, 3–43, 3–44
preferred participating ordinary shares, 3–40, 3–41
rights, 5–38, 5–39
Organic growth
funding, 1–26, 1–27
Past performance
investment criterion
competitive marketplace, 2–09
early stage investments, 2–10
generally, 2–07
improvements on, 2–07—2–09
plant facilities, 2–09
production facilities, 2–09
start-ups, 2–10
Pension schemes
due diligence, 8–33
shortfalls, 12–28
warranties, 9–44
Personal representatives
shareholder rights, 5–35, 5–36
Phases of an investment
See also **Transaction management**
completion phase
conditions precedent, 2–65
due diligence, 2–66
generally, 2–65, 6–44
conditional offer, 2–62—2–64
generally, 6–01
offer phase
generally, 6–03, 6–05
offer letter, 2–63, 2–64, 6–05
preparatory phase, 2–55—2–58, 6–02
Pre-emption rights

buy-outs without private equity, 9–136
share transfers, 10–14, 10–15, 10–16, 10–17, 10–29, 10–33
Pre-pack administrations
restructuring, 12–54
Preference shares
cumulative, 5–49
dividends, 3–46, 3–48, 5–44, 5–46, 5–50
meaning, 5–44
non-cumulative, 5–52
part of equity share capital, 5–48
participating, 5–53
ranking of, 3–45
redeemable shares, 1–32, 3–47, 3–48, 5–59—5–65
rights, 5–01, 5–44, 5–54, 5–55, 5–56, 5–57, 5–58
use, 5–44, 5–45, 5–46, 5–47, 5–71
winding-up, 5–51, 5–54, 5–55
Preferred ordinary shares
dividends, 5–41—5–43
rights, 5–40
Preparatory phase
phase of investment, 2–55—2–58, 6–02
Private equity
advantages, 1–35
disadvantages, 1–35
equity gap, 1–15, 1–16
generally, 2–01
growth of the industry, 1–36
investment ranges, 1–15, 1–16, 1–17, 1–18
meaning, 1–01
overview, 1–36
product categories, 1–06—1–14, 1–36
trends, 1–15—1–19
types of firms, 1–02—1–05, 1–36
use, 1–01
Professional advisers
financial advisers, 2–37—2–38, 2–74
restructuring, 12–19, 12–32, 12–33, 12–34, 12–44—12–50, 12–50, 12–77
role, 2–42
solicitors, 2–41
tax advisers, 2–39, 2–40
Profiling
management due diligence, 7–16, 7–17
Property due diligence
See also **Due diligence**
generally, 8–34
leaseholds, 8–39, 8–41—8–45
liabilities, 8–34
searches, 8–39, 8–40
title to land, 8–35—8–37, 8–39
warranties, 8–38
Publicity
flotations, 9–110
Purchase of own shares
companies, 5–34

453

Index

Quorum
  articles of association, 10–61
  board meetings, 10–61, 11–83
Ratchets
  See also **Internal rate of return**
  contingent consideration, 10–57
  deferred consideration, 10–57
  deferred shares, 5–66
  directors' powers and duties, 13–16
  early realisation, 10–56
  exits, 3–51, 10–43, 10–51—10–55
  generally, 10–59
  incentivisation, 3–49, 10–40
  negotiating tools, 10–42
  performance measurements, 10–44
  performance related, 3–49—3–51
  problems, 3–51
  profit related, 3–50, 10–51
  purpose, 10–38, 10–39
  valuation gap, 10–41
  warranties, 10–58
Ratification
  directors' breach of duty, 11–70
References
  management due diligence, 2–62, 7–11—7–15
Register of directors
  disclosure, 11–75
Registers of members
  information required, 5–31, 5–32, 5–71
Registration
  articles of association, 10–02
Relationships
  choice of investment offers, 2–70—2–71
Remuneration committees
  corporate governance, 9–92, 9–93
  negotiations over, 9–84
Repayment profiles
  debt finance, 3–29
Reports
  accountants, 8–13, 8–15
  due diligence, 8–13, 8–15, 8–74
  management due diligence, 7–18
  transaction management, 6–24—6–26
Rescues
  generally, 1–09
Resignation
  directors, 11–89
Restrictive covenants
  investment agreement, 9–82, 9–103
  service agreements, 9–82, 11–102—11–107
Restructuring
  See also **Insolvency**
  administrators, 12–61, 12–62
  advice, 12–19
  "Armageddon calculation", 12–37, 12–63—12–66
  bank support, 12–84
  before insolvency, 12–10, 12–14, 12–83
  business plans
    approval, 12–36—12–43
    "Armageddon calculation", 12–37
    delivery of promises, 12–37
    disclosure, 12–31
    generally, 12–29
    negotiations, 12–35—12–43
    preparation, 12–31
    professional assistance, 12–32, 12–33, 12–34
    unsecured creditors, 12–37—12–41
  collective decision making, 12–49
  commencement, 12–17—12–19
  cost savings, 12–05
  creditors, 12–12, 12–13, 12–42—12–43
  de facto directors, 12–57, 12–59, 12–60
  dilution of equity, 12–06—12–07
  directors' conduct, 12–46, 12–50
  divisible parts of the business
    closure, 12–05
    cost savings, 12–05
    identification, 12–04
    retain or sell, 12–04
  downsizing, 12–04
  fraudulent trading, 12–80
  generally, 12–01, 12–02
  need for, 12–03
  new businesses, 12–09
  new equity, 12–07—12–08
  opportunities, 12–51—12–53
  pre-pack administrations, 12–54
  problems, 12–82
  process, 12–16, 12–17, 12–18, 12–19
  professional advice, 12–19, 12–44—12–50, 12–50, 12–77
  purchases from possible insolvent companies, 12–51—12–53
  reviews, 12–21
  secured creditors, 12–42, 12–43
  senior management, 12–85, 12–86
  shadow directors, 12–57, 12–58, 12–59
  shut downs, 12–05
  solvent restructurings, 12–20
  time required, 12–81
  trigger events
    disclosure, 12–22
    failing financial covenants, 12–26
    litigation, 12–23
    loss of key customers, 12–25
    loss of key employees, 12–24
    pension shortfalls, 12–28
    profit drop, 12–27
  winding-up petitions, 12–81, 12–82
  wrongful trading, 12–67—12–79
Risk assessment
  transaction management, 6–30—6–31
Secondary purchases
  existing shareholders, 1–11
  exit route, 2–23, 9–129—9–130
  generally, 1–10
  other private equity firms, 1–10

Index

shareholder disputes, 1–11
warranties, 9–130
Semi-captives
private equity firms, 1–03
Sensitivity analysis
accountants, 2–67
Service agreements
benefits, 11–95
conflict of interest, 11–29—11–31
directors, 1–33, 11–02
directors' powers and duties, 11–29—11–31, 13–17
disclosure, 11–76
garden leave, 11–100, 11–101
generally, 11–94
importance, 11–94
investment agreement, 9–83
negotiations, 9–89
notice periods, 11–96, 11–97
remuneration, 11–95
restrictive covenants, 9–82, 11–102—11–107
termination of contract, 11–98, 11–99
Shadow directors
directors, 11–04, 11–06, 12–55, 12–56, 12–57, 12–58, 12–59
meaning, 11–04
Share buy-backs
exit route, 2–21—2–22
Share capital
generally, 5–01, 5–03, 5–71
maintenance
breach, 5–09
capacity of company, 5–26—5–28
corporate gifts, 5–09
dividends, 5–11—5–18
"dressed up" remuneration, 5–09
excessive interest payments, 5–09
ordinary course of business, 5–10
principle, 5–02—5–30
sale of property at undervalue, 5–09
ultra vires, 5–26—5–28
Share issues
consideration, 5–06—5–08
Share transfers
articles of association
compulsory transfer notices, 10–18, 10–19—10–22
controlling interest, 10–29—10–31
employee benefit trusts, 10–24, 10–25, 10–27, 10–28
forced sale provisions, 10–32—10–34
generally, 10–14, 10–15, 10–16
"good and bad leaver" provisions, 10–19, 10–20, 10–22, 13–14
market value, 10–17
pre-emption rights, 10–14, 10–15, 10–16, 10–17, 10–29, 10–33
restriction clause for managers, 10–19
termination of employment at crucial times, 10–23

warehousing, 10–26
wrongful dismissal, 10–21
satisfaction of warranty claims, 9–27
Shareholders
agreements to become members, 5–33
disputes
secondary purchases to fund a settlement, 1–11
eligibility, 5–34—5–36
limited liability, 5–05
registers of members, 5–31, 5–32, 5–71
rights, 5–01
sale of business
order of preference, 5–70
Shares
classes, 5–37
nominal value, 5–02, 5–03
purchase of own shares, 5–34
rights attached, 5–01
shares issued at premium, 5–03, 5–04, 5–08
Solicitors
role, 2–41
Specialists
early phase and start-up firms, 2–31
private equity firms, 1–04
product exclusions, 1–05
sector exclusions, 1–05
Start-ups
funding, 1–13, 2–10
new markets and products, 1–14
specialist funds, 2–31
Substantial property transactions
conflict of interest, 11–32—11–34
directors
conflict of interest, 11–32—11–34
Swamping rights
equity, 3–38
negotiations, 9–88
Syndicates
articles of association, 10–14, 10–15
private equity firms, 2–27, 9–104—9–107
Tax
See also **Employee share schemes; Enterprise Investment Scheme; Venture capital trusts**
business asset taper relief
abolition, 4–02
business property relief, 4–30—4–33
capital losses, 4–28—4–29
close companies
interest paid on investment borrowing, 4–25, 4–26, 4–27
disputes, 8–68
entrepreneurs relief
tax relief, 4–02
inheritance tax
business property relief, 4–30—4–33
limitation periods, 9–16
management shares, 4–34, 4–35
mitigation, 8–72

455

Index

reliefs, 4–01
trade sales, 9–123
Tax adviser
  role, 2–39, 2–40
Technology sector
  funding, 1–19
  investment criterion, 2–15
  start-ups and early stage investments, 2–31
Title to land
  certificate of title, 8–36, 8–37
  due diligence, 8–35—8–37, 8–39
  investigations, 8–39
  warranties, 8–37, 8–38
Torts
  directors' liabilities, 11–68
Trade sales
  all shareholders, 9–122
  benefits of, 9–118
  confidentiality, 9–127
  earn-outs, 9–120
  exit ratchets, 10–52
  exit route, 2–20
  flexibility, 9–124
  loss of independence, 9–126
  price, 9–119
  size, 9–121
  tax, 9–123
  vendor control, 9–125
  warranties, 9–128
Transaction management
  See also **Completion phase; Offer phase; Preparatory phase**
  action checklist, 6–35, 6–48
  banks, role of, 6–21
  client satisfaction, 6–18
  communication, 6–19, 6–22—6–23
  costs and fees, 6–45, 6–46
  documentation, 6–20, 6–21
  generally, 6–06, 6–48
  international transactions, 6–36—6–43
  key points, 6–49
  lead partners
    leadership skills, 6–14
    responsibilities, 6–13
    support of manager, 6–12
  list of documents, 6–35, 6–47
  managers
    establishing client's requirements, 6–16
    leadership skills, 6–12, 6–14, 6–15
    performance management, 6–17
    responsibilities, 6–14
    role, 6–11, 6–16, 6–23
  meetings
    agendas, 6–29
    "all parties" meetings, 6–27
    control, 6–28
    documents, 6–29
    types, 6–28
  negotiation of the agreement, 6–32, 6–33
  reporting and update system, 6–24—6–26

resources management, 6–09
risk assessment, 6–30—6–31
team membership, 6–09, 6–10, 6–12
time management, 6–34
timetables, 6–07, 6–08
Trustees in bankruptcy
  shareholder rights, 5–35, 5–36
Ultra vires
  gratuitous dispositions, 5–26, 5–27
  validity, 5–28
Vendor finance
  deferred consideration, 1–30, 1–31
Venture capital trusts
  conditions for approval, 4–19
  dividends, 4–21
  interest relief, 4–23—4–27
  private equity firms, 1–03
  qualifying companies, 4–05—4–09
  qualifying investments, 4–03, 4–04, 4–19
  reinvestment relief, 4–26
  smaller investments, 1–16
  tax relief, 4–03, 4–04, 4–18
Voluntary arrangements
  generally, 12–83
  insolvency, 12–83
Voting rights
  investor controls, 9–76, 9–97, 9–98, 9–103
Warranties
  accounts, 9–37—9–38
  acquisition agreement, 9–10—9–13
  assets, 9–46
  borrowings, 9–39
  claims, 9–18, 9–19
  development capital investment, 9–36
  directors' powers and duties, 13–09—13–13
  directors' waiver, 9–34
  disclosure letters
    complete disclosure, 9–54
    completeness, 9–54, 9–56
    corporate records, 9–60
    correspondence, 9–61
    disclosure bundle, 9–64
    effective date, 9–49
    form, 9–48
    general disclosures, 9–57—9–63
    information contained, 9–51
    investment agreement clause, 9–51—9–52, 9–53
    legal professional privilege, 9–65
    negotiations, 9–50
    precision, 9–55
    process, 9–49, 9–50, 9–51
    property inspection, 9–59
    public domain, 9–62
    qualifying warranties, 9–48
  due diligence
    impact, 8–11—8–12
  employment issues, 9–43
  environmental issues, 8–48, 8–53
  events since balance sheet date, 9–38

Index

exit, 13–13
financial limits, 9–21, 9–26
freeholds, 9–45
generally, 8–01
insurance, 9–20, 9–28, 9–29, 9–30, 9–31, 9–40
intellectual property, 9–47
investment agreement, 9–08, 9–09, 9–14—9–15, 9–81, 9–137
investment costs, 9–47
investor's knowledge, 9–32, 9–33
joint liability, 9–23, 9–25
joint and several liability, 9–21, 9–24, 9–25
leaseholds, 9–45
legal matters, 9–41—9–42
liabilities, 9–17
limitation periods, 9–16
litigation, 9–42
management, 13–09—13–13
management buy-ins, 9–11, 9–12, 9–13, 9–36
management buy-outs, 9–12, 9–13, 9–36, 13–09—13–13
management limitations, 9–101
pension schemes, 9–44
projections and forecasts, 9–36
property, 8–38
proportionate liability, 9–26
ratchets, 10–58
scope, 9–35, 9–36
secondary purchases, 9–130
several liability, 9–22
termination of agreement, 9–21
third party payments, 9–19
title to land, 8–37, 8–38
trade sales, 9–128
trading arrangements, 9–40
transfer of shares in satisfaction of claims, 9–27

Winding-up
petitions, 12–81, 12–82
preference shares, 5–51, 5–54, 5–55
restructuring, 12–81, 12–82

Written resolutions
directors, 11–86

Wrongful dismissal
compulsory transfer notices, 10–21

Wrongful trading
directors, 11–49, 11–50, 11–51, 12–67—12–79